Beyond *the* DSM Story

Beyond *the* DSM Story

Ethical Quandaries, Challenges, and Best Practices

Karen Eriksen
Argosy University, Orange County

Victoria E. Kress
Youngstown State University

SAGE Publications
Thousand Oaks ▪ London ▪ New Delhi

For information:

Sage Publications, Inc.
2455 Teller Road
Thousand Oaks, California 91320
E-mail: order@sagepub.com

Sage Publications Ltd.
1 Oliver's Yard
55 City Road
London EC1Y 1SP
United Kingdom

Sage Publications India Pvt. Ltd.
B-42, Panchsheel Enclave
Post Box 4109
New Delhi 110 017 India

Printed in the United States of America

Library of Congress Cataloging-in-Publication data

Eriksen, Karen.
Beyond the DSM story : ethical quandaries, challenges, and best practices / Karen Eriksen and Victoria E. Kress.—1st ed.
      p. cm.
Includes bibliographical references and index.
ISBN 0-7619-3032-9 (pbk.)
   1. Diagnostic and statistical manual of mental disorders—Evaluation. 2. Mental illness—Diagnosis. 3. Mental illness—Classification. I. Kress, Victoria E. II. Title.
RC469.E75 2005
616.89′075—dc22

                                                        2004010089

05   06   07   08   09   10   9   8   7   6   5   4   3   2   1

Acquiring Editor: Arthur T. Pomponio
Editorial Assistant: Veronica Novak
Production Editor: Kristen Gibson
Typesetter: C&M Digitals (P) Ltd.
Copy Editor: Richard Adin
Indexer: Sheila Bodell
Cover Designer: Glenn Vogel

Contents

Acknowledgments

There are several people who helped us in developing and completing this book. First, we would like to thank Victoria's former graduate student, Laura McCormick, for always being willing, eager, and able to secure resources and references that were critically important in writing this book. Laura McCormick and Brandy Kelly were also very helpful in developing several of the cases in Chapter 5. Additionally, we would like to thank Brandy Kelly, Renee Anderson, and Rachel Hoffman for their help in procuring book-related references. Thank you to our editor, Art Pomponio, for believing in this book, and spurring us on to improve it in necessary ways. Thanks to Garrett McAuliffe for his editing assistance.

Introduction

I sit in my office and listen to the couple's story. They are looking to me, as their mental health professional, to help them. I have been here before; I have heard a similar story. In some ways what they are telling me is familiar; it fits into what I have learned and what I think I "know." In other ways, this couple, like all others, is unique. The wife will tell me about her struggles to simultaneously pursue her career and take care of their two children. She will express guilt about not being a "full time" mother, and guilt for not putting more energy into her career. She will talk about feeling angry with her husband for not helping more with household and childcare tasks. The husband will talk about being tired: tired of the pressures of being the main "breadwinner," tired of changing diapers, tired of fighting with his wife.

When the couple leaves my office, I am aware that in order to receive reimbursement for the services that I render, I must pull my DSM (*Diagnostic and Statistical Manual of Mental Disorders*; when used in this way, we are referring to any version; American Psychiatric Association [APA], 1980, 1994, 2000) off of the shelf and apply a diagnosis. I ask myself how the DSM might contribute to my helping this couple. The thought crosses my mind that the DSM is likely to be of little practical use in this case, and will most likely play an insignificant role in the counseling process. Other fleeting thoughts cross my mind: If the DSM will be of limited help in my work with this couple, why must I use it? Will it be more harmful to deny this couple services that could help them or to apply a DSM diagnosis? What are the implications of my using a DSM diagnosis? Will I harm these clients by applying a label that could follow them for life, becoming part of their self-definition and perhaps later preventing them from changing their health insurance policy? What ethical responsibilities do I have in using the DSM with this couple? What should I tell this couple concerning any ascribed DSM diagnoses? This couple's case raises questions that ethical mental health professionals regularly tackle. However, although the questions related to mental health professionals' use of the DSM are clear and abundant, answers and resolutions to the questions are fewer, and generally more uncertain.

THE DSM'S INFLUENCE

Despite our own and other people's quandaries and concerns related to the use of the DSM, the influence of its assessment system on the mental health field has been profound. In fact, it is difficult to overstate the magnitude of the DSM's presence; it looms large in all aspects of mental health work. The DSM's multiaxial assessment system has become the primary language of communication regarding client problems, offering a "shorthand" for reducing complex information about clients into a manageable form (Seligman, Walker, &

Rosenhan, 2001). Students in most mental health fields are required to take courses in how to use the DSM (Commission on Accreditation for Marriage and Family Therapy Education [COAMFTE], 1997; Council for the Accreditation of Counseling and Related Educational Programs [CACREP], 2001; American Psychological Association [APA], 2002). DSM diagnoses are used to delineate which sorts of problems warrant referral for medication.

In particular, because of its economic "power," influence, and popularity, practitioners must use the DSM system in order to maintain an active and competitive presence in each of the mental health fields (Sturkie & Bergen, 2001; Russell, 1986b). It has been said that the DSM "is the key to millions of dollars in insurance coverage for psychotherapy, hospitalization, and medications" (Kutchins & Kirk, 1997, p. 12). Use of DSM diagnoses is required in order for mental health professionals to receive available funds from Medicaid, Social Security Disability Income, benefit programs for veterans, and Medicare (Kutchins & Kirk, 1997). Essentially, entry into almost any services in the mental health care delivery system requires the ascription of DSM diagnosis.

The DSM also affects researchers' questions and hypotheses, in that funding organizations tend to provide funds for research that focuses on established DSM categories. Relatedly, many forms of government funded research depend on the application of DSM categories (see, for example, http://www.nimh.nih.gov). When reflecting on the influence of the DSM, Kutchins and Kirk (1997) declare, "The DSM provides a template for new knowledge, shaping what scientific questions get asked—and which ones get ignored" (p. 14).

Some might say that the DSM's original intent of helping mental health practitioners to better classify, and thus ultimately understand psychopathology, has been overwhelmed by its market uses, so much so that one wonders if the proverbial "cart" is now leading the "horse." That is, some DSM challengers wonder whether the requirement that clinicians use the DSM in order to sustain their livelihoods may be leading practitioners to "invent" justifications for its use and for broadening its scope, rather than contributing to an ongoing and developing understanding about psychopathology (Schwartz & Wiggins, 2002).

Furthermore, the financial incentives inherent in DSM use draw advocacy groups, professional associations, and corporations to raise their voices in decisions about what should be included in the DSM, yet some of these groups may not always have client welfare at the forefront of their minds. For instance, drug companies provide substantial funding for conventions, journals, and research related to what is included in the DSM, because what is considered diagnosable directly impacts the sale of their drugs. Pfizer Pharmaceutical (Pfizer) paid for the development of Prime-MD, a symptom checklist for medical doctors, to assess whether patients have the DSM criteria that would warrant psychotropic medication. Pfizer also provides funding to train medical doctors in psychopharmacology. Although Pfizer may have a genuine interest in educating medical doctors, both of these aforementioned strategies clearly also serve to promote and encourage the use of Pfizer's medications and thus reflect Pfizer's understandable motivation to sell more drugs (Kutchins & Kirk, 1997). Others who have contributed to DSM inclusion and exclusion decisions are discussed throughout the book.

The DSM represents only one model, one story, for understanding human problems—the medical model—and as with any model, its limitations lie right beside its benefits. Although the DSM's medical model is currently the most popular and widely used assessment system, alternative and/or more comprehensive models of assessment, such as family and developmental models, are increasingly gaining status, respect, popularity, and grounding in research.

THE POTENTIAL HARM OF DSM DIAGNOSES

Right alongside the ostensible popularity of the DSM lie examples of harm that can occur to clients as a result of the DSM's diagnostic labeling system; these need to be acknowledged even when one embraces the need for diagnosis and recognizes the harm that may ensue from failing to diagnose. For instance, family therapists have often considered it problematic to label individuals because they believe that many symptoms result from problems in family systems, rather than originating within the individual. Family therapists frequently find these symptoms relieved by targeting systemic problems. The family that is illustrated in Napier and Whitaker's *The Family Crucible* (1988) is an example of such a systems problem. The teenager in that family was diagnosed with schizophrenia, as were many unruly teens of that era. Yet despite current evidence that schizophrenia is rarely curable, Napier and Whitaker were able to "cure" the child's "schizophrenia" by resolving family problems. It seems that the teen's symptoms resolved in response to the parents focusing on their own individual and marital issues.

The Napier and Whitaker case brings up another concern with the diagnostic process. It seems that each era has had its own "garbage can" diagnosis; that is, the diagnosis given to all who don't seem to fall into any other diagnostic category, or the most popularly ascribed diagnosis of the day. As hard as it might be to believe today, schizophrenia was one era's favorite diagnosis, borderline personality disorder belonged to the 1980s, multiple personality disorder claimed the 1990s, and today's favored diagnosis might be considered to be attention-deficit disorder (Blum, 1978; Hegarty & Baldessarini, 1994; Neill, 1990). Conversations with clinicians lead us to consider the possibility that different disorders may have been overapplied (or

possibly underapplied) during different eras. It could be speculated that "popular" diagnoses draw a great deal of attention (and medication) to those with the ascribed diagnosis, pay a great number of honoraria or speaker's fees to those with specialties in those diagnoses, and draw great numbers of participants to conferences on the particular problem area. The decrease in focus on such diagnoses as mental health services emerge into different eras, and the resultant diminishing of their ascription, should cause practitioners to question whether all such diagnoses were accurately ascribed, whether they should have been ascribed as frequently as they were, and whether their ascription resulted from factors other than careful examination of what might be helpful for the treatment of those so diagnosed. History should make clinicians wonder how the profession was so sure about diagnosing so many people as troubled when, as might be illustrated in cases such as the one cited in Napier and Whitaker's book, providers "should" have recognized that the problems existed somewhere other than in the individual, and that solving these other problems might have resolved the individual's symptoms.

In addition to past "popular" diagnoses, other diagnoses, such as homosexuality, also seem to have had their "eras." And during their eras of being considered "valid"—a validity founded only on their inclusion in the DSM—they caused significant and unnecessary harm (Cahn, 2003; Caplan, 1995). The current belief in the "invalidity" of what were historically considered "valid" diagnoses demonstrates the social construction of diagnostic labels, that they are artifacts of a time and place. Yet, unfortunately, diagnoses are not, and were not then, treated as artifacts; rather they exist and existed in an essentialist paradigm that belies what we know of social and cultural contingency. The later rejection of these so-called "valid" diagnoses causes thinking people to pause when faced with the damage that was experienced by those so diagnosed, damage that was justified by people in power who decided, supposedly on the basis of evidence, that other groups of people were abnormal.

Kutchins and Kirk (1997) further claim that the DSM contributes to our overmedicalizing everyday problems and that it determines how we think about social and other problems. "Issues of psychiatric diagnosis, commentary by psychiatrists on all manner of social issues, and the use of medical authority are so ubiquitous in our lives . . . [that we are finding] psychopathology where there is only pathos, and [pretending] to understand phenomena by merely giving them a label and a code number" (p. x). According to these authors, the ease of doing this (and the financial incentives for doing so), mean that the DSM defines how we think about our troubles, which behaviors should be considered the result of illness or disorder, and which problems fall under the purview of psychiatrists and other mental health professionals. In many cases, Kutchins and Kirk claim, we are allowing the DSM to reorient our thinking about important social matters, which, in turn, affects our social institutions.

IMPORTANCE OF UNDERSTANDING PSYCHOPATHOLOGY

Concerns about the DSM do not invalidate the existence of serious problems in living, problems that tremendously impact individuals, families, and society. Some peoples' problems do result from organic or physical illnesses or brain disorders. The severity of the impact of these mental illnesses makes it critical for mental health professionals to continually engage in creating knowledge about these problems and their necessary treatment. For example, individual problems in living, which may sometimes justifiably be considered mental illnesses, create suffering; life failures; relational failures;

stigma because of bizarre or unconventional behavior; incarceration in prisons and hospitals; financial struggles because of treatment costs and work loss; and homelessness.

For families, the consequences of such problems in living or mental illnesses include the loss of dreams for their children; fears about aggression; fears for their loved one's safety and well-being; a lifetime of care-taking; financial stresses; concerns about what happens when the caretaker is no longer around; lability and unpredictability in the child's emotions and behaviors; blame for problems; siblings' needs going unmet because of the attention needed by the child with problems; the need for spouses to take on unexpected financial and household and childcare responsibilities; the requirement that children grow up before they are ready in order to make up for parental deficiencies; and the "yo-yo" experiences of their loved ones alternating between using medications and not using medications depending on their denial or acceptance of the illness.

For society, the consequences of problems in living and mental illness include loss of worker and family productivity; increased criminalization of problems in living or mental illnesses; increased incarceration, which is far more expensive than treatment; increased demands for medical services by those with problems in living or mental illnesses; tremendous costs of hospitalization; increased private insurance costs to subsidize those with chronic problems; increases in public mental health usage as health maintenance organizations (HMOs) try to contain costs by limiting treatment, leaving those who need treatment to run out of reimbursable services (Seligman, Walker, & Rosenhan, 2001).

A clear understanding of the impact of mental health problems takes on new proportions when one considers the frequency with which Americans experience such problems and the costs of such problems: Twenty percent of Americans are diagnosed in any given year and one-third of their problems persist beyond a year. Six percent of Americans are addicted to alcohol and various drugs, with $100 billion per year being spent on treatment and $80 billion per year being lost in productivity at work and school (Seligman et al., 2001).

The costs to people and to society mean that researchers and practitioners need to find and disseminate any means to reduce, resolve, and treat problems in living and mental illnesses, and find any means to identify early predictors so as to intervene early, either preventing problems or preventing more serious problems. The question is how to accomplish these goals while helping individuals to maintain their dignity, as much independence as possible, at least minimal material resources, their privacy, their families, and their work—in short their quality of life (Seligman et al., 2001).

ETHICAL AND LEGAL DILEMMAS FACED BY PROVIDERS

Because of the potential for harm in diagnosing, and because of the equally strong imperative for understanding, treating, and reducing the negative impacts of mental health problems, many mental health providers struggle with the role of diagnosis in their work. A vivid example occurred in Virginia as family therapists pursued licensure (the first author was involved in this policy process). Family therapists were forced by professional counselors to include a diagnosis course in their licensure requirements. Professional counselors were worried, as a result of their experiences with family therapists, that family therapists who were untrained in diagnosis might fail to refer members of families with mental illnesses or mood disorders for needed medication. Family therapists included the course quite reluctantly, citing that their professional worldview considered symptoms to be expressions of systems, rather than individual problems, and that diagnosis courses would focus on individual diagnoses. In fact,

one survey of marital and family therapists indicated that one-third of a national sample of marital and family therapists completely avoid the use of individually focused, pathology-oriented diagnostic systems (Doherty & Simmons, 1996).

On the national level, COAMFTE, the accrediting body for marriage and family therapy training programs which is affiliated with the American Association for Marriage and Family Therapy (AAMFT), included the diagnosis course as a requirement for marriage and family therapists in training, despite paradigm considerations (COAMFTE, 1997). Some clinicians with whom the authors have had conversations believe that this shift occurred because of market demands, that is, that AAMFT and its affiliate, COAMFTE, recognized that marriage and family therapists would be unlikely to receive insurance reimbursement for their services without providing individual diagnoses for their clients. COAMFTE's decision will most likely be reflected in future marriage and family therapy licensure laws because professional organizations' standards typically impact licensure laws (Eriksen, 1999).

Other groups of mental health practitioners who may question the paradigm that underlies DSM diagnosis include professional counselors, counseling psychologists, and other more humanistically or developmentally oriented providers. Professional counselors, for example, claim an identity that includes a focus on wellness, mental health, development, and prevention (Myers, Sweeney, & Witmer, 2001; Neukrug, 2003). Thus, counselors sometimes wonder how a medical model approach with a static focus on pathology can be relevant to much of their work. More humanistically and developmentally oriented psychiatrists and psychologists (e.g., Breggin, 1995) also question the relevance of diagnosis, as they also focus on growth, potential, and authentic healing relationships (Ivey & Ivey, 1999; Leitner, 2003). As a result of these struggles, some mental health providers choose not to generate individual diagnoses at all, despite the loss of insurance money and other funding that may result from that decision. More often, however, those providers—with whom the authors have had conversations at state and national conventions—who find themselves in dilemmas about the diagnostic process, choose to use the least-stigmatizing individual diagnoses possible in order to, as they call it, "play the insurance game" (Glosoff, Garcia, Herlihy, & Remley, 1999; Sperling & Sack, 2002).

The limitations of DSM diagnosis (Parker, Georgaca, Harper, McLaughlin, & Stowell-Smith, 1995) and the life-altering and far-reaching uses and results of DSM diagnosis (Kutchins & Kirk, 1997) raise serious ethical questions with regard to its use. For instance, consider the following impacts of diagnosis: It can be used to commit people to hospitals, to medicate them, and to persuade them to pursue therapy, a relationship in which there is a power imbalance and in which the person in power may make important decisions about the client's life (see Hornstein, 2002, for examples of how this power may be abused). Serious personal, legal, and social stigmatization may occur for some people with certain diagnoses. In the judicial system, diagnoses can affect decisions about guardianship, child custody, criminal liability, fitness to stand trial, and the determination of the extent to which defendants have the capacity to understand the consequences of their acts. In schools, diagnoses can result in children being labeled, placed in special classes, medicated, or dismissed from school. The impact of diagnosis on public policy is striking. The government uses statistics on people suffering from various mental disorders to fund mental health programs, and the public epidemiologists who provide those statistics rely on the DSM categories to count the mentally ill. If the DSM's categories are flawed or if the people who use the DSM err in their diagnoses or fail to use the diagnostic criteria as they were intended, then those who depend on these statistics will

make flawed public policy decisions (Kutchins & Kirk, 1997). The power associated with diagnosis thus raises troubling questions about whether those who diagnose can protect the welfare of their clients, and whether they can avoid perpetuating some of the status quo perceptions about abnormality that have historically served to oppress those with less power (Caplan, 1995; Ridley, 1998; Sue & Sue, 1990). These concerns, often expressed by those who propose alternative perspectives to the DSM medical-model system of diagnosis, point out the urgency of exploring the ethical quandaries raised by mental health professionals' use of DSM diagnoses.

As a means toward that end, we have surveyed and summarized all of the available literature on challenges to traditional diagnosis, DSM diagnosis in particular. The literature on this topic is limited, and there is no other source that comprehensively presents all of the challenges. We augment the literature with knowledge that results from our 30 years of combined clinical experience, and our conversations with other professionals who have extensive clinical experience and have engaged in years of professional association leadership. We also use current professional association ethical guidelines to analyze the ethical dilemmas raised by those who challenge the DSM model. We propose possible solutions or best practices for addressing ethical quandaries, offer experiential opportunities to think critically about both the problems and the solutions, illustrate the complexities and possibilities with case studies, and propose a possible model for incorporating alternative models *with* DSM assessment.

Our aim is *not* to provide a balanced view of the DSM model of diagnosis. The DSM model of diagnosis dominates mental health practice, textbooks on diagnosis and psychopathology clearly declare its value to clinical practice, and many people espouse its value. The DSM has no further need for advocates or for those touting its benefits. Thus, our aim is to instead consider the other stories about assessment and diagnosis, to raise clinician consciousness about the challenges to DSM diagnosis, to consider the ethical dilemmas posed by these challenges, to stimulate critical thinking about the DSM and its use, to offer opportunities to consider solutions to the ethical challenges, to propose alternative stories to the DSM's story about human behavior and problems, and, hopefully, as a result, to trigger ideas about improving diagnosis and clinical practice. Despite our strong feelings about the problems with the DSM system, we consider it one among many possible stories about clients' experiences. Unfortunately, the financial benefits associated with the DSM story sometimes drown out the voices of other stories. It is our hope that this book will foreground their voices so that they can be added to the dialogue about what may be helpful for clients.

This book is intended as a supplemental text for abnormal psychology and diagnosis and treatment planning courses, courses in which the DSM or other texts on abnormal psychology already present standard information about the DSM system of diagnosis and about psychopathology. It is also intended for use by clinicians and supervisors in practice. Chapter 1 outlines the hypothesized benefits of DSM diagnosis and provides an overview of the challenges to traditional uses of diagnosis. Chapter 2 explores specific ethical dilemmas that can arise when using DSM diagnosis while attempting to follow ethical mandates related to informed consent/confidentiality, competence, accuracy of diagnosis, dual relationships, values, the obligation to promote growth and development, and the importance of including families in counseling work. Chapters 3 and 4 examine the concerns about DSM diagnosis that have been raised by feminists and people of color. Chapter 5 offers possible solutions to ethical dilemmas, as well as many cases, activities, and exercises that are designed both to increase awareness of the dilemmas surrounding the diagnostic process and to encourage practitioners, supervisors, educators, and students to use systemic and holistic thinking to more meaningfully understand and use diagnosis and assessment. The next three chapters offer actual cases and the means by which professionals around the country suggest incorporating this book's suggestions into the diagnostic process with the clients in these cases. Chapter 9 offers a model for contextual, developmental, and holistic assessment that includes diagnosis as a part of the client's context.

1

The Price of Diagnosis

Mental health professionals would clearly not engage in diagnosis or use the *Diagnostic and Statistical Manual of Mental Disorders* (DSM; when used in this way, we are referring to any version; American Psychiatric Association [APA], 1980, 1994, 2000) diagnostic systems were it not for this model's perceived benefits. The DSM system of diagnosis is the "gold standard" for diagnosis in mental health practice, textbooks on diagnosis and psychopathology clearly articulate its value to clinical practice and to understanding abnormal behavior, and its economic power would not have emerged without many people knowing and espousing its value. Consequently, in this chapter, we do not aim to rearticulate the dominant beliefs about the diagnosis of mental health problems nor do we intend to provide a balanced view of the benefits and limitations of the DSM system. Instead, we move quickly to discussing the DSM's limitations after offering only a brief summary of the benefits of using the DSM diagnostic categories, both for clients and for mental health providers.

BENEFITS OF DSM DIAGNOSIS

Some of the benefits claimed for the DSM make inherent sense, and thus have face validity. For instance, the DSM's categories reduce complex information into a form of "shorthand" that facilitates communication within and among professional groups. Also, by categorizing people's psychological problems, researchers and theorists can compare various treatment approaches to particular problems; they can evaluate counseling, psychotherapy, and other psychiatric treatment effectiveness; and they can research underlying causal mechanisms and processes of particular diagnoses (Harari, 1990, as cited in Ivey, Jankowski, & Scheel, 1999; Hinkle, 1999; López-Ibor, 2003; Maniacci, 2002; Mead, Hohenshil, & Singh, 1997). The DSM further provides information about the course, prevalence, and cultural, gender, and familial issues related to each diagnosis— information that may be helpful to practitioners who are struggling to fully understand clients' experiences. Additionally, DSM diagnosis can help practitioners to identify those clients

1

whose problems extend beyond the clinician's areas of competence (Seligman, 1990).

Other claims about the DSM's benefits are more controversial, and literature exists that espouses conflicting sides of the arguments (when we discuss the DSM's limitations later, we explore the "con" side of the arguments). For instance, some mental health practitioners believe that diagnosis enables effective referral and/or planning of counseling, psychotherapy, and other psychiatric treatment strategies, planning that is based on accurate conceptualizations of client problems (Duffy, Gillig, Tureen, & Ybarra, 2002; Mead et al., 1997; Waldo, Brotherton, & Horswill, 1993). Other writers state that the DSM's diagnostic system allows professionals to summarize complex information about clients for use in a variety of activities (Cook, Warnke, & Dupuy, 1993). Furthermore, just as in medicine, advocates claim that the DSM increases comprehension of the pathological processes involved in disorders, improves control over the outcomes of psychiatric disorders, and promotes prevention of the disorders (e.g., as a result of conducting research on etiology [APA, 2000]). Although the DSM does not address treatment, the APA has published many books that propose treatment guidelines that are based on the DSM criteria (see http://www.appi.org/). Consequently, identifying a DSM diagnosis allows practitioners to find and use information about empirically supported treatment and prognosis. Another reported advantage is that "the DSM's non-etiological and descriptive nature is purposefully intended not to alienate potential users with diverse theoretical orientations" (Hinkle, 1999, p. 475). However, although the DSM does not state that its diagnoses are rooted in biological processes, many believe that it reflects a medical-model approach to helping. Therefore, it is understandable that those operating from a medical model might vouch for the aforementioned claims. However, those mental health providers who stand on different theoretical ground might, because of a different perception

of what causes and "cures" problems, question whether a diagnosis reflects an accurate conceptualization of client problems or is more a reflection of the worldview of the person who conceptualizes the clients' behaviors (Clark, Watson, & Reynolds, 1995; Nathan & Langenbucher, 2003).

The DSM may benefit clients in more personal and direct ways. For example, sometimes clients benefit from a concrete "explanation" for their behavior and experiences. They may find it freeing to have their experiences labeled (Shergill, Barker, & Greenberg, 1998; Wetterling, 2000). One client known to the first author struggled with depression for many years. A psychologist who tested her said that she would be in psychiatric hospitals for the rest of her life. During counseling sessions, she kept "thrashing" herself with messages like "I should be better," "I shouldn't keep struggling with this," "I am such a loser compared with everyone else." When the therapist shared the diagnostic labels of major depression and borderline personality disorder with her and urged her to think of these disorders as physical, like having diabetes or like being a paraplegic, the client was able to refocus her efforts toward managing the problems, coping with them, developing realistic expectations of herself, and garnering appropriate kinds and levels of support for herself. Having a label to hang onto actually freed her from the paralysis of self-blame and helped her to invest her energy more productively in activities that, in the end, were successful in keeping her out of the hospital.

Diagnostic labels may also focus clients and their families on an identified external enemy and away from blaming one another or themselves. Family members of someone who is labeled schizophrenic, for instance, may put less pressure on the one so labeled about idiosyncratic behaviors, such as social isolation. Family members who learn that a member has a psychiatric illness may increase their motivation for the therapy process as a result of decreases in mutual blame and experiences of guilt (Anderson, Reiss, & Hogarty, 1986). For instance, a family who brought their adoptive child into counseling, secondary to the child exhibiting a great deal of acting out and causing trouble in school, was worried that their parenting would be blamed for the child's problem. In fact, the couple had struggled for a while with their own conflicts about which one of them was to blame for their son's behavior. When the counselor diagnosed some developmental problems resulting from physical abuse and neglect in the biological family, the adoptive family breathed a collective sigh of relief and buckled down to rectify and manage the problems that they had inherited.

In another family known to the first author, an adult daughter who had recently experienced tremendous trauma was very depressed and angry, and was increasingly nasty and abusive toward the very people who were trying to help her. When family members would urge her to do things that might help her, she would become very argumentative and put down all of their ideas. When a cognitive behavioral therapist explained that she was suffering from depression, that "thought disorders" (Beck, Rush, Shaw, & Emery, 1979; Burns, 1980) were associated with depression, and that depressed people were often very persuasive in expressing these thought disorders, the family members were able to let go of trying to convince the daughter to change her mind, were able to feel less hopeless and discouraged themselves in response to her anger, and were able to redirect the conversations with their daughter toward more productive topics. Accepting the notion that their family member was suffering from depression, as defined by cognitive behavioral thought, reduced the family's tendency to want to avoid their daughter, a tendency that would only have confirmed their daughter's current "awfulizing" beliefs.

Furthermore, knowing that a person "bears" a clinical diagnosis may even positively change practitioners' feelings toward those so diagnosed. In a human development course, the first author invited panels of people of various ages to come into class to talk about what it was like to "be that age." The students found one 50-something woman quite offensive and difficult, and challenged the instructor on why the woman had been invited to the class. The next semester, when the same students were taking a diagnosis class with the first author and the same woman volunteered to come in to share her experiences with generalized anxiety disorder, their feelings dramatically changed. Of course, the woman's conversation with the students included more than merely a diagnostic label; it included the rather vulnerable sharing of a lifetime of struggle. But somehow, when the students knew how long and hard she had struggled with the problem, they were more understanding, more forgiving, and more willing to engage with the woman.

Most practitioners with whom we have had conversations, however, seem more aware of the financial and occupational benefits of using the DSM. That is, the DSM has become the most widely used system for the diagnosis of mental disorders. As a result, various governmental agencies use the DSM categories for census purposes, for specifying target populations whose treatment may be funded by grants, and for determining who is eligible for specially funded programs (Holden, Santiago, & Manteuffel, 2003; Regier, First, & Marshall, 2002). Almost all settings in which mental health providers work currently require a *Diagnostic and Statistical Manual of Mental Disorders,* 4th ed., Text Revision (DSM-IV-TR) diagnosis for reimbursement of services (e.g., hospitals, private practices, community mental health agencies, and residential settings; Mead et al., 1997; Sperling & Sack, 2002). Consequently, without knowledge of diagnosis, mental health providers may lose credibility and status in their professional fields, may not be able to fulfill their employment requirements, and may lose credentialing opportunities (Chambliss, 2000; Sperry, 2002a; Waldo et al., 1993). Students in the first author's diagnosis course, when challenged to think critically about the DSM system of diagnosis, responded, "Look, we have to use the DSM. We don't have a choice. What good does it do to think about it? We just do it and get it over with so that we can have the funds to treat the clients in the best ways that we know how."

It is clear that the DSM has positive uses, and is the dominant story about mental health diagnostic classification. It also appears that the DSM system of diagnosis is "here to stay" (Hinkle, 1999, p. 45; Hohenshil, 1993; Schwartz & Wiggins, 2002). Yet despite its staying power and benefits, the DSM has many limitations that should be considered and addressed. Those who espouse different stories about diagnosis, assessment, and treatment often bring these limitations to light. Perhaps considering the DSM to be one story among many can help practitioners to open up to other stories that might, in certain circumstances, add breadth and depth and helpfulness to assessment and to mental health practitioners' attempts to benefit their clients.

LIMITATIONS OF DSM DIAGNOSIS

Some of the limitations of DSM diagnosis were mentioned in the introduction to this book; the remainder of this chapter expands on the introduction. The concerns about the DSM as a diagnostic system that are overviewed in this chapter and discussed further in chapters that follow can be categorized as the following:

- The DSM diagnostic system fails to *predict* treatment outcomes or to *promote understanding* of underlying pathology.
- DSM diagnostic categories can lead people to accept a *self-fulfilling prophecy* that their situation is hopeless and that they are sick.
- DSM diagnoses can *narrow a mental health professional's focus* by encouraging the

professional to only look for behaviors that fit within a medical-model understanding of the person's situation.
- DSM diagnosis fails to include a full understanding of *contextual factors* that may more aptly illuminate both etiology and helpful treatment.
- The application of diagnostic labels has historically *stigmatized* and hurt those who are different from the mainstream. This practice continues today.
- Serious problems exist in the *"science"* of the DSM diagnostic process.
- DSM diagnosis implies the imposition of a certain set of *values* on clients and the counseling process.
- Diagnostic categories can minimize peoples' individual *uniqueness*.
- The diagnostic process takes the focus away from clients' reality and understanding of their problems by directing clients away from an internal and subjective way of understanding their experiences, instead putting the focus on *external conceptions about* them.

This chapter offers brief explanations from the literature to help provide an overview of these concerns. Future chapters offer more in-depth literature reviews on these issues, analyzing each of them from practical and ethical perspectives.

Communication, prevention, prediction, and understanding. Spitzer (1975), an advocate of properly used diagnosis and a central figure in the development of many editions of the DSM, claims that, although diagnosis has been somewhat effective in enabling professional communication and quite helpful in predicting the usefulness of particular treatments for particular diagnoses, it has, as of yet, been woefully inadequate in helping practitioners to comprehend the pathological processes involved and to prevent the disorders from developing (see also Albee, 1999; Tsuang & Faraone, 2002; Tsuang & Stone, 2000). In fact, Spitzer recommends against the use of diagnostic categories for outpatients who are not seriously ill. Sarbin (1997) counters some of Spitzer's claims, indicating that there is actually a weak connection between psychological diagnosis and treatment choices (that is, in predictive value), despite the stronger connection between medical diagnosis and treatment, the paradigm upon which the founding notions of the DSM diagnostic system are based. Seligman et al. (2001) indicate that predictive value (that is, the degree to which patients receive a certain treatment based on a particular diagnosis) is higher for some disorders than for others. For instance, those patients who are diagnosed with bipolar disorder generally receive a drug such as lithium as treatment. Clients who suffer from premature ejaculation tend to receive and respond well to specific behavioral and social learning treatments. "In these instances, the diagnosis indicates a treatment that has a high probability of succeeding. However, in most diagnostic situations, merely having a diagnosis is of limited use" (Seligman et al., 2001) in dictating a helpful or particular course of treatment with a predictable outcome (Acierno, Hersen, & Van Hasselt, 1997; Clarkin, Kernberg, & Somavia, 1998; McWilliams, 1998; Ogrodniczuk, Piper, & Joyce, 2001). Although some authors indicate that connections between the DSM and treatments will be made in the near future (Gunderson & Gabbard, 2000), others consider a search for such connections to be misguided (Sarbin, 1997).

Self-fulfilling prophecies, contextual factors, narrowing the provider's view. The potentially negative impact of diagnostic labeling on both the clients and the caregivers is also troubling. For instance, the results of Rosenhan's famous experiment (Rosenhan, 1973; Seligman et al., 2001) challenge us to carefully consider the self-fulfilling prophecy and contextual nature of diagnosis. He and his colleagues were admitted to psychiatric hospitals after pretending to have a single symptom. They claimed to have "heard voices that said 'empty,' 'meaningless,' and

'thud.' From the moment they were admitted, these pseudo-patients abandoned that symptom and acted the way that 'normal' people do. However, Rosenhan and his colleagues were labeled as crazy and 'treated that way'" (Seligman et al., 2001, p. xv). As a result of this experience, Seligman and Rosenhan concluded that the setting in which diagnoses are made influences what diagnoses are ascribed to clients. For example, the hospital context (the site of their experiment), in which all residents were assumed to be abnormal, contributed to interpreting all patient behaviors or verbalizations in light of the patients' diagnoses. This bias toward abnormality subsumed other observations to the point that "normal behaviors" were overlooked or misinterpreted. Additionally, once a diagnosis was given, it was very difficult for the client, the mental health professional, or the hospital staff to shift their focus away from that diagnosis. Russell (1986b) indicates that this sort of a situation reduces a client's self-esteem. In the Rosenhan experiment, then, the diagnosis created its own reality for all involved, influencing others' perceptions of the patient and the patient's behavior, despite later evidence that contradicted the initial diagnosis. However, the array of complex stimuli that surround hospital mental patients, stimuli that many would consider to be quite "sick," are typically ignored in diagnostic systems (Rosenhan, 1973). Rosenhan concludes that because the DSM model locates the sources of aberration within the individual, once those diagnosing believe that they have an understanding of the patient, it is difficult for those around the patients, or even for the patients themselves, to concede that their behavior has changed, or to entertain alternative or different views. Rosenhan challenges mental health personnel instead to consider anyone who actually "fits into" dysfunctional systems—such as these hospitals—to have a disorder.

Similarly, Jensen and Hoagwood (1997) discuss the inaccuracies and contextual nature of the DSM assessment process. For instance, they claim that as the practitioner obtains diagnostic information, the information shapes the ensuing assessment process. Furthermore, clients engage in their own shaping process. During the initial assessment, they are usually in an exploratory mode. They probably begin an initial session by thinking that only certain revelations are relevant. As they hear their own voices revealing certain symptoms, clients shift what they consider necessary to reveal. Their revelations are further shaped by the questions that the practitioner asks. White and Epston (1990) call the process by which the client and assessor create an assessment *storying*, and write that "the sense of meaning and continuity that is achieved through the storying of experience is gained at a price: that is, a narrative can never encompass the full richness of our lived experience" (p. 11). Therefore stories require a selective process in which "we prune . . . those events that do not fit with the dominant evolving stories that we and others have about us" (pp. 11–12). Those selections, in turn, shape our future stories (see also Denton, 1990; Jones, 2003). Such storying clearly affects all assessment and treatment procedures, not merely DSM diagnosis. However, those who hold the more narrative theoretical perspectives do not claim that these stories reflect "reality," and are not searching for "truth." Instead, they evaluate a story on the basis of its helpfulness to the client or the therapeutic process. If it is not helpful, practitioners assist the client to rewrite the story into one that might be more helpful (not more true or closer to reality; Neimeyer & Raskin, 2000). In contrast, the DSM developers' and users' pursuit of truth and accuracy promotes a reification of the diagnostic category, that is, using it inflexibly whether or not it is helpful to the client or to the treatment (Duffy et al., 2002).

As Rosenhan's (1973) experiment illustrated, Jensen and Hoagwood (1997) also claim that beyond the behavior and contexts brought into the assessment process by the practitioner and the client are the expectations brought to bear by the assessment "setting" (e.g., agency, hospital). Organizations design procedures that specify the length of time available for assessments and place other boundaries around informants' reporting of data. When clients have had many prior experiences with diagnostic and treatment services, they may express only what they are "supposed to say" in order to acquire treatment, a process that limits and distorts the diagnostic process and its results. Furthermore, organizational needs for market success or for justifying its existence to funding sources may pressure practitioners to offer diagnoses that fit the program's funding requirements or that warrant insurance reimbursement. The setting can thus impact both the client and practitioners' behavior in ways that perpetuate invalid diagnoses. Again, although such setting factors may impact assessment and treatment more broadly, beyond the selection of a DSM diagnostic label, such shifts in awareness or revelations can flexibly be incorporated into treatment during comprehensive assessment or ongoing treatment. However, the initial ascription of a DSM diagnosis impacts whether or not clients will receive treatment or to which program they will be assigned, decisions that are far more difficult to reverse or shift (the contexts of culture are discussed more fully in Chapters 3 and 4).

Stigma. Rosenhan (1973) further points out that the stigma associated with some diagnoses should challenge us to question the ethics of diagnosing. In his experiment, the stigma attached to those with diagnoses warranting hospitalization resulted in negative responses by hospital staff, such as avoiding interactions and eye contact, treating patients abusively or as if they were invisible, and responding in other dehumanizing ways. Hinshaw and Cicchetti (2000) indicate that "stigmatization of mental illness continues to be a problem of deep importance and lasting impact" (p. 557).

The media continue to portray those with mental disorders as bizarre, socially incompetent, and violent. Such stigma results in problems obtaining housing, job discrimination, lack of medical insurance and care, deplorable conditions in many institutional facilities, deinstitutionalization practices driven by cost savings rather than maintaining of human dignity, self-blame, silence, shame, exclusion from society's mainstream, and family mistrust. Children and the elderly are disproportionately and particularly affected by such stigma (see also Harman, Crystal, Walkup, & Olfson, 2003; Penn & Wykes, 2003; Ramchandani & Stein, 2003).

The stigma associated with mental illness has also been institutionalized in social policies, such as insurance reimbursement and grant funding for mental health programs. In turn, the DSM and diagnostic decisions continue to impact social policy (Sarbin, 1997). For instance, Sarbin points out that the DSM systems have contributed to the increasing medicalization of everyday transactions between people. If one has a medical disorder, as defined by the DSM, that entitles one to services, money, treatment, and, according to the Americans with Disabilities Act, an excuse from "normal" behavior in one's job (see also Double, 2002; Mulvany, 2000).

Science versus consensus. If the risk of such stigmatization is so great, one would presume that great caution would be exercised in developing the diagnostic system, and that any decisions made would be based on research. Yet, some authors have challenged the use of psychological classification systems, in general, and the reliability and validity of the "science" upon which the DSM classification is supposed to rest, more specifically (Blashfield & Breen, 1989; Brown, 1992; Frances & Widiger, 1986; Jensen & Hoagwood, 1997; Spitzer, Williams, Kass, & Davies, 1989; Szasz, 1974; Widiger & Sankis, 2000).

Szasz (1974) and Jensen and Hoagwood (1997), for instance, point out that DSM classifications cannot be considered reflective of the "true nature" of what is observed. Instead, they claim, classifications are largely indications of the nature of the observer in that particular time and place, the nature of the questions being asked, and the goals of observation and classification. These authors explain their assertions in the following way: Diagnostic classifications reflect the human need to simplify complex phenomena. Thus, classification systems are imposed upon some unknowable "reality" for purposes of efficiency, that is, for reducing the number of things that an observer needs to look at. Classification thus censors out many of the features of those who are being observed and requires decisions about how to simplify. The question is, how does such censoring affect classification and the eventual use of the classification system? Might we make different classification and treatment decisions if we held different assumptions about what should be censored out? Ussher (2000) claims that in diagnostic classification systems, such censoring means that people are made to fit the researcher's or clinician's model of specific syndromes.

Classification also assumes that symptoms either exist or do not, rather than assuming that they exist on a continuum or that they are sometimes evident and other times not evident (Livesley, Jang, & Vernon, 1998; McLemore & Benjamin, 1979; Widiger, 1993). Furthermore, categories become reified as discrete, consistent, and homogeneous clinical entities that are assumed to have identifiable causes, causes that in turn, create symptoms. As a result, such classification denies the social and discursive nature of human experience and the gendered nature of science (Sarbin, 1997; Sperry, 2002a; Ussher, 2000).

Sarbin (1997) further questions the science of the DSM method for its lack of precision and, thus, its lack of reliability. For instance, he claims that practitioners use their own judgment to decide how often is "often," how frequent is "frequent," or how dysfunctional is "dysfunctional," determinations that are required by the DSM's system. Russell (1986b) asks how one decides that symptoms are in excess of a "normal and expectable reaction" as is required to diagnose an adjustment disorder. She asks how one knows whether someone's "paranoid" statements are actually false, or how one decides that enough instability is present to warrant a "borderline personality disorder" diagnosis. Yet, as Sarbin (1997) claims and we have observed, practitioners make such judgments daily when deciding on the presence or absence of DSM criteria, using such determinations in ways that are clinically useful, rather than scientifically replicable. Russell (1986b) expresses the further concerns that the subjectivity in deciding on the presence of diagnostic criteria may affect women particularly, as they may be more likely to be "persuaded, cajoled or forced to submit themselves for assessment by psychologists or psychiatrists" (p. 91).

There is limited evidence of the reliability with which practitioners make such decisions in the process of ascribing diagnoses (Widiger, 2002), although reliability improves when highly structured interview methods are used (Frances & Widiger, 1986; Miller, 2002). (We explore the DSM's reliability problems in more depth in Chapter 2.) How then can research that is based on practitioner diagnoses be considered valid? Such informal decisions, claim Sarbin and others, leave diagnosis in the realm of a subjective rather than scientific enterprise.

Other problems exist with the "science" behind the DSM. For instance, biases in sampling exist in the research upon which some of the DSM is based. The nonprobability samples that were often used in such research were obtained largely by convenience, despite researchers' ostensible awareness that convenience samples are highly susceptible to selection biases. For instance, such samples typically contain disproportionate representations of one or the other sex as a result of factors other than etiology (e.g., disproportionate treatment seeking by females, greater acknowledgment of problems by females, negative reactions of others to the problems of males, presence of comorbid conditions in males that result in greater referral for treatment; Hartung & Widiger, 1998). As a result of sampling bias, a disproportionate number of males become experimental subjects in investigations. Yet, researchers and practitioners apply the conclusions drawn from studies of male behavior to women, as though guided by some assumption of "universality" (Hartung & Widiger, 1998; McLaughlin, 2002; Worell, 2001).

These and other concerns about the science behind the DSM have led some challengers to claim that the DSM is more a political consensus document than a scientifically valid one (Denton, 1990; Figert, 1995; Gunderson, 1992; Laungani, 2002; Sadler, 2002). Denton (1990) considers it likely that DSM developers have been invested in obtaining a consensus about a classification system because they will then have achieved agreement about what is known, what is important to know, and whose knowledge is most important, in other words, what is or is not a mental disorder and the domain of mental health practice. This "convergence" tendency results in incorporating the positions and cultural biases of the creators into the DSM, biases of which the DSM creators may not have been aware. Unfortunately, a convergence tendency means that those whose perspectives are not included in the decision making run the risk of disempowerment and disenfranchisement by users of the classification system (Caplan, 1995; Crowe, 2000; Denton, 1990).

Some challengers expand this argument by claiming that the DSM is a mechanism of social control. Sarbin says, "Every society creates procedures and practices for marginalizing persons whose public actions fail to meet propriety norms. . . . Behind these . . . are implicit premises about maintaining order. Authority figures . . . make the initial judgment whether any particular item of conduct [is] unwanted" (1997, p. 241; see also Caplan, 1995; Cermele, Daniels, & Anderson, 2001; Crowe, 2000; Summerfield, 2001). One doesn't have to journey too far back through history to remember decisions that were made by authority figures that resulted in damage to certain groups of people. More specifics on such damage are considered in Chapters 3 and 4.

Imposing values. Related to the scientific defensibility of the DSM are concerns about the values inherent in the DSM system, despite its developers' claims of theoretical neutrality, and the failure of the DSM to be clear about and to examine the values that contribute to decisions about impairment (Russell, 1986b). In modern times, Woolfolk (2001) points out, the mental health professions have been dominated by the economic and ideological perspectives of such institutions as pharmaceutical companies, government agencies (such as the National Institutes of Health), managed care and health insurance companies, and academic psychology and psychiatry. These institutions largely support the notion that problems in living can be explained from a biomedical perspective. That is, they believe that peoples' problems should be conceived of as analogous to physical diseases, and they thus conceptualize therapy as a medical technology. Research from this perspective focuses on discovering the underlying genetic, chromosomal, or biochemical causes for people's difficulties (Woolfolk, 2001).

This way of thinking about people, called the medical model, is also reflected in the DSM; in fact, it may be the guiding paradigm of the DSM. To a degree, this is understandable because the DSM was originally created largely by psychiatrists who are, of course, medical practitioners. Other professionals have been included in more recent versions of the DSM; however, as Tomm (1989) points out,

the very notion of "diagnosis" is part of the medical illness and cure tradition, a tradition that conflicts with many schools of counseling and psychological thought. In the medical illness–cure tradition, says Tomm, clients are "diagnosed" with a "mental disorder" and subsequently obtain "treatment" to "cure" their "illness." He claims that clients who are envisioned from this perspective become identified with the mental disorder. That is, they refer to themselves, and others refer to them, as, for example, "depressed" or "borderline." When a problem-saturated identity is developed, or further solidified and reinforced, says Tomm, it becomes increasingly difficult for those who are so diagnosed to escape the label (see also Fewster, 2002; Laungani, 2002; Russell, 1986b).

Furthermore, the medical model's individualistic, reductionistic, mechanistic, static, and objectivist explanations of experience (Denton, 1989, 1990; Duffy et al., 2002; Sarbin, 1997; Sperry, 2002b; Sporakowski, 1995; Stravynski & O'Connor, 1995) are particularly antithetical to the values of some groups of mental health practitioners and of some clients, despite the continuing use of the DSM by members of these groups. For instance, family therapists and feminist and multicultural practitioners think contextually and systemically, and thus struggle to find relevance within the DSM system. They would say that any illness or problem exists within a context, and the medical model's practice, as expressed in the DSM, of separating social context from discussions of pathology and disorders excludes critical systems, relationships, and cultural perspectives. In the "pure" form of the diagnostic model, there is little room for developmental models, multicultural concerns, and strength-based counseling (Graybeal, 2001; Hershenson, Power, & Waldo, 1996; Ivey & Ivey, 1998; Rigazio-DiGilio, Ivey, & Locke, 1997; Sperry, 2002b; White, 2002). This narrowness of focus on the individual is likely to encourage the diagnosis of "mental disorder" when there is far more disturbance in the social environment, and when the "treatment program" ought to be directed toward that environment (Russell, 1986b, p. 93).

Feminists and multicultural mental health practitioners also point to other conflicts between the DSM's values and those of women and people of color, claiming that the DSM's definitions of normal and abnormal behavior have hurt both groups of people. Feminists and multicultural mental health practitioners may thus find themselves challenging the relevance of diagnostic categories for people of color, women, and others who differ from the mainstream, claiming that such categories are social myths that serve to justify existing social systems (Shields, 1995), that "pathologizing certain emotions and practices has served as a means of social control over women and members of other social groups, such as immigrants, poor people, and ethnic minorities" (Marecek, 1993, pp. 117–118). When one examines history, it becomes apparent that although we now consider many of the behaviors that are characteristic of women and people of color to be "normal," we previously diagnosed many of these people as abnormal. (We examine further the DSM's relationship with women and people of color in Chapters 3 and 4.) This means that we now judge the sometimes very recent past behavior of diagnosticians to have been unethical and expressions of societal discriminations (see, for example, Bohan, 1995; Mulvany, 2000; Sadler, 2002). How will we ensure that our current assertions are free from such bias in a discipline that is so value laden when we have clearly failed so recently?

Of course, this discussion is not meant to discredit the medical model as applied to physical illnesses, although even within medicine, alternative practitioners and others are challenging the notion that the medical model is the only story that should be given credit (Conroy, Siriwardena, Smyth, & Fernandez, 2000; Knaudt, Connor, Weisler, Churchill, & Davidson, 1999). This

discussion is also not meant to imply that all medical practitioners subscribe solely to the medical model. Those in behavioral medicine, for instance, target individual behaviors that contribute to medical problems (Hermon & Hazler, 1999; Okonski, 2003). Those in psychoneuroimmunology consider the client's emotional state and relational patterns paramount to understanding disease (Hirst, 2003; Kiecolt-Glaser, McGuire, Robles, & Glaser, 2002). And perhaps medicine is changing. However, the response of traditional medical practitioners to questions about contextual and systemic factors seems to resemble the discrediting response received by the first author when questioning a medical researcher about the psychological factors that might contribute to infertility. He asked, in response to her question about such factors, "Have you been reading *People* magazine?," as though any factors in infertility beyond genes, hormones, and physical damage were the stuff of popular culture, fairy tale, or wishful thinking.

There seems to be a similar disconnect between the DSM's expression of the medical model and the values of some mental health disciplines: counselors, family therapists, social workers, counseling psychologists, and other humanistically, developmentally, and systemically oriented mental health providers who often subscribe to alternative orientations, or stories, beyond the medical model (Phemister, 2001). In fact, accreditation standards often require training programs to present a range of therapeutic approaches, in concert with an understanding of their underlying values, and to help those in training to develop their own theoretical approaches to working with clients (e.g., Council for the Accreditation of Counseling and Related Educational Programs [CACREP]). The DSM's fundamental focus on mental illness does not fit easily with this diversity of worldviews.

Alternative systems of diagnosis have been proposed. Family therapists, in particular, have proposed a relational diagnostic system

(Ivey et al., 1999; Kaslow, 1993, 2001; Rigazio-DiGilio, 2000). Even the DSM has begun to recognize the intersection of relational issues and individual symptoms by including the so-called "V codes" at the end of the DSM and the Global Assessment of Relational Functioning (GARF) Scale ratings in the appendix of the DSM. However, these "diagnoses" by themselves are not typically reimbursable by insurance; they thus lose their economic value for both clients and practitioners. Therefore, the inappropriate-but-nevertheless-common use of DSM codes that are reimbursable (Bacon, Collins, & Plake, 2002; Patterson & Lusterman, 1996; Sperry, 2002a), rather than accurate reflections of relational issues, creates numerous ethical and legal dilemmas for family therapists, particularly when clients cannot afford treatment without insurance reimbursement (see Chapter 2 for further discussion of this practice).

CONCLUSION

Clearly, many of the authors cited in this chapter believe that the "noble aims" of diagnosis have not been and may never be realized. Over two-thirds of the mental health professionals responding to a survey in one study expressed the belief that there should be an alternative manual to the DSM (Duffy et al., 2002; Sarbin, 1997; Smith & Kraft, 1983; Sperry, 2002b). According to Robins and Helzer (1986), "At best, diagnoses are imperfect descriptions of reality" (p. 430). Eysenck (1986) makes an even stronger statement in reacting to the DSM-III:

> It is clearly necessary to throw out the whole approach, hook, line, and sinker before anything better can take its place. DSM-IV, if ever such a misshapen fetus should experience a live birth, can only make confusion worse and make the psychiatric approach to classification even less scientific than it is at the moment. What is needed is a complete rethinking of the whole approach, a consideration of the underlying problems, and an attempt to formulate experimental and psychometric approaches to these problems which may generate a universally agreed answer in due course. (p. 96)

Whether one agrees with Eysenck's bold statement or not, the concerns brought forth by the authors in this chapter clearly raise questions about whether the problems in knowing and using diagnostic procedures exceed their use for helping clients, questions that may create ethical dilemmas for mental health providers. In the effort to increase practitioners' awareness about ethical dilemmas related to diagnosis, we next examine the American Association for Marriage and Family Therapy (AAMFT, 2001), the American Counseling Association's (ACA, 1995), the American Psychological Association's (APA, 1992), and the National Association of Social Workers' (NASW, 1999) codes of ethics as they pertain to diagnosis.

2

Ethics Meets Diagnosis

Ethics represents the search for best practices, not just the prevention and remediation of delinquency (Mezzich, 1999a, 1999b). For the mental health professions, ethics implies the inclination or motivation toward behaving with integrity. As such, practitioners' ethical behavior is fundamental in facilitating clients' mental health (Welfel, 2002). Furthermore, rather than it being just a professional clinical concern, we consider ethics to be a critical component of practitioners' personal life, and a factor that ultimately contributes to the well-being of society. Ethics is, then, not a static entity, but one that contributes to a "dynamic state of complete physical, mental, spiritual, and social well-being, and not just the absence of disease or infirmity" (Mezzich, 1999a, p. 137). With such a framework in mind, we now explore the ethical dilemmas that may emerge when one becomes conscious of or agrees with some of the challenges to traditional diagnosis, in relation to informed consent and confidentiality, competence, accuracy of diagnosis, dual relationships, values, and the obligation to promote growth and development and to include families. As we stated earlier, we are not attempting to provide a balanced view of diagnosis, merely to thoughtfully consider the ethical ramifications of challenges to the *Diagnostic and Statistical Manual of Mental Disorders* (DSM) system. Related and more specific discussions about the interplay between gender and cultural sensitivity, the DSM, and ethical issues are addressed in Chapters 3 and 4.

INFORMED CONSENT AND CONFIDENTIALITY

Ethical practice requires that mental health professionals obtain informed consent and maintain their clients' confidentiality (American Association for Marriage and Family Therapy [AAMFT], 2001, Standards 1.2, 2.1, 2.6; American Counseling Association [ACA], 1995, Standards A.3, B.1–B.6, E.3; American Psychological Association [APA], 1992, Standard 4.02; National Association of Social Workers [NASW], 1999, Standard 1.03). Both obligations contribute to the development of a trusting relationship; that is, a relationship in which the client can depend upon the practitioner to do as the practitioner says she or he will do, and can depend on the practitioner to keep the intimate experience of therapy private. Thus, mental health professionals inform their clients about the process of counseling and about the risks and benefits of engaging in or refusing to engage in the process of counseling. They inform their clients about confidentiality and the limits of that confidentiality. Then, based upon the information given, they gain their client's consent, usually in writing, to participate in counseling. Diagnosis, along with its risks and benefits, is a counseling procedure for which practitioners should obtain clients' consent.

Informed Consent and Diagnosis

Ethical dilemmas related to informed consent emerge any time mental health professionals think critically about how to briefly explain the process of counseling, and how to explain benefits and risks in a way that realistically portrays counseling yet does not unnecessarily deter clients from pursuing needed help. However, providing information and acquiring consent about the diagnostic process—which is almost always a part of the counseling process and which, as we pointed out earlier, brings with it risk—magnifies the complexity of these dilemmas.

Denton (1989) and others (e.g., Corey, Corey, & Callanan, 2003; Reich, 1999; Van Hoose & Kottler, 1985) raise concerns about the risks associated with diagnosis. For instance, Denton (1989) claims that diagnosis provides an excuse for irresponsibility; robs people of their uniqueness by reducing their individual totality to a single word; and leads clients to resignation about who they are, with accompanying despair or self-fulfilling prophecies. Denton further claims that giving a client a diagnosis makes it easier to see the client as different from the practitioner, thereby excusing distance from or dismissal of the personhood of the client and

encouraging treatment that clinicians would not consider giving to those who are more like themselves.

Other practitioners struggle with informed consent because they believe that an individual, pathology focus may actually harm the counseling process (Fernald, 2000; Graham, 2001; Ivey & Ivey, 1999; Sperry 2002a). In family therapy, as an example, often the first task is to persuade family members to accept systemic explanations for problems, to help them to move away from a position of blaming one person (i.e., the identified patient) for the problem just because that person has become associated with the symptoms. This strategy is considered necessary to destabilize families from their usual ways of thinking and to encourage them to work together as partners in resolving the problems (Patterson, 2002; Walsh, 2002, 2003). How, then, does a family therapist explain the "necessity" of giving an individual diagnosis after working so hard to help a family think systemically? If, as often occurs, the diagnosed person is the scapegoat in the family (Yahav & Sharlin, 2002), a diagnosis may reinforce the family's perceptions that the identified patient is "the problem," thus reducing the likelihood of family efforts at change (Denton, 1989).

In other clinical approaches, for example, positive psychology (i.e., a belief in clients' strengths and resources and the use of these resources in therapy; Seligman, 2003; Snyder & Lopez, 2002) or competency-based approaches (Walters, Carter, Pap, & Silverstein, 1988; Worell, 2001), often the first task is to move the client from a focus on the problem, a problem that the client may be accepting as an identity, to an understanding of the functionality of the symptoms or of competencies that may contradict the adopted problem identity. From such perspectives, discussing diagnosis during the process of gaining the client's consent for treatment may be counter to or impede therapeutic goals. Other authors cited throughout this book have also raised concerns—some researched, some observed in clinical situations—about the impact of diagnosis (Rosenberg, 2002; Van Hoose & Kottler, 1985).

Should practitioners inform clients of all of these possibilities during an initial session? As with many counseling procedures, the risks and benefits of diagnosis may not be grounded in research; yet a lack of research has never excused practitioners from discussing risks and benefits. Consider the following example: In a university known to one of the authors, students receive extra credit for receiving counseling from counselors-in-training. The arrangement allows counselors-in-training to practice counseling skills prior to their practicum or field training experiences. The services are provided in an on-campus training clinic and no third-party payers are involved in paying for the provided services. The "clients" who receive counseling services are informed about confidentiality and about the status of their counselors, and they consent to participate. However, they are not formally informed that they will receive a DSM diagnosis and are not provided with any information concerning the ramifications of receiving a diagnosis. The "clients" are also not given information about their ascribed diagnosis. This sort of arrangement is fairly common in practitioner training programs and doesn't differ too much from actual practice settings in the failure to inform clients about the diagnostic process or the ramifications of receiving a diagnosis. This sort of situation raises many questions: What are the possible ramifications of these clients/students receiving a diagnosis? What if the clients/students do not fully understand the diagnosis and happen to become involved in court proceedings (e.g., related to a custody hearing or to domestic violence) or other situations in which their clinical records might be subpoenaed? Is it enough to mention that a DSM diagnosis will be ascribed on an informed consent form (in writing), but fail to verbally process the implications and risks of receiving a diagnosis? In a training situation, in which a diagnosis is not required to receive reimbursement for counseling services, and in which the "practitioners" are students-in-training, should formal DSM diagnoses even be applied? Or should the clients/students have a right to decide if they would like a DSM diagnosis ascribed? How should mental health professionals inform clients of the risks and benefits associated with diagnosis? Although discovering the answers to these questions may be complex, it is important that clients be made aware of the risks and benefits associated with practitioners' ascription of DSM diagnoses, just as with any other counseling procedure.

Confidentiality and Diagnosis

Other ethical questions emerge as a result of the harm that clients might experience should counseling information, including a diagnosis, be unwittingly revealed to certain third parties (see examples of potential harm in the Introduction and Chapter 1). Examples of the ways in which client information, including diagnoses, might be revealed inadvertently or with inadvertent effects follow: If a client signs a release of information on a job application that allows an employer to check into the client's counseling history, and the employer does not want to employ people with certain diagnoses, the client may lose the opportunity for a desired job (Corrigan, 2003; Couture & Penn, 2003). For example, when one author worked in placement services, she discovered a number of large companies that regularly asked questions about counseling or psychiatric history and who administered psychological assessments as part of the interview process. When asked about the ethics of this practice, they justified it by saying that they wanted to identify prospective employees who were drug addicts or were antisocial, and who they thus believed were more likely to steal or lie. Clearly, they were looking for particular diagnostic patterns as a means to eliminate certain prospective employees from consideration.

A record of mental health treatment could also be used against clients in custody hearings or other legal proceedings, causing social embarrassment or rejection (Denton, 1989; Woody, 2000, 2001), loss of custody of a child, or loss of a litigated case (Scott, 2000). In a case known to one author, a woman who was struggling badly during the period following a major trauma was also having to battle with a former husband to keep custody of their child, custody that she had maintained for all 13 years of the child's life. In addition to the woman's emotional struggles, she was unable to work for a period of time, and thus the former husband was in a position to challenge her custody on the basis of her inability to financially provide for her child. One means to rectify the financial problems was to apply for disability benefits, and she did qualify for these on the basis of a psychiatric diagnosis. However, her lawyer advised her that should she receive disability for such a diagnosis, she would run a higher risk of losing custody of her child.

Should a mental health professional reveal these risks related to the confidentiality of a diagnosis during an initial session? Would there be time to do counseling and the necessary relationship building if one were to fully discuss such risks and help the client to make a truly informed decision? Clearly such risks do not apply in all situations, and a clinician would use her or his judgment to determine when such risks would be more likely. However, because it may not be possible to predict the development of all risky situations, these are questions that ethical practitioners need to consider. It would seem best when working with clients who are at a particularly high risk of being negatively influenced by receiving a diagnosis (e.g., clients involved in custody hearings or otherwise involved in the legal

system) that the client be provided a more thorough and detailed education about the risks and benefits of diagnosis as part of the informed consent process.

Problems related to the confidentiality of diagnostic and other counseling information might appear to be resolvable if clients simply did not reveal their participation in counseling to others. However, clients may not have full control over what others know about their counseling. For instance, in many states, a civil or criminal court can require mental health professionals to release a client's records, which generally include a diagnosis (Luepker, 2003; Scott, 2000; Woody, 2000). This means that even though practitioners have an ethical responsibility to maintain confidentiality, clients may not concurrently have the legal privilege of privacy (APA, 1992, Standard 5.05; Fisher, 2003; Jenkins, 2002). Furthermore, in the specific instances in which clients participate in group or family counseling, courts generally do not uphold individual clients' privilege (Paradise & Kirby, 1990; Swenson, 1997; Woody, 2000). This means that family therapy or group counseling clients may have what they have said during counseling revealed by their practitioner during a civil or court action. Of just as great a concern, and perhaps applicable to a greater number of clients, any coparticipant in family or group counseling could choose to reveal a client's diagnostic information, despite cautions against such revelations. Some types of clients may offer greater risks for failing to exercise wisdom in deciding when to disclose information. Again, the risks may not be relevant to all situations, particularly risks related to disclosure of diagnosis in situations in which it is not necessary to discuss diagnoses with all participating clients (e.g., group members are unlikely to know the diagnoses of other group members). However, just as they would when other counseling information might be revealed to a third party, clinicians need to carefully consider when such risks exist so as to have conversations with clients about potential threats to the confidentiality of their diagnosis and how they might manage these threats (Fisher, 2002; Jepson & Robertson, 2003; Luepker, 2003; McGivern & Marquart, 2000).

A further complication in the area of confidentiality in family counseling occurs when spouses or family members wish to know the DSM diagnosis of their partners or other family members. Parents have the right to see their children's records (Koocher & Keith-Spiegel, 1990; McGivern & Marquart, 2000; Woody, 2001) and guardian spouses or family members have the right to see the records of those for whom they are guardians (Welfel, 2002). Clinicians are to be present when people are reviewing such records so as to explain the material in a manner that is understandable to those requesting the information (Campbell, 2000). In many situations, family members' knowledge about a client's diagnosis might not cause problems and might even help family members to better understand the person who is diagnosed. However, in other situations, clients might be seriously harmed by family members who use another's diagnosis for an agenda that is inconsistent with the therapeutic agenda (Woody, 2000). It is the clinician's responsibility to ensure that such harm does not occur.

Another risk to the confidentiality of diagnosis lies in the very common request of one member of a family or group for counseling after or in addition to the current family or group sessions. In these special counseling circumstances, records usually include information about more than one counseling participant. When the new mental health professional requests clinical information about the client, diagnostic information about other group or family members could be released with the written records or with other referral information. For instance, one author often included family members in counseling when another member of the

family was hospitalized for mental health or substance abuse problems. During such sessions, it frequently became apparent that the symptoms of other family members met the DSM criteria for a diagnosable disorder, and these disorders became part of the counseling content, along with the struggles of the person who was hospitalized. In one instance, as an example, the hospital therapist discovered that the patient's depression was at least partially related to the spouse's alcoholism, and family counseling sessions included discussions of both the depression and the alcoholism. In the process of referring the client to an outpatient practitioner for aftercare, the spouse's diagnostic information was shared as part of the reason for the referral, and when the aftercare practitioner requested hospital records on the previously hospitalized patient, information about the spouse's diagnosis was also released. Yet the spouse had not signed all of the consent forms for releasing information, either at the hospital or with the new outpatient therapist. It takes a great deal of attention to ensure that such lapses do not occur and that consents are obtained from all whose information may be revealed.

In another situation, a lawyer called one of the authors to ask for records to support his position in a case that included a former client of the author's. Clearly the client would have had to reveal participation in counseling for the lawyer to have been calling; however, the practitioner told the lawyer that any client information was confidential and would not be released. The lawyer then sent a court order for the release of the counseling records, with the client's name as defendant. The lawyer also communicated to the practitioner that her client did not have privilege in civil cases in that state if the judge decided that the information was critical to the case. Clearly the judge had determined that the information was necessary because she had signed the court order. The problem was that the practitioner had seen the client in the context of couples therapy, and the records included counseling and diagnostic information related to both members of the couple. Yet, both members of the couple were not listed on the court order as defendants in the case. Although some practitioners might have released the records based on the court order, particularly considering the possible consequences of not doing so, this practitioner was clear that she would not release the information without both parties being named. However, she found herself in a dilemma about how to tell the lawyer the reason that she would not release the records—particularly since the lawyer was threatening subpoenas and contempt of court for failure to release the records—because of the breach of confidentiality that would occur should she tell the lawyer about the partner's participation in counseling. She decided to tell the lawyer that she could not release the records because the named defendant was not the only person participating in the counseling and that the records included information about another counseling participant who was not named in the court order. Evidently, the lawyer figured out who else had participated in counseling, as he did produce a court order with both members of the couple named, and the practitioner released the records. However, such an example brings to light the ethical complexities around releasing clinical information, complexities that clients *and* practitioners may be unaware of until they occur, and which may be difficult to discuss in an initial counseling session. As in many ethically challenging situations, practitioners may worry about their own risks in such situations, which further complicates the question of how they will make the best decisions for their clients.

Similar dilemmas may arise in group counseling situations in which the hospital's or organization's practice is to write one set of notes about the entire group's process and copy the notes—without names—for each group member's records (Moline, Williams, & Austin, 1998). Should records be ordered by the court or some other third party for one member of the group, or should one member of the group sign a release to have her or his records released to a third party, the practitioner may be concerned about revealing group information without the consent of all group members. Some might wonder whether releasing such information would really be a problem given that no names were attached to the information. However, in very public cases or in small towns, it might be easy to discover who was in the group. Furthermore, the group members might not want material released even without their names attached. Ethically, it should clearly be their right to decide whether the information should be released. To inform such situations, it is worthwhile for the practitioner to discuss possible access to such information early in therapy. In order to do so adequately, however, practitioners need to be aware of the range of possible disclosures of confidential material that could occur.

Finally, we recommend informing clients about the risks of revealing diagnostic codes to insurance companies. For instance, once insurance reimbursement requests are submitted with the required diagnosis, the client's diagnosis is entered into a central information bank. If the client changes employers or wants to change insurance companies, and submits another insurance claim form, the new company may consult this central information bank to discover if the client has a preexisting condition. If the new request has the same diagnosis as the request previously submitted, the employer or company may not pay for the preexisting condition at all, or may only pay for treatment after the client has subscribed to the current insurance plan for a certain period of time. In these cases, the client may not be reimbursed for services and may have to pay for counseling services as out-of-pocket costs. In other cases, if a client is searching for new insurance coverage and the new insurer consults the central information bank, the insurance company may refuse to sell individual insurance to the client because the client has received treatment for particular diagnoses (Ackley, 1997; Campbell, 2000). A number of practitioners known to one author, for instance, have struggled to find health insurance companies that would insure them for medical *or* psychiatric care, because these practitioners had in the past pursued their own counseling.

People's problems with obtaining approval to receive insurance reimbursement develop because some insurance companies do not want to pay for the treatment of disorders that existed before their policy was purchased. Although this position is understandable from the perspective of insurance companies who clearly must consider economics, clients often remain unaware that their future care or insurability may be affected by accepting a psychiatric (or any other) diagnosis and by receiving treatment for that diagnosis (Kjorstad, 2003; Peele & Lave, 1999; Sherer, 2003; Wittig, 2000). Practitioners and clients alike may simply accept the practice of billing insurance for problems that arise, without carefully weighing the long-term consequences of doing so. Of course, if practitioners informed clients of these potential problems, their clients could choose to pay directly for services (we discuss this further in Chapter 5); however, low-income clients usually do not have the advantage of such choices unless the practitioner offers pro bono services or uses a sliding scale to determine the cost of therapy.

In this age of technology, a newer complication related to the confidentiality of diagnoses submitted to insurance companies has emerged: One has to wonder whether insurance claim information that is stored or transmitted electronically is really confidential. Indeed, recent Health Insurance Portability and Accountability Act (HIPAA) standards were specifically developed by the U.S. Department of Health and Human Services (HHS) to safeguard electronic submissions and to protect the security and confidentiality of consumers' health-related information (retrieved December, 28, 2003, http://www. hhs.gov/ocr/hipaa/). The standards represent a uniform, federal floor of privacy protections for consumers across the country. State laws providing *additional* protections to consumers are not affected by this new rule, but in general, HIPAA standards provide privacy protections for consumers of health and mental health services where standards were historically lacking.

According to HIPAA, diagnoses are not protected health information. Treatment plans, progress toward goals, Global Assessment of Functioning ratings, session start and stop times, modalities of treatment, and testing data are also not protected information. Thus, third-party payers have access to this information. Clients must be apprised of what information will be released to third-party payers and how this information will be used.

Another potential issue relates to the financial merging of various companies. Insurance companies and managed care companies are frequently bought and sold, and some corporations choose to self-insure their employees. Some authors speculate that such mergers may have an impact on the confidentiality of employees' private information (Ackley, 1997; Jenkins, 2002). In a situation known to one author, a client was taken to the emergency room following an overdose of sleeping medication taken during her attempts to recover from a major trauma. Because the overdose was reported for reimbursement purposes, and because the employer was self-insured and had access to this information, employees in the company found out about the diagnosis and the client became unemployable in her industry because of an assumed "drug addiction." Although she surely has grounds to sue, that strategy has its own risks and expenses, particularly because a lawsuit might not quench rumors that have already spread. Adequately informing clients of the potential risks involved in such corporate strategies so that clients can make responsible choices about their care should, as this case demonstrates, also be a part of the informed consent process related to the confidentiality of diagnoses.

Most practitioners accept their ethical responsibilities to inform clients of such limits to confidentiality. However, the realities of deciding how, when, and how much information to reveal so as to facilitate rather than harm counseling efforts, are more complicated. Smith (1981) and others (Campbell, 2000; Fisher, 2002; Jenkins, 2002) indicate that many practitioners do not adequately address clients' rights to be apprised of diagnostic information, even though they carefully inform clients about treatment plans and converse about client and practitioner expectations. Mental health professionals may thus compromise their integrity by not informing clients of the risks of diagnosis. However, even if clients are informed, many clients may decide that they have no choice but to accept these risks, because without reimbursement, they would be unable to pursue counseling services (Talan, 2000; Wittig, 2000).

Informing About the
Risks of Not Diagnosing

Even though practitioners may be aware of concerns about informed consent and confidentiality related to ascribing diagnoses, practitioners must not make the mistake of deciding that ascribing diagnoses means only risks. Ethical codes also require clinicians to inform clients of the risks of *not* pursuing particular counseling processes, which should include the risks of *not* diagnosing. For instance, as pointed out in case examples in Chapter 1, in some situations, receiving a diagnosis is a relief to clients. Through diagnosis clients may develop a social construction, or a meaning system related to their experiences that allows them to stop "beating themselves up" for being the cause of their own distress, and, in turn, allows them to pursue more

helpful methods of managing their "disorder." Similarly, once family members know that a person has a diagnosable disorder, they may stop blaming that person. Also, once family members know that *they* will not be blamed, they may be more willing to participate with their family in treatment (see cases in Chapter 1; Denton, 1989).

Clients may also lose various benefits if they are not ascribed a diagnosis. For instance, clients' health insurance may not reimburse for counseling services without the client receiving a DSM diagnosis, and clients may then have to pay large sums of money out-of-pocket in order to receive such services (Anderson, 2000; Kjorstad, 2003; Sherer, 2003). Furthermore, without engaging in the diagnostic process, it may be difficult to tell if the client meets the criteria for a disorder for which taking medication would help to alleviate distress. In addition, without diagnosing a client, it may be difficult to adequately communicate with physicians or psychiatrists about clients who may benefit from such medication. Without a diagnosis, those in need of hospitalization who are unwilling or unable to decide to admit themselves would not be eligible for involuntary commitment to a hospital, which, beyond the harm that society might experience from those who are dangerous, often means that individuals become homeless or are incarcerated (Fisher, Packer, Banks, Smith, Simon, & Roy-Bujnowski, 2002; Winkleby, 1993). Without being determined by diagnosis to be incompetent to stand trial, those who have committed a crime as a result of a mental disorder may receive imprisonment rather than treatment (Fisher et al., 2002; Seligman et al., 2001). Without a diagnosis, children may not qualify for special services in school (Anderson, 2001; Phipps, 1982). Other clients may not qualify for other kinds of services such as social security payments for a mental health disability, participation in day treatment or clubhouse programs, or opportunities to attend special camps to learn basic living skills (Rogers, MacDonald-Wilson, & Massaro, 2003; Steyn, Schneider, & McArdle, 2002). The benefits that incur to those with DSM diagnoses are, as these situations illustrate, clearly too important to justify dismissing the diagnostic process out of hand or to justify failing to inform clients of the risks of *not* diagnosing.

Responsible Informed Consent

Given the benefits of diagnosis, the questions still remain: How comprehensive should disclosure be about such benefits? How can we balance information about benefits with those about risks so that clients can make informed decisions? Chapters 3 through 8 propose many approaches to using diagnosis helpfully. At this juncture, it seems most important to remember that withholding information from clients about the possible risks and benefits of diagnosis places mental health professionals in the powerful position of making decisions that will impact clients' lives without their full consent, decisions that clients might not choose themselves if fully informed (Campbell, 2000; Fisher, 2003, 2002; Luepker, 2003). Practitioners are generally informed about whether they should take on such a powerful role by their particular school of psychological thought; that is, some schools of thought place clinicians in more egalitarian roles with clients while others encourage practitioners to assume a more authoritarian relationship with clients (Avery, 2002; Corey, 2001; Peterson & Nisenholz, 1999). However, regardless of whether one's school of thought advocates that practitioners take on or give up powerful and authority-based roles, practitioners cannot avoid playing powerful roles in their clients' lives whether or not they actively choose such power (Haug, 1999; Rosenbaum & Miller, 1996). Therein lies the importance of critically reflecting on power imbalances, on the range of possible harms to clients, and on ethical decision making related to the dilemmas that arise.

Approaches or mental health disciplines in which mental health professionals recognize and give up as much power as possible, and in which practitioners empower clients to carefully make their own decisions include professional counseling, family therapy, and more humanistic and constructivist psychotherapies, all of which tend to espouse a more egalitarian approach to counseling than do the more traditional therapies (Corey, 2001; Rogers, 1951, 1961; Sweeney, 1998; Yalom, 2002). From our (the authors') perspectives as counselors and family therapists, therefore, we generally recommend that clinicians openly discuss facts that are likely to impact clients, and we favor offering assistance to clients as they carefully weigh their choices. In fact, rather than conceiving of informed consent as the "agreements to be reached before counseling begins," we imagine such discussions to be part of the ongoing assessment and counseling process. During this process, mental health professionals observe how clients currently make decisions and take care of themselves, and encourage wisdom and self-care when they are needed. Practitioners clearly need to exercise discretion in deciding when and how to "fully inform" clients (Fisher, 2002; Jepson & Robertson, 2003). Practitioners also need to guard against informing clients later in the counseling process of the potential harm of diagnosis, as such late information may damage a trusting relationship if clients have previously agreed to the counseling relationship on the basis of incomplete information (Fisher, 2003).

In summary, although there are no easy answers to the complex questions and issues we have posed, we are recommending that clients be made aware of the diagnostic process, the risks and benefits of receiving a DSM diagnosis process, and ultimately any diagnoses that they are given. We recommend that the extent to which one provides information about informed consent issues be based upon the setting the practitioner works in, the presenting client concern and client needs, and the personal ramifications to a client of receiving a diagnosis. The decisions about how much to discuss about diagnosis during the informed consent process is ultimately based on the practitioners' clinical judgment.

COMPETENCE

It is understood that mental health professionals are to practice only in their areas of competence. Although competence related to any counseling procedures may emerge from a combination of sources, professions generally assume that such competence generates from adequate education and/or training and supervision (AAMFT, 2001, Standards 3.1, 3.4, 3.7, 3.11; ACA, 1995, Standard C.2; APA, 1992, Standard 1.04; NASW, 1999, Standard 1.04). On the basis of such assumptions, competence to diagnose would also require relevant education and/or training and supervision. However, becoming competent to diagnose can pose a problem given the variations in training and licensure requirements for mental health providers.

If one accepts the assumptions of ethical codes and accreditation standards, one can assume that graduates of accredited programs whose standards require a course in diagnosis would become competent to diagnose upon receiving supervision in applying course material to clients, and that they would remain "competent" as long as they practiced diagnosis. For instance, the Council for Accreditation of Counseling and Related Educational Programs (CACREP, 2001) for community and mental health counseling, and marital, couple, and family counseling programs, and the APA Committee on Accreditation (2002) require such a course, along with the supervision of diagnosis during internships and practica.

We can also assume that professionals who practice independently are competent to diagnose if their license to practice requires education and supervision in abnormal psychology and/or diagnosis and treatment planning (Clasen, Meyer, Brum, Mase, & Cauley, 2003; Spaulding & Strachan, 2003; Ward, 2001). For instance, in many states, licensure laws for community, mental health, and other professional counselors, psychologists, clinical social workers, and psychiatrists require a course or courses in diagnosis (Saul, 2002). Although licensure or other credentialing procedures are not universally held as the minimum for all mental health practice, they are almost always required for post–bachelor-level professional counselors, psychologists, and other mental health providers who wish to practice independently and receive insurance reimbursement for their services (Glosoff et al., 1999; Scheidt et al., 1998).

However, some mental health curricula and licenses do not require courses in diagnosis. Mental health professionals who diagnose but who have not graduated from accredited programs that require a diagnosis course, who practice in states whose licensure processes do not require DSM courses, who are bachelor level practitioners, or who are not licensed, may thus be practicing diagnosis without adequate training (Kunik, 2002; Levin, Beauchamp, & Henry-Beauchamp, 1997). Additionally, a number of mental health practice specialties do not require coursework and supervision in diagnostic procedures. For instance, some social workers; and school, career, and college counselors; even those who graduate from accredited programs, may not receive such training (Levin et al., 1997). Couple and family therapy programs, licensure laws, and certifications have not always required couple and family therapists to take courses in diagnosis or psychopathology (Kaas, Suzanne, & Peitzinan, 2003; Levin et al., 1997). It is therefore questionable whether such practitioners can be considered competent to provide diagnoses or to defend diagnoses to insurance companies, in peer reviews, or in court (Denton, 1989).

More importantly, even if one assumes that such practitioners would not practice diagnosis without adequate training, one would still wonder how such practitioners would know when to refer clients who have more intensive needs than the practitioner can meet, for instance, those with bipolar disorders who need medication, or those with suicidal depression who need hospitalization (Spaulding & Strachan, 2003). Some states (e.g., Virginia) require couple and family therapists, for example, to receive training in diagnosis to become licensed because of the harm that can result to clients if family therapists do not recognize the significance of more serious individual symptoms (Bischoff & Barton, 2002; Denton, 1989; Kaas et al., 2003). Also, in one study, 93% of surveyed couple and family therapy training programs mandated training for students in the DSM (Denton, Patterson, & Van Meir, 1997). Some mental health education programs also require school, career, and other specialties of counselors to receive some training in diagnosis for the same reason (Hunt, Niles, Jaques, & Wierzalis, 2003). However, these decisions do not adequately address the problem of those practitioners who have not accepted the need for diagnostic knowledge or the absence of training for those in other mental health specialties.

Even if practitioners have received what licensure laws and accreditation standards consider to be adequate training in diagnosis, the question of competency remains. Many programs have at most one class that specifically addresses the content and process of using the DSM and ascribing diagnoses. The course material on all of the psychopathologies is so time intensive to cover that there is rarely time to cover controversies such as those illustrated in this book. Furthermore, examples of improper application of DSM diagnosis abound. For example, one author worked with a psychiatrist who regularly diagnosed clients as having both bipolar 1 disorder and dysthymic disorder, yet the DSM indicates that to be diagnosed with dysthymic disorder, one must never have had a manic episode, which is a requirement for bipolar 1 disorder. In addition, the other author has had regular conversations with clinicians who are unaware of the necessary criteria for particular diagnoses.

Clearly, professional disciplines focus primarily on training as the means to acquire a minimal level of competence. However, another issue related to competence emerges from the ethos of some subspecialties. That is, what happens to the ability to behave competently in diagnosing when the undergirding philosophy of a mental health discipline contradicts the whole notion of individual diagnosis? For example, although couple and family licensure laws often include requirements for training in diagnosis of mental disorders, they may do so for market reasons only, that is, to allow licensees to receive insurance reimbursement and to prevent other mental health professionals from limiting couple and family therapists' scope of practice, rather than because individual diagnosis fits into the usual family therapist's philosophy or tasks. Humanistic practitioners may consider the whole process of diagnosis to contradict their notions of dynamism and growth potential (Boy, 1989; Rogers, 1961). Psychoanalysts may consider diagnosis to add little to their dynamic formulations of clients (Schmolke, 1999). So, if providers' commitment to the diagnostic process is limited for philosophical and value reasons, would these professionals be inclined to invest in maintaining or upgrading their levels of diagnostic competence after an initial, required course in diagnosis? It seems possible that their skill might decline without such a commitment. They may be unlikely to keep up on current developments in diagnosis if their theoretical school of thought questions its relevance to their work. These concerns take on importance when one considers the reasons behind the ethical mandates to keep up on current developments in mental health practice (e.g., adequate client care; AAMFT, 2001, Standards 3.1, 3.11; ACA, 1995, Standards C.2f, E.5).

On the other hand, the value of a questioning stance lies in its relativizing of diagnosis (Cerullo, 1992; Owen, 1992; Raskin, 2001). That is, questioning the diagnostic process for philosophical reasons may facilitate an understanding of DSM diagnoses as only one way of making meaning of client experiences (Durrheim, 1997; Guterman, 1996; Neimeyer, 1998). A questioning stance might result in an ongoing willingness to stay abreast of all of the information on diagnosis; that is, the information criticizing it, as well as that encouraging its use (Guterman, 1996; Neimeyer, 1998; Owen, 1992). Such a skeptical practitioner might be able to deconstruct the use and misuse of diagnosis, rather than either becoming a "true believer" or dogmatic adherent to the DSM system or dismissing it out of hand (Guterman, 1994; Martin, 1993; Williams, 1998). Given the concerns expressed thus far about the DSM system, a relativizing stance might be a more helpful position for practitioners to adopt.

Such a questioning stance might also stimulate those who hold different philosophical positions to develop and fully actualize their own diagnostic systems. For instance, couple and family therapists may fully develop their proposed "relational diagnostic system" (Ivey et al., 1999; Kaslow, 1993), and may advocate for its full reimbursement by insurance companies. Practitioners from gestalt, psychoanalytic, or behavioral schools of thought may develop and research a sixth DSM axis that offers conceptualizations of problems that fit their philosophical positions (Denton, 1990). Acceptance of a more inclusive system of diagnosis may then free systemically, developmentally, and contextually oriented therapists, as well as others who would like a universal and formal diagnostic system that extends beyond a medical model, from the requirement to have such extensive knowledge about the

current, individualistic DSM. They would still, however, need some understanding of severe individual disorders for referral purposes (Denton, 1989).

ACCURACY VERSUS MISREPRESENTATION

Ethical codes also emphasize the need for accuracy in client diagnosis. Ethical mental health professionals thus develop accurate diagnoses and do not misrepresent their work to clients, to the public, or to others, such as insurance companies (AAMFT, 2001, Standards 3.5, 3.12, 3.13, 7.4; ACA, 1995, Standards A.3, C.5c, C.5d, E.5). However, the disillusionment of some mental health professionals with whom we have had conversations with the static pathology and individualistic focus of the DSM system, along with the market necessity of using it, has led some of these practitioners to only marginally invest in the diagnostic process, seeing it as a game to be played, and misrepresenting their work to third parties (Danzinger & Welfel, 2001; Kanapaux, 2003). For clients who are able to pay out-of-pocket, practitioners may feel less bound to DSM diagnosis when it does not seem therapeutically relevant. However, without third-party reimbursement (which requires a diagnosis), middle or lower socioeconomic status clients will unlikely be able to afford practitioners' rates, and practitioners are unlikely to be able to continue to practice on what such clients could afford to pay (Cohen, 2003; Danzinger & Welfel, 2001). Some have gone so far as to suggest that the use of the DSM system, and the ethical questions about misrepresentation, would decrease if it were not for the dependence of practitioners' livelihoods on funding sources that require DSM diagnoses (e.g., Denton, 1989).

The challenges of those practitioners who are only marginally invested in the required diagnostic process may be justified in some respects. For instance, how accurate is it to indicate only "major depression" as the diagnosis when high levels of resilience, wisdom, and the ability to generate family support are also present? How accurate is it to ascribe an individually focused diagnosis when a client is the victim of systemic oppressions that would make any normal person "misbehave" or feel depressed or crazy (Diaz, Ayala, Bein, Henne, & Marin, 2001; Travis & Compton, 2001)? Why should an individual be diagnosed when a system needs fixing (see Chapter 3 and 4 for examples)? One can see how mental health professionals who operate from a systemic or holistic perspective might find themselves in a double bind when seeking accuracy, because the DSM system does not really allow for "accuracy" from a number of philosophical perspectives (Crowe, 2000; Fewster, 2002).

On the other hand, if mental health professionals choose to participate in a system that only reimburses medically necessary treatment as defined by a DSM diagnosis— and often in order to continue practicing they must so choose—then they need to accurately indicate such a diagnosis. Failure to accurately diagnose may be done for pragmatic reasons (i.e., the ability to be reimbursed for services), but it is ultimately legally fraudulent.

It seems, however, that some practitioners do commit such fraud (Danzinger & Welfel, 2001; Kanapaux, 2003). Danzinger and Welfel's (2001) survey research indicated that 44% of respondents had changed or would change a client's diagnosis in order to qualify for additional managed care reimbursement.

Relatedly, Mead, Hohenshil, and Singh (1997) found that couple and family therapists often provide a diagnosis for reimbursement purposes even when there are no Axis I disorders in evidence, or they offer a diagnosis to one member of the family, even when philosophically they believe that it is the family that should be "diagnosed."

Practitioners who do this evidently reason that because a diagnosis is necessary for insurance reimbursement, diagnosing a member of the family is necessary if the couple or family is to pursue counseling (Danzinger & Welfel, 2001). Consider the following illustrations of such behavior: Mental health professionals with whom we have had conversations have ascribed a diagnosis to the child in a family because the family considers the child to be "the problem," even though the practitioner believes that it is really a parent who has a diagnosable disorder. They have done this because the family might resist coming in for counseling were they not to do so. Some practitioners reason that such a practice is the best way to continue the counseling and thus to help the child in need (Stratton, 2003).

Additionally, family counselors known to the authors have diagnosed the one member of a family who has insurance coverage, despite the presence of diagnosable disorders in others. For instance, sessions for dependents (spouses and children) of military personnel are reimbursable by CHAMPUS (the health insurance plan for military dependents), while sessions for active duty military personnel themselves are not. Consequently, a family counselor may "find" a diagnosis for a child or spouse of a military person to enable the family to pursue counseling, even when the practitioner believes that aspects of the military person's behavior are the "real" problem.

Denton (1989) also discusses ethical issues associated with mental health professionals underdiagnosing as a means of protecting clients from the stigma of certain diagnoses. Mental health professionals with whom we are familiar have ascribed less-stigmatizing diagnoses, even though the full criteria for another diagnosis exist and the criteria for the diagnosis ascribed do not (Cooper & Gottlieb, 2000; Glosoff et al., 1999; Mead et al., 1997). In still other cases, professionals report the diagnosis that they know will be reimbursed (Axis I), rather than one that will not (Axis II or V codes), despite the greater accuracy of the unreimbursable diagnosis (i.e., overdiagnosing; Cooper & Gottlieb, 2000; Danzinger & Welfel, 2001; Glosoff et al., 1999; Mead et al., 1997).

Why would mental health professionals participate in such misrepresentation? Some known to the authors do it out of an advocacy or moral stance, believing that insurance should pay for such problems, and that they are engaged in an act of civil disobedience, countering a system that is inherently flawed (Laungani, 2002; Mead et al., 1997). After all, they reason, revolutions to change systemic oppressions often take years of conscientious resistance. Others known to the authors engage in misrepresentation out of pressure from clients who maintain similar beliefs about the insurance system. Some providers with whom we have had conversations believe that their misrepresentations are a caring response to clients who feel desperate to receive services, but who are not able to pay for services out-of-pocket. Still others cynically respond to the market demand to provide a diagnosis; after all, says Denton (1989), the client will probably be able to find another professional who will assign a diagnosis.

Obviously, professional ethical codes and legal requirements conflict with some mental health professionals' moral and ethical stances when accuracy of diagnosis is under discussion, and this creates ethical dilemmas that are not easily resolved. Ignoring the issue because it is too difficult, because it will "never be resolved," or because one does not have the time certainly does not contribute to creating a system with greater integrity. Ongoing alertness to the ethical issues involved, dialogue with peers, and participation in professional associations that advocate about such issues may contribute to creating a better system or to resolving one's own personal struggles.

However, it is critically important that practitioners recognize that their (perhaps virtuous, perhaps financially "necessary") choices to misrepresent a client's diagnosis do not protect clients from the potential harms of diagnosis. That is, if a clinician chooses to "upcode" a child from a "parent–child relational problem" to an Adjustment Disorder with Depressed Mood or to a Dysthymic Disorder, the potential harms of labeling and stigma discussed thus far exist for the child, even if the diagnosis is a misrepresentation and even if the client's parent is willing to agree to the misrepresentation (Knight, Wykes, & Hayward, 2003). Informed consent about misrepresentation may be as ethically necessary as informed consent about an accurate diagnosis, despite the legal liability that might ensue from such discussions.

DUAL RELATIONSHIPS

Ethical codes have much to say about dual relationships. For example, the AAMFT's (2001) code of ethics dictates that couple and family therapists "avoid exploiting the trust and dependency" of clients, and so make every effort to avoid the multiple relationships with clients "that could impair professional judgment or increase the risk of exploitation" (p. 2, section 1.3). Couple and family therapists are not to use relationships with clients to further their own interests, especially at the expense of the client (section 1.7). Such relationships include business relationships. The ACA's (1995) code of ethics further stresses that "when a dual relationship cannot be avoided, counselors take appropriate professional precautions, such as informed consent, consultation, supervision, and documentation to ensure that judgment is not impaired and no exploitation occurs" (p. 2, section A.6.a; see also APA, 1992, Standard 3.05; NASW, 1999, Standard 1.06C). However, because mental health practitioners use diagnosis for business purposes—that is, to receive reimbursement from third parties, both insurance companies and grant sponsors—and, in some cases, for therapeutic purposes, the potential for unethical dual relationships exists. Many of the issues presented in this book thus far emerge from the challenges of such dual relationships. Yet little literature explores ethical dilemmas that may arise related to the dual relationships that are inherent in diagnosis (Fishman, 2003; Nigro, 2003).

The Therapeutic–Fiduciary Relationship Tension

The ethical mandates related to dual relationships draw attention to the primary purpose of therapeutic relationships, that is, to meet the client's mental health needs. When a mental health professional enters into any other type of relationship with the client, for other purposes, these purposes may conflict with meeting the client's therapeutic needs. If the other purposes benefit the mental health professional in some way (as in a fiduciary relationship), the professional may feel personally threatened by the conflict and such feelings of threat may interfere with the professional's ability to make the client's needs primary (Galambos, 1999; Ljunggren & Sjoden, 2001). For instance, in the case of diagnosis, if giving a diagnosis might be contratherapeutic, the professional may feel conflicted because of the loss of reimbursement for services that are provided without a diagnosis. Many of the potential risks of diagnosis that have been stated thus far emerge from the conflicts between a mental health professional's needs to generate funds for the counseling services and his or her judgments about the value of rendering a diagnosis (Ljunggren & Sjoden 2001).

Of course, even were clients to pay the practitioner directly rather than needing a diagnosis to apply for insurance reimbursement or grant funding, practitioners have a fiduciary relationship with their clients. That is, practitioners are invested in receiving money from their clients; they thus are invested both in keeping the client for financial reasons and in therapeutic change, investments that at times may conflict

(Catalano, Libby, Snowden, & Cuellar, 2000; Dewa, 2001; Galambos, 1999). It might seem that the problem of dual relationships could be eliminated were the clinician to work in and be paid by a hospital or other mental health agency. However, in those cases, the need to maintain the relationship with the employer may come into conflict with one's best therapeutic judgment (Proctor & Morrow-Howell, 1993; Ryan & Bamber, 2002). It may, in fact, be impossible to eliminate such dual relationships.

Ackley (1997) continues this line of thinking by raising the question of who decides what is therapeutically beneficial. He claims that when practitioners ask for money from third parties—whether insurers, grant sponsors, employers (or clients, we might add)—they are relinquishing control over therapeutic decisions to these third parties. For example, according to Ackley, clear indications of such control by managed care companies exist in the requirement that practitioners adhere to the medical model in diagnosis and treatment planning, that they shorten the length of treatment to between four and ten sessions, and that they submit intimate therapeutic details to insurance companies in treatment plans. From his perspective, to eliminate these potential "dual-relationship" risks of diagnosis, mental health professionals would need to stop diagnosing and give up all of the funding sources that depend on diagnosing. According to Ackley (1997), only then, with clients paying out-of-pocket, might clients truly control the counseling process. However, as discussed above, that does not eliminate the dual relationship. In Ackley's opinion, it just places control for the therapeutic process where it ought to be.

In our estimation, refusing to diagnose in order to eliminate dual-relationship quandaries related to diagnosis leaves only fee-for-service (i.e., paying out-of-pocket) options, charity-supported options (e.g., funded by religious organizations), or supportive counseling services, such as school and college counseling, that are financed in other ways and are not limited to remediation and "medically necessary" treatment. As mentioned, it does not eliminate the dual relationship, merely the dual relationship that is complicated by the possible risks of diagnosis. However, if available counseling services were limited to fee-for-service, middle class and lower socioeconomic status people would be unable, or less able, to pursue mental health treatment (Abas, Baingana, Broadhead, Iacoponi, & Vanderpyl, 2003; Hines-Martin, Malone, Kim, & Brown-Piper, 2003), because school and college counselors and charity-based practitioners could not provide all of the mental health services that are currently needed in our society. Therefore, mental health professionals are left to figure out ways to manage the dual therapeutic–fiduciary relationship.

Toward Solutions to the Dual-Relationship Dilemma

The ethical codes suggest that when facing ethical dilemmas, mental health providers should use informed consent, consultation, supervision, and documentation to ensure that the therapeutic relationship does not suffer (ACA, 1995, Standards B.4.a, C.1.e, E.3.a, H.1.b; APA, 1992, Standards 3.10a, 4.06, 6.01; Bradley & Ladany, 2001; NASW, 1999, Standards 1.03, 2.05a, 3.01a, 3.04a; Welfel, 2002). Informed consent has already been discussed, as have the difficulties in determining the extent of information to be offered about the risks and benefits of diagnosis. However, mental health professionals might, at a minimum, create space for open discussion with clients about both the risks and benefits of diagnosis and the potential risks of the dual relationship. Open and honest conversation about the issues increases clients' abilities to choose and decreases the chance of exploitation.

Consultation and supervision, also in the list of ethical recommendations, presumably should also be used to assure that an accurate

diagnosis is rendered, to fully determine the ramifications of such a diagnosis, to clarify what information to offer clients about the risks and benefits of diagnosis, and to decide how best to prevent damage to the client as a result of funding requirements (Galambos, 1999; Proctor & Morrow-Howell, 1993). Those practitioners who are unlicensed or who work in hospitals or agencies may already have a supervisor. Others may pay a supervisor for ongoing consultation about cases. However, all practitioners should have several, more experienced professionals to consult with when treatment questions or ethical dilemmas arise (ACA, 1995, Standard F.1.a; NASW, 1999, Standard 3.01a).

Not always, however, will such consultants offer unbiased advice. For instance, if the consultant works for the same organization as the practitioner, the consultant has a vested interest in receiving the same funding that is needed by the practitioner (Proctor & Morrow-Howell, 1993). Furthermore, even if the consultant or supervisor does not work for the same organization, the consultant/supervisor is likely to be invested in (bound by) the same funding and reimbursement system as is the mental health professional, and to regularly face the same ethical dilemmas, albeit not always with conscious awareness. Presumably the consultant/supervisor will have the benefit of time and experience in the profession to assist in the decision-making process. However, doubts must be raised about whether years of traditionally diagnosing clients, given the questions raised about such, contribute wisdom about how not to exploit or harm clients by diagnosing (DeJulio & Berkman, 2003).

Finally, as directed by ethical codes, we turn to a discussion of documentation as a means for discerning ethical behavior in the dual relationship that may be involved in diagnosing. Theoretically, documentation assists practitioners to remember details about clients, about issues that are raised during counseling, about the counseling procedures that have been used, and about client responses to these procedures (Cameron & Turtle-Song, 2002; Mellor-Clark, Connell, Barkham, & Cummins, 2001; Prieto & Scheel, 2002). Taking adequate time to reflect on one's work with a client through writing in the client record may also help practitioners to internally process the best ways to conceptualize and work with a client (Cameron & Turtle-Song, 2002; Prieto & Scheel, 2002). Clearly documentation about diagnosis that is used in this manner should help clinicians in their decision-making process about dual relationships, about whether the dual relationship has the potential for harm, and about how they might ensure that the dual relationship does not lead to harming the client.

However, much training about documentation seems to focus on using documentation to protect mental health professionals in case of a legal suit (Scott, 2000; Woody, 2001). In documentation used for this purpose, a mental health professional writes about what she or he has done, gives a rationale as to why it was done, provides some idea of the impact of what was done, and indicates what was discussed with the client prior to gaining the client's consent for what was done. Should the client later sue the mental health professional, the professional has a record of all activities and events to use in defense. If the mental health professional's rationale makes sense, if the client consented, and if what was done conforms to standard practice, then the mental health professional is unlikely to lose the case (Carelock & Innerarity, 2001; Scheflin, 2000; Slimak & Berkowitz, 1983).

However, the question still remains: What about the harm to the client that may have occurred as a result of diagnosis or the perceived harm that may have led to the case? That documentation and standard practice help to protect the mental health professional does not guarantee that harm to clients that may be caused by standard or traditional practices of diagnosis will be prevented.

Clearly, then, the four suggestions presented by ethical codes—informed consent, consultation, supervision, and documentation—have limitations for ethical decision making related to the dual relationships inherent in diagnosis. However, in the absence of other reasonable possibilities, these four are a considerable improvement over secrecy or over the refusal to participate in such professional endeavors. At least mental health professionals who pursue these means of managing the ethical dilemmas of dual relationships in diagnosis are engaging in reflection and in the process of pursuing greater integrity. They are opening up the closed system of the counseling room to the sunlight of closer scrutiny. Such open discussion with clients, colleagues, and supervisors, and the willingness to document one's choices at least increase the chances of an improved solution and decrease the chance of blatant or unintended exploitation of clients.

VALUES

Diagnosing, like therapy, is a political act; that is, it is one that involves power in relationships and is performed in a political and contextual environment that is not value-free (Brown, 1990a, 1990b, 1992; Diaz et al., 2001; Galambos, 1999; Haug, 1999; Rosenbaum & Miller, 1996). Ethical practice requires that mental health professionals become aware of their own values, attitudes, beliefs, and behaviors and how these factors influence their work in a diverse society. Practitioners also avoid imposing their values on clients (AAMFT, 2001, Standards 3.3–3.5; ACA, 1995, Standard A.5.b; APA, 1992, Standards 1.08, 1.09, 1.10; NASW, 1999, Preamble).

The key reasons for the ethical mandates about values are that (a) counseling is intended to help clients make decisions about their lives by helping them to carefully weigh *their* thoughts and feelings about possibilities and the consequences of those possibilities; (b) therapy is supposed to empower clients, not only to make such decisions, but to own such decisions and to feel confident in them; (c) mental health practice may be about issues unrelated to values controversies (such as a client's decision to have an abortion or become sexually active); for instance, gay clients may pursue counseling for reasons other than discussing struggles related to their homosexuality; and (d) failing to examine one's own value systems may lead practitioners to unintentionally impose their values on the client, causing harm to clients whose values differ from those of the mental health professional (Baker, 2001; Minsky, Vega, Miskimen, Gara, & Escobar, 2003; Rosenbaum & Miller, 1996).

In a diverse society, people adhere to many different values, some associated with various religious and political groups; some the result of family, cultural, or regional history; and others the result of personal choice and experience (Choi, 2002; Schmolke, 1999). The values controversies for mental health professionals that are often most in the limelight center around homosexuality, abortion, male–female relationships, the roles of women, and sexuality outside of marital relationships (Kutchens & Kirk, 1997).

However, practitioners less often consider the values inherent in the counseling theories that they choose, despite the fact that these values may conflict with the client's values (Baker, 2001; Minsky et al., 2003; Rosenbaum & Miller, 1996). Relatedly, some practitioners may not consider the values underlying the DSM with regard to its development and its application. In the following section, we discuss the values inherent in the DSM.

The Values Inherent in the DSM

At first glance, the DSM system appears to be and generally aims to be atheoretical and value free. However, many believe that it does not succeed in these endeavors (Denton, 1989, 1990; Mead et al., 1997; Mezzich, 1999a,b;

Sarbin, 1997; Sporakowski, 1995; Stravynski & O'Connor, 1995). The mere act of specifying what to observe asks practitioners to be both "objective" and to make judgments about what is normal versus abnormal behavior (Denton, 1989); values will always be central to making such important decisions. Sarbin (1997) indicates that, despite disclaimers in the DSM that the symptom descriptors exclusively focus on observed behaviors and avoid claims regarding etiology, the use of the language of symptoms carries with it the notion of underlying causes, and clearly, these underlying causes are assumed to be neurological or biochemical. The DSM as a diagnostic system seeks to mimic the medical approach, and so leaves many assuming that there is a palpable disease underlying each diagnosis (Denton, 1989; Double, 2002; Laungani, 2002; Stravynski & O'Connor, 1995).

Values associated with a biomedical model of abnormality and its therapeutic management are thus the foundations of the DSM (Double, 2002; Laungani, 2002; Stravynski & O'Connor, 1995). The core values expressed by the medical model are as follows: The medical model assumes that mental disorders are in a person, regardless of what is happening in the family or in wider social contexts (Denton, 1990; Double, 2002; Laungani, 2002). The medical model has also been criticized as being reductionistic, in that it tries to reduce complex information about people into a few words; mechanistic, in that it assumes that one can explain the wholeness of a person by describing the person's parts (symptoms); static, in that it fails to see individuals' lives as dynamic or people as engaged in a developmental and ever-changing process of living; and reliant on an objectivist science that pursues linear causality—that is, that a few factors that precede the problems in history can be assumed to lead directly to the problem—as an explanation of experience (Double, 2002; Laungani, 2002; Sporakowski, 1995).

The DSM has added an environmental/psychosocial aspect to its multiaxial system as evidenced by the inclusion of Axis IV. In other words, the understanding that life stressors may be a factor in symptomatology or result from symptomatology has been included as a factor relevant to understanding clients' functioning (Denton, 1990; Double, 2003; Mitchell, Parker, Gladstone, Wilhelm, & Austin, 2003; Sinaikin, 2003). However, the medical model's problem focus, the placement of the problem within the individual, and the failure to include more recursive causality will still trouble some practitioners.

The medical model may have value for some biological-curative endeavors and for "hard" science research; however, as mentioned briefly in Chapter 1, the medical model and the scientific method have come under fire in recent years as a means of explaining human behavior (Charman, 2004; Denton, 1989, 1990; Double, 2003; Kastrup, 2002; Sarbin, 1997; Sinaikin, 2003; Sporakowski, 1995; Stravynski, & O'Connor, 1995; Watzlawick, 1984). Some challengers focus on the limitations of biomedical explanations for understanding human factors such as emotions, relationships, and spiritual and other life experiences (Denton, 1989; Double, 2003; Mitchell et al., 2003; Sinaikin, 2003; Sporakowski, 1995), experiences that are central to the counseling endeavor. Others challenge the scientific validity of the DSM's classification system, claiming that it is based more on consensus, and thus on the values of those who agree, than on science (Caws, 2003; Denton, 1990; Double, 2003; Stirman, DeRubeis, Crits-Christoph, & Brody, 2003; Stravynski, & O'Connor, 1995). Still others challenge the notion of linear causality directly (Sinaikin, 2003; Stirman et al., 2003; Watzlawick, 1984). We extend Chapter 1's discussions of the challenges to the science of the DSM in the paragraphs that follow, keeping in mind that as with all ways of knowing or making meaning, the DSM system is inherently value laden. We challenge practitioners to make these values, as well as the values inherent to alternative ways of knowing, explicit, and to reflect upon the impact of such values on the counseling and diagnostic process.

Challenges to Biomedical Explanations

A number of major schools of thought challenge biomedical explanations as the sole means for understanding human behavior.

Family therapy. Rather than being individualistic and emphasizing linear causality and static pathology, family therapy focuses on multiple, interactive causation that is continually evolving (Gladding, 2002; Sporakowski, 1995; Walsh, 2003). Family therapy focuses on relationships among people as the roots of problems in living, and does not envision problems as rooted in individual people (Denton, 1989; Hawley, 2000; Ivey, Scheel, & Jankowski, 1999). Furthermore, family therapy traditionally tries to bring family strengths to bear on the problems at hand. As Hinshaw and Cicchetti (2000) indicate, mental illness is not a static process, but rather mental health and mental illness are dynamic phenomena. They state that mentally ill people are "not either 'ill' or 'well;' rather nearly all such individuals experience stages and phases of remission and relapse across the life course . . . individuals with mental disorders should not be reduced to their psychiatric diagnoses" (p. 578). Therefore, these individuals should have their strengths, assets, capabilities, resiliencies, faith, and support systems accounted for concurrently with their mental "disabilities" (Longo & Peterson, 2002; Patterson, 2002; Walsh, 2002, 2003).

Humanistic therapy. Humanistic practitioners argue that a person's psychological characteristics are unique and complex, and that they cannot be objectively labeled, judged, understood, or identified (Frankl, 1969; May, 1981; Rogers, 1951, 1961). For example, the person-centered approach emphasizes the client's ability to "diagnose" him- or herself, rather than being analyzed by the therapist (Miller, 1990). Rogers (1942, 1961, 1987) presented compelling evidence that the most accurate and reliable way to understand a client is to consider problems from the client's internal frame of reference. Consequently, Rogers (1951) developed a Client-Centered Rationale for Diagnosis, basing it on the following propositions, which direct attention to the client's internal experiences:

- Behavior is caused, and the psychological cause of behavior is a certain perception or a way of perceiving. The client is the only one who has the potentiality of knowing fully the dynamics of his [sic] perceptions and his [sic] behaviors.
- In order for behavior to change, a change in perception must be experienced. Intellectual knowledge cannot substitute for this.
- The constructive forces which bring about altered perception, reorganization of self and relearning, reside primarily in the client and probably cannot come from outside.
- In a very meaningful and accurate sense, therapy is diagnosis, and this diagnosis is a process, which goes on in the experience of the client, rather than in the intellect of the practitioner. (pp. 221–223)

Other psychological schools of thought. In many ways, Adlerian (Mosak, 1991), Psychodynamic (Schmolke, 1999), Reality or Choice, and Solution-Focused (Duffy, Gillig, Tureen, & Ybarra, 2002) theories are also philosophically incompatible with a medical-model or DSM approach to assessment and diagnoses. For instance, Glasser (1984), the founder of choice theory, expresses concern that diagnostic labels enable clients to evade responsibility for a disorder, because, according to the medical model, clients do not play a role in causing or maintaining the disorder. Thus, the client is able to react to a psychological label with the same lack of responsibility and detachment as a medical patient. Glasser maintains that the

very cause of psychological problems is a lack of taking responsibility for oneself, and that using diagnostic labels perpetuates such irresponsibility (Boy, 1989).

Mind–body connection. Other practitioners challenge the medical model and its individualistic perspective because they claim that focusing within the person, whether on cognitions or biology, assumes that the body is more fundamental, real, or important than psychosocial variables; that somehow bodily experiences can be separated from or understood without sociohistorical knowledge, experience, or subjectivity; that the only things we are allowed to know "are those which meet the criteria of the measurement tools currently in use," which have their limitations (Ussher, 2000, p. 212; Sadler, Wiggins, & Schwartz, 1994). Even current medical opinion, particularly the field of psychoneuroimmunology, supports the seamless connections between mind and body, offering evidence for the influence of psychosocial factors on both disease and recovery (Ader, Felten, & Cohen, 2001; Johnson & Kushner, 2001; Zittel, Lawrence, & Wodarski, 2002).

Challenges to the hegemony of the medical model. Still others challenge the medical model because of the results of overreliance on it (Laungani, 2002; Schwartz & Wiggins, 2002; Sperry, 2002b). For instance, Ackley (1997) points out that "medical necessity" is an insurance term rather than a clinical term. It is a term that has led to suspicions about care that is *not* medically necessary. He claims that we have become reliant on "medical necessity" as a standard for reimbursement because as a society we think it is wrong to withhold medical care that is necessary. Beyond such arguable "necessity," we disagree about what services we should pay for. For instance, what will we decide or have we decided about the prevention of future medical problems, that is, medical care before the problems actually exist? It seems that society perceives that some preventive medical care saves lives and reduces remedial care costs. Vaccinations, well baby checks, and regular cholesterol and blood pressure checks, for example, are routinely employed and perceived by society and insurance carriers as valuable. Yet, why have we decided that learning life skills is not medically necessary, despite their key role in persuading young mothers to bring their children in for well baby checks and vaccinations? Why have we decided that ongoing nutritional and lifestyle counseling is not medically necessary to prevent the cholesterol, blood pressure, and other problems of obesity? Why have we decided that parenting training and anger management courses are not medically necessary, when we know that ongoing family conflict and poor parenting contribute to greater illness and injury in children? Although it is understandable that, for economic reasons, the insurance industry must limit what it is willing to pay for, its decisions powerfully impact what treatment will be provided, for what sorts of problems, and for whom. Being able to claim that a treatment is medically necessary has been the only way, in the current health care delivery system, to justify treatment, claims Ackley, which leaves many nonmedical professionals clamoring to be let into the medical model, whether it benefits their clients or not.

Ackley (1997) also claims that overreliance on the medical model results in overmedicalizing everyday problems in living, and underfocusing on competencies that might solve such problems. For instance, for struggles with anger, sadness about a death in one's family, disappointment that one is not more popular with one's peers, or stress about providing for one's family when one has lost a job, clients must be diagnosed with a specified illness and must have a practitioner document the specifics, all of which draws undue attention to one's symptoms and pathology. Such a focus, Ackley claims, results in clients and practitioners

spending less time correcting life situations that may be causing the symptoms, attending to developmental factors in order to prevent temporary problems in living, and developing skills in problem-solving. The client thus invests more energy on perceived deficits than on internal resources for change and growth, a focus that might promote helpful change (Fitzsimons & Fuller, 2002; Schott & Conyers, 2003; Sperry, 2002a; White, 2002).

Ackley (1997) further points to the implied status differential between the practitioner and the client that exists in the medical model, and to the impact of this differential on both the client and the practitioner. That is, the client is assumed to be sick, and the practitioner is considered to be well or without problems. Yet, identifying oneself as sick undermines a client's sense of general competence, making it harder to think clearly, to learn new things, and to move forward. The medical model may promote personal helplessness in clients, who may maintain an internal belief that, "I can't help it. I am sick!" The further need for mental health practitioners to prove that they themselves are personally well in order to maintain their position may lead practitioners to attempt the impossible feat of demonstrating that they are free of illness, which can only result in hiding the truth and failing to work on issues that need attention. Ackley claims that all human beings struggle with challenges to remaining personally well. Unfortunately, the medical model defines such "learning opportunities" as "disease," despite everyone's needs to engage in this sort of lifelong learning.

Finally, according to Ackley (1997), and in the experience of clinicians with whom we have had conversations, reliance on the medical model and the insurance industry to fund treatment limits people's choices of providers and installs initial obstacles to getting help, because clients must now get referrals, get preauthorization, and go through gatekeepers before seeing a provider who can help them (Daniels, 2001; Smith, 1999).

Challenges to Scientific Validity

As was seen above, many who challenge the medical model, the scientific method, and linear causality indicate that so-called scientific or objective decisions are really values decisions, and that authoritatively declaring these decisions usually implies imposing them on people, some of whom do not share those values or who will be devalued as a result of such imposition (Caplan, 1995; Kutchins & Kirk, 1997; Laungani, 2002; Sadler, 2002; Sarbin, 1997). Others who challenge the science of the DSM question the scientific method more generally. Still others claim that the DSM is a consensus document or "negotiations guided by ideological objectives" (Sarbin, 1997, p. 233), rather than a scientific document. They thus question its validity and reliability, pointing out the risks inherent in making judgments about people based on consensus.

Criticisms of the scientific method. Postmodernists and constructivists challenge the ultimacy of the scientific method, claiming that its aim of discovering reality will always be hindered by the biases inherent in any process of living; that is, that researchers' cultural and experiential lenses impact all that they do (including the questions they ask), making the scientific process far less objective and reality far less discoverable than scientists typically believe. A complete discussion of challenges to the scientific method or the philosophy of science is beyond the scope of this book; however, including postmodernist or constructivist challenges is not meant to discount science entirely, or to present those perspectives as a new "truth" to be adopted (Bracken & Thomas, 2001; Heath, 2002a). Instead, their challenges ask us to consider knowing that extends beyond what science can tell us and to consider the mediating role played by the contexts within which science operates and discovers. Also, because the "truth" that is assumed from any perspective is limited,

whether that perspective is that of constructivism or that of objectivist science, constructivist and postmodernists would ask us to adopt a tentative stance, one that learns from dialogue with other stances, in the hope that what will be most useful in the current time and place may be discovered (Bracken & Thomas, 2001; Fireman, 2002; Gergen, 1985; Harari, 2001; Heath, 2002a; Rorty, 1979; Sadler et al., 1994; Segal, 1986).

For instance, in Watzlawick's (1984) book, *The Invented Reality,*

> Experts from various fields explain how scientific, social, individual, and ideological realities are invented (constructed) as a result of the inevitable need to approach the supposedly independent reality 'out there' from certain basic assumptions that we consider to be 'objective' properties of the real reality, while in actual fact they are the consequences of our *search* for reality. (p. 10)
>
> All we can ever know about the real world," Watzlawick claims, "is what the world is not. (p. 14)

Von Glasersfeld (1984) speaks further of what we can "know" about the real world. He distinguishes "match" from "fit": match means that our knowledge replicates the real world, and fit means that knowledge allows functioning in the world. Knowledge, he claims, is not the world but merely one key that opens the lock, allowing us to function. He indicates that many other keys exist that will also probably open the lock. Thus, science only leads us to "one viable way to a goal that we have chosen under specific circumstances in our experiential world" (p. 24). It does not lead to the objective "truth" about the world as a whole, he says.

Ussher (2000) criticizes the realist/positivistic epistemology of the scientific method as reductionistic, and indicates that it marginalizes historical and cultural factors, methodologically appropriating for social sciences what has been helpful in natural sciences (naturalism).

This appropriation leads, she claims, to artificiality. It limits the variables that can be studied; it focuses on the individual only; and it supports an unrealistic belief in objectivity. She further challenges the notion that facts and values can be objectively separated. For instance, she points out that any inconsistencies in clinical data are usually assumed by researchers to result from the unreliability of clients' subjective accounts. Why, she asks, would women's (or other clients' or respondents') accounts be biased or subjective, while the researchers' would not be? Why are the researcher's choices of questions, choices of methodology, and interpretations of data not considered to bias the findings? Why is the researcher the only one qualified to "know"?

As another example of the difficulties of a realist/positivistic epistemology, Ussher (2000) points out that psychological symptoms are not always visible, and therefore their existence has to be ascertained through subjective accounts, "which may fall outside the required standards of objectivity and replicability" (p. 211). So researchers use standardized instruments, which ignore the complexity and contradictions evident in women's (or any other clients' or respondents') subjective accounts because they leave rich qualitative data unexamined.

Finally, she claims, positivism requires the client to be a passive sufferer, despite the fact that people are not passive objects, and that "seeking treatment for mental health problems is a process of active, reflexive negotiation with symptomatology, current life events, and lifestyle, and cultural, medical, or psychological ideas about madness" (Ussher, 2000, p. 211).

Our report on challenges to the scientific method is not meant to disqualify science. Clearly the scientific method has added much to psychology, to mental health practice, and to many other areas of our lives, and is a considerable improvement over many previous ways of knowing. Furthermore, many mental health practitioners will not choose to embrace constructivist or postmodern epistemologies in their practice, and thus may be less concerned about questions posed by those who espouse such ways of knowing. However, those who tell other stories, beyond or in addition to the scientific method, challenge us to think critically about our ways of knowing, about procedures that we have used unquestioningly, in particular about our use of the DSM system of diagnosis (Rosenberg, 2002). Thinking critically requires standing back from those things that we have always "known," making them "object" (Belenky, Clinchy, Goldberger, & Tarule, 1986; Kegan, 1982, 1994; Knefelkamp, Widick, & Parker, 1978; Kohlberg & Wasserman, 1980; Loevinger, 1976; Perry, 1970). In the words of metaphor, it is only by getting out of the water that a fish realizes that water exists and what its value or limitations are. It is our hope that dialogue among those whose strategies, worldviews, theoretical perspectives, and ways of knowing differ might advance thinking, research, and practice.

Determining causality. Linear causality expresses the goal of the scientific method; that is, to determine the causes of particular effects, and to draw direct predictive lines between such causes and their resultant effects (Sexton, 1994; Wilkinson, 1998). In the case of diagnosis, linear causality implies that researchers should eventually be able to point directly to the causes of each discrete mental disorder. More recently, such strategies as path analysis have allowed researchers to determine the relative contributions of a variety of causes, although it is still assumed that these causes precede their effects (Gana, Martin, & Canouet, 2001; Golier et al., 2003; Thatcher, Reininger, & Drane, 2002). Clearly, if causality could be confidently determined, particularly if causes were relatively simple to identify and change, then we could try to eliminate the causes of mental illness and save many people from a great deal of distress and heartache. In general, the notion of linear causality gives people a sense of constancy, stability, and assurance that there are "reasons" that can explain the unknown. These explanations provide comfort against the threat of unpredictable and unforeseen change.

Many, however, have challenged the assumption that causality can be determined. Such researchers and theorists indicate that linear causality is undone by the complicated relationships and interactions that exist between the observer and observed (Brown, 2002; Raingruber, 2003; Szasz, 1974). Family therapy theorists, for instance, often speak of reciprocal causality or recursiveness to explain people's difficulties. These interactive processes, claim family therapists, have greater explanatory power for family, religious, and other human experiences (Frances, Clarkin, & Perry, 1984). Some authors point out that hope for the future influences the present as much as past experiences do (Collins & Cutcliffe, 2003; Riedl, 1984); however, linear causality does not allow for such future motivators.

Watzlawick (1984) claims that in a world based on linear causality, there is a split between observer and observed and an ordering of the world into pairs of opposites (life–death, health–illness), neither of which ever "wins." In fact, he claims, in the pursuit of "victory" or perfection, each polarity ends up causing the opposite of its intended ideal (e.g., when medicine contributes to illness or when increasingly comprehensive welfare programs contribute to the mounting incompetence of the average citizen).

Ussher (2000) furthers these criticisms of linear causality by drawing attention to the social and environmental factors that interrupt the "line" and therefore make linear causality impossible. For instance, relative to DSM diagnosis, there is more frequent reporting of mental health problems in women who are (a) married than in single women or married men; (b) in caring roles, looking after small children or elderly relatives; (c) not working;

(d) lacking in social support and economic or social power; (e) more feminine; or (f) victims of sexual violence and abuse. Yet, Ussher believes that these contextual factors are not considered important in the DSM's medical-model assumption that brain disease causes mental illness.

Ussher (2000) continues her argument by criticizing the assumptions and behavior of scientists who pursue such explanations. For instance, she points out that often causal assumptions are inappropriately made on the basis of treatment effectiveness (i.e., there must be a biological cause because medication helped). Researchers have assumed that if a serotonin uptake inhibitor helps a person to feel less depressed, then depression must be caused by excesses in serotonin uptake (Bailey, 2002; Valenstein, 1998). Yet, as she points out, we do not assume that because aspirin effectively cures headaches, the absence of aspirin causes headaches. We also do not assume that because smoking or ingesting marijuana relaxes a person, marijuana's absence in our system causes stress. She asks why we persist in using such logic to defend the notion that mental disorders are biologically caused.

Ussher (2000) also criticizes researchers and readers of research because they often confuse correlational findings with assumptions of causality. That is, researchers who find higher correlations between certain chemicals in the body and a particular mental disorder jump to the conclusion that those chemicals cause the mental disorder, rather than honoring the statistically appropriate conclusion that there are higher levels of the chemical in the bodies of those who have the disorder.

Other researchers have proposed that mental disorders may actually cause the presence of certain chemical reactions. For instance, people who are exposed to traumatic events experience dramatic changes in the discharge of neurotransmitters such as endorphins, and in the central and peripheral sympathetic nervous system and hypothalamic–pituitary–adrenocortical axis (James & Gilliland, 2001). These neurological changes may become long-term, and because neurotransmitters play a critically important role in the affective, behavioral, and cognitive functioning of individuals (Armsworth & Holaday, 1993; Kolb & Whishaw, 1990; van der Kolk, 1996), those exposed to such trauma may experience subtle, degrading effects on emotions, behaviors, and cognitions (Burgess-Watson, Hoffman, & Wilson, 1988; van der Kolk, 1996).

Again, researchers may appropriately ask questions that lend themselves to causal answers. However, from our perspective, it seems that the complexities of factors involved in people's emotional, psychological, and behavioral lives, and in the counseling and other psychological processes used to respond to these lives, raise questions about how far social science research can go in answering causal questions, and how helpful the answers that they find will be to real people and real-life counseling situations. Although the challenges do not invalidate all such efforts at discovery, they certainly ask us to consider other ways of knowing that may be helpful to clients *in addition* to what can be discovered scientifically. This may be particularly necessary because of a common struggle that clinicians known to the authors have with scientific discovery, that is, that science lags behind clinical knowledge, that sometimes what clinicians read in scientific journals as a "new" discovery has been known about and/or practiced effectively by clinicians for years.

Criticisms of "consensus" as the DSM's criteria for inclusion. One of the most important challenges to consider is the criticism of the idea that the DSM is based purely on science, when it appears that consensus has also played a significant role in decisions about DSM inclusions and exclusions. If the DSM has been influenced by consensus as opposed to being solely grounded in science, concerns arise related to the impact of giving such importance to a document developed by so few people. We here address some of the history of the DSM's development and its reliability and validity problems as a means of considering these challenges.

As long ago as 1977, the Council of Representatives of the American Psychological Association (APA) created a task force to assess the need for an alternative diagnostic system (Miller, 1990). The task force concluded that the DSM approach was unsatisfactory because (a) its specific categories showed consistently high levels of unreliability, and (b) the categories had either been eliminated from the DSM or included in the DSM on the basis of committee vote rather than on valid scientific data.

Kutchins and Kirk (1997) trace the progression of DSMs and demonstrate that, in many ways, the DSM continues to be a consensus rather than a scientific document. They offer substantial evidence of the fragility of science in the face of political advocacy. They describe an absence of attempts by DSM developers to justify the many changes in the DSM on the basis of scientific evidence. "Twenty years after the reliability problem became the central focus of the DSM III, there is still not a single multi-site study showing that the DSM (any version) is routinely used with high reliability by regular mental health clinicians. Nor is there any credible evidence that any version of the manual has greatly increased reliability beyond the previous version" (Kutchins & Kirk, 1997, p. 83). Although the DSM is ostensibly based on scientific evidence, Kutchins and Kirk (1997) claim that "barely concealed beneath the surface is an intricate process that involves old fashioned political horse-trading, complex economic considerations, elaborate systems for consensus building, and other mechanisms for mobilizing power and negotiating social conflicts" (p. 16). Although stakeholders have been involved in the process to some degree, developers have also kept an eye on public opinion when considering inclusions or deletions.

According to Kutchins and Kirk (1997), such political activity has resulted in professional and public biases, particularly racial and gender bias, being translated into definitions of normality and abnormality (Bhugra & Bhui, 1999; Caplan, 1995; Chrisler & Caplan, 2002; Laungani, 2002; Sadler, 2002). Kutchins and Kirk (1997) go on to state that culturally normative behavior has been deemed "mental illness," and data has been distorted to serve the purposes of those in power. They further claim that status, reputation, and turf have had more impact on DSM decisions than has science. The development of the DSM "involved negotiations among contending interest groups of theoreticians, researchers, practitioners, hospitals, clinics, and drug companies—and, at times, potential patients. Changing the psychiatric nosology involved struggles among constituencies and required a balancing of conflicting interests" (p. 37). Each new edition has created mental disorders, eliminated others, and radically redefined still others. Yet, the "revisions can seldom be explained by advances in science;" instead they are better explained "by the shifting fortunes of various powerful factions within the American Psychiatric Association" (p. 37). New categories have been included on the basis of "whether the diagnosis was used with reasonable frequency, whether interested professionals and patient representatives offered positive comments about it, and whether the new condition maximized the manual's utility for outpatient populations.... The mentally ill were by definition those seen by psychiatrists. DSM-III desired for every client a reimbursable diagnosis" (p. 43). Thus, claim Kutchins and Kirk, the DSM developers erred on the side of the inclusion of new categories, at least partially because they were concerned with capturing more fiscal coverage from third-party reimbursement.

Some practitioners might not object to such a consensus-building process as long as it was not called "science" and intentionally or unintentionally viewed as descriptive of objective "reality." For instance, social constructivists would consider such a political process to be a true expression of developing "socially constructed truth," and as further evidence that "truth" really cannot be known, despite our claims of scientific objectivity; that truth can only be created by the various participants in a dialogue (Brown, 2002; Duffy et al., 2002; Harari, 2001). The goal, from such a perspective, might be to increase the number of people who participate in such a political process, so that better decisions can be made, and a better, more workable "truth" can be created. However, as we point out in Chapters 3 and 4, most of the discussants involved in the process, particularly initially, were White males, which leaves less-powerful and often-discriminated-against groups to be acted upon by a very influential document that was developed by a powerful few (Caplan, 1995; Cermele, Daniels, & Anderson, 2001; Sadler, 2002). History testifies to the harm that can occur to the less powerful when decisions are left to a small, dominant-culture, homogeneous group of people (Barstow, 1994; Bhugra & Bhui, 1999; Dudley & Gale, 2002). Women and people of color have struggled to have their voices heard in the development of the DSM, and although they are heard more often now, they often found their voices silenced as the DSMs were developed. Consequently, the consensus that has formed the basis of the DSM cannot be said to represent the input of all of those who have valid points to make about the diagnostic process (Chrisler & Caplan, 2002; Larkin & Caplan, 1992).

Reliability of the DSM. The strongest claim that has been made in support of the DSM system is that its criterion-based classification system has solved the problem of diagnostic reliability (Butler, 1999). Despite these claims, when controlling for the proportion of interrater agreement that could be expected by chance alone (i.e., kappa [κ]), the reliability evidence of the DSM systems is weaker than desired for a manual of such importance. In a classic and often-cited study on the reliability of the ascription of *Diagnostic and Statistical Manual of Mental Disorders,* 2nd ed. (DSM-II) diagnoses, Spitzer and Fleiss (1974, p. 344) identified kappa-coefficient values for each of six studies by 18 major diagnostic categories and found kappa-coefficient values ranging from .10 to .90 with a mean of .52. The authors concluded, "There are no diagnostic categories for which reliability is uniformly high. Reliability appears to be only satisfactory for three categories: mental deficiency, organic brain syndrome (but not its subtypes), and alcoholism. The level of reliability is no better than fair for psychosis and schizophrenia and is poor for the remaining categories" (p. 344).

The *Diagnostic and Statistical Manual of Mental Disorders,* 3rd ed. (DSM-III) was generally hailed as being more reliable than its predecessors because of its use of more explicit diagnostic criteria. In an article published by the developers of the DSM-III, they stated that "... the reliability of the major diagnostic classes of DSM-III was extremely good" (Hyler, Williams, & Spitzer, 1982, p. 1276). However, no empirical data have been provided to substantiate this strong statement. In fact, despite the DSM-III developers' claims of greater reliability, reliability appears to have improved very little. For instance, in a more recent study of the reliability of the *Diagnostic and Statistical Manual of Mental Disorders,* 3rd ed., revised (DSM-III-R) (Williams et al., 1992), researchers found that that this version of the DSM was about as unreliable as its predecessors. In a carefully controlled study conducted under ideal conditions (e.g., trained raters and the use of structured interviews), the kappa-coefficient values ranged from .40 to .86 and had a weighted average kappa of .61.

Among two of the community clinical sites, the kappa-coefficient values ranged from .19 to .59 and averaged .37. Further doubt is cast upon the reliability of the DSM when it is considered that the reliability statistics were computed only based upon the groups of diagnoses, rather than upon the specific diagnoses; that is, a perfect kappa (κ = 1) would have been obtained even if one clinician ascribed a diagnosis of borderline personality disorder and another clinician ascribed a diagnosis of paranoid personality disorder *to the same client.*

Reliability thus seems to shift depending on the diagnosis. For instance, studies on the DSM-III showed great variability in reliability for specific diagnoses, from quite reliable (for diagnoses such as panic disorder, agoraphobia, and obsessive-compulsive disorder) to utterly unreliable (for simple phobias and for generalized anxiety disorders) (e.g., Mannuzza et al., 1989). Reliability studies on the DSM-IV indicate that reliability increases if clinicians are at the same clinical site (because of allowed consultation about the clients) for such disorders as major depression, sleep disorders, and mixed anxiety and depression, but falls precipitously to poor or worse when the clinicians operate from different sites (Buysse et al., 1994; Keller et al., 1995; Zinbarg et al., 1994).

Despite the DSM developers' attempts at making the diagnostic process more rigorously objective, much subjectivity is involved in ascribing DSM diagnoses. For example, the DSM-IV states: "The specific diagnostic criteria are meant to serve as guidelines to be informed by clinical judgment. For example, the exercise of clinical judgment may justify giving a certain diagnosis even though the clinical presentation falls just short of meeting the full criteria" (APA, 1994, p. xxiii). Sarbin (1997) states that this is "strange advice" (p. 235) given that the developers of the manual are striving for greater reliability. Sarbin (1997) also indicates that the DSM developers further contradict their calls for reliability by indicating that users should use their clinical judgment with regard to cultural and subcultural patterns of behavior. Other examples of the potential unreliability of clinical judgment were pointed out in Chapter 1, such as those involving the need for practitioners to decide how often is "often" (Sarbin, 1997). According to Sarbin, these types of language ambiguities abound in the DSM, and as a consequence of the nuances and various perceived meanings of language, the issue of unreliability can never be fully resolved.

Kutchins and Kirk (1997) suggest the following reasons for the DSM's reliability problems. First, context influences the interpretation of behaviors, so the context in which the diagnosis is performed will influence the understanding of a client's behavior, as will the cultural lenses through which the client and the practitioner view the client's behavior. Second, diagnoses, once given, limit observers' perceptions, questions, and interpretations; practitioners may, thus, fail to notice behavior that falls outside of the diagnostic criteria, or to recognize behavior that indicates another diagnosis. Third, expectation influences judgment, and theory and setting influence expectation; for example, because family therapists define and understand problems differently than do psychiatrists, family therapists are more likely to develop different diagnoses than psychiatrists for the same clients. Fourth, as noted previously, the terms used in DSM criteria give practitioners' considerable latitude in decision making. Fifth, practitioners and clients are susceptible to suggestions by credible sources; so if the agency treats particular problems, a funding source pays for certain problems, or a supervisor is specially trained in particular problems, these are the problems that are likely to be noticed by practitioners and focused on by clients. As an example of our susceptibility to such suggestions, when the first author was attending a conference on Millon's test for personality disorders, a colleague noted, correctly or incorrectly, that Millon defined all problems as personality

disorders, and that when we finished the conference, we also would see personality disorders in everyone that we treated. It was certainly my observation that conference participants fulfilled his predictions, in that after encountering Millon's information, they regularly referred to the personality disorders noticed in the other conference participants.

If the reliability of DSM diagnosis is limited, Kutchins and Kirk (1997) ask on what basis we can claim that treatments that have been developed, particularly for specific diagnoses (e.g., medications), are valid. Without reliability, they claim, we will diagnose as mentally ill those who are not and fail to diagnose those who are, we will misuse reimbursement systems that are tied to diagnosis, we will have inaccurate estimations of the numbers of those who are mentally ill and the numbers of those who fall into particular categories, and, based on these statistics, we will create misguided public policy to address the problems of the mentally ill.

More evidence is clearly needed to substantiate the reliability of DSM diagnoses in different populations under varied conditions. Reliability studies are difficult and cumbersome to implement; but until greater reliability can be accomplished in DSM diagnosis, an awareness of the limitations of the reliability of diagnosing is important, as is appreciating the impact of context on the DSM diagnosis process.

Validity problems in the research supporting the DSM. Addressing the issue of the validity of DSM diagnoses is a daunting task. Indeed, this 943-page book (i.e., the *Diagnostic and Statistical Manual of Mental Disorders,* 4th ed., Text Revision [DSM-IV-TR]) is full of detailed information and a great deal of research, and many advisers were and are involved in the evolution of the DSM system. Sarbin (1997) states:

In one way or another, more than 1,400 professionals provided input that influenced decisions to include or exclude a diagnostic category and to include or exclude criteria for each diagnosis. The guiding task force was made up of 27 experts, assisted by 248 advisers. Ninety-six experts participated in work groups, aided by 875 work-group advisers. The DSM IV lists 167 international advisers, not to mention a large number of field trial and expert-phase participants. (p. 234)

The scope of such a project is certainly awesome. The amassing of such a prodigious amount of data and the input of so many advisers is an impressive feat. To develop the DSM-IV, the Task Force on DSM-IV and members of the DSM-IV Work Groups participated in a comprehensive empirical review of the literature, which ultimately led to the changes in the DSM IV. The *DSM-IV Sourcebook* (Widiger, Frances, Pincus, First, Ross, & Davis, 1994), published in five volumes, documents the rationale and empirical support for the text and criteria sets presented in DSM-IV.

A discussion of the reliability of the DSM is irrelevant if the diagnostic system itself is not valid. Yet Sarbin (1997) indicates that the issue of validity of DSM categories is not as important as reliability: "Even a cursory acquaintance with the manuals makes clear that validity issues receive short shrift; improvement in reliability is the acknowledged goal" (pp. 235–236). Sarbin goes on to state that the authors of the DSMs offer no data to warrant "assumed validity," that the "problem of validity is handled implicitly by the authority of expert consensus," and that this "authority by expert consensus is the source of an implied content validity" (p. 236).

It is beyond the scope of this book to even attempt to review or critique the vast amount of literature involved in revising the current version of the DSM. To be sure, much of the research base for the DSM-IV is sound. As stated earlier, the issues we raise are related to the bias that is evident in the questions people

ask when implementing research, the role that consensus plays in deciding which diagnoses stay and go, and the values associated with the DSM approach to assessment.

The issue of diagnostic bias—that is, the biases that people demonstrate when ascribing diagnoses—in DSM diagnosis is one validity-related issue that has been addressed in the literature (McLaughlin, 2002). It might be assumed or deduced that these same biases affected both the clinicians who were used by the researchers and the investigators whose research was used as the basis of the DSM-IV. McLaughlin (2002) identifies and discusses a body of research indicating that practitioners are not free of diagnostic bias when applying DSM diagnoses. The sources of these biases include stereotyping (i.e., making diagnostic judgments based on one or a limited number of common features; e.g., only males can have antisocial personality disorder); data availability and vividness (i.e., categorizing a diagnosis based on its familiarity, ease of recall, or salience; e.g., overdiagnosing people who self-injure with borderline personality disorder [BPD] as this is a relatively uncommon presenting behavior and this is also a possible criteria of BPD); self-confirmatory bias (i.e., categorizing by only focusing on conformity information; e.g., upon finding out that someone self-injures, one thinks the client has BPD and then focuses or looks for any behaviors that might be construed as related to BPD); self-fulfilling prophecy (i.e., acting on an expectation in a way that confirms it; e.g., Rosenhan's [1973] study in which non-mentally ill people were diagnosed based on the mere fact that they were in a psychiatric hospital); and diagnostic criterion bias (i.e., when diagnostic criteria are more valid for one group than another; e.g., the proposed inclusion of "premenstrual dysphoric disorder" has been argued to be prejudicial against women because only women can be diagnosed with it; McCurdy-Myers & Gans, 1992; Caplan, 1995). That humans are unable to ever be fully free of bias is another issue that must be considered in understanding the validity of DSM diagnoses. Chapters 3 through 5 address biases more intensively and provide ideas on how to limit or reduce diagnostic bias.

With regard to validity, Axis I and Axis II diagnoses are not the only components of the DSM system that have come under scrutiny. In a study of practitioners' ability to assess Axis V (i.e., Global Assessment of Functioning [GAF] ratings), Moos, McCoy, and Moos (2000) found that Axis I diagnoses and psychiatric symptoms were better predictors of ascribed GAF ratings than were social and occupational functioning, the intended assessment focus of Axis V. Additionally, Moos et al. (2000), found that GAF ratings were only minimally associated with patients' one-year psychological, social, and occupational functioning outcomes.

Others have also challenged the validity of the DSM (Halling & Goldfarb, 1996; Kutchins & Kirk, 1997; Laungani, 2002; Rosenberg, 2002; Sarbin, 1997; Skene, 2002). Kutchins and Kirk (1997) indicate that one reason it is difficult to establish the validity of the DSM is that the characteristics/ definition of disorders provided by the DSM cannot separate disorders from nondisorders. They point to the DSM's own definitions of disorder to support their point. The DSM indicates that disorder resides in the individual and is neither transactional nor an expression of social deviance; something in the individual must have gone wrong and become dysfunctional; the dysfunction must cause harmful effects to the individual in the form of distress, disability, or pain; the etiology of the disorder does not need to be identified; and the disorder does not need to be understood through the lens of a particular theory of psychopathology (APA, 2000). Kutchins and Kirk (1997) reason that the validity problems caused by this definition or statement of the characteristics of DSM disorders are as follows:

1. According to the definition, disorders cannot be expectable responses to events, and are therefore rare and unexpected. Yet some rare things that cause distress and disability, like "extreme selfishness, cowardice, slovenliness, foolhardiness, gullibility, insensitivity, laziness, or lack of talent" (p. 32) are not considered mental disorders despite being includable by definition. Therefore, the definition is too broad to be valid. Furthermore, disorders that are expectable responses to environmental events, such as depression in response to major loss, antisocial personality in response to socialization into a criminal subculture, and post-traumatic stress disorder, which by definition is a response to external events, are included in the DSM as mental disorders, despite not being includable by definition. In such cases, the definition is too narrow to be valid.

2. The definition claims that impairment must be evident. And yet, illiteracy, a short person's "inability to play professional basketball, a clumsy person's inability to work as a waiter, an intellectually below-average person's inability to become a scientist, or a very selfish person's inability to form intimate relationships" (p. 33) are not considered mental disorders by the DSM despite their clearly being impairments. In each case, internal conditions impair functioning, and therefore should, by definition, be considered mental disorders; yet such impairment has been considered by DSM developers to be insufficient to claim mental disorder. Some may claim that these examples are physical impairments or limitations, not mental or emotional ones. However, the DSM does consider the physical impairments such as reading and math-learning disabilities, mental retardation, dementias, and other pervasive developmental disabilities to be mental disorders.

3. The definition requires that the problems be internal to the individual, not responses to the external environment. This conceptualization excludes many problems that are

clearly responses to external situations and that usually result in the ascription of a DSM diagnosis: a child who is fearful or depressed because she has been abused by a parent; a widow who feels hopeless and depressed because she has been left penniless; a woman who has a sleep disorder because she is being battered. Again the definition is too narrow to be valid.

4. Dysfunction means that something that was designed to do something else has failed in its natural function. However, if symptoms are functional, that is, they were designed into human beings to help them in some way (e.g., grieving, not working, and not eating after a loved one has died; psychological escape from an abusive family member), how can practitioners call them dysfunctional?

What to Do With DSM Values

In sum, from an ethical perspective, several problems emerge related to the values that are inherent in the DSM system's medical model foundations. They lead to questions about the limits of DSM diagnosis for practice. First, should the values of the medical model (or for that matter any theoretical model) be imposed on clients? Of course, this question poses less of a problem for practitioners who realize the impossibility of operating in a value-free manner. Second, if certain values might harm people or have questionable scientific validity, shouldn't practitioners be even more cautious about bringing them into the counseling relationship? Operating from a theoretical framework, with its inherent values, is typically considered a necessity for competent professional practice (Spruill & Benshoff, 2000). However, operating exclusively from the medical model has been challenged consistently by those in the counseling, family therapy, and other systemically, developmentally, and humanistically oriented mental health fields (Honos-Webb & Leitner, 2001;

Ivey & Ivey, 1999; Ivey, Scheel, & Jankowski, 1999; Laungani, 2002; Schwartz & Wiggins, 2002; Sperry, 2002b; Walsh, 2002, 2003).

Such ethical dilemmas might be resolved by adhering to principles of informed consent and standards of professional practice, and by adopting a more egalitarian, tentative, and constructivist approach to diagnosis and assessment (Heath, 2002b; Mahoney & Marquis, 2002). That is, practitioners need to ensure that their theoretical procedures fall within the range of typical standards of practice (Daniels, 2001; Fireman, 2002). They can also talk openly about their counseling procedures, giving clients a chance to examine the values inherent in such procedures, as part of the informed consent process (Gambrill, 2003; Nelson & Neufeldt, 1996). Mental health providers can accept that there are many ways of making meaning, that none are sufficient explanations of human behavior, and that the medical model is one way of making meaning (for insurance purposes, for research, and for certain aspects of practice), albeit one that needs the addition of other explanations to be useful in counseling (Bracken & Thomas, 2001; Brown, 2002; Ivey & Ivey, 1999; Raingruber, 2003; Sperry, 2002a). Finally, practitioners can adopt a dialogical, egalitarian, and tentative approach with clients, checking out clients' perceptions about the developing counseling process, posing ideas gently, and encouraging clients to participate fully in the choice making process, not only about counseling goals and behaviors to be changed, but about the counseling process itself (Bilsbury & Richman, 2002; Fitzsimons & Fuller, 2002). Although not all practitioners will find such approaches congruent with their theoretical choices or personality styles, such strategies may provide one way to preclude the potentially damaging effects of mental health professionals imposing the value system inherent in DSM diagnosis, or any value system for that matter, onto their clients.

PROMOTING
GROWTH AND DEVELOPMENT

This section discusses the conflicts between the DSM model and the professional identity of some mental health professionals, an identity that centers on facilitating client growth and development and on wellness. We delimit our discussion by stating that we believe that there are few mental health professionals who are fully identified with one orientation, for instance, fully wellness-oriented or fully medical model-oriented. Indeed, most practitioners' probably practice in gray areas between approaches, and draw on case conceptualizations that integrate more than one philosophy. However, we approach this discussion from the perspective of comparing two rather well-defined positions.

Developmental Professional Identities and Ethical Mandates

The DSM's static, illness-oriented approach to understanding problems in living poses a challenge to ethical practice for members of mental health disciplines that espouse developmental perspectives for understanding problems and change, such as professional counseling, family therapy, and positive psychology. For instance, according to the ACA (1995) ethical codes, counselors are to encourage the growth and development of their clients (Standard A.1b). Professional counselors' and other similarly inclined professionals' undergirding philosophies promote a developmental focus and ascribe many client problems to normal developmental struggles and transitions (Caplan, 1995; Cermele et al., 2001; Duffy et al., 2002; Kutchins & Kirk, 1997; Sperry, 2002b). The developmental focus depicts people as dynamic, not static, organisms (Sexton, 1994; Sperry, 2002b), and points to people's natural inclinations toward growth and health (Hansen, 2000). Such perspectives are hopeful and do not consider

client problems or positions in life to be permanent; instead, they consider change and growth to be ever occurring and always possible. Inherent in these perspectives is the understanding that people have the capacity to move forward, to change, to adapt, to heal, and to attain optimal mental health or wellness (Fitzsimons & Fuller, 2002). One might argue that, from a developmental perspective, the focus of observation is actually change and trying to understand the processes of adaptation over time in an ever-changing context (Ivey & Ivey, 2001).

As part of their developmental focus, family therapists, counselors, and positive psychologists, among others, aim for wellness, rather than merely the absence of infirmity, which is the aim of the medical model (Myers, et al., 2001). In pursuing such a goal, they commandeer whatever resources, assets, or characteristics that clients might possess (Fitzsimons & Fuller, 2002; Saleebey, 2001; Schott & Conyers, 2003; White, 2002; Worell, 2001). Positive psychology, for example, identifies the "unique strengths that an individual has and amplify[ies] those strengths, helping the patient to use his [sic] strengths as buffers against the troubles that beset him" or her (Seligman et al., 2001, p. 692). Positive psychology focuses on increasing positive subjective experiences, such as "well-being, contentment, and satisfaction (past); hope, faith, and optimism (future); and flow and happiness (present)" (Seligman et al., 2001, p. 692). It further seeks to increase positive individual traits, such as "the capacity for love and vocation, courage, interpersonal skill, aesthetic sensibility, perseverance, forgiveness, originality, future-mindedness, spirituality, high talent, and wisdom" (Seligman et al., 2001, p. 692). Finally, it celebrates such civic virtues such as "responsibility, nurturance, altruism, civility, moderation, tolerance, and work ethic" (Seligman et al., 2001, p. 692). Developmental practitioners might also intervene early with prevention programs that teach cognitive and coping skills in order to decrease the risk of depression, anxiety, and violence (Seligman et al., 2001).

A developmental, wellness focus thus extends beyond the problem marriage, or the problem job, or the problem emotions as the client initially describes them. It extends into the whole of the client's life. As Mezzich (1999a) indicates, diagnosis should be "understanding fully what happens in the mind and body of the person who presents for care" (p. 138), not just identifying a disorder or differentiating one disorder from another. Additionally, as Lain-Entralgo (1982) points out, there are two parts to diagnosis: identifying the problem and doing an assessment, and then committing to attain the ultimate goal of diagnosis—the client's wellness. So, for example, if a client claims to be feeling depressed, a holistic mental health professional not only assesses the extent and possible etiology of the depression, but also determines what assets the client may bring to recovery from depression, and in what areas of life the client may be depression free (Crowe, 2002). Further still, even if the depression has emerged as a result of being in a dead end job, for instance, a wellness- oriented professional would want to extend the assessment beyond the client's job situation into the client's social life, spiritual life, relational life, physical health, and leisure experiences (Myers et al., 2000). Not only is health in all of these areas necessary to overall wellness, but healthy practices in any of these areas may transfer to the troubled life area.

The DSM's Developmental Performance

Recognizing the developmental and wellness identities associated with a number of mental health professions raises questions about whether traditional DSM diagnosis can ever be developmental enough, and if not, what professionals operating from these perspectives are to do in order to practice with integrity. For instance, with regard to developmental and strength-based clinical practice, the previous discussion raises such questions as: Does the DSM focus on the possibilities for change, and if not, what are the implications for practice? Do DSM diagnoses foster movement toward optimal mental health, and if not, what does this mean for one's clinical practice? Does the DSM focus enough on a person's strengths, on how well the client is, and on the rest of the client's life beyond the diagnosis? Does the ascription of a DSM diagnosis preclude the ability to focus on the clients' strengths and resources, and if so, how could this affect the services rendered?

Jensen and Hoagwood (1997) indicate that the DSM begins on the wrong foot, because "mental disorder," as used in the title of the DSM, implies a "mind–body dichotomy that is outmoded and not embraced by most present day neuroscientists and developmental neurobiologists" (p. 232). The DSM continues this dichotomy throughout, by seeing the practitioner's job as deciding on the presence or absence of a category of pathology based on the presence of enough of the relevant symptoms. Although its expanded multiaxial format examines the broader context of a person's life, it still asks about medical *problems* and life *stressors,* rather than asking about how a person is well and what assets the person possesses (Saleebey, 2001; White, 2002).

Rosenhan (1973) also draws attention to the failure of the DSM to assess the whole person by pointing out that diagnostic labels only reflect part of the person and part of the person's behavior. Sanity and insanity overlap: The "sane" are not sane all the time, nor are the "insane" insane all the time. Yet diagnostic labels draw attention to the "insane" part, rather than affirming the other parts. The general public's responses to the mentally ill—fear, hostility, suspicion, and dread—make it clear that others also respond primarily to the insane part and not to the rest of the person (Hayward & Bright, 1997; Honos-Webb & Leitner, 2001).

Developmentalists also respond to the above questions by claiming that, because the DSM does not focus on the developmental change process, its static descriptions do not contribute to an understanding of people's problems (Ivey & Ivey, 1998). Rosenhan (1973), as a result of his experiment, for instance, claims that the diagnostic process promotes permanent explanations about people, not developmental ones; that once labeled, there is really nothing the client can do to overcome the diagnosis. Once a person is designated abnormal, all of the person's other behaviors and characteristics are colored by that designation, even to the point that professionals overlook or misinterpret normal behaviors. The label thus becomes a self-fulfilling prophecy, promoting a reality that might not have occurred without the diagnosis (Hayward & Bright, 1997; Jussim, Palumbo, Chatman, Madon, & Smith, 2000; McLaughlin, 2002).

Monetary considerations may also influence the seeming permanence of diagnostic categories (Cooper & Gottlieb, 2000; Wylie, 1995). That is, a mental health professional might, for example, decide that a diagnostic category was indeed only one way of making meaning about problems and that, as a result of this decision, the professional will incorporate multiple perspectives on problems into understanding the client and into possible treatment strategies. However, to continue treatment, the mental health professional may need to maintain the diagnostic category that warrants payment for services. If the client "develops," that is, recovers from symptomatology, the client may not qualify for insurance coverage or funding from a grant source, and thus would have to terminate counseling as soon as symptoms were no longer present (or pay out-of-pocket; but the authors' experience is that many clients terminate counseling when such funding is no longer available).

Absence of symptoms, however, is not the end of counseling for those operating from a developmental perspective. It is merely one step in the journey toward optimal mental health or wellness (Lependorf-Palmer & Healey, 2002; Worell, 2001). Therefore, because "accurate" diagnosis would require changing the diagnosis as the client progresses, and because this would most likely result in a lack of funding and the resultant termination of counseling when symptoms were relieved, traditional diagnostic systems cannot be considered developmental.

Developmentalists must probably conclude that the DSM does not do enough in acknowledging developmental and growth possibilities for clients, and thus it would seem that an overreliance on traditional diagnosis does not fit within the worldviews or ethical mandates of family and other developmentally oriented mental health professionals. To garner insurance reimbursement, mental health professionals have had to portray problems in living as medical disorders that require "medically necessary" treatment, thus elevating pathology to the forefront of importance and demoting attention to health and wellness and strength (Demmitt & Oldenski, 1999; Saleebey, 2001; Sperry, 2002b). A holistic focus is not economically viable at this time for most mental health professionals (Lammers & Geist, 1997). The only apparent way for the DSM to be used developmentally is, as Seligman et al. (2001) indicate, to attend (a) to which disorders are more likely to occur at what age, (b) to what the progress of a disorder is likely to be throughout the life span, and (c) to the differential impact of illness on people of different ages.

Where, then, does this leave developmentally focused practitioners in their pursuit of ethical diagnosis? A constructivist approach to the ascription of diagnosis may be helpful in resolving some of the aforementioned questions and issues; that is, if a developmentally focused provider offers a permanent, provisional, or temporary diagnosis, the provider may also add a phasic or stage developmental story (see Chapter 9 as an example), or other stories. The provider may further engage a dialogue among these stories, perhaps in the client's presence, perhaps not, in the attempt to discover what might be most useful to the client at this time and place. The practitioner might then tentatively try one of the possibilities considered, using her or his clinical observation skills to determine the usefulness of the problem definition and resulting intervention. Feedback from these observations and from the client could then add to the stories as the practitioner and client develop in their ability to find useful interventions.

SYSTEMIC AND CONTEXTUAL UNDERSTANDINGS

A further ethical challenge for counselors, family therapists, and other systemically and contextually oriented practitioners is how to integrate an individualistic diagnostic system with their notions that families and broader societal influences are important to understanding people's experiences and problems in living.

Family Therapists

According to ACA and AAMFT ethical standards, mental health professionals are to enlist families as a positive resource to the counseling process (ACA, 1995, Standard A.1d; AAMFT, 2001, Standard 1.8). In fact, the discipline of family therapy began because of the observation that people in psychiatric hospitals became more symptomatic when their families visited. It seemed likely that the families themselves might be contributing to the existence of the problem, rather than that the problems possessed a life of their own, independent of the surrounding environment. As family therapy progressed as a discipline, it grew beyond its initial focus on families as the

cause of people's problems to more recursive understandings of problem development and maintenance and to beliefs that broader cultural factors influence families and individuals in important ways (Christian, 2002; Gladding, 2002).

Other Systemic Perspectives

Other theorists and researchers have also proposed macro-level explanations of mental disorders. For instance, Gottschalk's (2000) proposal that modern day society, as mediated by the media, is likely to create borderline, schizoid, and antisocial tendencies, as well as other problems, takes systemic thinking beyond family therapy and multicultural practitioners' usual focus on the influences of family and cultural groups on problem development and places the blame on large, broader, societal influences. According to Gottschalk (2000), if one lives in a crazy society, and that craziness is constantly expressed on television and in movies and newspapers, the distance between normal and abnormal grows less. From his perspective, what could be diagnosable may only be adaptive.

He offers examples of "usual" or "reasonable" responses to today's societal environment. For instance, Gottschalk (2000) indicates that the oscillation between "complete indifference and passionate involvement, between intense idealization and devaluation, between terror and chronic boredom" (p. 29) that the DSM might call "borderline personality disorder" is easily understood when one examines society's demands. He points to the quick and recurrent replacement of yesterday's products, ideas, styles, and desires with the newer ones of tomorrow. He observes the same about people's frequent change of spouses and physical space, and points to expert knowledge that becomes so quickly obsolete. From his perspective, to remain passionate about anything when it will be passé tomorrow is to obsess (which would be abnormal). Society, then, seems to require the oscillation in order for people to stay "with it," or up-to-date. He calls this a "normalized assault on a sense of constancy" (p. 29), but claims that those who are "keeping up" are actually demonstrating borderline personality characteristics, which would have to, then, be considered an expectable response to society's demands.

Another example of society's influence on problems in living is the creation of paranoid symptomatology, says Gottschalk (2000). He claims that interpersonal *transactions* have replaced interpersonal *interactions,* and that these transactions are mutually exploitive, partial, and fragmented. For example, he says, many people's energies seem to be directed toward getting as much as they can and then, when "no more" is apparently available, they sever relationships. People experience a fiercely competitive, highly mobile, threatening daily experience; it is a "jungle out there without any rules," he and others have said, a situation that might lead to understandable paranoid behaviors. He describes our social system as paranoid, and gives as examples surveillance in public spaces and gated communities ("paranoid architecture"; p. 30). If social systems can be paranoid, then he believes that individual diagnoses are unlikely realities. Instead, "mental 'disorders' should be . . . apprehended as changing interpersonal strategies individuals develop, rather than as fixed and internal 'diseases' they fall prey to" (p. 24). From his perspective, then, paranoia is also expectable given society's demands.

Gottschalk (2000) also describes other societal causes of problem behaviors. He points to television's models of schizophrenic communication patterns and schizoid behavior. The invisible and debilitating force of speed—speed with which we now electronically communicate and with which we are expected to engage others and everyday life—could cause a variety of addictions, exhaustion, inappropriate emotional reactions, and accidental death. Antisocial personality tendencies—an intense individualism unrestrained by social bonds that results in compulsive lying, manipulation, and deceitfulness—are regularly observed on TV. People also repeatedly watch gruesome acts of violence on TV; might this be sociopathy, he asks? He claims that it is no surprise, given what is observed in an ongoing way in the media, that some people's life strategy is emotional anesthesia: saying "whatever," offering a "postmodern shrug," displaying chronic coldness, radical indifference, objectification of others, and/or a lack of empathy.

Fee (2000) presents a slightly different take on the influence of systems on people's conceptions of self and of their "disorders." She indicates that as depression (or other disorders) become popularly discussed, they take on a life of their own, that is, a story, separate from clinical symptomatology. Such a societal "storying" confounds clinical understandings of disorders. For example, because lay people now know about depression, they can use what they know to construct their autobiographies. These autobiographies, or self-interpretations as mediated by popular knowledge, influence both symptoms and what is told to those who must decide on a diagnosis. Thus, Fee indicates, it is difficult to maintain a "coherent and relatively continuous 'narrative of the self' amidst the incessant refashioning and uprooting of the cultural milieu" (p. 86). It is also difficult to "have" depression as some sort of consistent self-definition; practitioners will need to assess the person's own story about depression as mediated by all of these external cultural elements. As she concludes, people never experience depression (or other disorders) by themselves without these influences; thus, a disorder is never an individual or solely biological problem.

Some might ask at this point why it is that certain people seem to develop more problems than others, when we know that most people experience "society" and its ills. Of course, this brings up the question of whether people's biological heritage or their environment makes them vulnerable to personal struggles (Mohar, 2003; Pilgrim, 2002; Valenstein, 1998). Most scholars, researchers, and others believe that all of our experiences generate from some combination of the biological and the psychosocial (Raingruber, 2003; Rutter, 2002). However, social constructionists, multiculturalists, and perhaps others would add the notion that those with less power in a society experience a greater quantity of life's difficulties, and therefore, have their biological predispositions activated more frequently than those from the dominant race, ethnicity, age, sexual orientation, or gender (Belle & Doucet, 2003; Rigazio-DiGilio, Ivey, & Locke, 1997). Those from nondominant cultural groups also garner fewer of society's resources, and thus, meet potential interventions later in the problem cycle, which may allow problems to develop more frequently into full-blown diagnoses. In addition, because those with less power are less likely to seek help, they may come to the attention of mental health providers only when the problems have reached a greater intensity.

Mental Health Training

As a result of grounding philosophical beliefs about the importance of cultural and societal forces, professional societies' ethical mandates, and the aforementioned types of family and societal observations, mental health training programs have incorporated systemic and cultural understandings into their curricula. Family therapy trainees are required to become fundamentally systemic, rather than individualistic, in their worldview and focus (Commission on Accreditation for Marriage and Family Therapy Education [COAMFTE], 1997). Most mental health providers now receive training in the cultural foundations of behavior (APA, 2002; CACREP, 2001; COAMFTE, 1997). Such

training includes knowledge about different cultural groups, skills in counseling people from diverse cultures, and awareness of one's own biases and stereotypes (AAMFT, 2001, Standard 1.1; ACA, 1995, Standards A.2, A.5b, E.5b; APA, 1992, Standards 6.01, 6.02; NASW, 1999, Standard 1.05). This training also often helps students to think critically about the intersection of client and practitioner cultures, and the impact of that intersection on the counseling relationship.

The DSM's Systemic Performance

Despite the clear intersections of family and cultural systems with individuals and their problems, and despite the resulting need for and actualization of training in these areas, we question whether traditional diagnostic systems effectively incorporate systems and/or contextual thinking. We do acknowledge improvements in recent versions of the DSM over past versions. For instance, the DSM *has* progressed to a multiaxial system that requires practitioners to indicate life stressors and medical conditions that may have a bearing on the development or maintenance of clients' disorders, or on their treatment. Recently, beginning with the DSM-IV, a Global Assessment of Relationship Functioning has been added as an appendix to the DSM and can be used by practitioners if they choose (Mottarella, Philpot, & Fritzsche, 2001; Ross & Doherty, 2001). These changes improve on past DSMs by acknowledging that the environment may contribute to the development or maintenance of a disorder.

However, as Parker et al. and Stowell-Smith (1995) indicate, taxonomies (classification systems) are by nature descriptive, static, and unidimensional. They provide relatively little context for understanding how psychopathology emerges within the broader surround. The focus on signs and symptoms of disorders omits many portions of clinical reality, such as the contextual and interactional realities that we have just described (Bilsbury & Richman, 2002; Hawley, 2000). Such a focus also draws attention away from clients' subjective attributions about their life experiences and symptoms. Currently observable behaviors are the focus, as intended by the DSM developers, and meaning and peoples' motivation are not addressed (Crowe, 2002; Fireman, 2002; Wehowsky, 2000). As we previously noted, "psychopathology" may be the person's attempt to adapt to a dysfunctional context. However, for various reasons, the DSM system is not capable of incorporating this more competency- based, contextual notion (Demmitt & Oldenski, 1999; Hodges, 2003; Parker et al., 1995; Pilgrim & Bentall, 1999).

Jensen and Hoagwood (1997) also question whether practitioners can say that mental disorders reside in minds, which reside in brains, which reside in the individual body, and by that logic therefore, do not reside in the social world. In fact, in their words, all "'mental disorders' reside in communities, neighborhoods, and families" (p. 238). Agreeing with Gottschalk (2000), Jensen and Hoagwood believe that, in many circumstances, communities, neighborhoods, and families, rather than the individual, should be described as dysfunctional. It is also possible that dysfunction might reside in the transactions among the individual and environmental factors. Yet the DSM focuses on defining mental health and illness as a matter of individual characteristics rather than collective conditions, despite the idea that the collectives may at times be more dysfunctional than individuals.

In addition to the DSM's failure to incorporate the critical role of context into understandings of problems in living, the DSM system does not suggest or require contextual input into the diagnostic process itself. The practitioner is still the person who "does" the diagnosing to the client (Caplan, 1995; Ivey et al., 1999; Kutchins & Kirk, 1997). A promising and more integrated approach to diagnosis has been offered, however, by The World Psychiatric

Association (Mezzich, 1995). Their International Guidelines for Diagnostic Assessment indicate that, in addition to the contextual focus of a standardized multiaxial formulation, comprehensive diagnosis needs to integrate the multiple perspectives of the client, the practitioner, the patient, and the family. Including a wider range of perspectives should decrease the experience of diagnosis being done *by* one person *to* another. Regularly soliciting these multiple perspectives may also overcome the tendency toward diagnostic permanence (Mezzich, 2002).

In conclusion, the current DSM system of diagnosis, with its minimal focus on social or contextual factors related to disorders, does not meet the ethical standards of counselors family therapists, and other similarly inclined mental health providers that require, recommend, or include a contextual or systemic focus. Nor does it fit within the systemic or contextual worldviews or undergirding philosophies of these disciplines because (a) it still ascribes individual diagnoses only, demoting relational, systemic, or contextual problems to nonreimbursable V codes; (b) it does not require multiple contributors to the diagnostic process; and (c) it does not consider systems as possible targets for diagnosis or treatment. The conflict, then, between traditional diagnosis and current professional mandates for systemic and contextual competence requires practitioners to rethink their use of DSM diagnosis (Benson, Long, & Sporakowski, 1992; Denton, 1989).

Systems-oriented practitioners approach the conflict between their undergirding systemic worldview and an individualistic diagnostic system in various ways. Purists may believe that individual and systemic approaches and theories are incompatible (e.g., Haley, 1987), and may thus refuse to ascribe individual diagnoses or to participate in a reimbursement system that requires such diagnoses. Other systemically oriented therapists may find themselves conceptualizing clients from a systems perspective, yet using a medical, individualistic perspective solely for the purposes of reimbursement (Denton, 1989; Sperry, 2002b). For example, a therapist may believe that a child's behavior problem serves the function of diffusing tensions between the parents. Yet the therapist may still apply a DSM diagnosis to the child in order to receive reimbursement. Still other practitioners consider it important to acknowledge and integrate understandings of various systems levels and types of interactions (Goldenberg & Goldenberg, 2004; Herring & Kaslow, 2002; Nelson, 2002). For instance, they may consider the impact of the physical body's system—wherein may lie individual medical and mental health diagnoses—to be just as important as the impact of global economics on an individual or family. Other systems therapists consider most "disorders" to be expectable responses to abuse, stress, loss, and trauma, that is, to abnormal environmental events (e.g., Bracken, 2002; Casey & Long, 2003; Crossley, 2000; Kutchins & Kirk, 1997). These events are painful and people want relief from distress, but this does not mean that people are disordered or out of touch with reality. Because the DSM indicates that a mental disorder has to be internal, and *not* an expectable reaction to an external event, such therapists might consider it unethical to ascribe a DSM diagnosis.

CONCLUSION

Although the reader may find some of these challenges to be more salient than others, it is our hope that at least some of this information provides mental health practitioners with questions to ponder, reflect on, pursue supervision for, and engage in conversation about. In our experience, few of the ethical dilemmas that arise from these questions are explored adequately during mental health training. Instead, practitioners-in-training read, and perhaps memorize, the DSM, read a text on psychopathology, watch videos or read cases

about people with various diagnoses, practice diagnostic discernment, and consider what treatments might be most useful for various diagnoses (White, 2001). Frankly, having taught the one DSM course that is offered in counseling programs, it is difficult for us to imagine being able to add more content to this already packed course. Yet failure to attend seriously to resolving some of these dilemmas has and will continue to negatively affect clients, particularly those with less power in our society (Caplan, 1995; Duffy et al., 2002; Kurpius & Gross, 1996).

In its review of principles related to informed consent and confidentiality, competence, accuracy of diagnosis, dual relationships, values, and the obligation to promote growth and development and to include families, this chapter has indicated the principles behind ethical mandates, has applied them to diagnosis, and has considered whether ways exist to resolve ethical dilemmas that arise related to these areas. In some ethical areas, more potential resolutions seem to exist. With respect to the obligation to promote growth and development and to include families and contextual understandings, fewer resolutions seem apparent with the current diagnostic system.

But lest the reader think that we hold only negative views with regard to using the DSM, we commit Chapters 4 through 9 to ideas for integration of the DSM with contextually sensitive practice. In the additional chapters, students and practitioners are offered opportunities to increase their awareness of ethical dilemmas and their resolutions, to consider how mental health diagnosis might progress to more ethical practice in the future, to hear how practitioners across the country have dealt with ethical dilemmas related to diagnosis, and to delve into an integrationist perspective, one in which diagnosis is placed within an assessment that honors context, development, and personality styles. We now turn to considering feminist and multicultural challenges to DSM diagnosis, and related ethical mandates for practitioners.

3

Multicultural Challenges to the DSM

Critiques of the *Diagnostic and Statistical Manual of Mental Disorders* (DSM) diagnostic process have been particularly intense from women and people of color (Bhugra & Bhui, 1999; Caplan, 1995; Cermele, Daniels, & Anderson, 2001; Chrisler & Caplan, 2002; Duffy, Gillig, Tureen, & Ybarra, 2002; Sadler, 2002). Because of the strength and vastness of their objections, we devote two chapters to the question of how mental health providers can both diagnose *and* attend to the principles behind ethical standards that mandate cultural and gender sensitivity. We begin with the ethical mandates and the principles behind them, then discuss the controversies over determining who is normal or abnormal, including the negative impacts of mistaken decisions on women and people of color, move on to specific challenges to the DSM system by people of color, and conclude with multiculturally sensitive diagnostic and treatment strategies. We follow a similar pattern in Chapter 4, when we address feminist challenges to the DSM. Case studies and possible best-practice strategies, as related to the issues addressed in these chapters, are outlined in Chapter 5.

As we review multicultural and feminist challenges to the DSM, we are conscious of potential reactions that may be evoked, reactions that may dismiss our inclusion of such challenges as mere attempts to be "politically correct" or as too political for discussion in a scholarly work. Some scholars have stated that discussions of feminist and multicultural concerns as related to the DSM can be perceived as overly political and are better left untouched (Fabrega, 1996; Griffith, 1996; Kutchins & Kirk, 1997). As Fabrega (1996) states:

To allow cultural factors to affect psychiatric illness determinations is to [in fact] risk politicizing the psychiatric enterprise. Having said this, one cannot but acknowledge that such kinds of conflicts are and have been implicated in the criteria for the definition of many Axis I and Axis II disorders. One has but to review quandaries involving definitions of psychosis, neurosis, homosexuality, and the sexually assaultive male syndrome, adjustment disorders, and personality disorder to appreciate how often psychiatric concerns intrude into, contaminate, and in some instances locally implicate sociopolitical concerns. In most instances, the potential problems of untangling medical–psychiatric and sociopolitical concerns are never allowed to materialize, or if they do materialize, are bypassed or ignored. (p. 8)

It is our intent to counter this historical tendency; that is, we hope to at least begin and deepen the dialogue about what it means to be diagnostically skilled, knowledgeable, or multiculturally aware, and about how intentionality about cultural and gender sensitivity may connect the realm of scholarship or clinical competence to political concerns.

We are also aware that many discussions related to multiculturalism—which includes, from our perspective, sensitivity about differences related to race, ethnicity, age, (dis)ability, gender, religion, sexual orientation, social class, geographical area of residence (region of the United States), and urban/suburban/rural living locations—are initiated or engaged in by those on the political left. This raises the question, cited by McAuliffe (1999), "Is there a liberal or left leaning bias to multicultural counseling?" Given our attempts to be culturally sensitive and to include all participants who might have something important to offer to discussions about DSM diagnosis, we do not want to dismiss the voices or stories of anyone, regardless of where they fall along the political continuum. However, these questions punctuate the relationships between such discussions and politics. Therefore, we openly acknowledge our bias that any discussions about the plight or conditions of groups that have been historically oppressed have political, social, and public policy ramifications. We personally think that it is impossible to separate politics from any area of life, including mental health services. However, even if our readers do not agree, we hearken back to ethical mandates to which all mental health providers must give account, for multicultural and gender sensitivity and for overcoming biases (American Association for Marriage and Family Therapy [AAMFT], 2001, Standards 1.1, 3.1; American Counseling

Association [ACA], 1995, Standards A.2, E.5b; American Psychological Association [APA], 1992, Standards 1.08, 1.09, 1.10; National Association of Social Workers [NASW], 1999, Standards 1.05, 6.01), and to various lists of multicultural competencies that have been developed by and for the mental health professions (American Psychological Association [APA], 2003; Garcia, Cartwright, Winston, & Borzuchowska, 2003; Liu & Clay, 2002).

Furthermore, we believe that there are lines regarding healthy versus unhealthy behavior that are shared almost universally by all cultures. For example, most societies would probably consider it abnormal for a person to randomly murder people, and would subsequently develop some type of label to describe a person who behaves in such a manner. Our intention is not to relativize all human behavior and experience or to say that no judgments about behavior should ever be made. Our discussion of cultural and feminist challenges to the DSM system is intended to bring to light information that increases readers' multicultural and gender sensitivity and ethical decision-making capacity as related to DSM diagnosis.

ETHICAL MANDATES AND CHALLENGES

All ethical codes prohibit mental health professionals from discriminating on the basis of such factors as age, disability, sex, race, ethnicity, religion, socioeconomic class, sexual orientation, or any other difference of the client from the mainstream. As stated earlier, all ethical practitioners are also to commit themselves to gaining knowledge, personal awareness, sensitivity, and skills pertinent to working with a diverse client population (AAMFT, 2001, Standards 1.1, 3.1; ACA, 1995, Standards A.2, E.5b; APA, 1992, Standards 1.08, 1.09, 1.10; NASW, 1999, Standards 1.05, 6.01). Yet how do these mandates play out in the actual practice of mental health providers?

According to some authors (Mezzich, 1999a,b; Mezzich, Kleinman, Fabrega, & Parron, 1996b; Tseng, 2001), being competent to work with diverse client groups when diagnosing and providing subsequent services means knowing how to do an overall cultural assessment. From their perspective, this means understanding the cultural framework of the client's identity, cultural explanations of illness experiences and help seeking behavior, cultural meanings of adaptive functioning and social context, and cultural elements in the practitioner–patient relationship. Although it seems unlikely that a provider could accomplish these ideals relative to too many cultures, providers certainly should develop these abilities for the cultures of the clients whom they predominantly serve, and should develop a referral base of practitioners for clients from cultures with which they are less familiar (Welfel, 2002).

Furthermore, it has been stated that practitioners should try to avoid jumping to conclusions about clients on the basis of their cultural group, should acquire knowledge about different cultures' norms and interaction styles, and should commit to ongoing awareness about their own biases, assumptions, and cultural encapsulation (APA, 2003; Sue, Ivey, & Pederson, 1996; Ivey, D'Andrea, Ivey, & Simek-Morgan, 1999; Sue & Sue, 1990; Welfel, 2002). As mentioned above, such cultural awareness extends beyond the usual attention to race and ethnicity into the differences related to religion, age, socioeconomic class, gender, ethnicity, disability, and sexual orientation.

Yet fully actualizing such knowledge, skills, and awareness can be challenging. Culturally sensitive diagnosis, in particular, is easier to talk about than to do, particularly when diagnosing those from cultures different from the host culture. Wide variations exist among people from different cultures in perspectives about how interpersonal relationships should

be conducted, especially in families. In some cases, the ways in which relationships are to be conducted—for instance, parents using physical discipline with children or males physically abusing women because their wives "belong" to them as mere possessions—differ from those of North American culture or are in conflict with North American laws (Garcia et al., 2003; Lo & Fung, 2003; McGoldrick, Giordano, & Pearce, 1996). How then can mental health professionals from the dominant culture become competent when diagnosing those from different cultures? How is it possible, for instance, for men to become free of bias when diagnosing women? Can they ethically diagnose women if they have not deconstructed their own positions of privilege in society? Can women become free of bias and gender role expectations when diagnosing men? Is it ever possible for White, middle-class mental health professionals to be accurate when diagnosing a low income, non-White client? These difficult questions perhaps indicate that the journey toward cultural and gender sensitivity cannot help but be a lifelong process of discovery rather than an accomplishment made after a short period of effort (Arredondo et al., 1996).

Related questions are as follows: Can mental health providers ever completely eliminate the influence of systemic oppressions, such as institutionalized racism and sexism, on themselves, the client, or the relationship, when diagnosing people who differ from the majority (Bhugra & Bhui, 1999; McLaughlin, 2002; Seem & Johnson, 1998; Nakkab & Hernandez, 1998)? How does one assign the necessary significance to expectable reactions to such systemic oppressions when only an unreimbursable "V code" is allowed? What forum is available for discussing the "illness" or diagnosis of contexts or systems? How do mental health providers find funding for correcting such systems, rather than expecting individual clients to correct the oppressions that are weighing them down?

However, questions about the practitioner's cultural and gender sensitivity are not the only questions raised by those pursuing culturally sensitive diagnosis. They also question the relevance, given the methods of development, of the DSM diagnostic system for people who differ from the dominant culture. They ask whether practitioners can draw any definite conclusions about people of color, gay or lesbian people, or women based on a diagnostic system whose development was grounded in the knowledge of European American men and that claims to be based on "scientific" evidence from research studies that did not include diverse participants (McLaughlin, 2002; Rogler, 1996; Skodol & Bender, 2003).

It is to these questions that we devote this chapter, which can only be considered a first step in a much longer journey. Some may wonder whether any counseling or diagnostic system can be free of such potential problems. This is a legitimate query. From our perspective, viewing the DSM as one story among many, recognizing that no story contains the whole or absolute "truth," and tentatively exploring a number of stories in a more egalitarian manner with clients, rather than imposing our "truth," may help us to counter the harm that has and could potentially continue to be caused by applying the DSM diagnostic system to historically oppressed groups. These ideas will be discussed in more depth in later segments of the book.

NORMAL VERSUS ABNORMAL

The most significant questions about the DSM that are raised by those who are concerned about gender and multicultural issues are, "Who gets to decide what is abnormal, what is mental illness, and where the line is between normal and abnormal?" and "On what basis do they get to decide these things?" As Fabrega (1996) indicates,

Each society incorporates standards of normality, deviation, and abnormality with

respect to human behavior. . . . The system of description and diagnosis of psychiatric illness reflects conventions about the normality versus abnormality of behavior and about personhood, social behavior, and the nature of illness. (p. 11)

Thus, as Marecek (1993) claims, "the field of abnormal psychology has intrinsically to do with definitions of the good life, and judgments about proper and improper forms of behavior and social relations" (p. 114).

Who Decides and How?

The question of who establishes these conventions and definitions, particularly with respect to psychiatric diagnosis, was briefly raised before, but is of critical importance. As stated earlier, these decisions do not seem to be grounded in science. Richardson (1999) asserts that people in power make the decisions. Sarbin (1997) points to a time in history when those people were medical doctors; they were considered responsible for explaining and controlling unwanted conduct. At one point, they grouped certain undesirable behaviors under the diagnosis "hysteria" when they couldn't explain such behaviors on the basis of underlying biological conditions. History then, according to Sarbin, links the psychiatric labeling process with the moral decision of deciding who is displaying unwanted conduct. Kutchins and Kirk (1997) add that agreements about such decisions change over time, depending on who is in power, and on the zeitgeist of the times (Caplan, 1995; Cermele et al., 2001; Duffy et al., 2002; Sadler, 2002). Fabrega (1996) further points out that "Each society has available systems and traditions of medicine that involve knowledge structures; this knowledge is produced, passed on, and applied by socially appointed experts" (p. 11). As Kutchins and Kirk (1997) state, these experts

incorporate [into clinical work the] prevailing and traditional cultural standards and conventions about behavior. The illnesses described, the modes of their diagnosis, and the technologies of their treatment reflect conventions of how people should behave, how they (should or can) misbehave, what meanings are to be ascribed to behavioral alterations, how such aberrations are to be shaped into normal channels of behavior, and how persons showing these behaviors are to be regarded and handled in the event "normal" behavior is reinstated. (p. 11)

So, who are these "experts" or "people in power" and how do these decisions get made? Szasz (1974) and others express a rather depressing-if-true perspective that those primarily in power are psychiatrists who are interested in expanding their treatment domain. He says, "the concept of mental illness and the social actions taken in its name serve the self-seeking interests of the medical and psychiatric professions, just as the notion of witchcraft served the interests of the theologians, acting in the name of God" (p. 304) to root out and kill witches. A number of authors agree that by framing certain ways of being as "mental illness," psychiatrists expand their domain and their earning power (Burr & Butt, 2000; Caplan, 1995; Kutchins & Kirk, 1997), claiming that the more "problems in living" that psychiatrists can decide are mental illnesses, the broader their domain.

Whether one agrees with such demonizing of psychiatrists or not, adding disorders to the DSM certainly means that more people qualify for reimbursable treatment and more practitioners *of all disciplines* will be reimbursed by funding organizations. One then needs to ask whether adding disorders is really a problem. Kutchins and Kirk (1997) believe so, complaining that these additions have led to the increased pathologizing of everyday life (Chrisler & Caplan, 2002; Duffy et al., 2002; Pilgrim & Bentall, 1999; Sperry, 2002b). Common human experiences, such as worry, feeling blue, obsessive thoughts, bearing grudges, lack of sexual interest, not sleeping,

smoking, being alone, having trouble at school, being hung over, are translated into evidence of mental disease.

Burr and Butt (2000) concur, saying that an important feature of this pathologizing is "psychologization" (p. 186), or placing daily difficulties into the framework of psychological theory and thus locating them at the level of the individual. Psychologization of daily difficulties, in turn, means that the responsibility for problems and for change belongs solely to the individual person, despite the availability of alternative, more social explanations and remediation. Constructing problems as existing only or largely at the level of the individual draws attention away from the effects of social conditions, such as the results of sexism, racism, and poverty, that are inevitable contexualities in individual experiences.

Burr and Butt continue, "Therapeutic vocabularies have over-sensitized people to their faults and misfortunes—and helped them to be defined as such" (p. 195). If the prevailing cultural beliefs are those of illness, they say, then clients will interpret life experiences as evidence of illness, themselves as passive sufferers, and the practitioner's job as treating the illness. This increasing "pathologization of everyday life" and the expansion of the boundaries of abnormality mean that it becomes harder and harder to be assessed as "normal" and more and more likely that individuals, rather than dysfunctional social systems, will be blamed for abnormality (Cermele et al., 2001; Chrisler & Caplan, 2002; Duffy et al., 2002; Kleinman, 1996; Lewis, Lewis, D'Andrea, & Daniels, 1998/2003). Many readers will recall a poster that illustrates popular culture's perspective on the difficulty of being declared or considering oneself to be normal. The poster reads, "Convention for Children of Non-Dysfunctional Families," and one person sits in an auditorium that has a capacity for hundreds.

As noted in Chapter 1, Kutchins and Kirk (1997), in their book, *Making Us Crazy,* detail the political process that they claim has been and is currently involved in deciding who gets included or excluded from the DSM, and thus considered abnormal or normal. They extend the political process beyond the psychiatric profession in their tracing of the debates and battles over the inclusion of homosexuality, masochistic personality disorder, borderline personality disorder, and post-traumatic stress disorder. They quite convincingly persuade readers that the political process involved in DSM development has consisted of debates, hearings, pressure by interest groups, keeping track of and worrying about public opinion, "horse trading," protests, manipulation, invalid studies thrown together by those with conflicts of interest, and falsified research.

Kirmayer and Minas (2000) suggest that such political maneuvering, related to the inclusion of disorders in the DSM, indicates that psychiatrists and DSM developers may not be as powerful or autonomous as some authors think; in other words, psychiatrists and DSM developers may *also* find themselves subject to forces larger than themselves. For instance, Kirmayer and Minas state "the sponsorship of so much activity in psychiatry (research, professional meetings, and continuing medical education activities) by pharmaceutical companies raises disturbing questions about the forces shaping psychiatric knowledge" (p. 445). "Professional autonomy," they say, "takes a back seat to marketing" (p. 446). One wonders, then, about the potential effects of economic forces on DSM diagnosis, an influence that extends beyond that of the psychiatric profession.

Risks of Abuse

In *The Myth of Mental Illness,* Szasz (1974) points, as have others, to larger concerns about people in power deciding the boundaries of normalcy: that is, the risk of abuse of this power and the risk that practitioners become agents of social control by imposing

values about normalcy on others (see also Hoagwood & Jensen, 1997; Howard, 1991). Szasz pursues the following logic: In a private practice, in which a practitioner engages in one-to-one counseling with a client, the ethical practitioner's sole motivation is good practice toward the client, and the client's privacy is protected. As soon as a third party enters the relationship, such as an employer, a grant sponsor, or an insurance company, the practitioner's motivations must be divided between good practice toward the client and pleasing the third party. When the third party's opinion of the practitioner weighs more heavily on the practitioner than does benefiting the client (for instance, if the practitioner stands to lose employment, promotions, or money by not doing as the third party wishes), the practitioner imposes the values of the third party onto the client, deciding for the client what is appropriate behavior. This progression, claims Szasz, results in practitioners becoming the oppressors. Thus, says Szasz, in any clinical situation in which there are more than two parties, the relationship can be used as a form of social control. Szasz (1974) points to the former Soviet Union's practice of using "medicine" as a means of keeping nonconformists in line as an extreme example of such social control (see also Fabrega, 1996; Tseng, 2001).

Griffith (1996), however, wonders about the lack of consciousness about culture in the United States that would lead Szasz and other authors to assume that one would have to go as far as the former Soviet Union to find an example of diagnoses used for political or oppressive purposes. By bringing into focus the oppressive use of diagnosis with African American clients, he demonstrates that one cannot separate the political (race polarization in the United States) from the diagnostic process. For instance, African American professionals have been concerned about the overuse of antisocial personality disorder (among other diagnoses) for African American males. It is believed that this categorization keeps many clients from receiving help from the mental health system and facilitates their entry into the prison system. Why, ask these same professionals, is not "racist personality disorder" included as a DSM personality disorder? However, even without behaving in extreme ways (e.g., the former Soviet Union's practices), one can never assume that there are not "third parties" influencing practitioners. Mental health providers find themselves influenced by many larger cultural systems, and should thus be particularly concerned about consciously or unconsciously imposing socially mainstream values on those who fall outside of the mainstream (Griffith, 1996; Fabrega, 1996; Seligman, Walker, & Rosenhan, 2001). Such imposition of values should probably be considered unethical, oppressive, and abusive of power.

When discussing gender identity disorder, Richardson (1999) claims that ascribing diagnoses is inherently just this sort of abuse of power; that, although "psychological dysfunction, not statistical deviation, [ought to define] psychopathology" (p. 44), practitioners instead tend to label any deviations that they find upsetting or repellant as pathological solely because they trouble the practitioner. In fact, he says, it isn't even the degree of atypicality that determines pathology, but the social value placed on that atypicality. He claims that in many cases the atypical people don't have problems; instead, the people in power have merely decided that they do. As an example of Richardson's declaration, one author remembers the upheaval caused in 1986 by a cross-dressing man who, adorned in a brightly colored leotard, tights, and a matching women's linen blouse, awaited his counseling session in the reception room of a family counseling center. His complaint was primarily about his failure to fit in and be approved of by the society that he inhabited, rather than any dysfunction related to his lifestyle choices, or gender dysphoria. Interestingly, practitioners, office personnel, and clients (those also

waiting in the reception area) alike were shaken by his presence because of the degree of "oddness" of his behavior and their up-to-this-point-unexamined disapproval. Despite the work of advocacy groups to counter claims that cross-dressing behavior is "abnormal" (see Ellis & Eriksen, 2002, for a reference list), cross-dressing continues to be considered a disorder by the DSM, identified as either a sexual fetish, the result of gender dysphoria, or the attempt to ward off depression or anxiety (APA, 2000). Thus, the DSM offered little support for considering this client's cross-dressing to be a lifestyle choice rather than a dysfunction needing correction.

As a result of situations similar to this one, Kutchins and Kirk (1997) claim that the DSM has become an instrument "that pathologizes those in our society who are undesirable and powerless; this occurs not because of any malicious intent but because of unspoken cultural biases about what should be considered normal and what should be considered disease" (p. 16). They further claim that the "identification of mental disorder has been used to promote stereotypes and . . . such thinking continues to be used to promote bigotry long after it has been scientifically discredited" (pp. 222–223). Kutchins and Kirk document a long history of misuse of census data to perpetuate racist myths, concluding, "Psychiatric diagnoses have been used frequently as tools to promote racial injustice" (p. 223). They believe that the DSM continues to do so as a result of the biases about gender and race that are embedded within it.

After reviewing anthropological research, Lewis-Fernandez and Kleinman (1994) agree. They declare that "North American professional constructs of personality and psychopathology are mostly culture bound, selectively reflecting the experiences of particular cohorts—those who are White, male, Anglo-Germanic, Protestant, and formally educated and who share a middle- and upper-class cultural orientation" (p. 67). They further indicate that diagnostic criteria ignore 80% of the world's population, and the most rapidly increasing segments of United States society (see also Gaines, 1992; Kleinman, 1988). These culturally specific ways of viewing individuals and their personality development result in an ethnocentric psychology (Markus & Kitayama, 1991), ignore the influence of cultural norms and social context on human behavior (Nuckolls, 1992), and do not take seriously cultural diversity in relation to psychological symptoms (Mezzich, Kleinman, Fabrega, Good, et al., 1993).

Rogler (1996) also agrees. He indicates that Hispanic clients, particularly those who are newly immigrated, poorly acculturated into the dominant culture, and economically disadvantaged, rarely have cultural meanings about their distress considered in the diagnostic process. Rogler claims that research should work to identify the category fallacy—that is, the application of diagnostic categories to cultural groups for which they were not developed and have never been validated—and to clearly articulate cultural differences in diagnosis. Rogler (1996) also states, however, that advocacy on behalf of culturally sensitive assessment has had a negligible effect on research. Research, he says, can only be made culturally sensitive "through an incessant and continuing finely calibrated interweaving of cultural components and cultural awareness into all phases of the research process" (p. 41). He also recommends that procedures be developed that "strongly bias the classificatory schemes away from the researcher's presuppositions and toward the subjects' culture." He states that "procedures are needed that serve to distill the culturally patterned meanings of psychological distress out of the private, individualized beliefs and behaviors of persons" (p. 41).

Despite the noted problems with how disorders are included in the DSM and the potential abuses that might occur given who is making such decisions, Richardson (1999) is hopeful that practitioners can be principled enough to reach beyond cultural biases. As Richardson says, "Although social biases will inevitably inform our nosology, our responsibility as intelligent, self-critical theorists, researchers, and practitioners is to counter strenuously the effect of such biases insofar as that is possible" (Richardson, 1999, p. 45; see also APA, 2003; Mezzich, Kleinman, Fabrega, & Parron, 1996a; Tseng, 2001).

Other authors, however, are not so hopeful about the ability of individual practitioners to be so principled. Marecek (1999), for example, does not believe that practitioners can succeed in sufficiently countering their personal, and sometimes professionally trained, biases. She claims, "When students study abnormal psychology, they learn about historically-contingent, socially-situated moralities, disguised as medico-scientific verities" (p. 114), and they tend to accept these as "truths." Castillo (1997) agrees: "The formal study of a particular paradigm is what prepares a person for membership in a scientific community. That person learns the rules of the paradigm and also what constitutes deviance" (p. 13). The paradigm defines what questions will be asked; how they will be asked (methods); and what counts as an acceptable answer. The reification of the principles in the paradigm occurs because a group of people collectively considers their experiences to be reality. Their experiences lead to what their group calls a "natural attitude." The same objects can be collectively reified in different ways in different cultures, contradicting each other, but seem "completely true and real to the people in that culture" (p. 19). Their natural attitude is their own unique way of experiencing the world. It thus becomes very difficult for practitioners to free themselves of the paradigms that they "received" in school, particularly when such paradigms are presented as "truth."

Howard (1991) concurs, but takes it a step further, indicating that if practitioners or others can evaluate situations from a variety of different story perspectives, then mental health disciplines may consider them to be well-educated; except that only certain stories are considered legitimate. That is, if individuals tell stories that deviate to any great degree from those that they learned, they are labeled criminals or mentally disturbed (see also Brodsky & Hare-Mustin, 1980; Donzelot, 1979; Fabrega, 1996; Foucault, 1973; Good, 1996; Hare-Mustin & Marecek, 1990, 1997; Kovel, 1982; Sarbin & Mancuso, 1980; Szasz, 1974). Although clinicians may not be labeled so extremely, they may find that their stories are not accepted, that they are branded as troublemakers, that they are blamed for valuing the political over the therapeutic, or that they are considered less competent by those who operate from other schools of thought.

HISTORY AND CURRENT EXPERIENCES OF ABUSES

History seems to bear out Marecek and others' claims about the potential abuse of diagnoses with regard to those from nondominant groups. In the past, despite the existence of "principled practitioners," people who have not conformed to the then-current societal conventions have been psychiatrically hospitalized, ostracized from their communities as deviants and witches, and prevented from marrying and working (Bever, 2002; Forsythe & Melling, 1999; Porter, 2003). Consider the following list of those who did not (do not) fit social conventions: Until recently, homosexuals were diagnosable as mentally ill (American Psychiatric Association [APA], 1980; Penfold & Walker, 1983; Sadler, 2002); African Americans and other people of color were considered subhuman animals, so any pursuit of human "rights" or activities was considered abnormal (Szasz, 2002; Tynerm & Houston, 2002); African American slaves' pursuit of freedom was given the diagnosis of "drapetomania" (Woolfolk, 2001); women of the upper classes who masturbated (and were sometimes considering

divorce) were said to be treading on dangerous ground, risking idiocy, mania, and death, and therefore were "treated" with clitoridectomies (Chesler, 1973; Darby, 2003; Wright & Owen, 2001); more generally, masturbation was considered a diagnosable problem (Woolfolk, 2001); women pursuing higher education and/or athletics would become sterile, according to "objective" research (Chesler, 1973); women who chose not to marry, not to have children, to divorce, or to have sex outside of marriage were considered abnormal and were ostracized (Cohen & Casper, 2002; Gordon, 2003); those women who expressed left-leaning politics were considered disordered more often than left-leaning men (Brodsky & Holroyd, 1975). Christian European Americans sought to convert the "heathen savages" (i.e., Native Americans, Africans, Asians, etc.) who dressed differently, had different customs, and perhaps used opiates or other drugs in their spiritual activities. Few today would describe these groups of people who were diagnosed or marginalized as mentally ill, and yet, they were considered so during the 20th century.

Mental health practitioners have also had some dangerous ideas in the past about how to psychologically treat those whom they considered abnormal, ideas that were based on society's thoughts about what caused the abnormality. As reviewed in a well-accepted textbook on abnormality, practitioners have considered "hearing voices" or other "abnormalities" to result from such varied causes as earthquakes, tides, germs, illness, bad blood, interpersonal conflict, animistic spirits, the environment (social influences), pacts with Satan, the wrath of the gods, and demon possession. Their decisions about such causes have influenced whether the people displaying such behavior were "revered, feared, pitied, or simply accepted . . . honored, incarcerated, abandoned, or given therapy" (Seligman et al., 2001, p. 12). For instance, when it was believed that evil spirits caused the problem, practitioners let the spirits out by drilling holes in people's heads or burning people as witches (Barstow, 1994; Comer, 2001). Mental health professionals have kept "abnormal" people chained to walls, have bled them, purged them, and forced them to vomit because of beliefs that the mad can't control themselves, need to be severely controlled, are capable of unprovoked violence, and are capable of living without protest in miserable conditions because they have lost their reason and are therefore merely animals (Seligman et al., 2001).

Toward a Better Future?

Some readers may assert that such past "uncivilized" and "uninformed" behavior should not worry us, that now that science has advanced our knowledge, we no longer treat people inhumanely, that such misbehavior is part of the distant past. These objectors point to the advances in *medical* research that now save or prolong people's lives and have replaced some previous, less-humane treatments. However, more recent history indicates that the continuing lack of cultural and gender sensitivity has resulted in harm to those who differ from Western norms or the dominant cultural group, because of sampling bias and because of overdiagnosis, underdiagnosis, and misdiagnosis. (The following sections and Chapter 4 address these issues in more detail.)

Overdiagnosis, underdiagnosis, and misdiagnosis. The race and sex of the mental health client, for instance, critically influence diagnosis (Lewis, Croft-Jeffreys, & David, 1990; Loring & Powell, 1988). Because behavior that does not match Western norms is sometimes labeled as pathological (Blankfield, 1987; Draguns, 1985; Fabrega, 1989; Mwaa & Pedersen, 1990; Snyder, 1992), gay men, lesbians, African Americans, ethnic minorities, women, and nontraditional men may be overdiagnosed with certain disorders or are

misdiagnosed entirely (Cook, Warnke, & Dupuy, 1993; Enns, 1993; Robertson & Fitzgerald, 1990). Specifically, African Americans are overdiagnosed with psychosis and underdiagnosed with depression (Jones & Gray, 1986; King, Coker, Leavey, Hoare, & Johnson-Sabine, 1994). Afro-Caribbean patients who were actually suffering from affective disorders were found to be misdiagnosed with schizophrenia (Jones & Gray, 1986; Keisling, 1981). People of varying ethnic populations receive more frequent diagnoses of schizophrenia (Jones & Gray, 1986; King et al., 1994; Keisling, 1981; Lewis et al., 1990).

Jones and Gray (1986) propose some reasons that African Americans are overdiagnosed with schizophrenia and dementia, even when really suffering from depression or alcoholism. They believe that practitioners are more likely to attribute a diagnosis of a severe chronic illness to African American clients, and that such clinical prejudice reflects prejudices that pervade the broader culture. Jones and Gray (1986) further state that African Americans may use more extreme language to communicate their feelings of despair or frustration, and that because the language is more extreme than that used by European Americans, mental health providers may be tempted to diagnose them as having more severe disorders.

Block (1984) indicates that African Americans may also be overdiagnosed with paranoid schizophrenia because in cross cultural situations, many African American patients tend to be wary and reluctant to participate in self-disclosure. Paranoia may also be accompanied by blunting of affect. Block claims that such behavior has been necessary to survival in a racist society. However, practitioners may find it difficult in an initial interview to determine the difference between this hypersensitivity and various paranoid processes.

Block (1984) further challenges the overdiagnosis of African Americans with personality disorders. He indicates that activity is an important coping strategy for African Americans, and is sometimes interpreted by others as "acting out." "Perhaps one can only be truly introspective in areas of functioning where one is relatively free from outer reality pressures. Are individuals truly character disorders because they refuse to accept value structures that exclude and limit them?" Block asks, can individuals be correctly diagnosed as "'an inadequate personality' because they have failed to develop certain standards of behavior in a culture which does not support their personal and social advancement?" (1984, p. 52).

According to Block (1984), the underdiagnosis of depression in African Americans may result from the differences in ways of expressing suffering in African American and European American culture. Block (1984) states that research indicates that African Americans experience the same levels of depression as the rest of society, but that their expression of that depression tends to be more intense and tends to be more active and self-destructive. An African American person (a) may act in ways to confront a life problem that actually brings about the feared reaction, (b) may be more active or agitated when depressed, or (c) may express sadness through anger or somatic complaints. These behaviors may mask a depressed mood. However, these behaviors are more culturally condoned ways of expressing depression, and because of the realities of African American life, these behaviors may be safer for those from nondominant groups (Block, 1984).

Lin (1996) expands Block's discussion of the reasons for misdiagnosis of people of color into the realm of the Asian community. He indicates that greater degrees of subtlety or inhibition in Asian clients may make it difficult for non-Asian, Western-trained practitioners to accurately diagnose Asian clients. The cultural differences might lead to an underestimation of the degree of psychopathology, especially mood disorders.

Furthermore, Asian sociocentrism actually encourages behavioral patterns that Western society would identify as dependent, for instance, allowing others to make important decisions for one and not doing things on one's own. In addition, Western practitioners might view Asian clients' tendencies to focus on somatic symptoms as more primitive, or less psychologically minded because the Western mind–body dichotomy runs counter to Asian notions of a unity between mind and body.

According to Cook et al. (1993), the problem of misdiagnosis of those from nondominant cultural groups occurs because diagnostic decisions rely on mental health professionals' own judgments of excessiveness or inappropriateness rather than on more precise criteria, as pointed out in Chapter 1. Such ambiguity leaves the door open for the same sorts of gender and racial bias that exist throughout society (Cook et al., 1993).

Practitioner bias has, in fact, been empirically demonstrated (McLaughlin, 2002). A great deal of evidence indicates that such misdiagnosis occurs as a result of stereotyping and overlooking the perspectives of women and the poor (Good, 1993; Lin, 1990; Parron, 1982; Manson, Shorc, & Bloom, 1985). Furthermore, bias seems to occur when "in groups" and "out groups" mix, and when one cultural group tolerates a higher level of misbehavior than another (Fisher, Storck, & Bacon, 1999). Practitioners are vulnerable to errors in judgment when they collect and interpret client information, and these errors may result from the practitioner's theoretical orientation, classifying clients into "good" and "bad" clients (Morrow & Diedan, 1992), or classifying client characteristics into stereotypical categories (Brown, 1986). However, research also demonstrates that when practitioners become culturally sensitive, not only is treatment more effective, but mis- or overdiagnosing problems is minimized (Mwaba & Pederson, 1990).

An additional concern related to sex and diagnosis is that if mental health professionals view certain problems as more prevalent in one sex, they may not recognize their occurrence in the other sex (Cook et al., 1993). It is possible that they may stop gathering information too soon because of a lack of knowledge about or sensitivity to gender-related issues. For instance, no information regarding the gender ratio for Post-Traumatic Stress Disorder (PTSD) is provided in the DSM, despite the substantial amount of research that exists on this disorder. This deficiency may serve to misinform mental health professionals, who may not recognize, for example, that men who have been raped suffer from PTSD as much as women following rape (Brown, 1990a, 1990b). Also, men's depression related to a rape experience or other traumas may be denied or camouflaged by male clients because of masculine gender norms or biological imperatives (Warren, 1983). Mental health professionals who are unfamiliar with different gender experiences or ways of expressing trauma may not probe deeply enough to discover whether PTSD or depression that results from such trauma exist in their male clients (Cook et al., 1993).

Similarly, women's substance-abuse problems may remain hidden from those who are tuned in to the higher incidence of male substance abuse (Mintz & Wright, 1992). Studies on alcoholism in women, for instance, indicate that women can tolerate far less alcohol than men (Ely, Hardy, Longford, & Wadsworth, 1999), and that women alcoholics tend to isolate themselves rather than to act out when intoxicated (Boyd & Mackey, 2000). Mental health professionals without this important information might dismiss red flags about drinking problems when a woman discloses such clues, or about other disorders that men and women manifest differently.

Thus, because the models in which most practitioners are trained are traditional and Eurocentric, they only seem to meet the needs of a small proportion of the population (e.g., European American, male, middle- to upper-class). As a result, providers may do harm by mislabeling or misdiagnosing problems (Arroyo, Westerberg, & Tonigan, 1998; Dana, 1998; Flaskerud & Liu, 1991; McGoldrick et al., 1996; Ridley, 1995; Santiago-Rivera, Arredondo, & Gallardo-Cooper, 2002; Sue, Bingham, Porche-Burke, & Vasquez, 1999; Sue et al., 1998; Sue & Sue, 1999).

Sampling bias. Of further concern is the impact on women and those from nondominant groups of sampling bias in the research upon which many DSM claims are based. Research has ignored many of the people most in need of practitioners' services—poor people, women, non-Whites, and the unemployed (Graham, 1992; Osipow & Fitzgerald, 1993; Reid, 1993). Sampling has also included a disproportionate representation of the sexes. These research omissions raise questions about success in developing unbiased diagnostic criteria (Gannon, Luchetta, Rhodes, Pardie, & Segrist, 1992; National Institutes of Health [NIH], 1994), questions about the relevance of applying current diagnoses to women and people of color, and questions about the appropriateness and availability of treatments that are based on such diagnoses.

Such sampling bias also raises questions about power and social control. What impact might there be, ask Caplan, McCurdy-Myers, and Gans (1992), on truths about mental illness when they are created by a small group of predominantly White, middle- or upper-class males and when they are practiced largely on a female population? Caplan et al. (1992) claim that a small group of people maintain a great deal of sanctioned power over what happens to a less-powerful group. Caplan et al. (1992) define such disproportionate power as an exercise of social control and further claim that without addressing the social context of diagnosis, our culture will tend "to use any sign of difference in a low-status group as proof that it deserves its low status" (p. 31; see also Hoagwood & Jensen, 1997; Howard, 1991).

Other examples. In addition, authors point to other examples in which, even in the United States, what might be considered inhumane or unnecessary treatment continues to exist: the "drugging" of children for attention-deficit hyperactivity disorder, the widespread use of antidepressants, the use of conversion therapies to attempt to change homosexuality, and the use of electroconvulsive therapies (Bailey, 2002; Giles, 2002; Halasz, 2002; Miller, 2003; Palma & Stanley, 2002). These authors point to the differences between medical illness and psychological problems, particularly in terms of the difficulty of locating the "disease" of mental health problems, and in terms of the harder-to-pin-down societal influences on our perceptions of abnormality (Bailey, 2002; Valenstein, 1998).

Conclusions. Many practitioners' shock at what was believed in the past indicates that different choices are made today. The very fact that mental health practice has "emerged," and hopefully grown and developed, however, also draws attention to how beliefs about truth change. As Hoagwood and Jensen (1997) indicate,

> Naming things is never innocent nor without costs and consequences. The fundamental changes in the diagnostic classification systems since its inception suggest that what may appear to be unalterable facts are actually modifiable, whether by virtue of new knowledge, changing terminology, or political pressures. (p. 111)

Unfortunately, the harm done to those who differ from the mainstream is not limited to the past. One would hope that the harm experienced today is not perpetrated by mental health practitioners. However, multicultural- and gender-sensitive practitioners indicate that because multicultural sensitivity is still in its infancy, a great deal of unintentional harm may still be mediated by practitioners who are unaware, unknowledgeable, and unskilled (Acton, 2001; Kocarek & Pelling, 2003; Sue & Sue, 1990). Therefore, it behooves us to carefully consider what we will think about our current actions toward those with mental health problems when we look back 50 years from now.

For instance, might we in the future have different thoughts about what should or should not be included as a "mental disorder"? Consider our current "normalizing" of some horrendous situations by *not* perceiving them as "disordered" enough to include in the DSM. For example, sexual abuse experienced by women and discussed in therapy was considered until recently to be a fantasy that women needed to understand and work through (Gleaves & Hernandez, 1999; Hare-Mustin & Marecek, 1990; Powell & Boer, 1995). The DSM does not diagnose, except in some cases as unreimbursable V codes, problems such as family violence, physical abuse, various family problems, criminality, gender and racial discrimination (e.g., Ku Klux Klan, White supremacists, bigotry, misogyny), racial genocide (Bosnia, for instance), a Hitler-allowing society, or Jim Jones and his followers (Fabrega, 1996; Griffith, 1996). Consequently, these problems are not included as mental disorders, and services to people who commit or are engaged in these behaviors are not reimbursable by insurance companies or many grant sponsors.

We cannot predict the future for any discipline, much less psychiatric diagnosis. However, it is clear that decisions about who will be considered abnormal have tremendous impacts on those so deemed. We do not even have to journey back in history to find mainstream conventions that are causing many nonmainstream people a great deal of grief. Certainly practitioners in the not-too-distant past treated people in ways that we currently consider horrifying. Our definitions of what is normal and abnormal have clearly changed— we might consider our definitions "broadened" when we measure them against previous standards, but what will we think tomorrow?— and our perceptions will certainly change again. Is it possible to create a diagnostic system that is responsive to these changes without codifying and thus cementing our perspectives in a way that damages so many people? Certainly a more tentative, less reified perspective on diagnosis may help to reduce such harm.

RACIAL AND ETHNIC CHALLENGES

Importance of Culture

Those who articulate American minority group perspectives challenge the notion that culture can ever be eliminated from discussions of effective counseling and diagnosis. They point to the influence of culture on everything in life. Sayed and Collins (1998) speak of culture as "an integral, coherent, and systematic approach to life that guides, rationalizes, defines, and modifies responses . . . to environmental demands in any given situation" (p. 443). From their perspective, it is the major influence on the ways in which people "organize their activities and make sense of the world around them" (p. 442). Particular cultural groups provide their members with crucial clues and instruments needed "to guide [their] responses to environmental demands" (p. 442). Even if two cultural groups share a similar history, they do not manifest identical values or expressions. Furthermore, displays of identical cultural values or expressions are not expected from everyone in a particular cultural group. "Hence the notion of time and place becomes crucial in any cultural analysis" (p. 442).

Culture also "defines, rationalizes, and interprets for its members the dynamics of their system of beliefs, customs, and values,

and the consequential considerations in terms of explicit and implicit expressions. This conceptualization, in turn, dictates the adaptation and the creation of tools that ultimately may determine the premium placed on each expression" (Sayed & Collins, 1998, p. 443).

In addition, culture shapes the environment's responses to children as they develop, including how childrearing will be carried out, who will provide parenting and childcare, and how involved the larger group will be in the developing child's life (Cole & Cole, 1996). Cultural values determine the goals toward which caregivers are working in raising children, in particular influencing what is considered acceptable or unacceptable behavior at different ages (Harrison, Serafica, & McAdoo, 1984; Serafica, 1997). Cultural values specify the range of acceptable behaviors and what differences will be accepted, as well as dictate how the caregivers or other group members will respond when a member steps out of that range (Harkness & Super, 1990). "Across cultures some latitude is accorded to individual differences as a function of age, sex, and the behavior involved" (Serafica, 1997, p. 150). Different cultures allow different degrees of latitude (Triandis, 1994). As a result, cultures vary with respect to how flexible they will be in creating a "goodness of fit" with particular children as they develop (Serafica, 1997).

Cultural Influences on Psychopathology

Thus, the role of culture in labeling and responding to problem behaviors, which may be or may develop into psychopathology, can also be clearly seen. One's culture creates labels for and decides what will be considered problem behavior and at what ages (Krener & Sabin, 1985). The culture also offers explanations for that problematic behavior that are culturally congruent. Culture may influence what symptoms are allowed as expressions of suffering (Serafica, 1997), and how individuals will cope with distress (Cohler, Stott, & Musick, 1995). Culture determines how those around the individual will respond to distress or problematic behaviors, in particular deciding the intensity or severity of the problem that must be evident before intervention is necessary (Weisz & Weiss, 1991). Culture will prescribe acceptable help-seeking responses, as well as acceptable interventions and interveners (Harkness & Super, 1990). For instance, Asian Americans may prefer to let children manage problems by themselves (e.g., "Don't think about it"), may depend on family members to handle the problems, or may pursue help from community resources other than mental health providers (Serafica, 1997).

Within a specific culture, psychological sophistication and education influence the understanding and perception of problems, in addition to what should be done about them (Lambert et al., 1992).

> Cultural values frame a parent's observational lens and interpretation of behavior, specifying which behaviors are salient and ought to be monitored closely. . . . Cultural values, beliefs, expectancies, and childrearing practices may tend to suppress the emergence of problems in one domain (e.g., socioemotional) while endorsing or even facilitating the manifestation of problems in another (physical). (Serafica, 1997, p. 151)

In some cultures, parents may note that particular problems exist, but may demonstrate a different level of tolerance for them than will parents from another culture (Serafica, 1997).

Class and social position may also influence how people respond to psychological problems. For instance, Fordham (as cited in Sayed & Collins, 1998) speaks of cultural self-identity, which refers to how a particular cultural group envisions its place in a specific society, how they view themselves in relationships, and how they view themselves in relationship with other social group members. Such self-identity

is challenged when subordinate groups have to figure out or scrabble for position in relation to dominant groups within that society. Thus, Engelsmann (2000) urges practitioners to consider not only the interaction of race and ethnicity with the development of problems, but also the influence of "minority status, experiences of prejudice, social and economic disadvantages, and language and communication barriers" (p. 429).

Overall, then, culture influences clients in many ways, including clients' experiences of the problems and internal sense of distress, their interpretations of the problems after experiencing symptoms, and their presentation of the complaint (Mezzich, Kleinman, Fabrega, & Parron, 1996a,b). Tseng (2001) adds to and formalizes the influences of culture on psychopathology. He lists and defines six types of effects:

1. Pathogenic effects, or the ways that culture is the direct cause of psychopathology: For instance, culturally demanded performance may result in stress or anxiety—as in the expectation that a woman needs to give birth to a son to carry on the family lineage or pressure to do well on college entrance exams in societies in which success is heavily influenced by education. These effects tend to be unique to cultures that hold those beliefs, creating their own unique psychopathology.

2. Pathoselective effects: People in a culture tend to select particular types of psychopathology as ways of expressing emotional pain. For instance, "running amok" in Muslim societies might be what is chosen in response to environmentally stressful situations. Such a "choice" might result in a person hurting someone, ending his/her own life, or becoming a monk and living in isolation. These effects emerge from the power of culture to influence the choices that people make in reacting to stressful situations.

3. Pathoplastic effects: Culture shapes the way in which symptoms are manifested,

influencing, for instance, the content of phobias, obsessions, or delusions. For example, the individual who is expressing grandiosity would assume the persona of someone who is considered popular in her/his own society. The individual who is experiencing paranoia would report types of persecutors that would differ depending on the society in which the delusional person lived. Further, certain symptoms might be exaggerated or absent depending on one's culture. In some societies, guilt is emphasized heavily. In Argentina, hospitalized patients are more passive and socially oriented than the same population in the United States.

4. Pathoelaborating effects: Certain types of disorders seem to arise more frequently in certain societies. Traditionally, eating disorders have been unique to Western culture where attention to thinness is more prevalent. *Latah* attacks (a sudden onset of a transient dissociation induced by startling, in which people become uninhibited, sexually promiscuous, or entertaining) are more frequent in Malaysia where modesty is emphasized and the interactions between women and men are fairly conservative.

5. Pathofacilitative effects: Cultural factors contribute to the frequent occurrence of certain mental disorders in a particular society. The more frequent occurrence in some cultures of suicidal behavior, alcoholism, mass hysteria, and collective panic are examples of the influences of general life patterns and attitudes toward certain issues. For instance, in Belau, Micronesia, there is a high prevalence of schizophrenia, which is generally considered to result from the cultural encouragement of intramarriage.

6. Pathoreactive effects: Cultural factors affect people's understandings and beliefs about the disorder, how they react to the disorder—including their emotional reactions—and thus how they express their suffering. For instance, how a society responds to a post-traumatic stress disorder experience that is associated with war—with empathy, welfare benefits, or no help at all—affects whether people decide to disclose their symptoms and how severe they consider their symptoms to be.

Culture also impacts clinicians' perceptions of the disorder, their style of interviewing, their choice of theoretical perspectives, the classification system that they use, and the purpose for making a diagnosis (Cooper, Kendall, Gurland, Sartorius, & Farkas, 1969; Tseng, Assai, Kitanish, McLaughlin, & Kyomen, 1992; Tseng, McDermott, Ogino, & Ebata, 1982).

Cross-cultural studies offer specific examples of the ways in which diagnoses, the experience of suffering, the perceptions of symptoms, and the responses to those with problems are "culturally patterned and socially negotiated" (Kleinman, 1996, p. 17). Consider the following examples of the ways that distress is manifested differently in various cultures:

Depression: According to the DSM, the chief symptom of depression is sadness or feelings of depression. Yet in most societies, those who would be diagnosed with clinical depression do not complain of sadness. Instead they report such complaints as fatigue, backaches, headaches, insomnia, stomach upset, and loss of appetite (Kleinman, 1996). Those in non-Western societies may also experience depression as a feeling of emptiness, as a sense of soul loss, rather than the "down" feelings expressed by depressed people in North America (Schweder, 1985). For most depressed people around the world, these physical experiences are what is most real. As a result, they assume their problems are physical, eschew mental health professionals, and visit primary care doctors instead. Unfortunately, they are then usually neither diagnosed nor effectively treated for depression (Kleinman, 1986).

Hallucinations: Plains Indians hear the voices of recently departed relatives calling them from the afterworld. This is considered normative and not evidence of psychopathology. However, in an adult European American North America, practitioners would be concerned that hearing such voices was evidence of serious mental illness.

Anorexia nervosa: Anorexia nervosa primarily exists in Western societies "that regard slim female bodies as beautiful, sexually desirable, and commercially significant" (Kleinman, 1996, p. 18).

Schizophrenia: "Schizophrenia seems relatively uncommon in any society without a system of wage labor" (Kleinman, 1996, pp. 18–19; see also Jablensky et al., 1992; World Health Organization, 1979). Peasant societies have much lower rates of schizophrenia than "economically and technologically advanced, urbanized, and bureaucratized societies" (Kleinman, 1996, pp. 18–19). The World Health Organization has shown in several major studies that "schizophrenia, regardless of age at onset, is a less serious illness and has a better outcome in poor countries, despite their limited health services, apparently because families and communities provide better support for schizophrenic patients" (Kleinman, 1996, pp. 18–19; see also Hopper, 1991; Jablensky et al., 1992; Jenkins & Karno, 1992; Kleinman, 1988; World Health Organization, 1979).

Even within the United States, schizophrenia and its recovery are affected by the family system, but differentially by cultural heritage. Lopez & Guarnaccia (2000) cite research that demonstrated that the family's emotional climate influences relapse; that is, schizophrenics in households with criticism, hostility, and high expressed emotion experience higher relapse rates. Jenkins (1991, 1993) situated families' high expressed emotion within the patient–family social interactions. Lopez et al. (1998) examined prosocial aspects of family functioning and found that relapse differed in relation to different family characteristics

based on culture. Jenkins found that lack of family warmth predicted relapse for Mexican Americans with schizophrenia, whereas criticism predicted relapse for Anglo Americans with schizophrenia. Lopez concludes that culture influences the ways in which families relate to those who are mentally ill.

Castillo (1997) offers an additional explanation for the better prognosis of those with schizophrenia who are from less-developed countries. He indicates that the neuroleptics (antipsychotic medications) that are used to reduce symptoms in places like the United States also change the brain by creating more dopamine receptors. This change, in turn, results in a greater need for dopamine (and thus the medications), and in the subsequent escalation of symptoms and prolonging of the disorder.

Childhood disorders: Weisz, McCarty, Eastman, Chaiyasit, and Suwanlert (1997) found that culture influences how mental illness is expressed and whether and how people in the environment respond. For instance, when compared, Thai children were referred more for internalizing problems, whereas U.S. children were referred more for acting out their difficulties. When the referral factor was eliminated, it turned out that the two groups did not differ in their degree of acting out problems. However, Thai children were more likely than U.S. children to express psychological distress in a way that did not counter cultural norms. The researchers did find that gender and nationality affected whether a problem was brought to the attention of a mental health professional. They noted that adults are the ones who have to notice and do something about children's problems, and differing social roles result in differing definitions of whether a "problem" exists or needs attention. Thai teachers, for example, have lower thresholds for identifying problem behaviors in their students than do U.S. teachers.

Antisocial personality disorder: According to Kleinman (1986), this diagnosis lacks validity if applied to African American and Hispanic adolescents in high-crime inner-city neighborhoods where violence is routine and where many of the DSM criteria are considered normative coping styles that aid survival. In fact, from his perspective, such brutal behaviors may also represent the only available means of resisting authority figures who are perceived as unresponsive and biased.

Grieving: Grieving following the death of a loved one is typically seen as a one-year intense process in Western clinical literature. However, grieving might be considered abnormal after four months in some other cultures and after five years in others (Parkes, Laungani, & Young, 1996). This seems to mean that the appropriate length of time for grieving, or the time period after which it might be considered depression or an adjustment disorder, isn't biologically or genetically determined or scientifically determinable. Instead, it is culturally decided; the individual's grieving patterns had better fit within what the person's society considers to be normal, or else the person will be considered "disordered."

Ataques de nervios: Ataques de nervios is considered by the DSM to be an individual, culture-bound syndrome, principally reported in Latin cultures, that may include what appear as panic attacks, dissociation, amnesia, and out-of-control shouting, crying, trembling, and aggression. In research that involved a dialogue between ethnographic, epidemiological, and clinical research methods, Lopez and his colleagues demonstrated that in almost all studies, *ataques de nervios* is not really "a cultural syndrome or clinical entity that resides within individuals, but is a common illness that reflects the lived experience largely of women with little power and disrupted social relations" (Lopez & Guarnaccia, 2000, p. 581; De La Cancela, Guarnaccia, & Carillo 1986; Guarnaccia,

Rubio-Stipec, & Canino, 1989; Liebowitz et al., 1994). Therefore, they would agree with Brown (1990a, 1990b, 1991a, 1991b, 1992) that Latin women's life experiences include conditions that lead to understandable distress, and that it is society that should be considered disordered rather than any individual woman.

Schizophrenia, manic-depressive (bipolar) disorder, major depression, and some anxiety disorders (panic anxiety, obsessive–compulsive disorder, and certain phobias): These are the only four *Diagnostic and Statistical Manual of Mental Disorders,* 4th ed. (DSM-IV) disorders that research indicates are distributed worldwide (Kleinman, 1996). The rest of the DSM-IV adult categories are reported only in North American and Western European countries (Kleinman, 1996).

Pibloktoq: Pibloktoq, or arctic hysteria, was discovered among the Inuit. It was mentioned in psychiatric texts as a culture-bound syndrome that was characterized by sudden, wild, and erratic behavior. However, when Dick (1995) studied all the reports of pibloktoq, he discovered that the behavior resulted from the sexual exploitation of Inuit women by explorers.

Poverty and social conditions: The World Mental Health Report (Desjarlais, Eisenberg, Good, & Kleinman, 1995) also concluded that mental health and illness are inextricably tied to the social world. The social roots of poor mental health in women, for example, include hunger (60% of women worldwide are undernourished), poorly paid or dangerous work, and domestic violence (50–60% of women worldwide have been beaten).

Different "times": Clinical experience indicates that certain psychiatric disorders become prevalent at particular times and then fade away later. Conversion disorder is becoming less frequent in developed countries, and catatonia seems to be significantly declining. Borderline personality disorder was defined clearly only recently, yet has been on the rise in developed countries. Social circumstances have resulted in substance abuse, borderline personality disorder, eating disorders, and PTSD becoming prevalent enough to warrant inclusion in the DSM (Tseng, 2001).

Different countries' perceptions of mental illness: British psychiatrists tend to diagnose as affective disorders what American psychiatrists consider to be schizophrenia. French and Anglo psychiatrists classify disorders very differently: The French approach is more abstract, and the Anglo approach searches for concrete criteria and precise descriptions (Tseng, 2001). Other cultures consider diagnosis to be negotiable, because they do not maintain an emphasis on more rigid ideas of mental health problems (Littlewood & Lipsedge, 1989). Fewer than 1% of East African societies consider hallucinations as a diagnostic criterion for psychosis (Edgerton, 1966).

Research that compared White British people with Bangladeshi and Afro-Caribbean residents of Britain in terms of their perceptions of mental illness (in particular schizophrenia) found that in comparison with the White group, Bangladeshi participants were less likely to consider suspiciousness or hallucinatory behavior as indicative of mental health problems. The Afro-Caribbean participants were less likely to consider unusual thought content as evidence of mental illness. Although there were differences in perception related to religion, education, gender, and contact with people with mental illness, ethnicity was the best predictor of perceptions of symptoms of schizophrenia (Pote & Orrell, 2002).

Political ideology: Russia, during the era of the Soviet Union, focused on collective well-being, and as a result, had no room for antisocial and narcissistic personality disorders; these disorders were excluded from the official classification system. Also, the term *vague schizophrenia* was created for the purpose of hospitalizing political dissidents. The disorder included displays of unusual or abnormal thoughts or behaviors; that is, those thoughts or behaviors that deviated from the thoughts or behaviors of mainstream citizens in the society. Some of these dissidents were hospitalized; others were eliminated. China also denied the existence of any socially caused disorders because of the belief that their society could not cause the significant distress that would create a mental disorder (Tseng, 2001).

Avoiding stigma: To avoid stigma or legal responsibility for crime, some disorders are not given in particular societies. Japan, for instance, avoids using the diagnosis "schizophrenia," instead diagnosing with a medical disorder those who in other societies might be diagnosed with schizophrenia. Other societies use psychosis and multiple personality (dissociative identity) disorder to assist in insanity pleas (Tseng, 2001).

Societal structures: Castillo (1997) cites anthropological research that demonstrates the correlation between specific societal structures and the development of particular psychopathologies. He divides societal structures along three continua: (a) societies that are sociocentric (collectivist) versus egocentric (individualistic); (b) societies that are egalitarian versus incorporating dominance hierarchies (i.e., gender, class, age, race, ethnic dominance hierarchies) in which force or threat of force is needed to maintain dominance; and (c) societies that reflect premodern, modern, or postmodern meaning systems. We illustrate here the different correlations between societal structure and the development of psychopathology by summarizing what Castillo (1997) points to as the differences between societies that are more egalitarian and those that incorporate dominance hierarchies.

Dominance hierarchies allow "for systems of discrimination that reify social distinctions, thus legitimizing the status and privilege of the ruling groups" (p. 42). Low-status people can accept their status as inferior, incapable, and flawed, in which case, they might become or be described as having a dependent or avoidant personality disorder. They could hide the stigmatizing characteristics and try to pass as "good" people, but would then live in constant fear of being discovered, in which case, they might become or be described as having an anxiety disorder or phobia. Low-status people could try to copy the dominant group, in which case their attention to details and rules, deference to authority, and rigidity might become or be described as an obsessive–compulsive personality disorder. Low-status people could attempt to prove themselves as better through accomplishment, or they could pretend that they are better if they cannot sufficiently achieve, and they then might become or be described as having a narcissistic personality disorder. They could display violent resistance to an unfair and exploitive system, and thus victimize others before they themselves could be victimized, in which case they might become or be described as having an antisocial personality disorder. Finally, low-status people might engage in violence or threats of violence against themselves, in which case, they might become or be described as having a borderline personality disorder.

However, low-status people are not the only ones whose lessened mental health correlates with living in dominance hierarchies (Castillo, 1997). One need only consider the entitlement, superiority, and mistreatment of the "lesser" that are displayed by the Ku Klux Klan and by White supremacists to understand how being in the dominant—in these cases, racially—group may negatively affect one's mental health (as further illustrated in the ethical mandates of mental health professional societies that value tolerance of diversity).

Castillo (1997) offers examples of different cultures that display varying combinations of sociocentric/egocentric, premodern/modern/postmodern, and hierarchical/egalitarian societal structures. He persuasively illustrates the correlations among societal structures and personality development, as well as the diagnoses that are likely to arise within these cultures. Egalitarian, modern, and sociocentric societies manifest less violence, criminality, and other abuses of people. According to his model, the United States is neither egalitarian nor sociocentric. Consequently, according to his model, mental health practitioners ethically need to consider the role that the United States culture and values play in the development of personal problems and the ultimate ascription of diagnoses.

The research and theory thus far reviewed indicate that culture is inextricably linked to the development, experience, and expression of abnormal behavior, to the ways in which diagnosed people are perceived and treated, and to decisions about diagnosis and treatment, as well as to how one determines what is abnormal and normal. Because of this, a dissimilarity between patients' and practitioners' cultures, and failures to recognize the importance of these differences, may result in clients and their surrounding communities feeling alienated or even expressing disapproval of the practitioner's methods (Sayed & Collins, 1998). It is well documented that those from nondominant cultural groups underuse mental health services (Fugita, 1990; Root, 1985; Sue & McKinney, 1975). Perhaps diagnostic insensitivity to multicultural issues can be at least partially faulted for the alienation and failure of some cultural groups to receive needed psychological help.

Specific Cultural Biases

A number of authors challenge the effectiveness and ethics of counseling and diagnosis that fails to consider how values differ among cultures (Fabrega, 1996; Lewis-Fernandez & Kleinman, 1994; Kleinman, 1988; Markus & Kitayama, 1991; Sayed & Collins, 1998). They offer specific examples of values differences that may bias practitioners and thus interfere with the counseling and diagnostic process.

Lewis-Fernandez and Kleinman (1994) and Vontress, Johnson, and Epp (1999) point to four Western culture-bound assumptions that may contribute to cultural bias: (a) egocentricity of the self; (b) mind–body dualism; (c) people seen in parts rather than wholes; and (d) "culture as an arbitrary superimposition on a knowable biological reality" (Lewis-Fernandez & Kleinman, 1994, p. 67). Egocentricity of the self means an understanding of the self as a "self-contained, autonomous entity, characterized by a unique configuration of internal attributes that determine behavior" (Lewis-Fernandez & Kleinman, 1994, p. 67; see also, Fabrega, 1996; Markus & Kitayama, 1991; Sayed & Collins, 1998; Schweder, 1991). The more radical view of egocentricity sees psychological normality and abnormality as internal to the person, discounting "the social roots of psychiatric disease, the social course of mental illness, and the interpersonal patterning of personality" (Lewis-Fernandez & Kleinman, 1994, p. 67). In Western culture, in which people consider themselves self-sufficient and the determiners of their own destiny, the individual capacity and determination to fulfill one's destiny contributes substantially to the development of personal identity. Such a perspective frowns on dependency, values independence in relationship with others, values solid ego boundaries, and perceives a clear boundary between the self and the world. Psychotherapeutic interventions aim to resolve mental health problems by helping the individual to develop inner strength and capacity and firm boundaries. Mental health thus belongs to the individual and is the individual's responsibility to attain. Individual capacity to change enhances freedom and environmental mastery (Sayed & Collins, 1998).

However, such egocentricity runs counter to the more sociocentric ideology adhered to by most of the world, in which individual experience is nested "in networks of social relationship that become the locus of self-worth, self-fulfillment, self-control, and other attributes of the person" (Lewis-Fernandez & Kleinman, 1994, p. 67; see also Fabrega, 1996; Markus & Kitayama, 1991; Sayed & Collins, 1998; Triandis, 1994). For instance, in Middle Eastern worldviews, individual identity emerges from the collective group, from affiliation and belonging to others. People do not exist independently, but are encouraged to "find themselves" in interdependent systems. Tribal and family concerns transcend individual concerns. "Asabiya" or "powerful allegiance toward group aims and function" (Sayed & Collins, 1998, p. 445) is one's primary aim. "Paramount to a sense of collective responsibility and destiny is a sense of togetherness and a continuous need for group validation and approval . . . healthy identity is therefore based on a social system" (p. 445). In traditional Chinese, Indian, Southeast Asian, and African and South American groups, who compose more than 75% of the world's population, the boundaries of ego are seen as permeable; and the self is seen as fluid and capable of leaving the body, becoming possessed, and entering altered states (Kleinman, 1996). Therefore, egocentricity of the self and nonpermeable boundaries around the self can be seen as Western values that are shared by little of the rest of the world. Western practitioners who do not have adequate cultural training or sensitivity could impose these values by overdiagnosing more sociocentric clients or by working toward culturally contraindicated goals.

A second culture-bound assumption related to psychopathology, dualism, depends upon a division between the mind and body, such that some psychopathologies are organic and others are psychological. Western scholarship has moved away from lay conceptualizations and meanings about psychiatric disorder, and has moved into progressively more elaborate and impersonal biomedical understandings. This has resulted in objectifying the experience of people, that is, "objectively" describing their symptoms, without taking into consideration the situational or personal characteristics of the person. Western thought, therefore, emphasizes handling persons as "mechanical objects" and sometimes eschews or disregards the view that "persons are socially, culturally, and morally situated" (Fabrega, 1996, p. 12). Fabrega (1996) points out, however, that psychiatry needs to be viewed differently than medicine, because "indicators of psychiatric disorders are linked to symbolic behavior and hence to the self, [despite the fact that] the current mode of describing and defining psychiatric illness is viewed as but temporarily expedient until truly biological markers (which are disconnected from behavior) are uncovered and linked to discrete disorders" (p. 6).

The majority of the world's people eschew such dualism, however. They "experience human suffering in an integrated, somatopsychological mode: as simultaneous mind and body distress" (Lewis-Fernandez & Kleinman, 1994, p. 67; see also Fabrega, 1996; Markus & Kitayama, 1991; Sayed & Collins, 1998; Kleinman, 1988). Therefore, when people of other cultures experience psychological difficulties, they often report physiological symptoms. The disconnect between Western and other perspectives results in U.S. professionals who do not have cultural training or sensitivity and who consider such clients as lacking introspective ability and as having a primitive cognitive style—in other words, as using less-developed coping or defense mechanisms (Block, 1984). Thus, such professionals' (inappropriate) goal becomes helping the client to

develop more sophisticated coping strategies, including behaving more congruently (that is, acknowledging psychological distress rather than displacing it onto physical symptoms). Clearly such a goal is not respectful of the differing experiences of distress within different cultures.

Beyond the mind–body dualism of Western culture is a third, but related, cultural assumption that contradicts many traditional societies' more holistic focus, that is, that people exist in "parts" as opposed to as "wholes." Vontress and his colleagues (1999) observed that modern, technologically advanced societies categorize problems; these society's members approach specialists to treat different sorts of problems (e.g., doctors for physical problems, clergy for spiritual problems). However, traditional societies treat people more holistically, considering everything in the environment to be related. In Africa, the same healer might be consulted for a sore toe, problem crops, or a conflict with a relative. Furthermore, economic problems in disadvantaged communities, such as floods or crop failures, "often produce a ripple effect, creating a variety of psychological and social problems" (Vontress et al., 1999, p. 64). Vontress et al. thus propose that cross-cultural counseling particularly attend to Axis IV information, because psychosocial and environmental problems often impact diagnosis, treatment, and prognosis of Axis I and II disorders.

A fourth culture-bound assumption is that culture is epiphenomenal; that is, it is a set of beliefs, usually considered to be faulty or superstitious, that are superimposed on the invariant "bedrock reality of biology." Unfortunately, this assumption discounts "the disease categories, illness experiences, and healing practices of people in other cultures, reducing them to the status of obstacles in diagnosis, treatment compliance, and outcomes" (Lewis-Fernandez & Kleinman, 1994, p. 67). Lewis-Fernandez and Kleinman direct attention to cross-cultural studies in anthropology that point to interpersonal processes as the bridges between the social world and the body. They indicate that "individual reality is the lived experience of perceptions, meanings, affects, and actions that come together (aggregate) at different levels and shape an individual's insertion in the world as body, self, personality, and member of a family and a social network" (p. 67). So, for instance, political upheaval, which is a collective experience, may result in an automatic mob reaction at the community level, upset of previously functioning relationships at the family level, and dysthymia or major depression at the individual level. Similarly, individual experiences of depression also affect the experiences of family and community members. "The attributes of self and personality are thus more plural and fluid than generally described, dependent largely on a changing behavioral environment that is fundamentally cultural . . . the individualized perspective on personality reduces to internal manifestations what is fundamentally an interpersonally constructed experience of the self" (Lewis-Fernandez & Kleinman, 1994, p. 68; see also Hermans, Kempen, & van Loon, 1992; Kondo, 1990; Schweder, 1991). Lewis-Fernandez and Kleinman examine Japanese, Chinese, and Puerto Rican cultures as illustrations of how distinctively people express difficulties in living. The authors conclude by saying,

> Clinicians and researchers trained to contextualize behavior and experience as a function of radically different environments would be less prone to category fallacies, that is, the imposition of one culture's categories onto another culture, for which they lack validity. We would be less likely to explain, for example, the adaptational strategies of impoverished inner-city minority youth to highly dangerous predatory environments as antisocial personality disorder, a condition that has evolved out of a different class, ethnic, and historical

context. We would take relevant cultural and gender norms into account before raising the question of pathological dependency or lack of individuation among Chinese and Latinos. We would consider the relevant behavioral environment—which includes a normative discourse on spirits and gods—before speaking of a hysterical predisposition to possession trance among the people of India. We would also not seek to pathologize each instance of somatization or to talk about others' culture-bound syndromes as esoteric and exotic without considering the effects of mind–body dualism on our own professional but still culture-bound categories, such as anorexia nervosa and perhaps borderline personality disorder. And we might very well come across local indigenous categories, such as face and favor, that can be used to reformulate our leading models of personality formation and their relationship to psychopathology. (p. 70)

Valasquez, Johnson, and Brown-Cheatham (1993) specify the particular ways in which the DSM fails culturally: (a) No discussion exists in the DSM of how specific diagnoses present or manifest themselves in people of color; the DSM could include data about key features, unique symptoms, or prevalence of specific diagnoses in specific ethnic minorities; (b) no empirical evidence indicates that using the DSM is valid or reliable with ethnic minorities, but there is evidence that diagnosis of ethnic minorities is highly susceptible to human error, errors that are particularly compounded when diagnosing a linguistically different client; (c) there is an absence in the DSM of culture-specific syndromes or culture-bound syndromes related to alienation, acculturation difficulty, migration and immigration trauma, ethnic–racial identity confusion, gang involvement, PTSD caused by socially sanctioned racism or violence, or familial intergenerational distress; (d) ethnic minority professionals have generally not been included in the development of DSM, which may mean that minimal attention was paid to the role of ethnicity or culture in the development of the diagnostic system (this comment by Valasquez et al. relates to the *Diagnostic and Statistical Manual of Mental Disorders,* 3rd ed., revised [DSM-III-R]; more people of color were included in developing later editions; however, this would most likely not fully correct for the grounding of later editions in the "truths" of previous editions).

To summarize, because "psychiatric illnesses are human behavioral anomalies and breakdowns that are culturally shaped, explained, and dealt with in terms of established conventions and meanings;" because "societies differ greatly in terms of how they define and explain such breakdowns" (Fabrega, 1996, p. 3); because the DSM fails to legitimize (by including them as Axis I disorders and thus allowing for reimbursement) social, economic, medical, and other contextual factors that people from non-Western cultures would consider to be just as important as, as intricately entwined with, or as causing the individual problem; and because the DSM fails culturally in the ways described by Valasquez, we can only conclude, along with Kleinman and others, that the DSM represents Western thought and assumptions, and thus currently represents "a minority bias cross culturally" (Kleinman, 1996, p. 20).

Universal Diagnoses Versus Specific Culturally Based Distress

Cultural and diagnostic scholars seem to pursue two different poles or models: one that suggests that there are universal diagnostic categories and descriptors that apply regardless of situational and cultural factors, and the other that claims that "it is impossible to extract an individual's lifestyle from the culture that helps to mold it and through which it is expressed" (Thomas & Sillen, 1972, p. 59; for discussion of the two different models, see

Fabrega, 1996; Hoagwood & Jensen, 1997; Hughes, 1996; Kirmayer & Minas, 2000; Lopez, 1997; Sayed & Collins, 1998). "Science" has typically searched for universal truths that apply across cultures. However, as is probably clear by now, multicultural practitioners find limitations with the universal model.

For instance, multicultural providers indicate that the emphasis on large-scale epidemiological studies has often suppressed "the voices of small groups," which has, according to Kirmayer and Minas (2000), contributed "to the homogenization and standardization of world cultures and traditions of healing. What we gain in methodological rigor," they claim, "we lose in diversity" (p. 447). The relevance of culture is then undermined, which results in interpreting those behaviors that do not conform to a Western model as abnormal or maladaptive (Sayed & Collins, 1998). The question that is certainly clear by now is whether diagnosis can ever be truly free from cultural influence, and therefore be universally applicable. "Specifically," asks Fabrega "is not DSM-IV a product of the interplay of 1) special biosocial factors producing illness conditions; 2) Western academic conventions about rationalism, voluntarism, and autonomy; and 3) sociocultural standards about behavior?" (1996, p. 8). Authors cited in the previous section seem to answer "yes" to these questions.

Yet the "remedies" to these situations have not always been well received nor been considered workable. For instance, the National Institute of Mental Health (NIMH) Group on Culture and Diagnosis found their data dismissed as merely anecdotal by DSM developers when the NIMH group attempted to include relatively smaller voices in DSM-IV revisions by presenting information gleaned from ethnographic research data (Kirmayer & Minas, 2000; see ethnographic data in Mezzich et al., 1999). Lopez (1997) discovered that most cultural research has focused on culture-specific information, which doesn't account for the heterogeneity of people from the same broad cultural or ethnic groups. This, he claims, results in "minimizing actual pathology, misunderstanding the clinical behavior of one's client in therapy, and judging someone to be less impaired based on presumed culture-specific test results" (p. 573). Kirmayer and Minas (2000) further point out that cross-cultural research compares averages from the different countries, a procedure that ignores the internal diversity in those countries. They further indicate that cross-cultural studies use diagnostic measures whose categories have been developed in a Euro-American culture; thus, researchers rarely canvas symptoms that range outside such categories. Kirmayer and Minas (2000) thus conclude, "The absence of attention to meaningful social and cultural variables and parallel ethnographic research on the social and clinical realities of these populations leaves us with data that poorly reflect the local reality" (p. 439).

Even adding cultural data to the DSM has generated criticism. For instance, Hughes (1996) points out that separating culture-bound syndromes in the DSM and giving them special, restricted status puts them at risk or makes them vulnerable to being dismissed, discounted, or not taken seriously. It might also make it appear as though no one is aware that the DSM as it currently exists represents Euro-American, biomedically based psychiatry. By separating culture-bound syndromes into a separate section, claims Hughes (1996), DSM developers are assuming that the Euro-American perspective is somehow superior or the standard or point of reference against which all other psychiatry (including cultural psychiatry) is compared. In fact, suggests Hughes, what the DSM-IV considers culture-bound syndromes are simply cultural differences, not psychopathology. He believes that all of the culture-bound syndromes could be assimilated into the already existent categories if the categories were improved upon to make

them less culture bound. He urges psychiatry to "examine its own culturally structured roots, not only when the issue is that of assessing a patient from a different cultural background, but in all instances" (Hughes, 1996, p. 290).

Some authors point to the need to find common ground between the universal and the culture-specific models, proposing that assessment should apply two sets of cultural norms: those of the mainstream culture and those of the client's culture (Hoagwood & Jensen, 1997; Lopez, 1997). For instance, Lopez (1997) concluded, following his qualitative research on how student therapists incorporate culture into their clinical work with diverse clients, that

> cultural competence reflects moving between alternative cultural frameworks . . . balancing both culture- specific and culture-general norms . . . [and collecting] data to test hypotheses derived from both culture-specific and cultural-general frameworks. The culturally competent therapist does not assume that any one perspective is applicable. (p. 572)

Lopez (1997) thus proposed a "both/and" perspective that focuses on the process by which practitioners ascribe meaning, rather than what the practitioners know about specific cultural groups. "Content approaches to cultural competence," he claims, "can lead to either creating or reinforcing stereotypes of given groups. . . . [U]ltimately . . . we want to broaden, not limit, clinicians' thinking about specific cultural groups" (p. 574). The both/and approach focuses on "how clinicians know which cultural meaning to apply in specific contexts" and in this way "stereotyping can be significantly reduced" (p. 574).

Initially, Lopez (1997) considered the practitioner's framework to be the "universal" framework. However, he later decided that the practitioner's framework was also culture-specific. Because practitioners and clients both view the world through specific cultural lenses, it seemed presumptuous to assume a hierarchy in which the practitioner was closer to the universal perspective than the client. He proposed instead that the practitioner's cultural-specific model might be considered an alternative to that of the client, rather than something to impose on the client as somehow a better way.

Castillo (1997) offers an example of the both/and perspective with respect to the Indian experience of *dhat*. The Indian *dhat* syndrome manifests in weakness and fatigue, similar to what someone operating from Western models might diagnose as depression. Although a Western model might prescribe medication for the problem or a shift in destructive thinking (Burns, 1980), Indians believe that *dhat* results in males from loss of semen, and therefore believe that "cure" results from having less sex and masturbating less. If the client and practitioner were from the same traditional Indian culture, the practitioner would be likely to help the client to achieve "cure" in the culturally prescribed manner. Castillo offers case examples demonstrating that many clients do, in fact, find the symptoms relieved subsequent to such a "cure." If the practitioner and the client are not from the same culture, however, the practitioner might try to "educate" the Indian about the "truth," which would probably result in loss of the client and/or in lack of compliance with treatment recommendations. A culturally sensitive Western professional would be aware of the Indian perspectives on *dhat* and might have a dialogue about how to integrate the best of the two perspectives. For instance, the professional might help the client to contain his sexuality, and, should this not prove enough to assist the client with the weakness and fatigue, might concurrently or subsequently try an antidepressant, perhaps framing the medication as "enhancing the client's efforts to contain his sexuality." In Castillo's example, the practitioner blends respect for culture-specific information with respect for his own culture's strategies of assessing and treating depression. In some cases, the practitioner might go a step further and choose to engage in a dialogue with the client about the cultural differences so that they could mutually decide on treatment approaches.

Alternatives to Traditional Diagnosis

"Cultural Psychiatry" has led the way in challenging traditional diagnosis and in proposing more culturally sensitive alternatives. Kleinman heralded the beginning of this discipline in 1977, touting its abilities to integrate anthropological conceptualizations with those of traditional psychiatry and psychology. Cultural psychiatry has urged respect for indigenous illness categories and recognition of the limitations of traditional illness categories (Lopez & Guarnaccia, 2000). The field has also considered the impact of social and cultural differences on mental illness and treatment (Kirmayer & Minas, 2000). In particular, Kleinman (1977) distinguished between disease ("malfunctioning or maladaption of biological or psychological processes") and illness ("the personal, interpersonal, and cultural reaction to disease") (Kleinman, 1977, p. 9). Baskin (1984) reflected the field's beliefs in concluding, after a study of mental health across 20 nations, that without knowledge about how behaviors are perceived in different cultures, the application of Western nosological systems (such as the DSM) is specious (see also Lopez & Nunez, 1987). According to Kirmayer and Minas (2000),

> Cultural psychiatry has evolved along 3 lines: 1) cross-cultural comparative studies of psychiatric disorders and traditional healing; 2) efforts to respond to the mental health needs of culturally diverse populations that include indigenous people, immigrants, and refugees; and 3) the ethnographic study of psychiatry itself as the product of a specific cultural history. (p. 438)

The field has achieved major advances in psychological practice. For instance, leaders in cultural psychiatry contributed to the publication of the World Mental Health Report, and Parron and her colleagues developed cultural materials for the DSM-IV with a grant from NIMH (Culture and Diagnosis Group: Fabrega, Good, Kleinman, Lin, Manson, Mezzich, and Parron). The DSM now includes (a) how cultural factors can influence the expression, assessment, and prevalence of specific disorders; (b) an outline of a cultural formulation of clinical diagnosis to complement the multiaxial assessment; and (c) a glossary of relevant culture-bound syndromes from around the world. The DSM's cultural formulation includes ascertaining the cultural identity of the client, the cultural explanation of the individual's illness, cultural factors related to the psychosocial environment and functioning, cultural elements of the relationship between the individual and the practitioner, and overall cultural assessment for diagnosis and care (APA, 2000).

However, significant portions of the Culture and Diagnosis Group's recommendations were not included in the DSM-IV or *Diagnostic and Statistical Manual of Mental Disorders,* 4th ed., Text Revision (DSM-IV-TR). Therefore, the DSM currently only includes "a partial reflection of the significant and dynamic role culture plays in psychopathology" and includes it in a way that tends to

> exoticize the role of culture. . . . Cultural researchers object to the view that culture only pertains to patients from specific 'cultural minority' groups, which present with specific symptoms or syndromes. Instead cultural researchers view culture as infusing the presentation of all disorders among all people. (Lopez & Guarnaccia, 2000, pp. 576–577)

In fact, Sinacore-Guinn (1995) proposes a model that assumes that all counseling and diagnosis are multicultural.

The Culture and Diagnosis Group believes that a culturally sensitive DSM would include more extensive guidelines in the DSM's introduction about how to use the DSM in a culturally sensitive manner; a cultural axis; a cultural issues section under each disease condition or chapter; specific examples of culturally normative client experiences that might look like disease or of disorders that are expressed in unexpected ways for cultural reasons; culture-bound syndromes; and an appendix related to expectable problems in working with interpreters (Kleinman, 1996). Thompson (1996) further recommended that the DSM (a) include information to assist the practitioner to address the interactions between the client's culture and the practitioner's culture; (b) assist the practitioner to distinguish between pathology and culturally different, that is, normal cultural practices that appear strange to dominant-culture practitioners; (c) clearly state that pathology should not be dismissed just because it occurs with high frequency in a particular culture; and (d) encourage practitioners to avoid the temptation to assume that they cannot treat clients with culture-bound syndromes; that is, practitioners should clearly assess the part of a client's psychopathology that they can treat.

Sinacore-Guinn (1995) outlines what more culturally sensitive assessment would look like. For instance, she recommends that practitioners begin by exploring cultural systems and structures (community structure, family, schools, interaction styles, concepts of illness, life-stage development, coping patterns, and immigration history; Bahr & Sinacore-Guinn, 1993; Sinacore-Guinn, 1992; Sinacore-Guinn & Bahr, 1993a, 1993b), cultural values (time, activity, relational orientation, person–nature orientation, basic nature of people; Kelly, 1990), gender socialization, and the effect of trauma. In the process, the practitioner (and perhaps the client as well) would gain an understanding of the impact of race, class, gender, sexual orientation, and ethnicity on the presenting problem, on the client's understanding of the problem, and on the client's expression of the problem.

Serafica (1997), who has researched Asian refugee children, concludes that multiculturally sensitive diagnosis, especially for children, requires a

> unique conceptual framework, one that acknowledges: (a) the unitary nature of development, that is, the idea that psychopathology or development gone awry has to be understood from the perspective of normal development; (b) the interaction between protective and risk factors in development; (c) the life-span nature of development; and (d) the bidirectional relations existing among multiple levels of organization. In other words, it requires a developmental–contextual framework applied to the study of psychopathology. (p. 153)

She further claims, "before data on the prevalence of the major psychiatric disorders of infancy, childhood, and adolescence can be obtained, the validity for specific Asian American subgroups of the established nosological systems will have to be determined" (p. 152). Serafica points to the difficulties of applying the DSM to Asian Americans because of such things as "different mores for adolescent independence, a shared conviction that there must be a physical cause for failure to cope well, and the belief in the ontological status of spirits and devils" (p. 152). Krener and Sabin (1985) concur with Serafica that current diagnostic systems do not take into account cultural definitions of what is normal or abnormal behavior at different ages.

These authors' proposals offer hope for the future of multicultural diagnosis, assessment, and treatment, and a vision that may guide researchers and practitioners into greater cultural sensitivity and practice. One hopes that the controversies that accompany all change in professional disciplines will not derail individual commitments to personal growth in multicultural awareness, knowledge, and skills.

CONCLUSION

As mentioned previously, it is only by standing back from one's own beliefs and experiences, by taking oneself as object (Kegan, 1982, 1994), that one can truly evaluate the pluses and minuses of one's various assumptions and behaviors. The ability to do so is a developmental achievement (Kegan, 1982, 1994; Kohlberg, 1981; Loevinger, 1976; Perry, 1970; Rest, 1979). Experiencing other cultures often assists people to take their own as object; thus, cross-cultural research can be very helpful to those attempting to deconstruct DSM diagnosis (or any other mental health practice in the United States). Of course, reifying other cultures' structures or strategies for handling mental health problems may be no more helpful than reifying the dominant system in the United States. One must balance the benefits of other cultural systems against their problems with poverty, oppression of women and children, illiteracy, and other social ills. It would, of course, be wise to do the same with the systems currently in place in the United States. In fact, strategies of other societies may be effective only in that culture and may not be applicable universally. However, to discount another culture's successes because that society has limitations or because it is "developing," to assume that practitioners in the United States have nothing to learn from the "other" culture, would be ethnocentrism of the worst kind. We certainly would not want other countries to discount everything American because of some of our failures.

4

Feminist Challenges to DSM Diagnosis

In some ways, the field of abnormal psychology has also had a troubled and troubling relationship with women. From a feminist perspective, "Diagnoses such as nymphomania, hysteria, neurasthenia, eroto-mania, kleptomania, and masochism have served to enforce conformity to norms of female domesticity, subordination, and sub-servience to men's sexual needs; at times diagnoses have reaffirmed class distinctions as well" (Marecek, 1993, p. 115). Feminist theorists believe that women's anger, depression, and discontent have been reframed as medical or psychiatric symptoms, and that, as a result, the often difficult and distressing life circumstances of women have been disregarded. They state that it is often forgotten that the roots of women's so-called psychological problems have many times been social and political, rather than individual and intrapsychic in origin (Caplan, McCurdy-Myers, & Gans, 1992; Ussher, 2000; Cook, 1992a, 1992b; Koss, 1990; Wakefield, 1992). Feminists also point out the stigmatizing effects of diagnostic labels; the classist, sexist, racist, and homophobic assumptions that they consider to be embedded in both the International Classification of Diseases (ICD) and the *Diagnostic and Statistical Manual of Mental Disorders* (DSM); the resulting pathologizing of behaviors that may be normative within particular gender contexts; the underdiagnosing of problematic behaviors; and, finally, the inability to find any use of the classification system for treatment or for conceptualizing the counseling process (Brown, 1990a, 1990b). This chapter reports feminist concerns about the DSM's system of diagnosis and about diagnosis more generally. We include discussions of the prevalence of diagnoses by gender, research related to sex bias, concerns about particular diagnoses and their problematic impact on women, and the socialization and social conditions of women—particularly the trauma experience—that may lead to the overdiagnosis of women. We conclude by describing feminist analysis and how it may benefit women in therapy.

PREVALENCE DATA OF DIAGNOSES BY GENDER

Research on the prevalence of mental illness by gender yields contradictory results. Some authors cite evidence that more women than men are mentally ill and that women's prevalence rates are higher than those for men on far more disorders (Cook, Warnke, & Dupuy, 1993; Gove, 1980; Hartung & Widiger, 1998). Others indicate that men and women experience mental illness at comparable rates (17.4% and 18%, respectively; Horsfall, 2001; Bijl, deGraaf, Ravelli, Smit, & Vollebergh, 2002; Kass, Spitzer, & Williams, 1983, for personality disorders). The reasons proposed for the conflicting results include differing definitions of mental illness (Gove, 1980; Johnson, 1980), differing research strategies (Gove, 1980), and sex bias (Abramowitz, 1973; Brodsky & Halroyd, 1975; Broverman, Broverman, Clarkson, Rosenkrantz, & Vogel, 1970; Broverman, Vogel, Broverman, Clarkson, & Rosenkrantz, 1972; Cook et al., 1993; Cormak & Furman, 1998; Fabrikant, 1974; Maslin & Davis, 1975; Sherman, 1980).

However, when examining prevalence of specific diagnoses rather than overall rates of mental illness, it does seem fairly clear that men predominate in some disorders, while women predominate in others. For instance, men's prevalence rates are higher for substance abuse and sexually related disorders, while women's prevalence rates are higher for all forms of mood and anxiety disorders (Bijl et al., 2002; Hartung & Widiger, 1998; Wetzel, 1991). Horsfall (2001) found differences between genders for substance abuse (men, 11%; women, 4.5%), anxiety (men, 7%; women, 12%), and mood disorders (men, 4%; women, 7%). According to the National Institute of Mental Health (retrieved December, 31, 2003, from http://www.nimh.nih.gov/wmhc/index.cfm), woman are affected twice as often as men by anxiety and depression and are nine times as likely as men to develop eating disorders. Furthermore, women were found to predominate in borderline, dependent, and histrionic personality disorders in two studies (Frisch & Frisch, 1998; Nehls,

1998), although Reich, Nduaguba, and Yates (1988) found little difference between men and women on dependent personality disorders for any age groups other than 31–40 years of age. Men predominate in antisocial, compulsive, paranoid, schizoid, and passive aggressive personality disorders in all age groups except 31–40 years of age (Kass et al., 1983; Landrine, 1989; Reich et al., 1988).

Interestingly, gender prevalence studies indicate that there are few gender differences in diagnosis prevalence before school age. Once children begin school, however, boys are more frequently diagnosed in the elementary years, and girls in adolescence and beyond (Keenan & Shaw, 1997). McDermott (1996) found that hyperactive, aggressive–provocative, and aggressive–impulsive syndromes showed higher prevalence in the youngest children, with reductions in older children, a pattern that for males is particularly pronounced for aggressive syndromes. This pattern is inverted for avoidant behavior. For every syndrome except "diffidence," males predominate, showing a male-to-female ratio of approximately 2:1 or 3:1. He found no significant female prevalence for any type of maladjustment during childhood. Caplan (1992) further indicates that despite the widely accepted wisdom that more boys have learning disabilities than girls, research indicates that learning disabilities are equally divided among boys and girls (see also , Shaywitz, Feltcher, & Escobar, 1990) even though more boys are referred for problems in this area.

REASONS FOR DEVELOPMENTAL SHIFTS IN PREVALENCE RATES

Keenan and Shaw (1997), in wondering about the rather sudden shift from gender similarity to gender difference in prevalence from before school to school-age children, hypothesized that young girls with difficulties are socialized to channel it into internalized distress that is not as identifiable by teachers and parents, whereas boys are not. Therefore, they suggest, young boys' more externalized problems disrupt families and school rooms, resulting in the boys being diagnosed and referred for help (see also Caplan, 1992).

Caplan (1992) also discusses "noticing" and "referring" those with problem behaviors. She indicates that girls' problems are more likely to be overlooked and underdiagnosed (Caplan, 1973, 1977; Caplan & Kinsbourne, 1974). When discussing the reasons for overlooking girls' learning disabilities, she reflects that, in addition to the differential abilities to observe girls' and boys' distress, the traditional notion that it is less important for girls to succeed academically may result in failure to label lower academic performance as a problem for girls.

Clearly, the lack of ability to observe young girls' distress, should it actually be present, would result in young girls' mental health needs not being met (Caplan, 1992). The very apparent needs of boys would, in contrast, result in the overpathologizing of young boys, or, as Caplan (1992) notes, in boys with learning disabilities developing disruptive behavior in addition to the learning disability. However, should these hypotheses be true, it would be difficult to positively assert the existence of differential incidence of diagnoses during childhood as a result of sex. Despite such difficulties, the beliefs about these differences seem to affect policy and funding decisions, making less money available for services for those who do not seem to have learning disabilities and who do not get referred as a result of classroom disruptions, that is, for girls in need (Kimball, 1981).

A hopeful sign is that school intolerance for acting out behavior and subsequent referrals for treatment may be working to decrease some problematic behavior. McDermott's (1996) research demonstrated reductions in acting out behavior as children got older. However, avoidant disorders increased, which draws attention to the differential "noticing" behavior for some diagnoses. That is, because

avoidant children do not disturb anyone and thus do not warrant "controlling" behaviors by school authorities, they may not be referred for needed help.

For those whose problematic behavior does continue into adulthood, however, it is interesting that childhood mental disorders with male predominance, such as conduct disorder, oppositional defiant disorder, and attention-deficit hyperactivity disorder (ADHD), have only three correlates in adulthood that might be ascribed—antisocial personality disorder, ADHD, and intermittent explosive disorder (Hartung & Widiger, 1998)—only two of which are Axis I correlates (i.e., those considered "mental illness") and therefore reimbursable. Caplan (1995), after observing the multitude of diagnoses available for women, argued that "the failure to include [other reimbursable] diagnoses for adults with disorders of dyscontrolled anger or aggression has reflected a masculine bias in the recognition of psychopathology or denial of psychopathology that would be more common in men than in women" (p. 264).

Caplan's declaration is an attempt to explain those research results that indicate that more women than men are mentally ill; that is, she reasons, fewer men are considered mentally ill when they continue their problematic childhood behavior into adulthood because fewer Axis I diagnostic categories exist for men with such problematic adult behavior. Some such diagnoses have been proposed but were opposed because they might mitigate the criminal responsibility of aggressive, assaultive males (Widiger, 1995). One might thus conclude that young girls' problems seem to evolve into adult problems that can receive a range of DSM diagnoses, while young boys' problems seem to evolve into criminality; and therefore men's problems are not considered to be mental illness. In addition, because of the pressures of the current reimbursement system, the lack of diagnoses for men's problematic behaviors may result in more women being in treatment than men. Furthermore, from a developmental perspective, clients who are at a developmental level reflecting less socialization into normative behavior—that is, being criminals—are unlikely to initiate psychological care for themselves; they are likely to attend treatment only when mandated by someone external to themselves (e.g., wife, court, school; Kegan, 1982, 1994); this would also mean that women would be more likely to pursue treatment. Based on these observations, researchers could conclude, perhaps without cause, that more women are mentally ill.

SEX BIAS IN DIAGNOSIS

However, regardless of whether there are differential overall prevalence rates for mental illness in men and women, feminists cite a number of substantial criticisms of DSM and other proposed diagnoses, as well as of practitioners' judgments about diagnoses, because of their potential for harming both women and men. For instance, women seem to be given diagnoses for both underconforming and overconforming to sex-role stereotypes (Abramowitz, 1973; Brodsky & Halroyd, 1975; Broverman et al., 1970; Broverman et al., 1972; Cook et al., 1993; Cormak & Furman, 1998; Fabrikant, 1974; Maslin & Davis, 1975; Sherman, 1980). Broverman and her colleagues' research (1970), for example, demonstrated that the qualities that practitioners considered to be healthy male characteristics—independence, personal assertion, and goal-directed activity—were also considered to be healthy adult characteristics. However, both differed substantially from what practitioners considered to be healthy female characteristics. It seemed that healthy women were supposed to have characteristics that neither male nor female practitioners considered to be healthy in adults; that is, women were supposed to be "more submissive, less independent, less adventurous, more easily influenced,

less aggressive, less competitive, more excitable in minor crises, having their feelings hurt more easily, being more emotional, more conceited about their appearance, less objective, disliking math and science" (Broverman et al., 1970, p. 4). Thus, being a healthy woman in 1970, according to societal, or at least practitioners', standards made it impossible to be a healthy adult. Only men could be healthy adults. If women wanted to be considered healthy adults, they had to behave like men and lose their status as healthy (or desirable) women. Of course, men operating within this context also ran the risk of underdiagnosis; that is, they might have all of Broverman's identified characteristics of a healthy adult, but the very bias about these being "healthy" might cause practitioners to overlook males' suffering. Research in fact indicates that well-socialized White men run the risk of underdiagnosis with the possible implication that they do not receive the services that they may need (Ganley, 1987; Kaplan, 1983a, 1983b).

One would hope that the passage of time might have shifted this difficult conundrum to allow people, particularly women, out of the bind that they were clearly in. However, Sherman (1980), in a later study, found that the passage of time had not altered such stereotyping. More current research continues this line of evidence (see also Althen, 1981; Angermeyer, Matschinger, & Holszinger, 1998; Brown, 1992; Busfield, 1989; Chesler, 1972; Cook, 1992a,b; Hamilton, Rothbart, & Dawes, 1986; Kaplan, 1983a,b; Landrine, 1989; Pederson, 1987; Spence, 1985; Sue, 1999; Unger & Crawford, 1992; Usher, 1989).

Angermeyer et al. (1998) extended the research from practitioner judgments to general public judgments to demonstrate the influence of popular culture in biasing clinical judgments. They asked participants to respond to vignettes of men and women with alcohol dependence, major depression, or schizophrenia. Participants' responses to women with schizophrenia and alcoholism were the most aggressive and anxious and the least helpful. Their responses to women portrayed as having substance abuse problems were the most nonprosocial of all (from males) and the most anxious and second most aggressive of all (from females). The researchers concluded that women who act in unfeminine ways receive very strong negative reactions, but that men who behave similarly do not. Ritchie (1994) points to the importance of this research because these beliefs about proper manhood and womanhood, assumed to differentiate between the mentally healthy and unhealthy, are used in planning treatment, in evaluating the effectiveness of mental health treatment, and in the construction of psychological tests. As he points out, such sex bias would result in men and women being diagnosed inappropriately, in raising questions about whether appropriate treatments were being chosen for those so diagnosed, and in invalidating outcomes and testing research.

Feminists concur with Ritchie, believing that these masculine-biased assumptions about health and illness were codified in the early versions of the DSM, and have affected all DSMs since, which, in turn, affect practitioners' judgments when assessing clients (Kaplan, 1983a, 1983b). For instance, Cook et al. (1993) point out that mental health professionals have been found to label people disturbed if their behavior doesn't fit the professional's gender ideals. Those clients who behave in traditional ways may be considered disturbed by mental health professionals who have made nontraditional choices. In contrast, those clients who behave in nontraditional ways may be considered disturbed by more traditional mental health professionals, despite evidence of the negative psychological consequences of behaving in gender stereotypical ways (Broverman et al., 1970; Kimmel, 1990; Lopez, 1989; Robertson & Fitzgerald, 1990).

Researchers have also found that simply knowing a client's sex can influence the diagnostic process, even among experienced practitioners (Loring & Powell, 1988). Female and male clients may earn different diagnoses even when they present with identical symptomatology (Becker & Lamb, 1994; Hamilton, Rothbart, & Dawes, 1986). These misjudgments about diagnosis may also result from the level of popularity of the particular diagnosis for a particular gender at that particular time and place, or within a particular mental health discipline (Becker & Lamb, 1994; McDermott, 1996). As Brown (1990a) indicates, "The impact of gender is to shape the perception of the assessor in ways that can yield quite different outcomes for the assessment process, unless the assessor is attentive to these potentially distorting influences of nonconscious gender effects on her or his judgment" (p. 15). As a result of studies like these, Ussher (2000) concludes that "Feminist critics have argued that misogynist assumptions about gender roles and normal femininity are used in diagnosing 'deviant' women. . . . Assumptions about the proper position of women within the institution of heterosexuality, furthermore, are used to prescribe notions of normality" (p. 217). However, as many feminist authors point out, men and women, boys and girls are harmed by over-, under-, and misdiagnosis (Becker & Lamb, 1994; McDermott, 1996).

WHO GETS SERVED BY COINING DISORDERS?

Feminists have identified and challenged the DSM diagnoses that seem to reflect a particularly masculine bias. They urge practitioners to think beyond the clear evidence that people struggle, to who gets served by labeling such struggles as diagnosable "disorders" (Marecek, 1993). Political ends might have driven the following examples, cited by Marecek (1993): that opponents of abortion developed the disorder of Post Abortion Trauma in their efforts to support their position; that those wanting to advocate on behalf of battered women who have killed their batterers have coined the disorder Battered Woman Syndrome; and that those who believe themselves to be falsely accused of sexual abuse coined the term False Memory Syndrome. She further claims that the pharmaceutical industry bankrolled efforts to include Premenstrual Syndrome; that psychiatrists wrested Premenstrual Syndrome away from gynecologists by coining Premenstrual Dysphoric Disorder; and that both diagnoses, should the latter be included in the DSM, will ensure that women will be buying drugs and paying for psychiatric services for a long time. Whether one agrees with Maracek or not, questions about such situations challenge practitioners to ask further whether such diagnoses are scientific verities or political and/or economic conveniences.

PREMENSTRUAL DYSPHORIC DISORDER

Diagnoses that have particularly been challenged for an androcentric bias have included premenstrual dysphoric disorder (PDD) (or late luteal phase dysphoric disorder [LLPDD]) and the borderline, self-defeating, histrionic, and dependent personality disorders, all of which have greater prevalence rates in women. Feminists have been particularly concerned with why the DSM developers have not identified or entertained (when they have been proposed) parallel diagnoses for men (Brown, 1991a; Caplan, 1992; Caplan et al., 1992; Gallant & Hamilton, 1988; Pantony & Caplan, 1991).

The battle over the inclusion of the "premenstrual dysphoric disorder" draws particular attention to the political and gender struggles inherent in the development of DSM classifications. Some believe that premenstrual dysphoric disorder has been supported as a "diagnosis under further study" with little scientific support for its becoming a classification (Caplan et al., 1992). Caplan et al. (1992), for instance, point out that, although

women may experience dysphoria related to their menstrual cycle, such dysphoria may result from culturally determined, negative associations with menstruation or from hormonal changes. Gallant and Hamilton (1988) continue this line of thought. After a review of the literature on premenstrual symptoms, they indicate that "the overabundance of methodological problems in this literature may simply reflect poor research. However, it is also possible that the quality of the research on premenstrual changes reflects tacit assumptions about the negative influence of the menstrual cycle on female functioning. . . . Such assumptions reinforce focusing only on negative changes, focusing only on the premenstrual cycle phase, and studying mood cycles only in women" (p. 273). As Caplan et al. (1992) point out, "there is no evidence that [women's hormonal changes] are any more severe than men's hormonally based mood or behavior changes [and yet] . . . there is no DSM equivalent for males" (p. 28; see also Caplan, 1992). Caplan and her colleagues thus question why women's changes in moods due to hormonal changes are considered psychiatric abnormalities, while men's are not.

Why, ask Caplan et al. (1992), is premenstrual syndrome (PMS) not merely continued as a physical, gynecological problem? As they point out, thyroid problems may lead to mood and behavior changes, yet there is no "thyroid dysphoria disorder." Such might be considered to be a "mental disorder due to a general medical condition" (American Psychiatric Association [APA], 2000), but it is doubtful that anyone would consider the person mentally ill; they would merely treat the thyroid problem medically so as to eliminate the mood and behavior correlates. Caplan et al. also indicate that depression may result from having the flu, and although one might (but probably wouldn't bother to) diagnose such a person as having a "mood disorder due to a general medical condition" (APA, 2000), again it is doubtful that anyone would consider the person mentally ill; they would simply wait for the flu to abate. Sadness can also result from terminating breast-feeding, and yet when doctors indicate to women that such sadness may be expected for a few days until hormone levels adjust, women feel relieved. "Why is this not the approach to PMS?" Caplan and her colleagues asked.

Caplan et al. (1992) and others (e.g., Gallant & Hamilton, 1988) further question the impact on women and society of failing to use more "normalizing, health-promoting, anxiety reducing" (Caplan et al., 1992, p. 28) approaches to this clearly biologically based experience? Caplan (1992) claims that

> abolishing the LLPDD [approximately equal to PDD] psychiatric label would not abolish the pathologizing of women with PMS, but having the explicitly psychiatric label formally and concretely legitimizes that pathologizing. Furthermore, the existence of a formal psychiatric label makes it incomparably more difficult for a woman branded with that label to convince her family, friends, co-workers, employers and prospective employers that she is psychologically normal. (p. 29)

Research on the impact of labeling by Schwartz, Weiss, and Lennon (2000) indicates, in fact, that those who are politically conservative attributed characteristics that are stereotypically associated with mental illness to women who were diagnosed with PDD. As Caplan (1992) points out, it does not take a large leap to move from defining women with PDD as mentally ill to keeping women out of well-paying, responsible jobs. She points out that men also experience cyclical hormonal changes that impact their functioning. Yet, because men's cycles are not tied to a marker like monthly menstruation, men continue to work in risky and highly challenging and dangerous jobs even when at low points in these cycles.

Gallant and Hamilton (1988) hypothesized that there might be benefits to including PDD as a disorder, although others disagree. For instance, Gallant and Hamilton indicate that a PDD diagnosis might reduce misclassification of women with premenstrual symptoms into more stigmatizing diagnoses, such as Somatization Disorder. However, they point out, dialectically, that including PDD may also interfere with full investigation into women's complaints or be used in a victim-blaming manner if contextual variables (e.g., women experience more symptoms when experiencing marital conflict) are not also investigated. Failure to fully investigate complaints may also result in failure to refer women for nutritional, vitamin, and exercise treatments that have been demonstrated to be helpful for PMS (Caplan et al., 1992). Brown (1991a) contends that the conceptualization of PDD or LLPDD has added nothing to anyone's understanding of mood fluctuations that result from hormonal cycling, and that such labels might contribute to missing true depression.

Gallant and Hamilton (1988) further point out that the proposed criteria for the PDD diagnosis indicate that the symptoms of those so diagnosed should not be merely an exacerbation of the symptoms of some other disorder. However, research on differential diagnosis (Stout, Steege, Blazer, & George, 1986; Endicott, Halbreich, Schacht, & Nee, 1981) indicates real difficulty in determining when premenstrual symptoms should be considered separate from another disorder. Finally, as when receiving other diagnoses, the PDD diagnosis may lead to feelings of powerlessness in women. Gallant and Hamilton thus conclude that women's premenstrual complaints can be sensitively dealt with within the current nosology without having to develop a separate diagnosis for these experiences.

PERSONALITY DISORDERS AND SOCIALIZATION

Personality disorder diagnoses have been examined more frequently for sex bias because they represent medical diseases least of all, and therefore could be more likely to reflect social conventions (Kroll, 1988). As mentioned previously, women seem to predominate in borderline, dependent, and histrionic personality disorders, and men seem to predominate in compulsive, paranoid, antisocial, schizoid, and passive–aggressive personality disorders. Horsfall (2001) indicates that each of the symptoms listed in the criteria for the disorders in which women predominate could be seen as an exaggeration of socially promoted feminine characteristics that are embedded in many cultures' beliefs and practices (e.g., excessive worrying, low self-esteem, feelings of worthlessness, overdependence, passivity, seductiveness). In fact, it is easy to see the correlations between Broverman et al.'s (1970) list of feminine characteristics and the criteria for dependent, borderline, and/or histrionic personality disorders.

Caplan (1992), when challenging the self-defeating personality disorder (SDPD), which at one time was a proposed addition to the DSM, paralleled it with the "good wife syndrome" (p. 74), or the ways that North American women are socialized to be unselfish and to put others' needs ahead of their own. She declares that it seems unreasonable to raise women to behave in certain ways and then to diagnose them for complying. Kaplan (1983a, 1983b) similarly questions the assumptions underlying the dependent personality disorder diagnosis, which also reflects characteristics of well-socialized women. In addition, she questions the notions that dependency is unhealthy, that extreme dependence in women indicates a disorder rather than merely that the woman lives in a subordinate position in society, and that women's dependency deserves a diagnosis, but that men's dependency (e.g., relying on others to clean their houses, cook for them, take care of their children) does not.

It seems a major concern to many feminists that women who are well-socialized receive a diagnosis, but that men who are well-socialized do not (Brown, 1991a, 1992; Caplan, 1992; Kaplan, 1983a,b; Pantony & Caplan, 1991; Russell, 1986b). Brown (1992) questions the tendency to label stereotypically female behaviors as pathology significantly more frequently than stereotypical male behaviors, which she believes equates masculinity with normalcy while considering femininity to be abnormal (see also Pantony & Caplan, 1991; Russell, 1986b; Wine, Moses, & Smye, 1980). Caplan (1992), for instance, questions why the DSM does not consider the inability to express a wide range of emotions— or other forms of extreme male socialization (e.g., macho personality disorder)—to be disordered. Kaplan (1983a, 1983b) jokingly comments that we don't seem to define as pathological the inability to write thank you notes, pick up dirty socks, and apologize for wrongs (male gender-stereotyped behavior), although we do pathologize the failure to leave cruel loved ones and difficulties in assertiveness (female gender-stereotyped behaviors, included in the criteria for Dependent Personality Disorder). Brown (1991a) suggests that "diagnoses are often proposed to describe the behaviors that irritate those writing the descriptions, and those with the power to write descriptions have tended to be members of the dominant group in North America: White, young, heterosexual, able-bodied, Christian, middle-class, well-educated, men" (p. 142). This means, she indicates, that the behaviors of nondominant groups are more likely to become diagnosable, and that dominant group behaviors are not likely to be considered problematic, even when they are dangerous to nondominant groups.

In reaction to what they consider an imbalance in pathologizing, Pantony and Caplan (1991) proposed "delusional dominating personality disorder" (DDPD) as a challenge to practitioners and diagnosticians to pay attention to those stereotypical male characteristics that harm men and those around them. The criteria include characteristics, among others, such as difficulties establishing and maintaining interpersonal relationships; difficulties expressing and attending to emotions; the choice of violent solutions or power, silence, withdrawal, and/or avoidance as solutions to conflict; the need to be around younger women who are shorter, weigh less, make less money, and are conventionally physically attractive; a tendency to be threatened by women who don't disguise their intelligence; and resistance to efforts to establish gender equity. One author's (Eriksen) response to the DDPD criteria was to be surprised that she hadn't considered these characteristics problematic enough to be diagnosed, despite her willingness to consider contrasting characteristics in women to be diagnosable. We wonder if readers had similar reactions. If so, then we believe that we must consider how firmly we are embedded in a culture that values male characteristics more than female characteristics, and how much we need greater awareness of gender factors in diagnosis and clinical treatment.

Landrine (1989), however, criticizes the above authors' focus on reasons for gender distribution in personality disorders because they have all focused on hypotheses about the two diagnoses that are prevalent for women, ignoring those that are prevalent for men. She claims that the hypotheses cannot be valid if they do not take into account why men experience prevalence in other personality disorders. She cites as support a number of studies that examine the above proposed hypotheses, studies that have not met with empirical success.

Landrine (1989) attempts to rectify this problem by proposing a hypothesis that accounts for observations of both genders. She notes that the personality disorders received by men most represent role stereotypes for men of a certain age, class, and marital status, while the personality disorders received most by women represent female role stereotypes for females of a certain age, class, and marital status. Her research has found support for her

"social role" hypothesis, a hypothesis that includes gender, age, and socioeconomic class as interacting variables. The research results indicate that stereotypes of young, lower-class men were labeled antisocial; stereotypes of single middle-class young women were labeled histrionic/hysterical; stereotypes of married middle-class middle-age women were labeled dependent; stereotypes of the "ruling class," that is, middle-class men, were labeled prototypically normal, or corresponded with the criteria for compulsive, paranoid, and narcissistic descriptions. Borderline and schizoid descriptions were not attributed to either sex. These results match the epidemiological distributions of the disorders. Landrine indicates, therefore, that the gender distribution of personality disorders does not result from the misogyny of practitioners, but from the overlap between personality disorder characteristics and role/role-stereotypes of both sexes.

Landrine does not stop, however, with these conclusions. She asks why personality disorders should so closely mirror stereotypes of these groups. Her answers point to the political nature of personality disorders. That is, she believes that the parallels indicate the tendency to focus attention on treatment of individually located issues and to define them as problems, rather than focusing attention on changing gender roles or eradicating gender stratification. If personality disorders are merely "a reflection of gender roles that serves to maintain gender stratification, then those [diagnoses] are political" (Landrine, 1989, p. 332). She further states that if new categories of personality disorder are added that merely reflect the current status of gender roles, adding them and reifying them as mental disorders results in the inability to engage in political or social analysis about these roles. Finally, she indicates that politically motivated hypotheses that do not account for the data fail to affect the political realities that motivated them in the first place.

The notion that male predominance personality disorders represent stereotypical male behavior and female predominance personality disorders represent stereotypical female behavior makes intuitive sense. However, as Landrine and others seem to point out, such a hypothesis begs the question, "Why are those who are well-socialized considered mentally ill?" Shouldn't the fact that such socialization causes problematic behavior direct our focus to society's behavior rather than to the diagnosis and treatment of individuals?

SOCIALIZATION AND MENTAL HEALTH

Research and theory on the mental health implications of socialization have further clarified some of the ways that gender-specific socialization harms people or causes them distress. For instance, Wirth-Cauchon (2000) points to society's contributions to so-called borderline characteristics. She claims that the "medicalized construction of women as borderline has the effect of pathologizing some of the fundamental conflicts women face in contemporary society, and within which they construct a sense of self" (p. 142). She offers a case example of a so-called borderline personality disordered person in which a male therapist and a feminist therapist constructed different meanings about the client. The male portrayed the client as alternating between being a sexy, bright, seductive woman and a passive, helpless, depressed woman. He discussed his own struggles to not be seduced by her seductive, strong side, but instead to assist the woman to integrate the two sides of herself.

In contrast, Wirth-Cauchon (2000) says, the feminist therapist situated the fragments of the borderline client within the "wider cultural splits and fragmentations that impact on women's construction of identity" (p. 157); that is, the struggles between cultural imperatives to be submissive and passive *or* sexy (not both) and the internal urges to buck free of such and be an "it." She points to the psychic and bodily costs for women in this struggle. Therefore, from a feminist perspective, Wirth-Cauchon (2000) indicates, the cultural imperatives that are transmitted through families and broader Western culture result in symptoms that "may be read as meaningful or intelligible responses to the double bind of feminine subjecthood . . . [they] manifest in a split or fracturing of self, a split between irreconcilable aspects of being" (pp. 157–158). Borderline women, from her perspective, are those who have lost touch with "any form of being outside of the boundaries of the mask, and thus manifest empty conformity" (p. 159) to cultural mandates about femininity that are superficial and empty. Borderline women may struggle because of the blurring of the image and the "real" in a world in which men continually expect women to be, and women try to be, the pornographic ideal of women. Thus, the cultural imperative requires women to be false, disembodied, and doll-like, as though this is "real" womanhood, and as if there are no other imaginable possibilities. Yet women have the haunting sense that there is something else, an authentic self "whose loss is memorialized in symptoms" (p. 159). Because these women may have lost themselves, they can't say, "I'm faking it." "Only a feeling of falsity remains. One may feel empty inside" (p. 159).

Gilligan and her colleagues (Gilligan, 1982; Brown & Gilligan, 1992; Taylor, Gilligan, & Sullivan, 1995), as a result of their research, direct attention to another aspect of female socialization. They found that girls silence themselves and their desires, abilities, and interests—that is, give up their "voice"—as they move into adolescence, because they believe that such silence is necessary in order to make intimate relationships possible. Smolak's (2002) research on "voice" and psychopathology found that voice was negatively correlated to femininity, and that the "lack of voice" and psychopathology link was documented more clearly for women than for men. She found that

> Silencing was a significant predictor in two of the five eating equations for women. . . . Indeed, even in the simple correlations, [silencing] is not related to any of the measures of problem behaviors among the men while it is related to all such measures among the women . . . voice measures are somewhat more related to depression in men than in women. (p. 238)

She also discovered that, rather than voice being related strictly to being male or female, higher voice ratings were related to higher ratings on masculinity, and lower voice ratings to lower ratings on masculinity and higher ratings on femininity. Her findings confirmed previous findings that higher levels of masculinity were related to better mental health (Murnen & Smolak, 1998; Whitley, 1995).

Kirsh and Kuiper (2002) discussed and researched individualism and relatedness, comparing these to masculinity and femininity, in their discussions of why women in North America as are twice as likely as men to experience depression in their lives. They explained the difference in prevalence rates as a function of cultural factors, claiming that such explanations are validated by the fact that in other countries such gender differences are not as dramatic (Nolen-Hoeksema, 1995). Such explanations are also supported because the gender differences seem to begin during adolescence, just at the time when girls' socialization becomes different from boys' (Sprock & Yoder, 1997; Steinberg, 1990). During adolescence, boys are taught that men are to be "active, masterful, and autonomous" (p. 77), whereas girls are taught that women are to be passive, compliant, and committed to interpersonal relationships (Helgeson & Fritz, 1998; Kaplan, 1987). Research has indicated that those boys and girls who operate against socialization as young children

experience depression later in life (Gjerde, 1996). Other researchers and theorists have examined the constructs of communion and agency, which are also parallel to relatedness and individualism or femininity and masculinity, concluding that communion is more pronounced in women and agency in men (Bakan, 1966; Helgeson, 1994; Mansfield & McAdams, 1996).

A series of qualitative research studies offer rich data about the cultural factors that may contribute to women's distress or depression. For instance, in Gammell and Stoppard's (1999; as cited in Kirsch & Kuiper, 2002) qualitative research, women described themselves as having two sides: their relatedness side that was weak and depressed, and their strong, confident, individualistic side that was not. McMullen (1999) concluded from similar research that women may also desire autonomy, and that those who are depressed somehow find that relatedness alone is insufficient. Such gender role conflict may also exist for men, although it is less well researched. That is, those men who experience conflict between their socialization into individualism and their desires for relatedness experience greater depressive symptoms (Good & Mintz, 1990). Heifner (1997; as cited in Kirsh & Kuiper, 2002) also found corresponding themes in depressed men of high performance expectations, being emotionally distant from others, and maintaining traditional gender roles. Heifner concludes, however, that "the mismatch generally appears to be much more evident in the case of women, resulting in much higher overall rates of depression for women, when compared to men" (p. 79).

Long ago, Bem (1974) indicated that suppression of the non–sex-typed part of oneself was unhealthy, and that androgyny resulted in better mental health and adjustment. Helgeson (1994) expanded these notions of balancing individualism and relatedness in her research, which indicated that poor health and relationship difficulties result from a lack of balance (Helgeson & Fritz, 1998). However, actually being male or female turned out to be less relevant than the person's degree of masculinity and femininity. Higher femininity scores and lower masculinity scores correlated with higher depression in both sexes. Higher levels of masculinity resulted in lower levels of depression in both men and women, which points to the mental health need for Broverman's (1970) list of male characteristics regardless of one's gender.

What then are women to do about the conflict between their needs to adopt masculine characteristics in order to be mentally healthy and society's demands that they adopt feminine characteristics (serious demands, as society punishes women who fail to be sufficiently feminine)? Feminist assertions seem well grounded that answers to these questions are unlikely to emerge from a focus on diagnosing and medically reducing the symptoms of these conflicts, that at least part of practitioners' focus ought to be on changing a biased and unreasonable society. Some of the more extreme feminists conclude from such DSM-related experiences that psychiatry is an institution that exerts social control over women by influencing and reflecting societal definitions of sex-role-appropriate behavior, definitions that reflect ideology rather than science (Caplan et al., 1992).

SOCIAL CONDITIONS

Beyond the typical socialization of men and women and its impact on the mental health of each are questions about the influences of societal conditions, in particular trauma experiences, on women's mental health. For instance, environmental factors that many researchers (Carmen, Russo, & Miller, 1981; Collins, 1998; Cook et al., 1993; Gove & Tudor, 1972; Horsfall, 1998; Howell, 1981; Jordanova, 1981; Miller, 1976/1991; Root, 1992; Rothblum, 1982; Vance, 1997; Weissman & Klerman, 1981; Wetzel, 1991)

have hypothesized to account for the high rates of depression and other disorders in women include: (a) the greater restrictiveness of women's roles, which would result in less financial, occupational, or social gratification; (b) the inability to measure up to standards of women who are held up as examples of those who have "made it"; (c) a lack of social networks and supports; (d) being married, as married women are more depressed than never-married women, possibly as a result of isolation and not having their needs met in their roles as housewives, or as a result of being employed yet carrying most of childcare and household responsibilities; (e) being separated or divorced (because women are less likely to remarry and more likely to live longer than men and women tend to "marry up" in age); (f) single motherhood and its attendant stresses (Rothblum, 1982); (g) more frequent experiences of gender-based discrimination (Cook et al., 1993; Root, 1992); (h) higher prevalences of living in poverty with its attendant ills and stresses; (i) inequities related to marriage, family relationships, reproduction, child rearing, divorce, aging, education, and work (Carmen et al., 1981); (j) work outside the home that is low status or low pay; and (k) women's roles being defined in terms of the needs of others, which means they tend to leave their own needs secondary and unmet. All of these social situations involve alienation, powerlessness, and poverty, conditions that epidemiological data link with increases in mental illness (Carmen et al., 1981, p. 1321). Vance (1997) concludes that attention to ecological and systemic contributors to psychopathology "does not preclude heritability but assumes that the heritability operates . . . through the avenues available to it developmentally and through the filters and pressures of one's ecology" (p. 223).

Feminists prefer to focus on ecological and systemic contributors to women's distress and depression, believing that the dominant focus on biological factors has resulted in overdiagnosis of women and misdirected efforts at solving women's problems. For instance, Russell (1986b) concludes that even though some problems may surface most visibly in particular groups of people, that does not mean that the problems are centrally located within those people. In fact, it may be more accurate to say that disorder exists in the relationships between certain people and those with whom they relate, or between those people and societal norms and demands. Focusing on the individual may result in failure to "cure" the problem, while focus on societal situations, for instance, providing child care, opening up employment for women, or changing the definitions of proper female behavior, may succeed in reducing the incidence of the problems. Russell claims further that the DSM practice of diagnosing the individual "amounts not simply to an error or an oversight; it contains a program of political policy disguised as humanitarian medical attention to the disordered" (p. 96).

An example of a feminist focus would be studying the effects of inequality on women's psychological Health. According to Carmen et al. (1981),

> Women's sense of identity is developed within a framework that defines women as a devalued group. . . . Girls' self-esteem remains dependent on acceptance by others. . . . Because men hold the power and authority, women are rewarded for developing a set of psychological characteristics that accommodate to and please men. Such traits . . . [have been] incorporated into some prevalent psychological theories in which they are defined as innate or inevitable characteristics of women [rather than as] learned behaviors by which all subordinate group members attempt to ensure their survival. . . . These survival skills exact a costly penalty because they are antithetical to the use of *active* psychic mechanisms for coping and resolving conflicts inherent in healthy psychological development. (Carmen et al., 1981, p. 1321)

Instead, girls and women develop more passive and indirect strategies for coping with difficulties, strategies that do not lead to favorable outcomes and may result in psychological and relational difficulties. Carmen and her colleagues (1981) believe that the current circumstances of inequality, circumstances that society considers normal, "set the stage for extraordinary events that may heighten vulnerability to mental illness: the frequency with which incest, rape, and marital violence occur suggests that such events might well be considered normative developmental crises for women" (p. 1321; see also Caplan, 1992; Chesler, 1972; Lee, Lentz, Taylor, Mitchell, & Woods, 1994; Libbus, 1996; Miller, 1976/1991).

Collins (1998) examines the effects of subordination directly, and indicates that the effects can be generated in any subordinate group, not only in women. She first summarizes Miller's (1976/1991) descriptions of "how the personality characteristics ascribed to subordinate and dominant groups develop as a result of prolonged exposure to a limiting role" (Collins, 1998, p. 99). All of the "symptoms" of those in subordinate roles, according to Miller, belong to DSM diagnoses that are typically ascribed to women. All of the "symptoms" of those in dominant roles belong to DSM diagnoses that are typically ascribed to men. Collins indicates that women are assigned to the subordinate role at birth, and men are assigned to the dominant role at birth; she further indicates that symptoms are particularly pernicious when dominance positions are permanent and long standing.

In Zimbardo's Stanford prison experiment (Musen, 1992), the effects of subordination and domination were artificially generated in White males. In the experiment, psychologically healthy White male college students were assigned to be prison guards or prisoners. The "prisoners" developed symptoms associated with the DSM diagnoses that are typically ascribed to women; they became depressed, suicidal, anxious, and developed eating problems. The "guards" developed symptoms associated with DSM diagnoses that are typically ascribed to men; they became verbally abusive, violent, and otherwise antisocial. In fact, the experiment had to be concluded after only six days because of the severity of symptoms that developed in both groups. Collins's (1998) conclusions from the experiment and from research using videotapes of the Zimbardo experiment were that "even psychologically healthy White males (who are typically perceived as dominants) will exhibit the 'psychopathology' that is typically ascribed to subordinates (women) when placed in a subordinate role, even for a short period of time" (p. 108). She remarks that the results of this experiment demonstrate that these disorders probably result more from social position (subordinate/dominant) than from biology, as is typically assumed. In drawing this conclusion, she differentiates the gendered disorders (those with symptoms that are typically associated with either males or females) from those in which biological substrates are most supported, and in which the prevalence is the same for men and women (e.g., schizophrenia, bipolar disorder).

In conclusion, evidence seems to have mounted that the social conditions that are a reality in most women's lives contribute to their psychological distress. Their high rates of depression and other "neurotic" disorders can be explained by factors as surprising and seemingly innocuous as marriage to factors that all of us would like to find remedies for, such as poverty, discrimination, and the trials of single motherhood.

WOMEN'S TRAUMA EXPERIENCES

The cited negative social conditions that surround female day-to-day existence could be viewed as trauma experiences, and some authors have indicated that the ongoing experiences of subordination and oppression are a type of insidious trauma (Root, 1989, 1992;

Brown, 1990b, 1991a, 1991b, 1992). The more dramatic effect of such social conditions, however, is to expose women to more frequent experiences of physical and sexual abuse, experiences that are more commonly considered "trauma." Gender differentiation in our society (Cook, 1992a, 1992b) results in these life circumstances being more likely to happen to those who are less powerful, particularly women and children (Cook et al., 1993; Finkelhor, 1984; Koss, 1990; Walker, 1979).

Statistics

Violence against women in the form of incest, rape, battering, observing the abuse of other women, and sexual abuse in childhood approaches normative status in girls and women. Men from nondominant groups are also repeatedly exposed to trauma and victimization (Brown, 1986, 1992; Committee on Women in Psychology, 1985; Rosewater, 1986, 1987; Russell, 1986a; Walker, 1985, 1986). For instance, Russell (1986a) discovered sexual abuse histories in 37% of a nonclinical random sample of women. In clinical samples, estimates of the number of women who are sexually abused is consistently approximately 55% (Jacobson & Herald, 1990; Lipschitz, Kaplan, Sorkenn, Faedda, Chorney, & Asnis, 1996; Wurr & Partridge, 1996). In a study of 108 homeless people with a dual diagnosis, women experienced very high rates of rape, assault, and sexual and physical abuse; 75% were mothers (Brunette & Drake, 1998). FBI estimates indicate that one in four women will be victims of sexual assault in their lifetime (Heppner et al., 1995). Some suggest that more than 50% of female murders are committed by a past or present domestic partner (Carden, 1994). Carmen, Reiker, and Mills (1984) reviewed charts of psychiatrically hospitalized women, and found the frequency of sexual and physical abuse histories to be 43%. Bryer, Nelson, Miller, and Krol (1987) and Herman, Perry, and van der Kolk (1989) found that women diagnosed with personality disorders had experienced sexual and physical abuse at extremely high rates. Jacobson and Richardson (1987), when using a structured interview with psychiatrically hospitalized patients, found that 81% had experienced at least one type of major interpersonal violence. None of these statistics include the more "minor" experiences of verbal or emotional abuse or observations of violence against property or others, which also result in traumatogenic impacts (Miller, 1984; Patrick-Hoffman, 1984; Walker, 1985). However, the statistics certainly point to high correlations between sexual and other abuses and homelessness and other psychiatric disorders.

Psychological Results of Abuse

The impact of sexual abuse and sexual assault on women's mental health and development is well-documented (James & Gilliland, 2001). Depending on the age and developmental level of the person who was assaulted, the extent of the abuse, the degree of violence used, the relationship with the perpetrator, and so on, sexual trauma has numerous impacts on human development and psychological well-being (Ferrara, 2002; James & Gilliland, 2001).

For instance, Brown (1992) points out that because the penalties for failing to behave as abusers require can range from verbal abuse to violent beatings, many from nondominant groups will choose certain behaviors or perceptions of self that allow an easier fit with the dominant and oppressive culture. These accommodations to oppression, she says, seem to be reflected in the higher rates of diagnosis with various problems in members of oppressed groups. The results of abuse can appear as severe psychological distress or psychopathology in their intensity and resistance to change. For instance, women and girls who have experienced such traumas display the expressions of despair, anger, and traumatization that result

from such abuse, which may result in diagnoses such as PTSD, depression, anxiety, eating disorders, and borderline personality disorder (Busfield, 1996; Gallop, McKeever, Toner, Lancee, & Lueck, 1995; Lego, 1996; Nehls, 1998). These disorders and experiences seriously impede women from "effectively performing and enjoying activities of daily living such as work, parenting, recreation, partnerships, and friendships" (Horsfall, 2001, p. 429). However, unlike the more serious disorders that these women's behaviors mimic (e.g., schizophrenia), symptoms usually abate in response to treatment that recognizes and responds to the trauma.

Borderline Personality Disorder

That women who have abuse histories are often diagnosed with borderline personality disorder (BPD) deserves further attention. Substantial research indicates that women are diagnosed more frequently than men with borderline personality disorder, with ratios ranging from 2:1 to 9:1 (Akhtar, Byrne, & Doghramji, 1986; Castaneda & Franco, 1985; Frances & Widiger, 1987; Gilbertson, McGraw, & Brown, 1986; Henry & Cohen, 1983; Kirshner & Johnston, 1983; Sheehy, Goldsmith, & Charles, 1980). Research also indicates that many clients who are diagnosed with borderline personality disorder have histories of sexual abuse (Barnard & Hirsh, 1985; Courtois, 1988; Herman et al., 1989; Ogata et al., 1990; Rieker & Carmen, 1986; Stone, Unwin, Beacham, & Swenson, 1988; Surrey, Swett, Michaels, & Levin, 1990; Westen, Ludolph, Misle, Ruffins, & Block, 1990; Wheeler & Walton, 1987). The DSM cautions against readily applying the borderline personality diagnosis to women who have been abused. However, very few practitioners ask their clients about abuse (Brown, 1991a; also see Firsten, 1991, for a review). So practitioners may observe the results of the abuse in behavior and emotions without understanding its context and may as a result potentially misdiagnose trauma reactions (Caplan, 1992).

Becker and Lamb (1994) point out that BPD may be diagnosed more frequently in women because of the tendency of practitioners to consider symptomatic behavior to result from intrapsychic problems in women and from environmental factors for men (see also Wallston & Grady, 1985). Becker and Lamb test out their hypotheses in a major study to discern what leads practitioners to diagnose BPD more in women and PTSD more in men. The study used case vignettes in which the symptoms for both BPD and PTSD were present, in which sexual abuse history was clearly evident, and in which the same symptoms were presented for either a man or a woman. The cases were sent to psychiatrists, psychologists, and social workers, who were asked to provide a diagnosis.

Becker and Lamb's research results indicated a substantial level of sex bias in the diagnoses. Overall, practitioners more frequently diagnosed the female clients with BPD, as was expected. Psychiatrists and younger psychiatrists and psychologists diagnosed women more frequently with BPD than did other practitioners. Becker and Lamb ascribe these results to the tendency of these practitioners toward a medical-model orientation, toward intrapsychic and biological explanations for behavior, and away from a focus on external causes. They also attributed the age differentials to the recent upsurge in information about the BPD diagnosis, information to which younger and ostensibly more recently trained practitioners would have had greater access. The researchers also found that female practitioners more frequently diagnosed the clients with PTSD than did male practitioners. Researchers attributed these results to the more frequent personal experience of female practitioners with trauma, which may heighten their sensitivity to these issues.

Male practitioners, particularly psychiatrists, underestimated the negative effects of sexual abuse on both male and female clients.

Blaming the Victim

Many authors challenge the notion that women who have been victims of sexual or physical abuse should be diagnosed or labeled as flawed in any way, because whatever distressed or distressing resultant behavior that they may display is usually understandable and normative in the context of the experience of trauma (Brown, 1991a; Johnson, 1980). These authors particularly challenge the tendency to consider such women mentally ill and challenge the concurrent failure to discuss the mental illness of their abusers (Johnson, 1980). In fact, the level of disorder of men and women involved in battering situations tends to be treated and perceived differently by practitioners, because the batterers seem to have the ability to behave in socially acceptable ways when around others and the battered tend to express anger that is outside the expectations for feminine behavior. For instance, Ganley (1987) indicates that it is hard to tease out pathology in male batterers who seem to be very able to demonstrate socially desirable behavior during clinical assessments. Contrastingly, Rosewater (1987) and Walker (1984) indicate that women who have been battered tend to be overdiagnosed because of the high levels of overt anger that they express about their batterers.

But Brown (1991b) names labeling or diagnosing women who have been victims of trauma "blaming the victim." She says she rarely encounters writing about the

characterological pathology of people who seek out flood plains or tornado alleys to live in, nor do those who wage war or go down to the sea in ships that can sink come under the sort of scrutiny we find given to battered women or survivors of rape or incest . . . the "self-defeating" woman who's been in a battering relationship is treated quite differently (and less well) than is the survivor of a train wreck, even when the presenting problems are similar . . . the former is assumed to have contributed to her problem . . . ; the latter is almost always seen as the innocent victim of a random event. (p. 102)

In Caplan's (1992) research, hundreds of women expressed that "their therapists told them regularly that they brought all their problems on themselves" (p. 75). She believes that this brings on depression in women, who then figure that there is no way out of living in damaging relationships or situations. In fact, DSM developers indicate that therapy makes these "self-defeating" women worse (Kass, MacKinnon, & Spitzer, 1986). Given the above findings, such therapy failures seem understandable.

Brown (1991b) goes on to say that if practitioners define a traumatic stressor as something that is outside normal human experience (as PTSD criteria previously required), by definition we exclude those experiences that occur so frequently in the lives of some groups that they have become normative statistically. The result is that the everyday experience of members of those groups is labeled pathological or disturbed, yet these people can't protect themselves from these events, events that result in experiences of psychological distress. Those who are not members of these groups are usually the ones who are consigning nondominant group members to the category of "less than human, less than deserving of fair treatment" (Brown, 1991b, p. 103), or disordered. "If we maintain the myth of the willing victim, who we then pathologize for her presumed willingness, we need never question the social structures that perpetuate her victimization" (p. 106).

In addition, Horsfall (2001) indicates that the women who receive these diagnoses are undertreated. This occurs at least (a) partly

because public mental health funding cuts result in only "serious" mental illness being treated in the public sector where lower income women can afford treatment, and perhaps (b) partly because women's tendency to internalize pain is not overtly dangerous or disruptive to society and is therefore less likely to be a priority in policy decisions. Substantial unmet needs exist in women who have suffered abuse related to being mothers, to family planning, and to sexual safety (Australian Bureau of Statistics, 1998; Brunette & Drake, 1998; Busfield, 1996; Perkins & Repper, 1998). The lack of attention and services for them may result in women feeling that "their distress and pain is rendered illegitimate, unreal, or inconsequencial" which puts them at further risk for "depression, anxiety, substance abuse, and social withdrawal" (Horsfall, 2001, p. 429).

Alternatives to Currently Used Diagnoses

Many authors offer alternatives to the previously cited diagnoses. For instance, Becker and Lamb (1994) indicate that clients who have been physically or sexually abused might be better served were they to receive a PTSD diagnosis, which is less stigmatizing, recognizes the trauma etiology of their distress, and directs practitioners toward interventions that are pertinent to recovery from trauma, rather than a BPD diagnosis, which results in greater stigma and poorer treatment by practitioners. A PTSD diagnosis allows for treatment and a "reconceptualization of the sexual abuse and its secondary effects without labeling the patient 'crazy'" (p. 56; see also Brown, 1992; Carmen et al., 1984; Courtois, 1988). The difference between "'severe psychopathology' and 'severe distress secondary to a history of lifelong hostile context' is meaningful from a feminist perspective, in that the latter most accurately describes the interactive effects of person and environment in the development of distressed affect and less-than-functional behavior" (Brown, 1992, p. 222).

Smith and Siegel (1985, as cited in Brown, 1992) advocate reframing rather than diagnosing. That is, they note that the behaviors of abuse survivors that have been labeled as passive or dependent by traditional practitioners can be relabeled as quite "skillful manifestations of personal power" (p. 217) in situations where other self-care choices may be punished. Brown (1992) also reframes such behaviors, proposing the alternative hypothesis that "such individuals are manifesting not a disordered personality, but a normative, functional, and at times creative (although distressed) response to potentially dangerous situations and oppressive cultural norms" (p. 220) because "attempts at what might be considered 'healthy' means of self-expression by members of culturally disenfranchised groups are often met with punitive responses" (p. 221).

Brown (1990b; 1992) further proposes an alternative DSM diagnosis for women and others who have experienced trauma: "abuse/ oppression artifact disorders." Specifically describing women's struggles as artifacts of abuse and oppression takes into account the repetitive nature of exposure to trauma (rather than the single discrete experience that is usually reflected in a PTSD diagnosis) that is an everyday experience for those in subordinate positions in society. It accounts for the effects of "multiple learning trials across many situations, with severe penalties for 'wrong' responses" (p. 219). It describes the intermittent reinforcement of behaviors that results in the tenaciousness of difficult behaviors, requiring many exposures to non-exploitive situations in order to relinquish behaviors that have been necessary to "surviving, coping with, or making sense of abuse or oppression" (p. 219).

Use of an abuse/oppression artifact disorder diagnosis would also help clients make sense of their behaviors, placing ultimate responsibility for distress on the oppression or abuse that they experienced. The diagnosis would clarify etiology for practitioners, so that no mistakes would be made by calling the disorder "pathology within the individual client" (Brown, 1990b, p. 57). Symptoms would be considered as understandable, "survival-oriented" (p. 57) responses to horrible circumstances, rather than as a form of pathology. The focus could then be on the "survival value" of the symptoms, which would be a "more affirming, less stigmatizing way of explicating their persistence" (p. 57).

Brown (1990b) further incorporates Benjamin's (1986) Structural Analysis of Social Behavior (SASB; a continuous assessment of descriptions of relevant interpersonal and intrapsychic interactions yielding directional understandings of which factors lead to others) to direct the practitioner's assessment procedures in abuse/oppression artifact disorder. For instance, the SASB would emphasize attention to the "interpersonal meaning and consequences of experience" (Brown, 1990b, p. 58). The practitioner would determine, in conversation with the client, what the stressor and its consequences meant to the person, helping the client to define her own experiences, which would allow the client to be the "expert about her own life, while also validating the expertise of the therapist in developing hypotheses about the meaning of those experiences" (p. 58). This proposed diagnosis "encourages diagnostic thinking, it increases awareness without adding stigma, it reflects the diverse realities of women's lives in a range of contexts, and it promotes a mutually respectful interchange between client and therapist" (p. 59).

An abuse/oppression artifact disorder diagnosis would also provide a way to account for what Maria Root (1989, 1992) calls *insidious trauma*, or the traumatogenic effects of oppression that do damage to the soul, but are not necessarily physically threatening at a given moment (as would be required for PTSD). She and Brown (1992) indicate that we live in a culture in which there is a high base rate of sexual assault of women, and that merely being part of that culture, being frightened by what might happen, and seeing on television what happens to other women exposes women to insidious trauma; that membership in a nondominant group means "a constant lifetime risk of exposure to certain trauma" (Brown, 1992, p. 108). If trauma is unusual, Brown claims, women can pretend that they are safe, pretend that if they don't draw attention to themselves, they will not be victimized. However, when trauma is usual, women must conclude that only an accident has spared them thus far.

Conclusion

I (Eriksen) frankly find myself horrified at the numbers of women and children who are physically or sexually violated. My clinical experience also bears witness to the long-term disruptions in life that result from these trauma experiences, as researchers have verified. Clearly, the levels of distress and disorder must be accounted for in some way, and in a way that allows for the reimbursement of very necessary services. It seems unreasonable to take any chances at further harm to these survivors by ascribing diagnoses that may increase stigmatization and blame, and that clearly don't reflect the reactive nature of these women's distress. I find the Abuse/Oppression Artifacts Disorder a substantial and ethical solution, one that I hope DSM developers will adopt.

However, solving the problem of trauma cannot be restricted to a focus on abused women. Clearly, practitioners and others need to broaden the focus of their interventions beyond 50-minute, individual, in-the-office, talk therapy. They need to expand their focus to family, community, and educational change creation strategies. I find it troubling that because women are more frequently diagnosed with mood and anxiety disorders, the less-serious disorders, and

because public mental health is currently funded only for serious mental illness and dually diagnosed clients, women are less likely to find public, low-cost services. One wonders, then, if some women will simply have to remain in distress. This may increase their life troubles, which, in turn, may make them "crazy" enough to attract the attention of service providers. Experiences of trauma that occur subsequent to women's distress or experience of troubling social conditions may be one example of such a phenomenon.

Furthermore, substantial focus needs to be placed on diagnosing and treating the abusers, and on the societal institutions that allow, promote, or fail to intervene in the violence against women and children. As feminists claim, once we have the information about the damage that women suffer in our society, we are wrested from our comfortable offices and from a reliance on caring listening into a maelstrom which has no easy answers.

FEMINIST ANALYSIS

The feminist challenges to diagnosis might be encapsulated in perhaps a somewhat simplistic nutshell: If you beat someone regularly, she may get angry, anxious, "crazy," and/or depressed. If you then decide that she should be referred to counseling for treatment of her anger, anxiety, craziness, or depression, there are a number of treatment choices. A practitioner might assume that her depression and anger result from constitutional, biological, or genetic predispositions to emotional disorders that have been activated by the beating, and then one would treat her with antidepressant medications (DSM and medical-model assumptions). The mental health practitioner might assume that she has a past history that predisposes her to choosing a relationship in which she will be repeatedly beaten, and such a perspective would direct the clinical work toward having her explore that past history and reconnect emotionally with past predisposing experiences, hoping that the catharsis and insight gained would enable her to make better choices in the future (psychodynamic and some humanistic assumptions). The practitioner might assume that anger, anxiety, and depression are "bad" things that the woman needs to eliminate or decrease so that she can adapt to her current life situation (traditional assumptions about marriage and male-female relationships), perhaps recognizing that if she thought differently about her life circumstances, she would feel less distress (cognitive behavioral assumptions). A practitioner might further assume that having a healthy, congruent relationship with a practitioner (or with others) would free the client's growth potential and that as she grew, she would be more able to make responsible, self-affirming choices (humanistic assumptions).

Any of these treatment choices assumes an individually located "illness" or "disorder" of some sort (whether disordered biology, thinking, relational ability, or past history); assumes that the anger, anxiety, and/or depression are "the problems" to be fixed; and places the responsibility for change or adaptation to the situation on the individual woman. The choices fail to locate the problem in the person who is doing the beating, or in the society that allows (encourages?) such beatings to occur. The choices fail to insist on diagnosing the batterer and referring him to counseling (or prison), or to insist on reforming the society that supports such behavior. And the choices fail to recognize that anger, anxiety, and/or depression are expectable reactions to such abuse; that to react differently would, in fact, be "crazy." Some argue that the therapeutic options suggested above actually further victimize the woman by discounting the reality of her experience; that is, that she has been beaten repeatedly and that her feelings are justified.

One might argue here that the woman could leave the abusive situation and then she would

no longer be beaten. However, if we believe the data presented above, "beatings" in the form of sexual and physical abuse and other forms of interpersonal violence are normative experiences for women, with very high prevalence rates for the clinical population. The experience of other forms of discrimination, abuses of power, and other results of subordination and oppression are almost universal for those in nondominant groups. Therefore, it would seem that it is impossible to escape from repeated victimization until society changes. It seems that a need exists to proactively work to change the beatings and the beaters, to change a society that "values" hierarchies of dominance and subordination, and perhaps, also, to empower the clients to understand their position vis-à-vis an abusive society and to become active in the same ways. These are the beliefs and proposals of feminist analysis.

Gove (1980), in a rather early treatise, indicated that

> when an individual is so distressed or disorganized that his or her functioning is impaired, both society and the people directly involved with that individual have an interest in seeing that he or she is restored to a state in which he or she can function effectively. If the individual's emotional disturbance is in part a reaction to aspects of the social system, then society has a particular concern with the way in which the therapist goes about alleviating the person's disturbance. The therapist who uses procedures that alleviate the disturbance by helping the person to adjust to characteristics of the social structure as it exists is correctly seen as an agent who helps maintain the status quo. In contrast, the therapist who uses procedures that lead to a change in aspects of the person's environment that are reflective of the basic social structure is correctly seen as an agent of social change. (p. 357)

Gove (1980) believes that some mental illness is clearly individual and related to idiosyncratic life experiences, biology, or personality traits. However, when the problems "reflect societal conditions, the way the woman is treated inevitably has consequences for the maintenance or change of the societal structure, and her therapist, is then, in the broadest sense of the word, a political agent" (p. 357).

Feminists, indeed, begin from the position that the personal is political, and so make no apologies for envisioning the therapy process as a political process as well. In contrast to the traditional hypotheses about etiology and treatment, feminist analysis indicates that personality develops in a "complex web of interaction between the internal, phenomenological experiences of the individual and the external, social context in which that person lives" and that we need to attend to the constant interplay between the two in understanding people and their distress. Feminist therapy "eschews the sort of dichotomous thinking that characterizes much of mainstream psychology in which there tends to be an overemphasis on one or the other perspectives to the detriment of a more integrated view" (Brown, 1991b, p. 103).

Johnson (1980) indicated that feminist therapy offers distinct advantages to women over traditional therapies, for nonfeminists and feminists alike. For instance: (a) Defining oneself as a feminist makes clear up front what one's values are, which, in turn, identifies one's political stance, so that the client knows what she is "buying." In contrast, in traditional therapy, those values are covert, often unacknowledged, and therefore may be imposed on the client despite claims to the contrary. Feminists, in fact, believe that it is impossible and undesirable to operate in a value-free environment. (b) Feminist therapy also offers an egalitarian relationship that counters the usual submissive position expected of women in society. (c) It interprets the client's symptoms in terms of their sociopolitical context. (d) It supports anger, assertiveness, aggression, and initiative taking

when indicated, even if their expression causes problems with significant others. As Miller (1976/1991) points out, seeking self-definition and self-determination may upset current relationships, but "women are not creating conflict, they are exposing the fact that conflict exists" (p. 126). Furthermore, as Johnson (1980) points out, "Emotional pain [or such interpersonal conflict] is not always psychopathology; it may result from movement toward growth" (p. 368). (e) Feminist therapy also encourages trust and respect for other women and attends to the shared nature of emotional problems. The shared experiences of women result in relief, sometimes rage, and the oft shared, amazed realization: "So it isn't just me. I am not crazy."

Brown (1990a) urges all practitioners to conduct feminist clinical assessments, and includes pointers for doing so. For instance, practitioners need to take on a mind-set that continually questions their own assumptions about what is usual or normal with respect to gender and that attends to factors that may influence the expression of gender. The meaning of gendered behaviors to the client and to the practitioner become equally important in gender role analysis, and are determined in a cooperative manner, along with their impact on the final assessment. "This requires that the clinician be prepared to have her or his assumptions about what a behavior implies challenged and that she or he be willing to accept and privilege the client's constructions of her or his own gendered behaviors" (p. 14).

Feminist analysis also asks practitioners to consider the demand characteristics that enter the assessment process as a result of gender. For example, during clinical assessments, both men and women are penalized for deviation from gender role norms, because those gender norms reflect value judgments held by the practitioner (Carmen et al., 1981). If the client behaves in ways that irritate the practitioner, and the practitioner does not assess what contextual variables may lead to such irritation, the practitioner may miss gendered experiences that normalize the client's behavior. In the opposite way, if the practitioner is attracted to the client, the practitioner may also behave in ways that distort the assessment, either positively or negatively (Brown, 1990a).

Practitioners conducting feminist clinical assessments also purposefully ask about gender issues and experiences. For instance, the practitioner needs to assess what it means to the client to be a failure or a success as a man or a woman. Practitioners need to include an analysis of gender meanings and roles within the client's milieu and an analysis of clients' experiences of culture and cultural oppression (Brown, 1990b). Gender-sensitive assessment also considers and questions deviance and compliance with mainstream gender roles. A person who demonstrates a lifetime of deviance from prescribed gender roles may be experiencing severe pathology. However, that person may also be expressing a very healthy level of ego strength and inner directedness in the face of unhealthy gender-prescribed norms. The clinician thus needs to assess whether the deviance is functional and serves positive purposes, or if it fails to be useful to the individual in her or his social context (Brown, 1990a).

The practitioner conducting a feminist analysis also needs to be aware of issues, patterns, or behaviors that occur with high frequency in one gender or the other, of the cultural reasons for men and women's positions in a society, and of the resultant impact on men and women's expressions of distress or types of problems (Brown, 1990a). Feminist practitioners reach beyond awareness, however, into direct inquiry into life events whose base rates are related to gender—for instance, experiences of interpersonal violence, sexual assault, or covert discrimination—because women rarely volunteer this information, and may, in fact, have repressed their memories of these experiences (Bass & Davis, 1988;

Brown, 1990a; Bryer et al., 1987). These assessment strategies require a substantial level of cultural literacy, because the North American White middle-class gender assumptions of most practitioners are not shared by those clients who differ from that cultural group. Awareness of different cultural assumptions, therefore, may require ongoing and intentional inquiry by practitioners. Such inquiry should also focus on historical changes that have occurred in gender roles during the client's lifetime (Brown, 1990a).

Additionally, a feminist approach to assessment (Brown, 1992) (a) differentiates between those behaviors, affect, and thinking that result from gender-role socialization and from high-frequency and psychologically traumatizing life events and those that result from other personality traits or disorders; (b) intentionally takes into account the organizing function in a woman's life of interpersonal relationships; (c) takes "into account the lifetime learning experiences of living in a sexist, racist, homophobic, ageist, and otherwise oppressive cultural context" (p. 220); and (d) inquires into the gender and other characteristics of the people involved, including the power differentials between them, and the repetitive interactions or reality experiences of the person being diagnosed, in particular taking into account the behavioral options and limits that result from social roles.

When feminists move beyond assessment into treatment, they deliberately create interdependent egalitarian relationships (Brown, 1990a,b, 1991a,b, 1992; Rothblum, 1982) with their clients, thus reducing the impact of society's power differentials, increasing individuation, and reducing stereotyping (Fiske, 1993). In contrast, according to Carmen et al. (1981), traditional therapy relationships replicate "the inequitable power distribution most women have had in their relationships with men as fathers, husbands, employers, and health professionals" (p. 1325). This raises the question of whether men should counsel women, whether a male-practitioner-to-female-client relationship can ever allow a woman to fully experience the sort of relationship that allows her to reclaim her own power. As Collins (1998) points out, in egalitarian relationships, "When people need each other to meet goals, they pay more attention to each other, construct more detailed profiles of each other, and are less likely to stereotype" (p. 109).

Feminist practitioners also actively seek to counter women's experiences and the consequent emotional difficulties by "acknowledging the effects of oppression, considering the impact of socially prescribed female roles, aiming for egalitarian interactions, examining [their] own values, and exploring feelings and views about ethnicity, class, gender, and sexual orientation" (Steen, 1991, as cited in Horsfall, 2001, p. 430). The counseling process may include educating the client about women's issues, working to empower the client, and encouraging expanded roles for both men and women (Rothblum, 1982).

Because feminist therapy recognizes the role of the larger community on women's problems, it also encourages intervention in the larger community. Therefore, feminist practitioners may use family therapy to involve partners in therapy; to particularly address domestic, childcare, and occupational roles of both partners; and to examine more flexible and nontraditional alternatives (Rothblum, 1982). Hare-Mustin (1980) encourages redefining responsibilities, equalizing power, and rethinking sex role stereotypes as part of such family work.

Group therapy may also be useful in providing a social network for women; in reducing isolation; in providing an environment to share experiences, support, and encouragement; and in letting women know that they are not alone in experiencing such difficulties. Skills training, including assertion training, may assist women to counter socialization that is not helpful to them. Career counseling may

help women to become more gainfully employed (Rothblum, 1982).

Rothblum (1982) continues by pointing out that depressed people are not always in the best position to do things to change their own situations. Therefore, community interventions may be another option for feminist intervention. For instance, education programs in schools, businesses, and community organizations may increase the available information on all of the above women's issues. Feminist practitioners may work at changing, consulting with, and advising institutions about factors that do harm to women. They may also create programs that bring people together who have similar difficulties (mothers with young children, women in nontraditional careers), and may train health professionals about women's issues.

Clearly, then, the feminist perspective "requires us to move out of our comfortable positions . . . to a position of identification and action" (Brown, 1991b, pp. 108–109). Rather than the examination of trauma existing solely as a scholarly exercise, it becomes "a step in challenging and changing those social institutions that wound and keep wounds open" toward a vision of relationships "in which mutuality and respect are the norm rather than power and dominance" (Brown, 1991b, p. 109). The personal thus becomes the political, and the larger society becomes the focus, in the attempt to turn painful knowledge into an "ethic of compassion" (p. 110).

However, Brown (1990a) cautions that

> Gender in assessment and psychotherapy should not become a special interest reserved for the practitioners of feminist and other gender-conscious approaches to therapy. . . . Every person has bias related to gender; without an awareness of that bias and its impact on our clinical judgment, and with access to data concerning its sources in our personal experiences and professional training, the assessment that takes place may be socially irresponsible, whereby the

assessor acts out her or his unresolved countertransferential responses in the form of inaccurate or incomplete diagnostic inquiry and findings. (p. 16)

Adopting a feminist stance in diagnosis, assessment, and therapy, however, is not without risks. Working to change a woman's situation so that she is no longer experiencing inequities on a day-to-day basis, requires changes beyond her own goals and activities; that is, the attitudes and behaviors of others in her life must change as well. When practitioners conduct feminist analysis, they most likely will raise the woman's consciousness; however, some of those others may not want to change. Consequently, the combination of consciousness raising in the woman and the refusal of these others to change may result in the deterioration of the immediate situation, perhaps resulting in divorce, ending jobs, and the like. In turn, this may negatively affect a woman's mental health (Gove, 1980).

CONCLUSION

Clearly, not all practitioners share the perspectives offered by feminist authors. On some level, we wonder how practitioners can afford not to be feminists or can practice ethically without practicing many of the feminist therapy tenets. As Brown (1991b) indicates, "we must, if we have any morality, question a society that subjects so many of its inhabitants to traumatic stressors" (p. 108). Despite our personal convictions, we are aware of substantial resistance in professional and public quarters about adopting a feminist perspective.

However, critically reflecting on the data and the questions posed does draw attention to the broader societal influences on DSM development, on diagnostic decision making, and on the treatment, more generally, of those groups in our society who have less power. Furthermore, considering the possibilities presented here focuses attention on who

benefits from diagnosis. Ethical practitioners seek ultimately to benefit their clients with their counseling procedures. However, they cannot extract themselves from the broader social and economic milieus within which they operate. Constant attention to the impact of these broader milieus on their work and balancing the benefits to the multiple stakeholders may be fundamental to ethical decision making.

With such questions being raised about the cultural and gender limitations of diagnoses, it seems to us that it becomes more clearly necessary for practitioners to be tentative in diagnosing those from diverse backgrounds, and to, as part of a more egalitarian relationship, co-construct an understanding of the problem *with* the client, rather than imposing a diagnosis *on* the client. The questions of diagnostic accuracy raised in Chapter 2 also apply doubly to practitioners who diagnose clients from diverse backgrounds. That is, how can practitioners be accurate when assuming only an individual description of a problem, without describing strengths, support systems, and positive characteristics, and without including a broader understanding of the cultural contexts in which the person was raised and in which the person currently resides? Beyond diagnosing the client's context and its impact lies the broader social constructionist question of the impact of culture on the mental health professional and on the counseling relationship. Social constructionists, for example, indicate that the questions asked while diagnosing tell us more about the diagnoser and the culture in which diagnosis takes place than about the client (Parker et al., 1995; Dickerson & Zimmerman, 1995; Wakefield, 1992).

Mental health professionals therefore err if they harbor preconceptions based on their life experiences that do not allow for wide variation in normal people. For instance, they err if they assume that a male cannot have an eating disorder or that a woman cannot have an antisocial personality disorder. They err if they consider that a strong, assertive woman or a gentle man who is interested in the arts is not accepting her or his gender. They err if they push all gay people to reconsider their sexual orientation as the central counseling issue, instead of listening to the counseling issue that is chosen by the gay client. They err if they are too certain and not tentative when diagnosing people from cultures different from their own, assuming that "normal" in the client's culture will look the same as "normal" in the practitioner's.

So, what does culturally sensitive and feminist diagnosis mean? We have offered a variety of possibilities in these two chapters. But might it also mean not diagnosing? Might it mean more broadly assessing the problem situation in conversation with the client, without entertaining the DSM system? Does it mean considering the DSM as one minor part of the broader scheme of diagnosis and assessment—a part currently necessary for obtaining funding for services—while considering all of the parts of a typical intake interview to be the more important guides to further treatment? Might DSM diagnosis be considered one story among many and, in the particular case of clients from groups who have historically had less power, might that story be less relevant or more harmful than other stories? Might culturally sensitive and feminist diagnosis require mental health professionals to diagnose and act to change oppressive systems, instead of merely sitting in their offices and requiring clients to change? These are difficult questions, but questions that need to be asked, and asked, and asked again, as mental health professionals struggle with the ethical dilemmas posed by mandates to be culturally sensitive while engaging in the diagnostic process.

5

Toward Resolving the Quandaries and Pursuing Ethical and Contextually Sensitive Diagnostic Practice

It is unfair and unwise to expect the *Diagnostic and Statistical Manual of Mental Disorders* (DSM) to be all things to all mental health professionals. Yet, based on the issues that we have presented, issues that are currently associated with the use of the DSM, the question looms: What can be done about the inconsistencies between the ethical mandates of mental health professionals and the assumptions of the DSM model of diagnosis? In the literature, much of the critical discourse related to professionals' use of the DSM has focused on "what not to do" versus "what to do." This chapter attempts to change that focus. We delineate strategies and offer activities, exercises, and cases that are designed to increase practitioners' and trainees' awareness of the ethical dilemmas inherent in using the DSM, while at the same time increasing their competence in contextually sensitive and thorough assessment practices. We also suggest ways for practitioners and trainees to actualize their commitment to

responsible use of the DSM classification system. In particular, we challenge practitioners and trainees to incorporate into their practice systemic, developmental, and multicultural "stories" about client problems and solutions to these problems. There are no easy resolutions to the complex issues associated with practitioners' use of the DSM, but we hope that these awareness-building activities will stimulate dialogue about DSM-related issues and controversies—dialogue that may eventually lead to changes in professional thinking, education, and practice. For the duration of this chapter, students in training, supervisees, and mental health practitioners will all be referred to as practitioners.

INCREASING VIGILANCE AND AWARENESS OF THE STRENGTHS AND LIMITATIONS OF THE DSM

Little research exists on people's micro-level decision-making processes related to using the DSM (Hill & Ridley, 2001). However, consciousness of the DSM's much publicized advantages and disadvantages may increase cautious and thoughtful diagnostic technique and approach.

More specifically, DSM diagnoses could be viewed from the perspective that abnormal behaviors are historically contingent and socially situated values and moralities, rather than objective, biologically based facts (Marecek, 1993). Marecek makes several suggestions for how educators and supervisors might thoughtfully teach students and supervisees about the DSM and its context. Seasoned mental health professionals should also find Marecek's suggestions helpful. For instance, Marecek states that when presenting the DSM, educators and supervisors might *change the subject* by bringing what has been excluded into discussions, for instance, the perspectives of women and other underrepresented groups to DSM discussions. Marecek also suggests *breaking the textbook habit* by reaching beyond the DSM and traditional textbooks to other materials on abnormal behavior and on controversies surrounding diagnosis. The following activities, and the exercises in all other sections of this chapter, are designed to assist mental health professionals in discovering ways to follow Marecek's and other authors' suggestions for increasing vigilance. Some of the activities apply directly to practitioners and some are addressed to trainees.

Activity One

- Goal: To encourage empathy with client perspectives on diagnostic labeling. To reduce the tendency for detachment from and objectification of the client when applying diagnostic labels.

Exercise 1: Students or supervisees engage in an exercise in which they visualize and imagine what it would be like to be diagnosed with various diagnoses. They are then asked to consider what they would least like to be diagnosed with, as well as to discuss

attributional words that they associate with each diagnosis (e.g., good, lovable, concerned, bad, lazy, weak, struggling).

The instructor or supervisor then chooses several diagnoses and presents a comprehensive story of a person so diagnosed. The students or supervisees then reconsider their attributions and explore how their perspectives may have changed after the whole person was considered. The exercise might follow the steps below:

Step 1: Close your eyes and visualize a mental health provider presenting you with his or her assessment of your problem. The provider indicates that you are "borderline" (or have a multiple personality disorder, or schizophrenia, or an anxiety disorder, etc.).

Step 2: Open your eyes and discuss as a group what it was like to receive the pronouncement. What did you feel? Were your feelings more positive or more negative? What did you want to do? How did you feel toward the mental health provider? How did it change your perspectives on your life or on possible solutions to your struggles?

Step 3: Write out the names of 10 diagnoses, making sure to include the diagnoses for the cases in Figures 5.1 and 5.2. Next to them write any word (attribution) that comes to mind about these diagnoses. Continue until you have a number of words next to each diagnosis.

Step 4: Which diagnosis would you least like to be diagnosed with? Why? Which diagnosis might you prefer? Why?

Step 5: Read the cases in Figures 5.1 and 5.2.

Step 6: Process any changes in your attributions about clients with these diagnoses.

Exercise 2: If you could remove any diagnosis from the DSM for any reason, what would it be? What don't you like about this diagnosis? How would you feel about your closest friend receiving this diagnosis? If you could add any diagnosis to the DSM what would it be? What do you like about this diagnosis? How would you feel about your closest friend receiving

---

Case 5.1

DaShawn is a 7-year-old African-American boy who attends a primarily White school. A year ago he was diagnosed by his family physician with Attention-Deficit Hyperactivity Disorder (ADHD). On receiving this diagnosis, his parents and teachers began to attribute all of his undesirable behaviors to his ADHD. His teachers would frequently make him stand in the hall and would disregard much of what he said as being caused by his disorder. DaShawn became increasingly isolated from his family, friends, and school peers. Simultaneously, noting DaShawn's vulnerability and increasing isolation, a school "bully" began to tease and harass DaShawn. This harassment only increased DaShawn's sense of isolation. DaShawn was unable to express his pain and frustration, and he began to increasingly act out in order to get people to notice his increasing frustration.

- ❖ How might DaShawn's reactions be adaptive given his life circumstances?
- ❖ What impact did DaShawn's diagnosis have on his situation?
- ❖ How might the stigma of the diagnosis have made his situation worse?
- ❖ If DaShawn's situation continues, might some additional problems develop?
- ❖ What type of actions might you take in working with DaShawn to prevent additional problems from developing?
- ❖ How might DaShawn's situation be affected by his being in the minority at his school?
- ❖ How might DaShawn's ostensible ADHD behaviors be related to his being a person of color in a primarily White school?

---

this diagnosis? If you feel differently about your closest friend receiving either of the two diagnoses, why do you think this is?

Activity Two

- Goal: To increase awareness about common perceptions of mental illness and to explore the roots and sustainers of negative perceptions.

Exercise 1: Was there anyone in your family who everyone knew was a little "off"? What words were used about that person? "Special"? "Touched"? Others? How often do you or people you know use the terms nuts, crazy, mental, insane, obsessive, compulsive, manic-depressive, and the like in everyday language and daily conversations, whether as a joke or in all seriousness, to refer to someone's behavior that causes a problem? How do you think that those diagnosed with mental disorders view people's use of such vocabulary? How do you think this everyday slang language affects perceptions of the mentally ill? What do you think about these words being used?

Exercise 2: Make a list of five popular movie characters who have been portrayed as being mentally ill. How were they portrayed? How do you think these portrayals impact people's perceptions of mental illness? Are there any movie portrayals of the mentally ill that capture their positive contributions or characteristics? Practitioners might also view movie clips to trigger responses to these questions. For example, the movies *Girl Interrupted* or *Fatal Attraction* show negative portrayals of mentally ill women. More positive portrayals of people diagnosed as having mental disorders and/or mental retardation are: *Benny and Joon, A Beautiful Mind, Rain Man, Shine, Good Will Hunting,* and *I Am Sam.*

Activity Three

- Goal: To increase an understanding of the political nature of some DSM diagnoses by exploring who promoted the inclusion of the diagnoses, and what their reasons might have been for wanting the diagnoses included.

Case 5.2

Jordan is a 41-year-old African-American male. He has a long history of receiving services within the mental health system. Jordan meets with you during a recent hospitalization for a suicide attempt. He seems uninterested during the interview, is not forthcoming with information, and states he's "been through this a million times and that you can't help him." You are aware that you feel annoyed with Jordan.

In reviewing his charts, you see that he has historically been diagnosed with borderline personality disorder, major depression-recurrent, pathological gambling, impulsive self-mutilation, and adult antisocial behavior. Jordan has attempted suicide multiple times and is perceived by many health care providers as "difficult" and "manipulative." Jordan often fails to follow through on recommendations made by providers and can appear "needy," "volatile," and "helpless," as documented in many of his providers' progress notes.

Jordan is aware of the annoyance that many providers feel toward him. He is bitter about the multiple diagnoses and "uncaring" treatment he receives. He feels very misunderstood and has not been open with his providers about his past experiences. In reality, his father and mother were sexually and physically abusive. His football coach also raped him in the ninth grade. He suffers many trauma reactions secondary to his childhood experiences and many of his behaviors are attempts to keep him from committing suicide and spiraling into a deep depression.

- ❖ How might Jordan's reactions be adaptive given his life circumstances?
- ❖ What impact did Jordan's diagnoses have on his situation?
- ❖ How might the stigma of the diagnoses have made his situation worse?
- ❖ How might Jordan's diagnoses help him or the treatment process?
- ❖ If you were the practitioner, how would you manage your feelings of annoyance toward Jordan?
- ❖ What strengths or resources might Jordan have and how could you assess these and use them in your work together?
- ❖ How might Jordan's behaviors be expectable developmental reactions to abnormal situations?
- ❖ How might Jordan's gender affect his situation, his perception of his past and present situation, and your understanding of his situation?

Exercise: Why do you think that many groups are eager to have their viewpoints presented in the DSM? Why do you think some groups have advocated strongly for having certain diagnoses removed from or kept from inclusion in the DSM? For instance, why do you think that opponents of abortion have developed the disorder of Post-Abortion Trauma (e.g., to support their position that abortion should be illegal? to assure payment for psychological care for these women?)? Why do you think that those wanting to advocate on behalf of battered women who have killed their batterers have coined the disorder Battered Woman Syndrome (e.g., to reduce the blame and legal liability of those so battered? to assure payment for psychological care for these women?)? Why do you think that those who believe themselves to be falsely accused of sexual abuse coined the term False Memory Syndrome (e.g., to lend weight to their position in battling those who they claim have falsely accused them)? Why do you think Premenstrual Dysphoric Disorder was recently added to the appendix of the *Diagnostic and Statistical Manual of Mental Disorders,* 4th ed., Text Revision (DSM-IV-TR) as a diagnosis for future study (e.g., might its inclusion financially benefit those who would treat the ones so diagnosed)? Discuss the case in Figure 5.3.

Activity Four

- Goal: To develop an appreciation of the idea that diagnoses are not set "facts," but context ridden, ever-changing labels (e.g., at one point, the DSM labeled gays and lesbians

---

Case 5.3

You are an advocate and lawyer for women leaving domestic violence relationships and become aware that the developers of the newest DSM are considering a diagnosis entitled sadistic personality disorder. What political concerns strike you about the development of such a diagnosis? What might the ramifications and implications of such a diagnosis be? How would such a diagnosis impact your clients and perpetrators of sadistic crimes and behaviors?

Now consider how you might answer the same questions if you were a lawyer for a person who regularly assaulted his wife.

---

as mentally ill). To become aware of the ever changing line between what is considered to be normal or abnormal behavior.

Exercise: In order to understand the contextual issues associated with diagnoses, trace the development of a diagnosis through various editions of the DSM, paying attention to the historical events that were occurring at the time of publication. How is the boundary drawn between disorder on one hand and eccentricity and/or crime on the other? What kinds of circumstances surround the death of some diagnoses and the birth of others? What social contexts correlate with changes in or exclusions/inclusions of different diagnoses? Where does one draw the line between pathology and normal adaptation to stress? Which diagnoses that were previously included, but are currently excluded, might have merely been reflective of non-mainstream choices? Consider these questions as you review the case in Figure 5.4.

Activity Five

- Goal: To encourage awareness of and sensitivity to the complexity of the diagnostic decision-making processes.

Exercise: Invite people who are or have been in some type of counseling for various disorders to share their experiences (e.g., in a class or supervision group). Hearing personal stories can encourage practitioners to consider the layers of dynamics that affect therapists' diagnostic decisions. Such an experience can also provide a better alternative to the practice of many instructors in which trainees are asked to diagnose a fictitious person in a case study with the understanding that there is one "right" diagnosis. Guests can be given the following questions to think about before coming to class: (a) When did you become "diagnosed" with this problem? (b) What experiences did you have that led you to seek help or to find out what was wrong? (For example, what would you say your symptoms were? How did those symptoms affect your work, love, family life, etc.?) (c) What was your life like before you received the diagnosis? (d) What impact has the diagnosis had on your life? (e) How does the "disorder" affect you currently? (f) What kinds of help have you sought and what has been most effective? (g) What do you currently do to manage the problem? (h) What recommendations do you has for mental health professionals who may encounter people with your diagnosis? (i) What would you say are the most important things for mental health professionals to remember about people with your diagnosis?

BROADENING PRACTITIONERS' PERCEPTIONS OF DIAGNOSTIC ASSESSMENT: MORE THAN JUST THE DSM

Diagnosis should include "understanding fully what happens in the mind and body of the

---

Case 5.4

Amy is a creative, 19-year-old, fun-loving woman whose mother expresses concerns about her and asks you to counsel Amy. Amy prides herself in "doing whatever she wants whenever she wants." Amy says she really doesn't care about what other people think, as long as she is having fun and expressing herself.

Amy brags about her 25 tattoos and is eager to show you her arm, which is completely covered in tattoos. She explains that her favorite tattoo is the one on the back of her neck. You see that it is a date, and when asked, Amy points out that it is the date of her dad's death. She likes this tattoo because it is the most meaningful to her. She adds that she will put the dates of all of her family members' deaths on her body so that they will always be remembered.

As Amy speaks, you notice that her tongue is swollen. She says this is because she just got her tongue pierced; this is her tenth piercing. She has 5 of the 10 piercings in her back. They are big hoop rings that she can be suspended from. Amy loves being suspended by her skin because it gives her an invigorating feeling of freedom. She also says people call her a freak because she has pink and blue hair and extremely pale skin. She doesn't care because she prides herself on being unique.

Amy practices magic and belongs to a cult that worships the "Star Savior." Her cult believes that one must turn to the stars for all answers in life. They chant to the "Star Savior," asking the higher power for happiness and good fortune. Amy says that when you do something that the "Star Savior" likes, you will know, and it will speak to you in your sleep. It is important to Amy to do what she believes the "Star Savior" would want.

Like her grandmother, an Appalachian healer, Amy earns a living by reading the palms of people on the streets at night. She sets up a tent every night and people come to get their fortunes read. She says that she is a "witch," therefore, this occupation is her calling. She believes that she is a very good palm reader and that most of her prophecies come true.

Amy further adds that she does not come out in the daylight. Her cult believes that the light is dangerous and slowly kills people. Every night, after she is done reading palms, Amy hangs out in a Gothic bar. She likes to "hang out with her kind of people." She leaves the bar before the sun comes up and sleeps all day long until it is dark out again.

- ❖ What DSM diagnoses might apply to Amy's behaviors?
- ❖ What cultural/contextual issues might also be considered?
- ❖ What developmental issues might be considered in applying a DSM diagnosis?
- ❖ Where is the line between subculture and deviance drawn?
- ❖ Are Amy's behaviors different from those of any religious zealot? If so, how?
- ❖ How could your personal values affect your conceptualization of Amy's behavior?
- ❖ What if Amy does not want to be in counseling and does not want you to ascribe a diagnosis?
- ❖ If Amy states that she does not consent for you to diagnose her, but you have to diagnose her to be reimbursed, what will you do?
- ❖ What strengths and resources does Amy possess that could be used to help her in counseling?

---

person who presents for care" (Mezzich, 1999a, p. 138), not just identifying a disorder or differentiating one disorder from another. The World Psychiatric Association's *International Guidelines for Diagnostic Assessment* (in Mezzich, 1995) include two steps in diagnosis: identifying a diagnosis while doing the assessment and committing to attain the ultimate goal of diagnosis, that is, promoting the client's wellness. Furthermore, Mezzich (1995, 2002) and others (e.g., McLaughlin, 2002) suggest that a comprehensive diagnosis should integrate the perspectives of the client, the practitioner, and significant others, such as friends and family members. Consideration of and integration of many perspectives are essential to ethical diagnosis and represent an understanding of diagnosis as broader than the application of a label and a number.

Currently, as its developers intended, the DSM focuses only on problematic behaviors (Ivey & Ivey, 1998; Jensen & Hoagwood, 1997; Sperry, 2002b). As a result, practitioners should always be aware that the DSM diagnostic process is only a piece of a comprehensive assessment. Not only do other diagnostic considerations beyond the DSM exist, but the DSM can only be considered helpful to the degree that it helps practitioners in their work with clients (e.g., triggering referrals for medication or hospitalization or special programs). For example, Sadler and Hulgus (1994) and others (Lo & Fung, 2003; Nelson, 2002) state that for assessment to contribute effectively to client care, it must include a careful description and operationalization of all relevant phenomena (e.g., individual symptoms, functional abilities, family interactions, contextual factors, and longitudinal-historical information). They consider these phenomena to exist on three levels: syndromes of personal history, syndromes of the interpersonal environment, and syndromes of the "extrapersonal" environment. A practitioner might therefore consider the DSM as a first step toward helping clients, while being aware of the DSM's intended (and limited) scope, and extending the assessment process beyond DSM diagnosis.

Other conceptualizations of diagnoses, perceptions that consider the DSM in context, have also been proposed. For example, McAuliffe and Eriksen (1999) and others (e.g., Anderson & Goolishian, 1992; Tomm, 1989) state that diagnosis is a construction of meaning that is accomplished during a dynamic process and that diagnoses should be co-created together with all who are involved in the clinical relationship. Tomm (1989) also recommends considering diagnoses as case-and-situation specific, as there are a wide variety of potential descriptions and explanations for the presenting difficulties. These diagnoses should further be considered to be evolving as new information becomes available over time, rather than as static, objective truths. The practitioner is, then, according to Tomm and others (Dietz, 2000; Larner, 2000) not an expert *doing* diagnosis to the client, but a facilitator in forming diagnostic meanings.

Activity Six

- Goal: To encourage multiplistic and divergent thinking about the DSM and its uses.

Exercise: Debates are one way to encourage an understanding of the complexity of the DSM and to reduce dualistic thinking. In a class or another group setting, students or practitioners can be assigned a point to argue and can read, talk with people, and access other resources in order to be prepared to adequately support their argument. Debate topics might include such controversies as:

- Mental disorders are located within the individual versus disorders are located within society.
- Abnormal behavior can be differentiated clearly from normal behavior versus abnormal behavior cannot be distinguished clearly from normal behavior.
- Diagnostic labels hinder the effective treatment of persons with mental disorders versus diagnostic labels contribute to the effective treatment of persons with mental disorders.
- Women have higher rates of psychopathology versus selection bias and cultural definitions result in overdiagnosing women.
- We are overdiagnosing certain disorders (e.g., attention-deficit hyperactivity disorder) because of the "times" versus diagnosis is an accurate and objective process regardless of the "times."

Caution: People with a strong dualistic cognitive style can turn debates into combative and unpleasant experiences. Instructors and supervisors may need to set up ground rules to preclude such occurrences and to encourage listening and learning from others.

Activity Seven

- Goal: To encourage considering (or adding) alternative explanations for clients' experiences beyond a "mental disorder" conceptualization. To help practitioners view diagnoses as case and situation specific. To facilitate an emphasis on client strengths.

Exercise 1: Review the cases that have already been presented. Decide how you would, without deciding on a diagnosis, help the clients in these cases. What are your thoughts about *not* giving the clients a diagnosis? Could you provide services without a diagnosis? What would be the practical and theoretical limitations of doing so? Did your conceptualizations about the client and the client's treatment seem different without ascribing a diagnosis? If so, how? Might you have been more apt to focus on wellness and client strengths or on a particular theoretical conceptualization when not ascribing DSM diagnoses? Or did you feel the need for a diagnosis to clarify your treatment decisions?

Exercise 2: For the same cases, develop a DSM diagnosis. Next identify five alternative or additional explanations for the etiology of clients' presented difficulties—explanations beyond the DSM's medical model. Consider, for instance, systemic, developmental, multicultural, and feminist explanations. To assist with this process, develop a comprehensive assessment that includes family history, social history, educational or employment history, counseling and clinical history, substance use history, medical history, legal or financial history, religious/spiritual history, cultural

impacts on client, and strengths/wellnesses. After doing so, discuss how the alternative explanations differentially impact your thoughts about helping the client. How did developing a comprehensive assessment change your treatment decisions (that is, compared with trying to come up with treatment options before assessment)? To what degree did your explanation extend beyond the facts and into your theoretical or values orientation? It is helpful to do this exercise in a group in which practitioners espouse different theoretical positions so as to clarify the impact of different theory and values perspectives on the derived explanations.

Activity Eight

- Goal: To facilitate and practice deconstructing clients' language in order to understand clients' perceptions of their reality, rather than merely "accepting" the language and assuming that one knows what the clients mean.

Exercise: In pseudodiagnostic interviews conducted with colleagues or peers, listen for casual use of words (i.e., lingo) such as "depressed," "obsessive," "codependent," "overweight," "good communicator," "black sheep," or other words that clients use to describe themselves, words that could have multiple meanings. Help the clients to deconstruct—that is to take apart the meanings of these words by examining their context—the language that they use about themselves. For instance, ask questions of the clients such as, "What do you mean by 'obsessive' (or other words that they attribute to themselves)?" "When did you first associate that word with yourself?" "Was anyone else instrumental in making you think that you were 'obsessive'?" "In what context did you first consider yourself (or were you considered by others to be) 'obsessive'?" "How is your situation today different or the same?" After the interview, discuss as a group how your perceptions of the clients changed as the "clients" deconstructed the language that they used about themselves. How would your shift in perspective change your sense of the best way to help the "clients"?

Activity Nine

- Goal: To avoid making premature diagnostic decisions, as research illustrates that delaying diagnostic decisions leads to greater accuracy, and that once made, practitioners find it quite difficult to shift their diagnostic impressions despite new information (Elstein, Shulman, & Sprafka, 1978; Hill & Ridley, 2001).

Exercise: Review Part One, from an initial session, of the case in Figure 5.5. Provide a diagnosis. Next read Part Two of the case, which includes third session information, and again, diagnose the client. Finally, read Part Three of the case, which includes fifth session information. Process the (probably) different diagnostic results and what led to the different results. What do you think about how your attributions changed with more information? What does this tell you about the diagnostic process? How might you postpone final decisions about a client's diagnosis or avoid making static and premature decisions about such diagnoses? How might your later attributions help the counseling process? What will help you to consider diagnoses to be dynamic concepts that evolve with new information and time, rather than static, objective truths?

Activity Ten

- Goal: To encourage the consideration of strengths and how they can be used and emphasized in counseling.

Exercise 1: Identify a problem that you are currently experiencing. What strengths and resources do you possess that could help you in resolving this problem? Now, shift perspectives: What diagnosis might someone else give you at this point? Did such a diagnosis change the strategies for resolving or managing the problem from the strategies you previously considered? If so, how?

Exercise 2: Now review the case in Figure 5.6. Identify the client's strengths and resources and how these might be used to resolve or manage her problem. How might such an approach differ from or add to approaches developed on the basis of the diagnosis only?

Activity Eleven

- Goal: To explore the numerous issues and layers of considerations that contribute to diagnostic decision making, and to encourage advanced levels of conceptualization and thinking about diagnoses.

Exercise: Consider case examples that are ambiguous and not clear-cut, cases that have layers of issues. Diagnose these diagnostically "ambiguous" clients using the DSM system. Next, use a more comprehensive assessment system (such as that suggested in Activity Seven) to broaden your conceptualization of the client and the case. Begin, for instance, with the cases in Figures 5.7, 5.8, and 5.9.

UNDERSTANDING GENDER AND CULTURAL DYNAMICS IN THE DIAGNOSTIC PROCESS

Ethical practice requires practitioners to be sensitive to issues of diversity. How does one do this during the diagnostic process? Research indicates that students who are sensitized to gender issues from a feminist perspective are better able to avoid making sexist assumptions and interventions in working with and diagnosing clients (Leslie & Clossick,

Case 5.5

Part One: A 20-year-old woman, Jenna, who looks to be 60 pounds overweight, comes in complaining that she is fat, dislikes herself, doesn't fit in with the other college kids, can't attract the attention of any of the guys that she is attracted to, and despite many diets is not successful in losing weight. She says she sticks to the diets for a week or so, but then she "loses it" and stuffs herself. When in the midst of such "stuffing" she doesn't feel like she has any control, that the food has control over her. After such a binge, she feels depressed and guilty and more unhappy with herself.

Question: What diagnosis might you give this young woman?

Activity: Write down words that come to mind about a person such as this were you to meet her walking through campus or have her in one of your classes. Then share these words and write them on the board.

Question: What stereotypes do you have of obese people, and how do your values relate to these stereotypes?

Part Two: The counselor discovers during her assessment that interpersonally, Jenna is quite perky, cheery, and personable. She participates in student government, sings in the gospel choir on campus, earns great grades, and was nominated for student of the year by her professors. She is currently serving as a resident assistant in her dorm, and many of her residents come to her for "counsel" when they are hurting or are in bad situations. At Christmas time, on special occasions, or on people's birthdays, she makes lovely crafts as gifts and decorations, which others really appreciate.

Question: How might your diagnosis change given this information?

Activity: In a second column on the board, write down any new words that come to mind about this person.

Part Three: As the counselor explores the client's history, she finds that Jenna comes from a very close Southern Baptist family. Both of her parents came from small families in which religion was considered harmful by one of the spouses. They decided to raise their children Christian because of benefits that they had observed in Christian families. They had three children, of whom Jenna is the oldest. The mother was always watching her weight, as Jenna remembers, although Jenna never remembers her mother being overweight. The parents were very involved in their children's lives: science fairs, PTA, community sports events, taking the children skiing, camping, and to church. Jenna remembers that her parents had a lot of rules, many more than her friends seemed to have had. Other parents had described her mother as controlling and perfectionistic, although Jenna wasn't clear what they meant. Jenna's middle sister was somewhat of a "black sheep," running away during high school, becoming involved with drugs, and hanging out with older guys that her parents didn't approve of. This sister went to counseling to work on these issues. Jenna, on the other hand, graduated fifth in her high school class, received honors at entrance in college, took all advanced placement classes, was in student government, played after-school sports, was the president of her church youth group, and participated in many other extracurricular activities. She reports that throughout high school she was always struggling with her weight, would be on regular diets that she would "blow," and always thought that the skinny girls got dates when she didn't.

Activity: In a third column, write down any new words that come to mind about this person. Write these words on the board in a different column.

1996). Leslie and Clossick's research further suggests that training in gender issues alone, or in cultural issues alone, without the feminist perspective or without a review of power dynamics and oppression, is not enough to create such sensitivity. It seems, then, that

---

Case 5.6 (excerpted from White, 2002)

Your client Gabrielle meets the DSM criteria for Bulimia Nervosa–Purging Type (i.e., recurrent episodes of binge eating, compensatory behavior in order to prevent weight gain, self-evaluation unduly influenced by body shape and weight).

Gabrielle was asked to consider the ways that the bulimia influenced her. She stated the following: negative self-talk and feelings about her body, skipping meals, repeatedly weighing herself, binge eating, eating larger amounts of food than intended, vomiting after eating, and feeling ashamed.

Gabrielle was then asked to identify her strengths and resources. With encouragement and repeated questioning, Gabrielle was able to identify the following: enjoys writing/journaling, gets good grades/overall good school performance, manages her time well, keeps to a schedule, knows a great deal about nutrition, is highly motivated, and is a fighter.

Based on her perceptions of how the bulimia was influencing her, Gabrielle was asked to identify the goals she wanted to achieve. She indicated the following: decrease negative self-talk and negative feelings about her body, eat two meals per day and weigh herself once a month, increase feelings of control over her food intake and decrease feelings of being out-of-control when eating, and achieve zero episodes of vomiting behavior.

The counselor urged her to shift her goals into positive, active language (e.g., increasing positive self-talk about body), instead of negatively stated goals and language (e.g., decreasing negative self-talk about body).

- ❖ Help Gabrielle think about how to do this, and how to identify the strengths and resources that she might use in approaching the goals that she identifies.
- ❖ How is this strength-based approach different from a medical-model, pathology-oriented approach?
- ❖ What impact might her gender and culture have on her issues?

---

training in gender and other cultural issues that includes these critical factors may be necessary for greater cultural sensitivity in diagnostic decision making.

Valasquez, Johnson, and Brown-Cheatham (1993) contribute other ideas about how to become thoughtful and competent in diagnostic decision making when working with people of color. They indicate that people should be (a) trained in the basic fundamentals of the diagnostic decision-making process; (b) taught to be critical of the DSM, to recognize its imperfections, and to identify critical incidents in which DSM diagnoses can be unethical, dangerous, and oppressive to people of color; (c) encouraged to examine beliefs about normal and abnormal behavior; and (d) given opportunities to actually apply and use diagnostic skills with people of color. Such opportunities

offer mental health professionals a chance to learn about the wide variations that exist in (a) perspectives about interpersonal relationships, especially in families, (b) perceptions of power in relationships, and (c) cultural role expectations, all of which should be considered in diagnostic decision making.

Castillo (1997) contends that providing a culturally sensitive helping environment can help facilitate the development of a therapeutic alliance and provide an opportunity for the culturally different client to obtain optimal care. He claims that cultural assessment, or an assessment of the impact the person's culture has on the person's experiences, is critical because culture structures clinical reality: "mental illnesses can be constructed, maintained, exacerbated, and treated on several different levels simultaneously" (p. 55). For

---

Case 5.7

Lourdes is a 30-year-old immigrant from Puerto Rico who says that she is unhappy in her life because she has not made many friends in the United States. She feels very lonely and isolated. She is sad and would like to work on feeling more grateful and happy while learning how to become a better wife. She misses all of her old friends in Puerto Rico and longs to see them again.

Lourdes and her husband arrived in the United States 2 years ago. They have no children, but do have a few other family members who came to the United States with them. Lourdes is unemployed, but her husband owns a convenience store. She works for her husband at the store when he requests her service. When she is not working for her husband, she is at home cooking and cleaning and tending to home matters. She says that this is what women "do," and she feels comfortable with this arrangement.

However, she feels lonely being in the house for days at a time. She says that in Puerto Rico when she had to stay at home all day, she could at least socialize with her neighbors and family, but she has had difficulty connecting with her neighbors here in the United States.

Lourdes says that she is having trouble sleeping and has had appetite changes, as she is often worrying about various issues. She says that she worries that she did not make the right thing for dinner or that the house will not be clean enough for her husband. She also worries that she will never make any new friends. She indicates that she often is jumpy because she is afraid she is forgetting something or will make a mistake and upset her husband. She says that when she is not cooking or cleaning she feels lethargic, sad, and worried.

Lourdes wishes that her husband had more time for her, but "realizes" that she is being selfish with his time. She says that she knows that it is important for him to be at work and to tend to his social life. She indicates that her husband has several girlfriends and while she sometimes feels jealous, she would never challenge his behaviors. She is not upset that her husband has girlfriends. Her husband gets mad at her and sometimes becomes violent if she asks him to spend more time with her. She said she also feels guilty that she has not been able to provide her husband with children, and she notes that he often castigates her for not being able to get pregnant.

The next time Lourdes comes into the office she has a black eye. The counselor also notices several bruises on her arms. When questioned about the bruises, she says that her husband hit her the night before because she was in a bad mood and asked him to stay home instead of going out with his friends. She says that she came to this appointment to tell the counselor that it would be her last appointment. Her husband does not want her to come anymore because he feels that it is disrespectful to him for her to see the counselor. He also doesn't want her participating in anything that takes away from his time with her.

Without the context of domestic violence, what diagnoses might have best fit this client?

- ❖ How does the domestic violence context change your diagnostic impressions?
- ❖ How do you think that long-term contexts, such as living in a domestic violence situation, affect a client's DSM profile?
- ❖ How might your values affect your conceptualization of the client's situation?
- ❖ How might the client's gender/culture affect her perceptions of her situation?
- ❖ If the client ever needed to go to court to obtain a restraining order, press domestic violence charges, obtain a divorce, and the like, and the court ordered your files, what would the implications be of the different diagnoses you mentioned above?
- ❖ If the client continues in counseling, how might you play a preventative role with this client?

---

instance, emotions, he says, are connected with culture at three stages: the initial appraisal of the meaning of an event based on culturally determined norms and roles, the emotional sensation or experience, and a culture-based behavioral response. An accurate assessment

---

Case 5.8

You begin counseling Angela, a 28-year-old female. Angela reports that she'd like help in decreasing her anxiety. She indicates constant tension, irritableness, tiredness, worrying, and occasional panic reactions. She notes that she has a history of strained relationships and has difficulty trusting others. She also reports that she self-injures by cutting her arms and legs and has difficulty feeling at ease and "real." She states, "I don't know who I am or where I'm going. Life feels so chaotic." During your intake interview you notice that Angela is difficult to connect with and seems very distracted and agitated.

❖ At this point, what DSM diagnostic labels might apply?
❖ What additional information do you need before applying a formal diagnosis?

You obtain a release of information to talk with Angela's mom. "Since the rape and the time she moved in with me 3 months ago, she begs me every day to never make her leave," says Ms. Connor about her daughter.

❖ How does this information change your initial diagnostic impressions?

Angela appears to be somewhat restless and guarded during your second session, but when you ask about the rape and validate her experience, she relaxes and shares her story. She reports that she was raped while walking home from work 3 months ago, and the rape triggered memories of early sexual abuse inflicted by her father. Now driving everywhere rather than walking, she continues to function well at work, but finds herself unable to live on her own.

When asked what prompted her to pursue counseling, Angela reluctantly pulls up the sleeves of her shirt, revealing multiple slash type cuts and scars. In tears, Angela explains that when she feels overwhelmed by thoughts of her abuse as a child and recent rape, she distracts herself by making superficial cuts on her arms. She explains that she continually thinks about what has happened to her, especially when she's alone, and that she feels sad most of the time.

Angela reports that she was able to trust men earlier in her life. However, she has felt uncomfortable around men since her rape, and now believes that they are untrustworthy. She has recently begun working in a women's clothing store, and as a result rarely has to deal with men. Angela carries pepper spray in the event that she should ever find herself alone with a man.

❖ Based on this additional information, what DSM diagnoses best apply?
❖ What additional information do you need to make a formal diagnosis?

---

of emotion or behavior is not possible without an assessment of cultural schemas. The practitioner, therefore, needs to know what types of emotions a particular cultural group experiences, which emotions are elicited by what situations, what particular emotions mean to indigenous observers, what means of expression of particular emotions exist in that culture, what emotions are considered proper or improper for a person of a particular social status, and how unexpressed emotions are handled. Castillo further urges practitioners

to treat both the illness (client's subjective experience of being sick) *and* the disease (practitioner's diagnosis).

Castillo (1997) provides the following guidelines to enable mental health professionals to offer clients a culturally sensitive diagnosis:

1. *Assess the client's cultural identity.* For treatment to be effective, mental health professionals must first understand the client, and they cannot do so without understanding the client's position culturally. Cultural

---

Case 5.9

Case: Melanie, a 30-year-old secretary, recently began receiving counseling from her company's Employee Assistance Program at her employer's insistence. Because of her preoccupation at work, Melanie does not always complete the amount of paperwork that is required by her employer. Melanie admits that she usually has a lot on her mind, and that she sometimes feels distracted and anxious, especially when she's not at home. She has a good rapport with her coworkers, as well as a loving and supportive husband.

Melanie grew up and, until recently, continued to live in a very poor neighborhood and had limited resources (food, money, clothes, etc.). She recalls a winter night when one of her neighbors was actually murdered. More recently, Melanie was able to leave her neighborhood, and with her husband, move into a safer area. She began working as a secretary one year ago.

Melanie keeps three locks on the door to her home and often worries that she forgot to lock one. She sometimes finds it hard to go to work because she is so worried that she'll forget to lock one of the locks. She reports, "Once my mind starts going, I think of one thing after another, and I worry about everything." She continues, "What if someone breaks into my home, or something inside catches on fire, or I forget to refrigerate some food, or my car dies and I can't get home before dark?" She also reports that on some days, she asks her husband to check the house on his lunch break, and she anxiously awaits his phone call.

- ❖ What DSM diagnoses might Melanie meet the criteria for?
- ❖ If you did not consider her context or history, what diagnoses might you ascribe?
- ❖ What role do her history, development, and context play in how you conceptualize her situation and ascribe a diagnosis?

---

beliefs often vary among individuals. The professional should never assume that a culturally different client has accepted the values and norms of his or her own culture. To understand the client culturally, mental health professionals should obtain information from the client about language, religious beliefs, educational status, societal norms, social status, and gender roles.

2. *Identify sources of cultural information relevant to the client.* Culturally sensitive professionals study the cultures of the clients whom they are likely to see in their practice; clearly, fully understanding all cultures is impossible. Information about a client's culture can be obtained through reading relevant books, visiting religious organizations, and consulting with key members of a cultural community, among other methods.

3. Assess the *cultural meaning of a client's problem and symptoms.* If a mental health professional only treats a client's symptoms and not the cause of the symptoms, the course and outcome of the case is likely to be poor. The mental health professional must understand the client's beliefs about the development of the illness. What does the client believe to be the cause of the symptoms/problem, the problem's effects on self and others, and the symptom's treatment? Views of mental illness vary in different cultures, as do beliefs about the professional's role in treatment. In some cultures, for instance, problems are perceived to be caused by spirit possession, bad luck, or excess semen. Without responding to these perceptions, a clinician is unlikely to succeed in forming a working alliance with the client, a necessary precursor to successful treatment.

4. Consider the *impacts and effects of family, work, and community on the complaint, including stigma and discrimination that may be associated with mental illness in the client's culture.* Mental health professionals should assess clients and their illnesses within the total sociocultural context.

Clients, even those with severe mental illness, are sensitive to the cultural meanings and responses to their illnesses that are experienced in their social environment. It is important for the professional to learn about the client's experiences with stigma and discrimination.

5. *Assess personal biases.* In treating the culturally different client, professionals should be aware of their own biases, values, and stereotypes. If professionals are not aware of their own cultural schemas, these schemas may be projected onto the client, and may result in improper diagnosis and treatment. Mental health professionals should attempt to see the situation from the client's perspective as much as possible.

6. *Plan treatment collaboratively.* The mental health professional and client should collaborate on developing counseling goals and methods for reaching those goals. When the goals are understood and are significant to the client, the client will have more incentive to reach for them.

Castillo adds the following suggestions for culturally sensitive assessment and counseling:

- adjust the interviewing style (i.e., eye contact, personal space, rate of speech) to the norms of the client;
- do not use symptom scales without validating them in the new culture; remember that different symptoms mean different things in different cultures;
- consult with and work in collaboration with qualified folk healers;
- use symbols from the client's culture as part of the treatment;
- reduce the unknown by supporting the client's own understanding of the illness, as long as his or her understanding includes the possibility of treatment and eventual cure; Castillo (1997) considers this ethical, even if the client's understanding is not "true," and he points out that very few of our widely promoted understandings are empirically based;

- increase the manageability or the client's sense of "control or competence to meet the demands of the illness" (p. 80);
- increase understanding of the function of the illness, its purpose, and the moral or religious reason behind it;
- use symbolic, ritualistic healing in order to shift clients' cognitions about the problem, the clients' meanings, and thus their emotions.

According to Castillo, following these steps gains the culturally different client the opportunity to obtain optimal care and outcomes from counseling and other interventions.

Activity Twelve

- Goal: To increase practitioners' awareness of the impact of culture on the diagnostic process. To broaden the perspective of culture beyond race into other cultural experiences.

Exercise: In a group setting, one person role-plays an initial counseling session with a colleague, class member, or supervisee. Part way through the session, the person stops and asks the group, "What cultural groups does this client belong to?" If the group members don't know, they ask the client about her or his race, religion, ethnicity, gender, disability, sexual orientation, socioeconomic class, and age. They may also want to ask the same questions of the practitioner.

The practitioner resumes the session, now assuming that these cultural groups are at the forefront of everyone's mind. After the session, the group discusses the difference such cultural questions and understandings had on their subsequent experience of the client, the professional, and the session.

Activity Thirteen

- Goal: To explore the issues of gender as they relate to conceptions of normal and abnormal behavior. To identify value influences on what is included or not included in the DSM.

1. Failure to conform to social norms with respect to lawful behaviors as indicated by repeatedly performing acts that are grounds for arrest.

2. Deceitfulness, as indicated by repeated lying, use of aliases, or conning others for personal profit or pleasure.

3. Impulsivity or failure to plan ahead.

4. Irritability and aggressiveness, as indicated by repeated physical fights or assaults.

5. Reckless disregard for safety of self or others.

6. Consistent irresponsibility, as indicated by repeated failure to sustain consistent work behavior or honor financial obligations.

7. Lack of remorse, as indicated by being indifferent to or rationalizing having hurt, mistreated, or stolen from another. (APA, 2000)

Figure 5.1   Antisocial Personality Disorder

1. Has difficulty making everyday decisions without an excessive amount of advice and reassurance from others.

2. Needs others to assume responsibility for most major areas of his or her life.

3. Has difficulty expressing disagreement with others because of fear of loss of support or approval.

4. Has difficulty initiating projects or doing things on his or her own (because of a lack of self-confidence in judgment or abilities rather than a lack of motivation or energy).

5. Goes to excessive lengths to obtain nurturance and support from others, to the point of volunteering to do things that are unpleasant.

6. Feels uncomfortable or helpless when alone because of exaggerated fears of being unable to care for himself or herself.

7. Urgently seeks another relationship as a source of care and support when a close relationship ends.

8. Is unrealistically preoccupied with fears of being left to take care of himself or herself. (APA, 2000)

Figure 5.2   Dependent Personality Disorder

Exercise: Consider the two diagnoses in Figures 5.10 and 5.11. Imagine a man diagnosed with Antisocial Personality Disorder and then imagine a man diagnosed with Dependent Personality Disorder. Now imagine a woman diagnosed with Antisocial Personality Disorder and then a woman diagnosed with Dependent Personality Disorder. How do your perceptions of men and women differ even when they are diagnosed with the same disorder? What would the opposite of each of the disorders be? Develop the specific "opposite" criteria. Why are there not DSM diagnoses associated with these opposite criteria? What are some other "opposites" that are not included in the DSM (e.g., stoic to parallel histrionic)? Why do you suppose such opposites are left out?

Activity Fourteen

- Goal: To explore social constructions of gender related to normal and abnormal behavior.

Exercise: Complete the following statements as they apply to your gender:

As a woman/girl, I am a failure if I don't . . . *or*

As a man/boy, I am a failure if I don't . . .

Real women/girls do . . .

Real women/girls don't . . .

Real men/boys do . . .

Real men/boys don't . . .

How might the diagnostic process be influenced by a practitioner's responses to these statements? Based on your responses, consider the following questions: What diagnoses might you be more likely to give to men than to women because of the beliefs inherent in your responses to these statements? What diagnoses might you be more likely to give to women than to men? What behaviors would you be likely to consider abnormal or "diagnosable" in men, but not in women? What behaviors would you be likely to consider abnormal or "diagnosable" in women, but not in men?

Activity Fifteen

- Goal: To consider the sociopolitical context associated with past diagnoses.

Exercise: In the late 19th century, Dr. S. Weir Mitchell garnered praise for his treatment of female neurasthenia patients (i.e., those with fatigue, loss of energy and memory, and feelings of inadequacy), treatment that involved overfeeding the women patients and depriving them of intellectual and social stimulation. During a similar time in history, Dr. Isaac Baker Brown advocated and practiced clitoridectomy as a cure for female masturbation (Hare-Mustin & Marecek,

1997; Marecek, 1993). Why do you suppose such treatment was practiced and praised? What other "treatments" have been practiced in the past that we now consider incomprehensible? What are some diagnoses that were included in the DSM that we now have decided are not mental health problems? What are not included now that perhaps should be? What diagnoses that are now included do you think might be excluded in the future? Why do you suppose such inclusions or exclusions are deemed appropriate at one time in history and inappropriate at another time occur? How will we know in future DSMs whether we are inappropriately including or excluding diagnoses? If we can't know, what might an appropriate response to our lack of confidence be?

Activity Sixteen

- Goal: To explore the role that gender and culture play in conceptualizing mental disorders.

Exercise: Read the case study in Figure 5.12. Provide a diagnosis. Then change the gender, race, and socioeconomic status as directed, and discuss any different or additional diagnostic impressions that are generated. Next, create case studies with and without different environmental stressors and contexts (e.g., sociopolitical and economic context of diagnosis) and follow the same procedures.

CONSIDERING THE SOCIAL AND ENVIRONMENTAL CONTEXTS IN ASCRIBING DIAGNOSES

Mental health professionals who use the DSM system responsibly also take into account the role of social and environmental contexts and the impact these contexts may be having on the person's experience (Jensen & Hoagwood, 1997; Marecek, 1993; Shields, 1995). However, practitioners may also experience limitations in the DSM system around how to fully include such social and environmental influences

---

Case 5.10

Part One: Jada is a 17-year-old girl brought to counseling by her parents because of the concerns and anxieties that Jada has about her English class. She indicates that it is hard for her to pay attention because her teacher is boring. She adds that she does not like her teacher because the teacher calls on her when she doesn't have her hand up. She says that the teacher tries to pick on her knowing that it will upset her. Jada is embarrassed when this happens because she does not like to be put on the spot when she doesn't know the answer. She says that it is not normal for teachers to call on girls in class; she indicates that in her other classes, it is the boys who mostly talk in class.

Jada feels that it is not important for her to learn English. She says she speaks English just fine and doesn't understand the point of the class. She adds that she doesn't plan on working when she graduates and has no intentions of going to college. She wants to get married and support her husband in his work while she develops as a homemaker.

Jada says that she hates school because she has no friends and people pick on her because she is different. She wishes she could drop out of school, but her parents won't let her. She says she has only one friend, but that she and her friend don't have much in common. Jada says that the only reason that they are friends is because they are both "losers." Jada adds that she is used to being a "nerd," so this really doesn't bother her. The only problem is her mean English teacher.

Jada indicates mounting anxiety prior to attending her class. She says that her stomach starts to hurt about 1 hour before English class everyday. She used to go to the school nurse instead of going to class, but the nurse told her that she couldn't come anymore. She says that sometimes she doesn't even want to come to school because she hates English so much. When she's in English class her palms are sweaty and she has trouble breathing. She says that her chest feels tight and she is afraid she is going to have a heart attack.

She says she has trouble eating lunch because she is so nervous about going to English class. She also says that if she thinks about English class before bed, she cannot sleep and often has nightmares about going to her class. Jada wishes that she could drop out of English class and take something else so that she can get rid of her anxiety.

- ❖ Reread the case inserting "boy" and "he." How does your assessment differ if the client is a boy?
- ❖ Now reread the case with the assumption that Jada is Asian from an upper-middle-class family. Her father is a doctor and her mother is a housewife. How does that change your impressions?
- ❖ How would your reactions have been different if this client were from the "barrio"?
- ❖ How would ascribing a DSM diagnosis potentially impact the client?
- ❖ How would your values impact your conceptualization of the client's situation?
- ❖ How might some of the client's issues be related to developmental issues?

---

in the multiaxial system. For instance, the following questions may arise: If we maintain a contextual perspective, can we consider any disorder to be located within the individual? Can we say that mental disorders reside in minds, which reside in brains, which reside in the individual body, and, therefore, do not reside in the social world? It would seem that mental health professionals who fully consider social and environmental influences, rather than locating dysfunction in individuals, will extend their assessments beyond the individual to communities, neighborhoods, and families, and will define the "problem" in terms that include such entities (Gottschalk, 2000; Jensen & Hoagwood, 1997).

When thinking systemically, practitioners may also realize that what the DSM considers to be psychopathology may actually be a very functional attempt on a person's part to adapt to or cope with a dysfunctional context (Allwood, 2002; Ivey & Ivey, 1998, 1999; Webb, 2002; Yahav & Sharlin, 2002). A compulsively overeating teenager may be offering herself nurturance when she experiences negative emotions because no one in her family is able or willing to comfort her when she needs it. A little boy may hide under his bed and refuse to see or speak to anyone as an escape from incessant parental fighting and abuse. A firefighter may dissociate following the horror of having removed bodies from the collapsed World Trade Center. Including the context—for example, traumas such as rape, incest, abuse, and battering—in the diagnostic discussion creates a very different diagnostic picture than considering symptoms without the context (e.g., posttraumatic stress disorder versus major depression).

Conceptualizing symptoms as adaptations or coping strategies may result in a different practitioner–client relationship than might emerge within a medical-model assessment relationship. That is, when viewing symptoms as coping strategies that are already being employed, a counselor might acknowledge and recognize the value of the symptom, might appreciate all that the client is doing to manage, and might encourage the client to use the symptom until another, less damaging or more helpful coping strategy becomes apparent or useful. When viewed traditionally, the practitioner immediately focuses on how to reduce symptoms, viewing the client's way of handling her or his life as inadequate or as filled with deficits (Jensen & Hoagwood, 1997). The DSM may thus be seen as only one way of making meaning or one way of assessing clients' experiences (Ivey & Ivey, 1998). If mental health providers realize the limitations of the DSM system, they can proactively include additional ways of understanding that increase the range of treatment possibilities.

Activity Seventeen

- Goal: To foster an ability to use strength-based language that communicates an

understanding of the impact of context. To decrease pathology-based language during client assessment.

Exercise: This exercise uses role-plays to explore the use of language. Begin the role-play with one practitioner playing the client and various group/class members offering counseling interventions. Stop the role-play periodically and ask what the group members think is "going on" with the client. Whenever assumptions are negative or judgmental or use pathology-based language, point that out and ask what else could be going on that might lead to more understanding and acceptance, rather than judgment, of the client. Point out possibilities. Continue the role-play while encouraging the group members to focus on such possibilities and to practice using language about clients and with clients that is strength-oriented and empowering.

Activity Eighteen

- Goal: To explore the importance of cultural context in the etiology and treatment of mental disorders.

Exercise 1: Research and/or discuss the relationship between a particular diagnosis and the cultural milieu. For example, in the United States during the late 20th century, anorexia nervosa was most commonly diagnosed in young White females. What contextual situations might contribute to this fact? The demographics of this diagnosis appear to be changing, with more people of color and males being diagnosed with anorexia and bulimia. What contextual situations might contribute to this fact? Other diagnoses that might be discussed are antisocial personality disorders, dependent personality disorders, and conduct disorders in children.

Exercise 2: Using the example of major depression (or other disorders such as phobias, generalized anxiety disorder, or conduct disorder,

---

Case 5.11

Michael, a 35-year-old man with no criminal record, was brought into a community mental health clinic after a verbal confrontation with a police officer. When asked why he refused to pay a parking fee for a local event, he responded angrily, "I offered the parking attendant my credit card, and he said that they only take cash. I never carry cash! Why does everyone have to make things so difficult?"

Michael noted that he does not like to go to banks, and he refuses to ever enter a bank. He handles all of his finances over the phone and through writing and depositing checks at an ATM. Furthermore, he indicates that he never carries or handles cash.

"When I have to use an ATM," Michael reported, "I have a pocket knife in the passenger seat, ready to use, just in case." Michael also reported that he is leery of others and becomes suspicious when discussions involve the subject of money. He has one credit card and his driver's license in his wallet, and he carries a list of his allergies just in case he is ever wounded and unconscious. He has also posted on his refrigerator the phone number for the local police, as well as the phone number of the credit card company, in the event that his card is ever stolen.

Michael's suspicious behaviors appear bizarre, and you begin to suspect that he may be paranoid or psychotic.

- ❖ What diagnoses might you be considering at this point in the interview?
- ❖ What additional questions do you need to ask Michael?

After further inquiry about past events, Michael explains that while he was in a bank approximately 2 years ago, he witnessed an armed robbery during which a man was shot and killed. Almost every night since then, Michael has nightmares about the event, so vivid that he can smell the money and feel the man's blood spatter onto his face. He indicates that he was afraid to tell the interviewer this because of fears that he would be found and hurt by the family of the bank robber.

- ❖ How does the context surrounding Michael's presenting problem change the aforementioned case scenario?
- ❖ What additional traumas might a counselor ask about when assessing a client and ascribing diagnoses?
- ❖ Discuss the importance of specifically asking clients about their context versus assuming that they will tell you?
- ❖ Why might clients not tell you about their varying contextual situations?
- ❖ How might Michael's ethnicity or gender impact his situation?

---

etc.), explore how sociocultural factors could legitimately lead to depression in anyone who experienced them. Consider what family dynamics, geographical region, language difficulties, religion, socioeconomic status, folk beliefs, quality of life, immigrant experiences, disabilities, discriminations, or work experiences might contribute to depression (or other disorders). Name all of the possible life circumstances that might lead someone to feel depressed. A discussion of these changes and contexts may help to

expand practitioners' ways of knowing beyond the typical perception that only certain people, with certain genetic predispositions, "get" certain "diseases" or diagnoses.

Exercise 3: Explore how seemingly less-significant details about clients' experiences may be significant to diagnosis and treatment. For instance, in considering the case in Figure 5.13, consider the impact of situational and contextual events and what a "usual" response might be to such experiences, explore alternative diagnoses, challenge preferred diagnoses, and require students or supervisees to give evidence for their diagnostic choices.

Exercise 4: Videos can encourage an appreciation of the complexity of diagnostic issues. In numerous videos, actor-clients who meet the DSM criteria for various diagnoses present their "symptoms." Instructors or supervisors can ask students or supervisees to decide what they don't know and to consider various situations that would lead them to different conclusions. Mental health professionals can be challenged to consider clients' situations as being more complex than might be initially presented or than might be presented in a limited time frame. Professionals can use Interpersonal Process Recall (Kagan, 1980) to discuss what students or supervisees are thinking at various points in the tape.

ADHERING TO PROFESSIONAL ETHICS WHEN USING THE DSM

Mental health education and supervision and good clinical practice include, by necessity, discussion of ethical issues; it is critical that diagnosis and the use of the DSM be included in these discussions (Haynes, Corey, & Moulton, 2003; Prieto & Scheel, 2002). Challenging students and supervisees to consider complex and dynamic ethical issues may contribute to greater complexity in student and supervisee thinking (Kegan, 1982, 1994; Knefelkamp, Widick, & Parker, 1978; Kohlberg, 1981; Loevinger, 1976; Perry, 1970), in general, and to greater complexity in thinking about DSM-related issues, more specifically (Haynes et al., 2003). Such considerations should include exploring the relationship between specific ethical issues, such as informed consent, confidentiality, accuracy versus misrepresentation, values, and dual relationships, and diagnosis. For example, clients have a right to informed consent

(Welfel, 2002). Responsibly using the DSM system of diagnosis requires informing clients that a diagnosis is required for the practitioner to provide services; in many states, providing such information is mandated by law (Welfel, 2002). Responsible diagnosis also requires sharing diagnostic information with clients (Mappes, Robb, & Engles, 1985; Welfel, 2002). Ethically, during this process practitioners should educate their clients about the ascription of potential DSM diagnoses, what the diagnoses mean, the advantages and disadvantages of receiving a formal diagnosis, and alternatives to receiving a formal diagnosis. This informed consent process should take place at the beginning of the first session, and questions or concerns that the client poses should be addressed then and as they emerge during counseling (Welfel, 2002).

As a way of making informed consent a dynamic, rather than static, process, practitioners might demystify diagnostic procedures by sharing diagnostic decision making with their clients, rather than "doing" the diagnosis to them. When both the client's and the practitioner's perspectives on the problem and the diagnosis inform the treatment process, a more collaborative counseling relationship may emerge (Anderson & Goolishian, 1992; Ivey & Ivey, 1998).

Ethical standards also include mandates about counselor values, and thus serve as one source of motivation for mental health professionals to stay aware of their own values, attitudes, beliefs, and behaviors and how these influence their work. The DSM incorporates its own assumptions and values, and so, practitioners also need to be aware of how the values inherent in the DSM diagnostic system may influence their work (McLaughlin, 2002; Sadler, 2002). Mental health professionals are not only to be aware of their values, but are to avoid imposing their values on clients (American Association for Marriage and Family Therapy [AAMFT], 2001, Standards 3.3, 3.4, 3.5; American Counseling Association [ACA], 1995, Standard A.5.b; American

Psychological Association [APA], 1992, Standards 1.08, 1.09, 1.10; National Association of Social Workers [NASW], 1999, Standard 1.05). Although the DSM was intended by its developers to be atheoretical, value free, and based on observable facts and symptoms, we extensively described in Chapter 2 the values that have been incorporated into the DSM and must conclude that value-free diagnosis is an oxymoron. Practitioners who behave ethically, therefore, need to be aware of the values and assumptions that are inherent in any diagnostic system, and need to avoid imposing them, inadvertently or not, on clients (McLaughlin, 2002).

Mental health professionals also need to be conscious of how values inherent in the school of thought that guides their practice intersect with the values inherent in the DSM. For instance, as stated in Chapter 2, the values of many specific schools of therapy do not mesh with a DSM medical-model approach to diagnosis (Ivey & Ivey, 1998; Miller, 1990; Sperry, 2002b). Thus, educators and supervisors need to assist students and supervisees to explore more philosophically related considerations, such as how to manage the values associated with the DSM that contradict the developmental, systems, or wellness orientations of some schools of thought in psychotherapy. For example, the counseling profession's focus on normal human growth and development (Myers, Sweeney, & Witmer, 2001; Neukrug, 2003; Sperry, 2002b) can be philosophically compared with the DSM's medical model philosophy, and discrepancies can be identified. Couples and family counseling's systemic focus (Gladding, 2002) might be compared with the DSM's individualistic focus. Person-centered and humanistic therapists' focus on growth potential and choice (Boy, 1989) might be compared with the DSM's more static and deterministic values. Alfred Adler's individual psychology perspective that focuses on one's phenomenological or idiographic reality experiences might be compared with the DSM system's focus on an absolute reality

(Maniacci, 2002). A psychodynamic perspective that emphasizes the subjective experience of clients and a belief that the evolution and development of client problems become clear as therapy progresses might be compared with the DSM system's focus on the objective behaviors that can readily be viewed and assessed (Schmolke, 1999). Mental health professionals can then use the discussions about conflicts and differences to launch efforts at reconciling the differences or at least deciding what to do about the conflicts. Such discussions may also include working to resolve ethical dilemmas that arise from potential demands to work concurrently from different philosophical orientations.

Finally, practitioners' professional development may include further training about issues associated with the DSM. Such training may be formal, or may take the form of reading or consultation with colleagues about various concerns related to diagnosis. Hopefully training will help practitioners to challenge their usual assumptions, and when necessary, to develop more sensitivity in the use of the DSM.

Activity Nineteen

- Goal: To use case studies to explore ethical and practical issues associated with the DSM.

Exercise: Develop and use different case examples that explore various ethics-related issues. For instance, consider the case in Figure 5.14 that includes informed consent dilemmas, values dilemmas, and professional identity dilemmas; answer the provided questions.

Activity Twenty

- Goal: To increase the ability to collaborate, involve clients in the diagnostic process, and facilitate the formation of diagnostic meanings.

Exercise: Practitioners divide into small groups with the goal of diagnosing and assessing the client in a specific case presentation. Each small

---

Case 5.12

Andrea, a married, full-time graduate student with a part-time job, entered counseling to work on career issues and to seek help in decreasing her "stress." You discover that Andrea meets the DSM criteria for Generalized Anxiety Disorder (GAD). Andrea is worried about whether she is in the right field. Among her concerns is whether she can continue to pursue a field that demands a high level of professional commitment. Both her husband and her husband's parents wish her to quit graduate school so that she can more adequately attend to matters at home, especially keeping the house in better order, cooking more often, and cleaning more adequately. From her perspective, much of her stress generates from the conflict between her husband and his family's desires, and her own desire to continue her education; but she is also upset that she can't handle her "duties" at home more effectively. Finally, you are also aware that in order for her insurance carrier to pay for her counseling services, you must give Andrea a DSM diagnosis.

❖ How will a DSM diagnosis impact Andrea's "stress" and what message will it communicate to her about her problem?
❖ What risks are associated with giving her the diagnosis?
❖ What risks are associated with not giving her the diagnosis?
❖ How much will you tell Andrea about such risks in the first session before obtaining her signature on your informed consent form?
❖ Is GAD an accurate assessment of Andrea's problem? What else needs to be included for accuracy?
❖ How will you handle the discussions related to payment and giving her a diagnosis?
❖ Change the gender in the case. Now the race and socioeconomic class. Next consider the case with her husband being disabled. Try other cultural varieties.
❖ What have you learned through this activity?

---

group creates a simulation that demonstrates ways to engage clients in a collaborative, co-constructive diagnostic process. One practitioner plays the client, another plays the professional, and the remainder of the group serves as consultants. Each small group presents its simulation to the larger group. The larger group, as it observes, creates a list of all the ways that the practitioner has been collaborative during the simulated diagnostic process.

Activity Twenty-One

- Goal: To encourage understanding of the ways that values may impact counseling and diagnosis.

Exercise: Write down 10 of your values, one on each of 10 index cards or pieces of paper. Now, on 10 other index cards or pieces of paper, write down 10 values that others might espouse but that you do not adhere to. Pair one of your values with a value espoused by someone else. Discuss how mental health professionals and clients who hold these differing values might struggle with or influence one another. How might such differing values affect the client's perceptions, the professional's perceptions, or the counseling relationship? Pair other cards together as though other professionals and clients with differing values were meeting together. Discuss how these differing values might affect your perceptions of the client's abnormality were you the professional. For example, if you value feminism and your client values a traditional family arrangement, how might this affect you as the professional, your client, and the counseling process? How might the differences impact your conceptions about the problem, the client, or the treatment of the problem?

Activity Twenty-Two

- Goal: To increase practitioners' understanding of the values inherent in different theoretical approaches and how they compare with those of the DSM.

Exercise: Identify different theoretical approaches to counseling (e.g., person-centered, cognitive therapy, reality therapy, family therapy, feminist therapies). List the values inherent in these approaches. Next compare these values with the values stated in Chapter 2 that are inherent in DSM diagnosis. During discussions, try to discover ways to reconcile (or not) any ostensible contradictions between the two value systems.

Activity Twenty-Three

- Goal: To encourage understanding of the relationships between the values of certain mental health professions and the values inherent in the DSM diagnostic system.

Exercise 1: Identify the values espoused by your profession (e.g., strength-based orientation, diversity, empowerment). Compare these values with the values inherent in a medical model approach to discover conflicts or similarities. If conflicts are discovered, process how to handle them.

Exercise 2: How do counselors, couple and family therapists, and other humanistically, systemically, or developmentally oriented mental health providers reconcile their professional identities with the medical model? Can they ethically operate outside the boundaries of such professional identities? For instance, consider the questions that follow in response to the philosophical orientations below, orientations that are associated with the medical model.

Illness orientation. Does a DSM perspective keep us focused on infirmity and its absence, rather than fully considering wellness and its absence? Do we, as a result, neglect assessing wellness, the things that people do that are well, the things that they need to do to be optimally healthy? Can we espouse the DSM's undergirding philosophy of illness while at the same time fully actualizing a wellness-oriented, strength-based professional identity?

Remediation orientation: Does the medical model's focus on diagnosis and either "cure" of individual illnesses or reduction of symptoms keep us from identifying ways to prevent problems that might be high risks in certain contexts? When such a "lens" focuses us on what happens after the problem develops, can we remember to invest in efforts that might prevent such problems in others? Or will we find ourselves so busy with remediation (and so much better reimbursed for it) that we will be disinclined to engage in working to prevent problems from occurring? Might focusing on eliminating symptoms also direct us away from appreciating the functionality of a person's symptoms and the symptoms' benefits to the person or to the person's family? Might a remediative focus direct us away from helping clients to use the symptoms when necessary to benefit them or their families?

Individual orientation: Does the DSM's focus on individual symptoms and illnesses interfere with systemic thinking? Can we truly (and ethically) give a diagnosis to one person in a family or one person in a high-risk community, and then, because we believe that these are the best ways to help the individual, shift paradigms to help families and communities to change unhealthy and damaging behavior?

Static orientation: If many DSM users find themselves believing that a person "has" a disease or "is" a disease (e.g., "borderline") once diagnosed, can we really maintain the developmental perspective that posits that some problems are "normal" life struggles at particular ages or in particular life situations, and that assistance at critical time periods can successfully help people resolve such struggles? Or that some problems are limitations in constructive developmental functioning caused by unhelpful environments, but that we can become part of a helpful environment that moves people ahead developmentally? Discuss how wellness, systems, developmental, and prevention orientations might result in different strategies than illness, individual, static, or

---

Case 5.13

Ann presents for counseling at the community mental health center where you work. She has been referred by the Women, Infants, and Children (WIC) program coordinator who is concerned for her safety. She is a 27-year-old single mother from a low socioeconomic background, and she struggles with many daily issues, such as providing food for her baby. She has few sources of income, and when she can find no other means of income, she occasionally works as a prostitute. It is difficult for her to obtain a job because she does not have a high school diploma; however, she has basic reading and writing skills. Ann and her baby currently live with her new boyfriend so that he can help to provide food and shelter for her and her baby. They have been dating for 1 month; he beats her on a regular basis and is very controlling. During the last abuse incident, he strangled her until she passed out. When questioned about her safety, her response was that at least she "isn't dead yet."

Ann and her boyfriend live in the projects, but she does not mind the location because the city bus stops a block away from her house. Ann loves her baby and will do anything for her. She will tolerate anything so long as she can keep her baby. She also points out that her current circumstances are better than many of her past living situations.

Ann is in need of medical assistance because she has AIDS. However, she has no health insurance and cannot afford to pay for her medications. She says she uses heroin to take the pain away. She doesn't like to use heroin, but it is all she has to prevent her from feeling terrible. Her boyfriend is a heroin addict, and he supplies her with drugs. Her boyfriend has also recently been diagnosed as HIV-positive.

Ann's only family is her younger sister, Julie, who is 24 years old. They have always been close. However, Julie has her own struggles to deal with, so she is unable to assist Ann financially. Ann and Julie lost their parents when they were 14 and 11 years old. They spent the rest of their childhoods in and out of foster care. Ann views her time in foster care as a positive experience. She feels terrible that her parents died, but she says that she did not miss being the recipient of her father's sexual abuse. Although, at times her various foster parents abused her, she says she always persevered because she knew it was only a matter of time before she would be sent to another home.

❖ What strengths does Ann possess?
❖ What resources does Ann have in her life?
❖ How might focusing on these strengths and resources result in a different treatment plan and attitude toward Ann, than solely focusing on the problems and pathology in Ann's life?
❖ How might you implement a holistic, wellness focus? How is this strength-based approach different from a medical-model, pathology-oriented approach?
❖ How might Ann's ethnicity or gender impact her situation?

---

remediation orientations as you consider the case in Figure 5.15.

FOCUSING ON ALL DSM AXES AND SCALES WHEN DIAGNOSING

A focus on Axis IV (Psychosocial Stressors), Axis V (Global Assessment of Functioning [GAF]), and the Global Assessment of Relationship Functioning (GARF) when one is diagnosing and developing interventions may somewhat reduce the limitations of the two-axis DSM classification system (Mottarella, Philpot, & Fritzsche, 2001; White, 2001). The intention of Axis IV, for instance, is to uncover stressors that may be contributing to the "development of a new mental disorder," "the recurrence of a prior mental disorder," or "the exacerbation of an already existing mental disorder" (American Psychiatric Association [APA], 2000, p. 31). This Axis IV conceptualization is similar to the stress-diathesis model that regards social factors such as life stressors as triggers of biological predispositions toward various mental disorders (Denton, 1990). By definition, a focus on Axis IV implies that practitioners will be more sensitive to clients' relational and social contexts.

Waldo, Brotherton, and Horswill (1993), in their efforts to direct clinicians' attention to the value of systems of categorization such as the DSM, stress that Axis III and IV "categories" may encourage practitioners to take a more holistic look at medical and psychosocial problems. Assessing problems more holistically may, in turn, suggest the use of more comprehensive, developmental, and systemic interventions. For instance, an Axis IV indication of family stress could lead to referrals for family therapy (Frances, Clarkin, & Perry, 1984; Ivey & Ivey, 1999), or evidence of work stress might imply a need for career counseling (Dollarhide, 1997).

An additional method of conceptualizing and understanding the uniqueness of clients' experiences is the GAF (Axis V). Although an Axis I or II diagnosis indicates that symptoms exist, it doesn't indicate the severity of the problem (i.e., severe post-traumatic stress disorder [PTSD] versus mild PTSD reactions). GAF ratings provide a numerical indicator of clients' levels of functioning across various areas of their lives, including social, occupational, and relational functioning. An increased focus on Axis V (GAF) may also help practitioners to clarify the areas in which clients are functioning well, allowing for attention to their various strengths. Strengths and assets can then be built on during counseling (Ivey & Ivey, 1999).

Furthermore, the DSM has become more relationally oriented as a result of efforts by the Coalition on Family Diagnosis (CFD), a multidisciplinary conglomeration of professionals representing mental health-related organizations (Kaslow, 1993). This organization encouraged DSM developers to expand the V Codes to include "Relational Problems" and "Other Conditions that May Be a Focus of Clinical Attention," as well as promoting the GARF (see also Mash & Johnston, 1996).

The GARF is located in the DSM-IV appendix, and focuses practitioners on clients' relationships. "The GARF scale permits the practitioner to rate the degree to which a family or ongoing relational unit meets the affective or instrumental needs of its members" (APA, 2000, p. 814). Like the GAF, the GARF's numerical ratings range from 0 to 100. Higher scores indicate satisfactory relationship functioning and imply that the client's perspectives are included in relational decisions. The GARF rates a family's levels of organization, emotional climate, and problem solving, and thus also offers direction to practitioners about these areas when they develop interventions (Ivey & Ivey, 1999; Mottarella et al., 2001; Sporakowski, 1995).

Activity Twenty-Four

- Goal: To increase awareness of the more positive perspectives of diagnostic labels, and thus to reduce the chance that professionals will fail to identify client strengths when assessing.

Exercise: Instructors or supervisors may teach or practitioners may focus on learning reframing skills. Reframing helps mental health professionals to recognize the positive function(s) of distressing symptoms and the positive intentions behind problematic behavior (Pesut, 1991). When clients experience reframing during counseling, they may experience a positive valence in their mental health professional's assessment of them. This, in turn, may reduce defensiveness and may lead to greater motivation to alter problematic ways of thinking and behaving.

As a first step in this reframing exercise, list the diagnostic criteria and associated features for a particular diagnosis (e.g., depression, dependent personality disorder, mania, avoidant personality disorder). Next, generate ideas about the positive features of these symptoms and positive intentions that may be indicated by the symptoms. Select those positive connotations that stand the best chance of promoting

---

Case 5.14

Ramos is a 21-year-old, Mexican-American community college student who presents for counseling at a local mental health agency. He is upset about his 40-pound weight gain over the past 2 years. Further exploration indicates that Ramos has been under a tremendous amount of stress during the past 2 years. Ramos has felt pressure, as a first-generation college student, to be academically successful. His stress also emanates from the recent death of his grandmother with whom he was very close. Despite his struggles, Ramos has been able to maintain a good grade-point average and full-time employment. He contributes part of his wages to his car's maintenance, and gives the rest of the money to his family. Ramos notes that he is tired from working so much. Ramos describes a recent increase in eating and notes that food is a comfort to him and is "always there for him" as he struggles to maintain his equilibrium. He reports that, at times, his eating feels "out of control"; he states that he cannot voluntarily stop eating even though he tries. Ramos denies any mental health related concerns and seems to demonstrate a relatively high level of functioning despite his recent stressors. He does indicate that his recent weight gain has kept him from feeling socially confident and pursuing new friendships or potential romantic relationships.

- ❖ What DSM disorder might best capture Ramos's experience?
- ❖ In what ways do the symptoms help Ramos manage his situation?
- ❖ How might Ramos's gender impact his perception of his situation? How might it impact your reactions to his situation?
- ❖ How might Ramos's situation be reflective of developmental issues?
- ❖ What might be the implications of taking a pathology focus versus a strength-based, developmental perspective?
- ❖ What types of holistic, wellness issues might be considered in working with Ramos?

---

change in the client's orientation to the disorder. Generate a list of the client's strengths and resources. Identify which of these strengths or resources may contribute most to client change. Apply this process to a case (for instance, the case in Figure 5.16).

DEVELOPING ALTERNATIVE DIAGNOSTIC SYSTEMS

Alternative diagnostic systems and approaches have been suggested that may correct for some of the noted weaknesses in the current DSM model. These alternative systems have emerged from the already cited and long-standing debates about whether mental disorders are discrete or continuous and whether they can be separated from relational or contextual factors. Thus, those debating have wondered whether mental health problems might be classified using a more relational system and/ or a more dimensional system of diagnosis (Shankman & Klein, 2002).

Dimensional Systems of Diagnosis

The criticisms leveled at the DSM system for being categorical have primarily challenged its "all-or-nothing" approach to classifying disorders. Kovel (1982), for instance, in a book review of the DSM III, questioned the premise that mental disorders are discrete entities, "like bodies in the physical world," that can be classified "as though they were elements in the periodic table" (p. 2). Other critics point out that many people have subclinical traits (i.e., below the threshold of actually meeting the diagnostic criteria) that suggest Axis I or II diagnoses, yet the categorical approach gives little credence to this type of information. Davanloo (1990), for instance, indicates that in clinical populations there are generally elements of depression, anxiety, and character disturbance that interact, and that each may be below the threshold for a full diagnosis at some point in a person's course of illness. Davanloo contends that during the course of a disorder, the various elements of the disorder shift. For example, a person who has chronic tension headaches, generalized anxiety, and obsessive–compulsive disorder may not have three discrete conditions but may have one condition with three elements. Similarly, two people may have the same diagnosis yet have differing severities of the various diagnostic symptoms.

It has been suggested that a dimensional approach to considering diagnoses may correct for the all-or-nothing categorical approach (Livesley, Jang, & Vernon, 1998; McLemore & Benjamin, 1979; Widiger, 1993). Theorists argue that dimensional systems may better reflect the "true" nature of mental disorders, have greater reliability, and convey more information to outside observers (Eysenck, Wakefield, & Friedman, 1983). A dimensional system should allow aspects of a person's situation that do not meet the threshold criteria for being a psychological disturbance to still be addressed as significant to the therapeutic interventions and process. Even the most current DSM, although still representing a categorical approach to diagnosis, has adopted some dimensional features (e.g., severity descriptors; Shankman & Klein, 2002).

Several specific dimensional models have been developed. Using such models for the diagnosis of personality disorders has received the most attention and the greatest degree of support (Benjamin, 2002; Livesley et al., 1998; Widiger, 1993). Although dimensional rating systems have been debated with regard to other mental disorders (e.g., depression), little consensus has been reached (Shankman & Klein, 2002). A dimensional approach to diagnosis may have enormous clinical and research potential; however, further evidence is needed of the reliability and validity of such an approach (Frances et al., 1984). Furthermore, some authors wonder whether dimensional models improve upon categorical models to a significant degree (Clark, 1995; Shankman & Klein, 2002; Widiger, 1997).

Relational (and Other Theoretical) Systems of Diagnosis

Jensen and Hoagwood (1997), in their review of the constraints of the current DSM system, conclude that the current system fails to address the complex nature of the interactions between individuals and their environments. In response to this criticism, some theorists have developed assessment models that more predominantly include relational factors that are pertinent to DSM diagnoses. For example, these theorists propose that it might be helpful to include an Axis VI for family evaluation as part of the traditional multiaxial system; such an inclusion would make the DSM more useful to family therapists (and other systemically oriented professionals) whose implicit paradigm currently contradicts that of the DSM (Denton, 1990; Kaslow, 1993; Mash & Johnston, 1996). The axis could include a narrative case formulation from a family systems perspective, a family typology, a global assessment of family health, or a rating of families on various dimensions such as enmeshment or power (Denton, 1990). Full multiaxial diagnosis that includes such an Axis VI on each family member would provide critical information to more individually oriented mental health professionals as well. In addition, inclusion of an axis relevant to their work might also challenge family counselors to fully use the DSM, and thus to add the "individual system" to their considerations of the family (Mash & Johnston, 1996; Sporakowski, 1995).

Other mental health disciplines might similarly develop their own separate axes to supplement the current DSM system, axes that reflect the group's particular areas of emphasis (e.g., positive psychology, gestalt, existential, psychodynamic; Cooper, 1981; Mundt, 2002). For example, Mundt (2002) states, "There are a number of concepts crucial to consider for psychologically informed classification, including personality structure, temperament, psychodynamic psychiatry, functional psychopathology, basic symptoms, anthropological phenomenology, and health psychology. In future diagnostic systems, one must critically consider objective measurement and subjective experience, as well as categorical and dimensional measurement" (p. 145). Denton (1990) suggests that perhaps independent research groups or professional organiations could take a leadership role in developing these axes or other sorts of inclusions, as by including the perspectives of various schools of thought, these groups have the potential for encouraging more accurate and helpful assessment.

The most ambitious systemically based alternative diagnostic system efforts have come from the Coalition on Family Diagnosis. The Coalition on Family Diagnosis was developed in the late 1980s and set as its mission the establishment of a relational diagnosis scheme that could be incorporated into the DSM's Axis I (Group for the Advancement of Psychiatry, Committee on the Family, 1989, 1995; Kaslow, 1993; Mash & Johnston, 1996). However, despite arduous, cross-disciplinary, and painstaking efforts to develop the relational system, it has been criticized for many of the same problems that the original DSM system has faced (Ivey, Jankowski, & Scheel, 1999; Kaslow, 1996). For instance, some have criticized the relational diagnostic system as being merely an additional layer of labels (i.e., mere semantics) that emanates from an alternative philosophy yet has the same inherent problems (Gergen, Hoffman, & Anderson, 1996). The critics have also stated that the use of a language of mental deficits is not helpful and may sometimes hinder practitioners from facilitating change and from resolving problems (Anderson, 1996; Gergen, 1990). Arguments abound for and against a relational diagnostic system (Ivey et al., 1999). Yet further development of these relational systems would provide a viable alternative or addition to the current DSM model for family therapists and others who work systemically. It

should also be noted that despite the current lack of success in their original mission, the efforts of the Coalition on Family Diagnosis have resulted in the development and inclusion in the DSM-IV of the GARF (discussed above).

Many consider the suggestions for more relational and/or dimensional systems of diagnosis to be naïve, voicing their beliefs that fully developing such axes and receiving reimbursement for them is unlikely because of the extremely intensive amount of work needed to develop such categorizations (Cooper, 1981; McLemore & Benjamin, 1979). Benson, Long, and Sporakowski (1992) also counter ideas about adding alternative axes to the DSM. They indicate, for instance, that the DSM can be used in a way that focuses on systems perspectives, claiming that how one uses the DSM is more important than the inherent limitations of the DSM (see also Carlson, Hinkle, & Sperry, 1993). If they are right, changing the DSM in the ways proposed above may be less necessary. Benson et al., in their attempt to bridge the gap between an individual focus and systems perspectives, developed a series of exercises that link the DSM and family systems theory. The Reciprocal Process (see Activity Twenty-Six below) is one example from their list of exercises. It challenges the linearity of causation that is assumed in the DSM's medical model and encourages practitioners to emphasize dynamic interactions between the individual and his or her environment and context. Benson et al. also state that the DSM classifies disorders and not individual people, that the DSM should *not*, thus, be viewed as limiting from a systems perspective (Sporakowski, 1995).

Activity Twenty-Five

- Goal: To encourage divergent ways of thinking about diagnoses.

Exercise: Practitioners respond to cases by thinking about problems in four ways: (a) as

DSM diagnoses, (b) as patterns co-constructed in a conversational process between therapist and client, (c) as cultural and personal discourses that influence others in ways that promote the development of problem stories, and (d) as stories in which people develop self-deprecating, problem-saturated versus success-oriented self-narratives (Dickerson & Zimmerman, 1995). After using each of the four conceptualization strategies, practitioners ask themselves: (a) What effect does thinking about the problem in this specific way have on the way I think about the person? (b) What effect might thinking about the problem in this way have on the way the client thinks about him-/herself? (c) What effect does thinking about the problem in this way have on the ways that I might act toward the client, and the ways that we together think about solutions?

Activity Twenty-Six

- Goal: This exercise challenges the linearity of causation that is assumed in the DSM and in the medical model upon which it is grounded, and instead, posits a circular or recursive way of understanding causes of problems.

Exercise: This exercise involves teaching the notion of "reciprocal process" (Benson et al., 1992). Practitioners list the defining characteristics of a particular disorder. They then reflect on the consequences of each symptom by asking how they and others might react to the symptom, behaviorally, emotionally, and cognitively. Practitioners then reflect on how these reactions might influence the maintenance of the symptoms.

Activity Twenty-Seven

- Goal: To encourage consideration of alternative methods of diagnosis and counter the notion that disorders should be conceptualized as being located solely in the individual.

Exercise: Develop a "Family Diagnosis" (Benson et al., 1992). First, identify at least two families with similar patterns (e.g., increased family conflict when one child is adolescent). Next, analyze the family interactional patterns to clarify their exact nature and to uncover their differences and similarities. From this analysis, discern the essential criteria that distinguish between families with the problem (diagnosis) and families without (i.e., develop the diagnostic criteria and associated features). Finally, consider the other types of information that are provided in the DSM, such things as sex ratio, prevalence, predisposing factors, and the like. Discuss what it might mean to include this diagnosis in a future DSM.

Activity Twenty-Eight

- Goal: To help practitioners to consider a dimensional versus a categorical perspective on diagnosis.

Exercise: Using case examples above, first ascribe a DSM diagnosis. Next rate the client's behaviors or symptoms on a continuum. Does the addition of a continuum result in a different sense of the client? If so, how? What are the implications of using a dimensional approach? Should people with low levels of a disorder receive the same diagnoses as people with high levels of a disorder? Can people have traits of a disorder without having the full disorder? How do you feel about the all-or-nothing categorical approach?

EXTERNALIZING DIAGNOSES

Social constructivists tend to eschew traditional diagnostic schemes and rarely spend time identifying and using diagnostic systems (Neimeyer, 1993). Instead, they try to provide a broader glimpse into the discourses that create the client's constructions of self or others; they also emphasize the client's unique set of personal constructs and the client's own multiple identities, as opposed to situating clients within an externally validated set of diagnostic constructs (Etchison & Kleist, 2000; Tomm, 1989).

One proposed resolution to managing the discrepancies between such a postmodern, context-sensitive use of DSM diagnoses and the realities necessary for professional survival is to find a balance between traditional clinical diagnosis and postmodern skepticism (White, 2001). A strategy for achieving such balance is the externalization of clients' diagnoses, which has been proposed as a means of using DSM diagnoses with clients in an empowering fashion (Dickerson & Zimmerman, 1995; White, 2002). Narrative theory offers techniques that may contribute to externalizing client's problems and/or diagnoses (Freedman & Combs, 1996; White & Epston, 1990). For instance, in narrative work, mental health professionals may encourage clients to externalize their problem by naming a problem (e.g., "The Angry Man," "The Sweet Young Thing") and talking about it as though it were someone else's problem, or as though it were an entity "out there" beyond the client (for examples, see Fristad, Gavazzi, & Soldano, 1999).

Externalizing encourages clients to objectify and, at times, to personify the problems that they experience as oppressive. Because a problem becomes a separate entity from the person or relationship, problems that have previously been considered to be inherent, as well as those relatively fixed qualities that have been attributed to persons and relationships, are rendered less fixed and less restricting (White & Epston, 1990). Although externalizing a problem began as a narrative therapeutic technique, mental health professionals practicing from a variety of theoretical orientations might use it.

Activity Twenty-Nine

- Goal: To externalize clients' diagnoses and internalize personal agency.

Exercise: Practice externalizing diagnoses during role-plays through the use of externalizing language. Have "clients" give the problem a name and discuss the problem as though it were external to them. Help clients decide how they can fight the influence of the problem. Perhaps clients can assign another person or object to "be" the problem, and can thus see and interact with it as though it were outside of themselves (see case in Figure 5.17).

BREAKING FREE OF DEPENDENCE ON INSURANCE

As is probably clear many times over by now, the issues discussed in this book might be considerably less problematic were it not for practitioners' reliance on a financial reimbursement system that is dependent on DSM diagnosis. With this in mind, Ackley (1997) suggests strategies for private practitioners to break free of their bondage to the insurance industry and to the medical model, strategies that by implication would mean that practitioners could choose whether or not to use the DSM system of diagnosis. They could be free to use whatever assessment system worked best in conceptualizing their clients and in suggesting treatment approaches, and these decisions would most likely be influenced by their theoretical perspectives. The freedom not to diagnose, Ackley suggests, grants practitioners the freedom to fully actualize, rather than compromise, their own beliefs about the best ways to practice. His book, *Breaking Free of Managed Care*, is filled with suggestions about how to do this, a few of which we present here.

Ackley (1997) suggests that practitioners need to believe in and persuade others of the value of therapy. In 1992, $800 billion was spent on traditional health care and $114 billion was spent on nontraditional, unreimbursed health care services, ostensibly because patients perceived value in these services. If similar benefits were perceived for counseling services, many people would pay regardless of insurance

---

Case 5.15 (excerpted from White, 2002)

Dina, a 24-year-old part-time college student, sought counseling because of her escalating binging and purging behaviors. She reported that she had been periodically vomiting after she ate for about two years, but that her vomiting behaviors had escalated over the past three months. She indicated that she was vomiting after she ate about 50% of the time. Dina had read many books about eating disorders and nutrition and currently identified herself as bulimic. She stated that she had read about how hard it was to overcome eating disorders, and she feared that she would never be able to stop binging and purging. She conceived of her entire life as related to the bulimia; she had internalized bulimia as a significant part of her identity. She expressed frustration, anger, and shame associated with thinking that she had no control over herself, and stated that she could change if she only had more discipline.

Dina met the DSM criteria for bulimia nervosa–purging type (i.e., recurrent episodes of binge eating, compensatory behavior in order to prevent weight gain, self-evaluation unduly influenced by body shape and weight). Dina was asked for a name that described the influence of the problem. She decided to name it the Food Monster because her perception of the influence was negative, and the influence felt like a frightening monster. Dina perceived the Food Monster influence as an intrusive monster telling her to binge eat, and then telling her to vomit.

After a few sessions, Dina was able to begin viewing herself as fighting the Food Monster. Her bulimic self-identity and anger at herself was replaced with anger at the Food Monster. She became increasingly angry at its influence in her life. This anger empowered her to become aware of when it tried to influence her and how she could effectively push the influence away. She was better able to identify her strengths and resources, and use these in fighting the influence of the problem.

---

reimbursement. For example, Ackley (1997) indicates that if most counseling is offered at $100 per session and takes 6 months to complete (a total cost of $2,400), 80% of people can afford to pay out-of-pocket. Many people would even end up paying less than this. He urges mental health professionals to help people to see what else they spend that kind of money on and to help them to compare values. For the 20% of clients who cannot afford to pay out-of-pocket, Ackley suggests that practitioners offer pro bono services, donate time to agencies, or find subsidies to ensure that these people receive services.

Ackley (1997) suggests that breaking free of dependence on insurance reimbursement, and thus from the medical model and the DSM, allows practitioners to:

1. Expand their market to the 100% of people who have problems, rather than only the 10% who are diagnosable.

2. Focus on problem solving/skill building as a model, with the result that people no longer

need to be ill—they can be competent *and* work on developing new competencies. The practitioners' work thus shifts, he says, from promoting helplessness to promoting personal responsibility for change.

3. Recognize the value of what they do that is not reimbursed by insurance: customized attention; individualized plans; a focus on quality and strengths; pursuit of optimal health and wellness.

By focusing on a broader market, Ackley says, practitioners can work at normalizing the use of their services so that 100% of people will see counseling and therapy as relevant. Mental health providers can also, in this way, eliminate the negative effects of diagnosis, many of which have been listed in this book.

Activity Thirty

- Goal: To imagine possible funding sources or methods of payment other than insurance.

Exercise: Think about how you pay for other things that you value in life (e.g., cars, furniture, food, vacations). How might you help clients to think about valuing and paying for counseling or therapy in similar ways? Discuss your ideas in a large group. (Discussion leader, instructor, or supervisor might want to point to sliding scale fees, scholarships, installment plans with interest, a modified orthodontist plan [estimate the number of sessions and the fee for that number of sessions; client makes regular payments on the total; client gets a rebate if fewer sessions are needed and can renegotiate for more sessions if needed]; prepay full amount for 10% discount; use credit cards; arrange with a local bank for low-interest loans [Ackley, 1997]).

Activity Thirty-One

- Goal: To increase awareness of the benefits that mental health professionals have to offer beyond traditionally reimbursed services.

Exercise: Think back to your mental health curriculum, to the topics that were surveyed as possible content areas for mental health providers and to the settings in which mental health practitioners work. Now make a list of the sorts of groups, trainings, or classes that you might offer in these areas. Discuss these in a larger group. (Discussion leader, instructor, or supervisor might want to point to an Attention-Deficit Hyperactivity Disorder [ADHD] clinic; an adult ADHD group; an adult children of alcoholics [ACOA] group; an ACOA parent group; breaking away from food dependence; marriage training; child and family stress; divorce mediation; psychological hardiness; children and divorce; facilitating the emotional divorce; premenstrual syndrome [PMS]; sex offenders; family violence/anger management; quest for meaning; the family meal; retreats for lawyers; preventing childhood depression; life span development consultation; grief work with parents who lose children; consultation with clergy; vehicle [mobile] therapy; smoking cessation, etc. [Ackley, 1997]).

Activity Thirty-Two

- Goal: To increase awareness of the value to employers of a mental health provider's knowledge.

Exercise: Brainstorm the ways in which what a mental health provider knows might be valuable to employers. Write down your ideas individually, and then share your ideas with a larger group. (Discussion leader, instructor, or supervisor might want to point to health promotion; trauma response teams; stress management/toxic stress seminars; leadership training; downsizing; individual employee dismissal; increasing worker productivity; increasing managers' interpersonal skills; family stresses interfering with work; decrease in work and increase in insurance premiums caused by psychological problems, which then cause physical problems, which then cause absenteeism; conflicts on the job; communication in troubled departments; working with troubled employers or employees [Ackley, 1997]).

Activity Thirty-Three

- Goal: To increase mental health providers' ability to advocate for and market themselves.

Exercise: Ackley (1997) suggests that mental health practitioners need to learn how to sell themselves just as other businesses do. Eriksen (1997) suggests the steps by which counselors might advocate for their profession, steps that are also applicable to marketing a business:

1. *Professional Identity*: Review your credentials and the training that you have received. What strengths do you bring to the world? What topics do you know more about? Why would people want to listen to you? (Remember that you are comparing yourself to the general public, so include your degree, any certifications, and any specialized training. Then include all of the topics that were covered in your college courses, any specialized conference

presentations that you have attended, and any books that you have read on particular topics.)

2. *Define Your Funding Needs in Terms That Payers Will Be Motivated By*: Next think of the sorts of people who could benefit from what you know and any people who might be able or willing to refer these people to you. Make a list of both. What do these people care about that you also care about? What do doctors, for instance, or pastors, or school teachers, or employers, worry about that you might be able to do something about?

3. *Evaluate Your Resources*: Decide how much money, time, expertise, passion (or other resources) you have or are willing to commit to your plan.

4. *Create a Strategic Plan*: After completing steps 1, 2, and 3, prioritize your list according to what you would like to tackle first. Think of the ways that other businesses get your attention. Has one particular business persuaded you to buy recently? How did it do it? Brainstorm ways that you might persuade clients to "buy" your services or referral sources to refer to you. Buy a book on marketing a small business and find the ideas that most attract you or that you consider most feasible. Consider advertising, flyers, personal contacts, phone calls, and "loss leaders" (offering a service for a reduced price to motivate people to attend and sample what you can provide). Decide what you will say in each strategy: first, you will need to name their need; then indicate that you have a way of meeting that need—list the particulars briefly; next, anticipate their objections and answer them; and finally, ask for their response.

5. *Create an Action Plan*: Develop a schedule for carrying out what you have planned. Perhaps you will want to keep index cards with ideas or contacts in a calendar file or database, so that you are reminded of your plan for particular days, and can check off your accomplishments.

6. *Celebrate Your Successes, Reevaluate Your Plan, and Plan for the Next Round.*

CONCLUSION

It is our hope that the activities and strategies that we have provided in this chapter will offer educators, supervisors, students, supervisees, and other professionals the opportunity to broaden their awareness of the benefits and limitations of DSM diagnosis, labeling, and other classification processes. We also hope that readers have taken advantage of the opportunities afforded by this chapter's exercises to brainstorm ways to include other stories about clients' problems in order to overcome the limitations of the DSM story, and in order to expand traditional ways of diagnosing into more usable, ethical, practice-relevant, inclusive, and respectful ways of making meaning of client problems. This chapter offers piecemeal strategies for examining the use of the DSM system. The next chapters offer actual cases and the means by which professionals around the country suggest incorporating this book's suggestions into their practice of diagnosing and treating the clients in these cases. The final chapter offers a model for contextual, developmental, and holistic assessment that includes diagnosis as a part of the client's context.

6

The Case of 9-Year-Old Janelle and Her Mother

MAX HINES, KY HEINLEN, WENDY K. ENOCHS,
COLLEEN A. ETZBACH, AND WILLIAM ETZBACH

CASE BY MAX HINES

I found the ethical considerations particularly challenging during the diagnostic process with a 9-year-old female client. Janelle came in at the insistence of her mother, Pam, who indicated that she was very worried that Janelle had become increasingly quiet and withdrawn at home. Janelle was an only child, and Pam was a single parent. Pam conveyed flat affect as she reported that Janelle's father was an alcoholic who had been verbally, but not physically, abusive with Pam. "That's why I left him while I was pregnant with Janelle, to get away." Janelle showed no emotional reaction when her mother said in Janelle's presence, "I am very worried because Janelle is depressed, has no friends, lacks social skills, and may even be suicidal."

Pam was clear from the initial telephone contact that she wanted to use her health insurance to pay for my services, a procedure that would require a DSM-IV-TR (*Diagnostic and Statistical Manual of Mental Disorders*, 4th ed., Text Revision) diagnosis. Pam also emphasized that she wanted to know the diagnosis. She said she was frustrated with previous providers, "They weren't cooperating by letting me know what my daughter's problem is." I told Pam that once I had completed the assessment phase, I would let her know the diagnosis. I informed her, however, that more than one session might be needed to complete the assessment and provide accurate diagnostic information. Pam said that she wanted an answer on the diagnosis by the end of the first session. I again reiterated to Pam that it could take two or three sessions before I could complete a full assessment and provide an accurate diagnosis. I told Pam that I felt that it was reasonable to provide diagnostic information by the end of three sessions, two if feasible. We agreed to this timetable before beginning counseling.

I proceeded with counseling Janelle and her mother. During the initial session, I gathered information from Pam and Janelle. Pam signed a release to exchange confidential information with Janelle's teacher. After Janelle's teacher received a copy of the release, I called her. The teacher reported that Janelle "talks enough" and was sociable and socially accepted at school. Janelle's teacher said that Janelle was doing reasonably well academically and went on to say, "If you want to know what I really think, I think Janelle's mother is the problem. She's just looking for a problem with Janelle, and there isn't one. She insists that Janelle is depressed and needs social skills. If you can just get the mother into a bowling league 5 days a week, that might solve the problem." I considered the possibility that the teacher might be engaging in mother blaming, a common problem in the diagnostic process (Caplan, 1989; Chesler, 1986). At the same time, her statements brought into question whether Janelle actually had a condition that met the criteria for a DSM-IV-TR diagnosis.

Further investigation raised the same question because the problems that were reported by the mother apparently occurred only in the home. In follow-up individual interviews, Janelle and Pam each reported that the only regular visitors in the home were Pam's sister and her two children, who were close to Janelle's age. Both Janelle and Pam indicated that Janelle came out of her room and played with her cousins whenever they came to visit. Janelle also stated that she tries to stay away from her mom. She stated that she avoids her mom at home because "My mom thinks I have a problem, and I don't. She's just making things up, and that's my only problem. There's no convincing her. Even worse is that it never ends and there's no way out."

RESPONSE BY MAX HINES

Although the mother was clearly intending that her daughter be diagnosed and receive treatment, I found no verification of a diagnosable problem in the daughter. A suicide assessment indicated that Janelle was at very low risk. Therefore, I shifted the diagnostic focus to the mother.

Given Pam's declarations about her daughter's problems, combined with no evidence that Janelle had these problems, I initially considered a diagnosis of Münchausen's, or factitious disorder by proxy, for the mother. That is, Pam appeared to be manufacturing symptoms in her daughter. Further confirmation of such a disorder emerged as I explored Pam's visits with Janelle to two physicians prior to pursuing counseling; Pam had expected the physicians to verify that Janelle had some medical problem. I obtained a release and called the physicians. The two physicians' responses were similar. Pam had told the physicians that she was convinced that Janelle had to have some problem with her hormones or thyroid, or to have some biochemical imbalance. Each physician completed a physical examination of Janelle, including specific medical tests, and then informed Pam that Janelle appeared to have no diagnosable medical (i.e., physical) problem. Each reported to me that they were a little concerned about Pam's insistence despite the relative lack of clear symptoms. When questioned about the physician's reports, Pam stated that she believed that the physicians were wrong. I asked Pam which she thought was needed at this point, another medical assessment or counseling? She indicated that she wanted to "give counseling a try."

In the first session, I met initially with the two of them, then with Janelle individually, and then with Pam alone. Janelle said that she didn't have any problems except with her mom. My heart went out to Janelle, and somewhat to Pam. However, I needed a consult in order to free myself from countertransference reactions toward Pam. Because I have a strong desire to protect and help children, I saw Janelle's suffering, and I felt angry with Pam.

My feelings aside, however, in my professional judgment, Pam's condition did not sufficiently meet the criteria for any DSM-IV-TR disorder, including 300.19 Factitious Disorder Not Otherwise Specified (i.e., factitious disorder by proxy), although it was a better fit than any other diagnosis. Considering factitious disorder as a possible diagnosis was complicated by the diagnostic criteria being relatively vague and nonspecific. For instance, the DSM-IV-TR includes only two sentences regarding 301.19 Factitious Disorder Not Otherwise Specified:

> This category includes disorders with factitious symptoms that do not meet the criteria for Factitious Disorder. An example is factitious disorder by proxy: the intentional production or feigning of physical or psychological signs or symptoms in another person who is under the individual's care for the purpose of indirectly assuming the sick role. (APA, 2000, p. 517)

The focus is not upon observable behaviors, but rather upon intention and motivation. Was Pam's behavior intentional? What constitutes intentionality? Can unconscious motivation be deemed intentional? Even if the answer is yes, was Pam's behavior for the purpose of indirectly assuming the sick role?

Other factors that contributed to my conclusion that factitious disorder by proxy did not apply included Janelle's age, Janelle having no diagnosable disorder, the general midrange magnitude and intensity of Pam's psychological need for her daughter to be in the sick role, and the fact, as noted in the DSM-IV-TR, that factitious disorder by proxy with psychological factors is rare. For example, if Pam were projecting these "disorders" onto her child, I would have expected the projection process to occur earlier in Janelle's life. It appears to have crested at the time that they came to me, rather than 4 to 5 years earlier when Janelle was much more dependent and vulnerable. Janelle also apparently had no medical disorder, and the magnitude of any projection of psychological problems by Pam was not great enough to induce symptoms that

were sufficient for an identifiable diagnosis in her daughter. Although the very nature of the disorder is that the parent would invent disorders in the child over time, I would expect the symptoms of those disorders to be clearly apparent to observers. In Janelle's case, they were not.

I also believe that it is important to consider the presenting problem in context. I gathered information about the mother–daughter relationship and found that the two had been close when Janelle was young, and that now the relationship was more strained. I considered the possibility that Pam was "binding her anxiety" by focusing on Janelle. I find it amazing how wide ranging people's responses can be to anxiety. Some people emanate their anxiety directly in anxiety disorders. Some people bind their anxiety and thus assuage it by eating more or smoking cigarettes. Some people work more, and others engage in physical activities to contain and/or work off their anxious energy. Pam did not exhibit any visible anxiety. I had little data that would serve as a foundation for the hypothesis that Pam was projecting anxious energy by feigning symptoms in her daughter. In my professional opinion, the truth of the matter was that neither Pam nor Janelle met the criteria for a diagnosable disorder.

My diagnostic conclusions themselves were distressing to me because I felt that they left me in an ethical bind. Pam was adamant that she wanted to use her insurance to pay for my services, and it seemed fairly probable that she would terminate counseling upon learning that, in my perspective as a licensed psychologist, no diagnosable disorder applied. I felt torn because of my worries about Janelle, and the knowledge that if I did not "please" the mother by doing as she wished, Janelle might not receive help.

Ethical Principles

The word *ethic* derives from the Greek *ethikos* or *ethos* which means character or custom

(Webster's, 1988). Ethics involves a system of moral standards or values manifested in the standards of conduct for our profession. It also involves the character of the counselor. In this case, I experienced a conflict between my character and the customs or standards of conduct in the counseling profession, a conflict that can better be illustrated from the context of an ethical framework. One such framework was described by Meara, Schmidt, and Day (1996). Building upon the earlier work of Kitchener (1984) and others, Meara et al. (1996) declared that the following six basic principles are involved in ethical decision making:

1. *Nonmaleficence:* Counselors should do no harm.

2. *Beneficence:* Counselors should do good and help the client.

3. *Autonomy:* Clients have the freedom of self determination.

4. *Fidelity:* Practitioners should be faithful to the client and should keep their promises.

5. *Justice:* Counselors should practice fairness and offer equal treatment.

6. *Veracity:* Mental health practitioners should be truthful and honest with their clients and with themselves.

Application of Ethical Principles

All six of these principles came to bear in my struggle regarding diagnosis while working with Janelle and Pam. Below I describe how I struggled with these ethical issues:

Nonmaleficence: Do No Harm. Above all else, do no harm. This is much more than an ethical standard. It is a fundamental commitment and a way of being in the world. There have been numerous situations in my life in which I have been powerless to do good, but at least I did not do harm. Whereas I can often live with sometimes not being able to do good in the world, I find it difficult to live with myself when my behavior results in harm to others. When I was younger, I would have a nightmare every few months (or at least that's how often I recall having had the dream) that I was driving an automobile and unintentionally ran over a young person. In this family, I saw Janelle being run over by her mother. The crushing weight was Pam's negative projection onto Janelle. I felt torn by my belief that Janelle was being harmed and could continue to be harmed. I was also aware that my choices around diagnosis and my approach with Pam could potentially contribute to her continuing to be harmed. My choices to help Janelle might be overridden by Pam's choices. Whatever people's concerns about labeling children—many of which have been cited in this book—situations like this case point out the dilemmas around not being able to provide a diagnosis.

Beneficence. Reflective of my character and values is a deep and fundamental desire to be helpful, a desire that resulted in my choice to become a counseling psychologist. There is a lot of pain in the world, and my choice to become a counseling psychologist was meaningful in that it reflected a means by which I could help others with this pain (I believe this is true for most counselors). Therefore, the ethical principle of beneficence, "doing or producing good" (*Merriam-Webster's*, 2001, p. 106) is much more than a standard of conduct: It is a core value that's innate to my character. I wanted to help Janelle. And yet helping Janelle, because she was a minor, depended on Pam's approval and agreement to proceed. Pam had set conditions on our ability to proceed; that is, she demanded to know her daughter's diagnosis and insisted that we use her insurance, which also required a DSM-IV-TR diagnosis. I was unable to fit Pam or Janelle into any DSM-IV-TR diagnostic grouping. I felt torn by my genuine commitment to helping Janelle that seemed in conflict with the reality that I might be relatively powerless to do so. I thought it was entirely possible that my feelings of powerlessness were parallel to Janelle's. I was aware that others, in order to ensure that clients obtained treatment, routinely ascribed diagnoses that were "close" or least stigmatizing with all of the criteria being met. I felt myself tempted to do the same for Janelle's sake.

Autonomy. Autonomy is highly valued in American culture. Freedom and self-determination are at its core. Autonomy with respect to counseling generally means that the client gets to decide whether to engage in counseling; I am usually quite comfortable with accepting a client's choice. When counseling involves children, however, the parent or legal guardian has decision-making authority until the child reaches the age of consent. Janelle was under the age of consent, and therefore, Pam had to make the decision regarding whether counseling would continue. Janelle was quite compliant and in all likelihood would have participated in counseling if her mother requested as much. In this situation, the legal right of the parent to determine whether counseling should be pursued seemed in conflict with the daughter's right to treatment that might assist her. I even briefly considered whether Pam's behavior constituted reportable abuse. Even if I understand the reasons for a parent's mistreatment of his or her child (i.e., past traumatic experiences or poor treatment by the parent's parents) or poor parenting, I really struggle with what to do when this "harm" falls short of actual physical or sexual abuse.

Pam's ability to choose whether to participate in counseling also required that I provide her with relevant information so that she could make an informed decision. I wished that I wasn't obligated to tell her that I could find no diagnosable disorder. In this situation, it was clear from the beginning that Pam would require me to disclose a diagnosis. But

in most situations, I would frame assessment information in terms that would be most likely to facilitate treatment, sometimes not explicitly stating a diagnosis. I wished that I had that option in this case.

Fidelity. Fidelity requires counselors to be loyal and faithful, which are critical behaviors and attitudes in creating a trusting relationship with the client. To form a trusting relationship with Janelle, I needed to first create a trusting relationship with Pam. I found it especially challenging to be loyal and faithful to Pam because I saw her as the primary source of the problem. I have been told by those close to me that my emotions are transparent: I am not the type of person who can hide his feelings or attitudes. If not verbally, then surely nonverbally, my feelings about this mother causing harm by attributing nonexistent problems to her daughter would get in the way of building a trusting relationship with Pam. I was genuinely committed to Janelle and had begun to develop a trusting relationship with her. However, I was aware that I first needed Pam's consent to treatment, and that meant I needed her to trust me. How could I be true to myself and remain loyal to Pam? Might I sacrifice a trusting relationship with Janelle if I were to do the things necessary to build a trusting relationship with her mother? I felt very confused and frustrated by these internal questions.

Justice. Justice means fairness and equal treatment for all clients. With my other clients, and in general, would I seriously consider giving a diagnosis that truly did not apply so as to be able to help the client? Consultation was very helpful in assisting me to answer this question. Of course, the answer was, "No, I would not." Therefore I needed to look at what my temptation to do so with Janelle and Pam was about. It was about my countertransference, my own experience of pain when I was about Janelle's age. It was about my sensitivity to the issue of parents causing harm to their own children. It was about my own woundedness and hypersensitivity regarding the pain and suffering of innocent children because of their parent's limitations. I wanted to be helpful to Janelle, yet I couldn't do for Janelle and Pam what I wouldn't do for any other client. This meant that I needed to base the diagnosis on the data not on the necessity for treatment.

Veracity. In my perspective, veracity means honesty and openness in my relationship with myself as well as in my relationships with others. In this troubling situation, I needed to start with myself. There are times when a new client will say, "I don't know how counseling works." In response, I often say, "Counseling is a process. Let's look at 'HOW.' 'HOW' is spelled H, O, W. H is for honest; O is for open; and W is for willing. Counseling works if you are honest, open, and willing. The process generally works if you work the process." It is sometimes difficult to walk my own talk, yet it's of fundamental importance. I was tempted in Janelle and Pam's case to stretch the truth and give a diagnosis when, in truth, the diagnostic criterion did not apply. I felt torn by my commitment to truth and honesty because it seemed in conflict with my desire to find a way to help Janelle. Sometimes the truth is difficult to accept and deal with. However, as Carl Whitaker (personal communication) once said to me, "The truth might hurt, but you can heal from that." Indeed.

Ethical Decision-Making Process

As is so often true, this case brought forth more than one ethical dilemma and the need to weigh them simultaneously during the diagnostic process. I began with identifying that I was experiencing ethical dilemmas. For me, consultation is generally very helpful in identifying and sorting through the ethical issues involved. In this case, by the end of the second session, it was clear that I was very angry with

Pam. Janelle was only 9 years old, and was very sweet, innocent, and relatively defenseless. She wanted her mother's approval, and she generally trusted her mother and others. Janelle was the type of person who engages people out of her own trusting nature, regardless of the situation. In a healthy, affirming family environment, this can be wonderful. In a toxic family environment, and especially with a parent whose dynamic is child pathologizing, Janelle's innocent trusting could result in damage to her. It had become increasingly clear that many, if not all, of Janelle's difficulties emerged from negative projections by the mother onto the daughter. My anger toward Pam grew to such an intensity that I could not have ignored it, even if I wanted to. I think it's likely that most counselors observing this situation would struggle with some negative feelings toward the mother. Regardless, my anger toward Pam was a red flag, warning me that I was in danger of unethical choices and indicating that I needed to focus on my own countertransference.

Once I recognized this need, I pursued supervision. I was very grateful that I had a supervisor with whom I could be honest and open, with whom I had had consistently constructive experiences. This supervisor was someone with a commitment to the highest ethical standards, yet someone with whom I also felt safe to explore my feelings toward Pam. Therefore, in consultation with the supervisor, I processed my countertransference and identified its source: my own personally harmful experience in relation to a parent when I was Janelle's age.

My supervisor's stated position was that although identification of the countertransference is often sufficient, sometimes it is not. If it is not, the counselor may need to explore the issue further in his or her own counseling, and/or may need to refer the client to another practitioner. In this situation, recognizing my countertransferential issues was sufficient because a few years earlier, I had resolved many personal issues while I was a client in long-term counseling. Therefore, near the end of the consultation session, I felt relieved to realize that I no longer felt so angry with Pam. I recognized and accepted that she had strengths as well as limitations.

Identification of my countertransference helped to free me emotionally. Nonetheless, I still needed to decide how to proceed. I wanted to do no harm. I wanted to help Janelle. I needed to respect client autonomy, that is, Pam's right to end treatment if she so desired. I needed to be honest and trustworthy. I needed to treat the client (and her mother) in the same manner that I would treat any other client. I discussed each of these considerations with my supervisor, and worked to clarify how these considerations conflicted with one another. I discovered that once I cleared myself of my countertransference, most of them did not seem to conflict any longer.

The most difficult ethical challenge that still remained was the clear evidence that Pam was harming her daughter. I was no longer overwhelmed by my own anger about it; nonetheless, there was reason to be concerned about the harm continuing. It thus became a clinical matter for discussion with Pam. I recognized that it would be inappropriate for me to be anything other than honest and open with Pam in regard to the matters of relevance for her. I felt grounded. I was ready to meet with Pam.

Proceeding Ethically

Because Pam was the decision maker regarding counseling, I considered it important to communicate directly with her regarding my diagnostic conclusions and ethical concerns. After my consultation, but prior to the already scheduled third session, Pam called and asked, "Do you have the diagnosis yet?" I responded by saying that I would like to talk with her about the diagnosis in our upcoming session. Pam said, "Can't we just discuss it by phone?" I asked her to come for one more

session and to bring Janelle with her. Pam said that she didn't want to meet again if her insurance was not going to pay for the session. I again offered a sliding fee scale arrangement, and Pam said, "No, I am not going to pay for any more sessions." I agreed to write off this one session if her insurance did not cover it. I would have done the same for other clients in such a situation. Pam agreed to come for one more session.

During the session, I dedicated myself to what I considered Janelle's best interests: Janelle was my client, and Pam was not interested in counseling for herself. I had previously suggested to Pam that we work collaboratively together to help Janelle. Pam had said that she didn't see Janelle's problems as related to parenting issues, and that she wasn't interested in being blamed for Janelle's problems. She had read that counselors often blame parents, and she wanted none of it. I had assured her that I was not interested in blaming her or anyone, that what I had in mind was helping her daughter. Despite my approach, Pam had remained closed and resistant to my efforts to reframe the therapy as a collaborative family effort.

So, when Pam and Janelle arrived for the third session, I met individually with Pam and began by engaging her in her role as Janelle's mother. Prior to this session, Janelle had given me permission to talk with her mom about anything that we had talked about in our time together one-to-one. I informed Pam that in my professional opinion, Janelle did not meet the criteria for any diagnosable mental disorder. "The good news is there's nothing wrong with Janelle." In response, Pam again insisted that her daughter was depressed because she did not have any friends and did not have social skills. "I think she might even be suicidal," she said. When asked again for specifics, Pam was vague and was not able to corroborate her concern that Janelle might be suicidal. I informed Pam that I had assessed Janelle for suicidal thoughts, behaviors, and associated factors. I informed her that in my assessment I found no basis for me to believe that Janelle was currently at risk of harming herself. We also dialogued about Pam's concern that Janelle was lonely and needed more friends. I encouraged her to foster Janelle's involvement with peers, yet also reflected that Janelle seemed much less concerned and distressed about the matter than she (Pam) did.

When it was apparent that I had made as much progress as I could with Pam, I asked her to invite Janelle in to talk with us. With Pam and Janelle present, I spoke with Janelle about her mom's concerns and that her mother had brought her in to see if there was any need for counseling. I said that I thought that counseling could be helpful for lots of people. I commented on how we are all learning and growing, and that counseling can be especially helpful for people who come in when there's a life concern, one that hasn't had time to develop into something more serious. I used the medical analogy that if a person gets an infection, it's a good idea to go to the doctor early. Then it can be treated effectively with an antibiotic, because if left untreated, many infections could develop into life threatening conditions. Pam would have none of it, saying "If she has a medical condition, I'll take her to a medical doctor. This is different." I agreed that it was different, yet noted its similarity as well. "For instance," I said, "if someone lacks social skills, counseling might help the person to gain such skills *before* the lack of skills results in no friends and before such isolation results in depression."

Pam became argumentative at that point. After hearing her out, it became apparent that Pam was not open to counseling without a diagnosable disorder for which her insurance would pay. I repeated an earlier offer of a sliding fee scale arrangement, saying, "I can appreciate your concern about the finances." Pam repeated her earlier insistence upon a diagnosis for Janelle. Although Pam had repeatedly rebuffed my efforts to explore her

perspectives further, I now clearly indicated the need to reconsider her position because I believed that it was harming Janelle. I stated kindly, but directly, that the problem was one that appeared to be present at home but not in other contexts, and that for this reason I considered it important that we explore this together, not to blame her or anybody else, but to understand it all better and to find some solutions that everyone could be happy with. Pam was insistent and adamant: The problem was not hers, but Janelle's. It became increasingly clear to me that any further discussion of the matter would meet with further resistance. I had made every effort to bring Pam into the counseling, and further efforts toward that end would not be helpful. Pam was clear and insistent in repeatedly stating her position. If there was no diagnosis, there would be no counseling. In my professional opinion, it was time for me to accept her decision.

I then turned my attention to Janelle. I told her that the good news was that, "There's nothing wrong with you." I then explained as best I could at a level that Janelle could understand what I meant in terms of DSM-IV-TR. Janelle smiled. Pam had a look on her face as though she were sucking a lemon. I invited them to continue working with me even though "You have no disorder, Janelle." Pam then indicated that this would be our last session. I said that I'd be glad to work with either or both of them if Pam changed her mind at any time in the future. I also noted to Pam that because she had already paid for two sessions and since I had completed the diagnostic procedure, my diagnostic report would be available if needed at any time in the future. The session ended with Pam softening a bit, but far from openly looking at her own contribution to this situation.

Even though I did the best I could at the time, I have continued to struggle internally over what I might have done differently so as to help Janelle. I recognize, too, that the reader may well have some good ideas about how I might have more effectively approached the case so as to ensure that Janelle received help. The counseling profession can be humbling sometimes, as this case has so vividly reminded me.

Conclusion

In closing, I would like to reflect upon some ethical implications of the larger mental health system, that is, the diagnostic and the insurance systems. I think it is important to recognize that the diagnostic and insurance systems often limit the counseling process in important and troubling ways. For instance, the DSM-IV-TR presents social constructs, not verities; that is, the mental disorders that it describes are socially constructed phenomena about clusters of symptoms, clusters agreed upon in the relatively political process that has accompanied the development of each edition of the DSM. I find these social constructs to be incomplete and not always helpful. For instance, they seem to define for clients (and sometimes professionals), as can be seen in this case, the boundaries of problems and counseling services, when clearly counseling can benefit people with a far wider range of problems than are included in the DSM and in many more ways than are reimbursed by insurance companies.

But of course, broadening the definition of "problems" and widening the scope of services brings up issues of cost. Insurance companies rightly aspire to contain costs because they are businesses whose customers, whether businesses or individuals, want to contain the costs of the health insurance policies that they are buying. Health insurance policies routinely pay only what they are legally mandated to pay or what their purchaser asks them to pay (of course, their purchasers often use insurance company expertise to decide on standards of care, reimbursement, and containing costs). For these reasons, insurance companies may not want to recognize a broader range of problems and services.

However, mental health practitioners do not have to be completely defined by insurance

company perspectives. I have counseled, and I suspect that other counselors have also counseled, many clients who do not have diagnosable disorders but who have benefited significantly from counseling. In my practice, these clients pay full fee or pay under a sliding-fee schedule. In either event, the client receives the same sorts of services that insurance pays for when clients have diagnosable disorders. One wonders how we might change the reimbursement situation so that we are not reduced to what Tom Lehrer (satirist, singer) refers to, that is, becoming "doctors" who specialize in the diseases of the rich, because they are the ones who can afford to pay full fee. For those of us who see some clients on a sliding-fee schedule, we find ourselves on occasion wondering how to pay the monthly bills. Where is the balance? What is and what is not ethical? What is one to do? Clearly, then, ethical decision making about Pam and Janelle cannot be separated from the larger social contexts of how one is to ethically balance one's own financial needs with the financial abilities of the client(s) and the current funding environment.

RESPONSE BY KY HEINLEN

The case of 9-year-old Janelle illustrates several of the essential ethical dilemmas commonly found in the diagnostic process. First and foremost, it reflects the quandary that clinicians find themselves in when they have to assign a diagnosis in order to receive insurance reimbursement for services. In addition, the case demonstrates some of the difficulties encountered when a diagnosis is to be made for a child. As with most cases that involve children, the case also reflects some of the problems encountered with diagnosis within the context of family therapy.

Reimbursement

The case of Janelle and her mother illuminates several of the problems encountered when a clinician is required to make a diagnosis for insurance reimbursement purposes. To receive mental health care benefits from an insurer, a diagnosis is usually required. It is not sufficient to simply identify appropriate V codes or Axis IV issues. Rather, the insurer mandates that the treatment be "medically necessary" and thus requires that an Axis I and/or II diagnosis be identified. Using the DSM to diagnose a disorder clearly reflects the influence of the medical model, and for some clinicians this in itself is problematic. Clinicians whose philosophical perspectives run counter to the DSM diagnostic process must make a decision about their willingness to make a diagnosis solely for the purposes of being reimbursed by an insurance company. Furthermore, as Kutchins & Kirk (1997) point out, the client's impairment must meet the criteria for a DSM disorder; in this case, symptomatology doesn't appear to exist that clearly meets diagnostic criteria.

The first task in approaching the ethical quandary related to insurance reimbursement is to decide whether there is sufficient evidence to warrant making a diagnosis for the child. The mother has reported that the child is depressed, has no friends, lacks social skills, and may even be suicidal. Each of these symptoms suggests a diagnosis of depression; however, without corroborating information from Janelle or her teacher, it is difficult to attest to the validity of these symptoms.

Second, it is important to consider the future ramifications of giving Janelle a diagnosis, whether it is warranted or not, and who benefits from the diagnosis. It is important to recall that information regarding a client's diagnosis will be maintained in a central information bank and may impact future insurability and mental health care. Assigning Janelle a mental health diagnosis of any kind will establish a preexisting condition for her that may necessitate that she maintain continuous medical care insurance or risk being denied coverage for claims relating to her mental health

condition. In other words, if a diagnosis is made for Janelle, she may have to keep medical insurance continuously for the rest of her life, assuming current medical insurance parameters, in order to have mental health services covered. If she has a lapse in medical insurance coverage, this preexisting condition may not be covered in the new coverage that she obtains. Furthermore, it seems that diagnosing Janelle will be a relief to Pam, rather than to Janelle. That is to say, the diagnosis will not serve the client but rather her mother. On the other hand, if no diagnosis is made, the clients' health insurance will probably not reimburse for counseling services, and the family may then not be able to afford to pursue counseling.

Third, clinicians need to avoid misrepresenting the facts when submitting claims to insurance companies. This mandate draws attention to another inherent dilemma that is faced by clinicians: that is, the challenge to not over- or underdiagnose. As previously mentioned, many clinicians choose to underdiagnose in an effort not to stigmatize the client or create future problems for the client. On the other hand, some clinicians may overdiagnose the client in an effort to be reimbursed and to enable the client to afford counseling services. In this case, Janelle does not appear to meet the criteria for major depression or dysthymia. Therefore, to receive reimbursement, a clinician may be tempted to overdiagnose in an effort to meet the diagnostic criteria of an Axis I disorder. This is misrepresentation and, although a common resolution to this ethical quandary, it is also one of the most frequent acts of financial misconduct brought before licensing boards (Peterson, 1996, as cited in Welfel, 2002). Another problem in assigning a diagnosis, even if the criteria are met, is the failure of the current diagnostic process to accurately reflect such things as client strengths, assets, support systems, and family dynamics. Thus, it might be said that those who use the DSM system by itself, although they may succeed in avoiding the legal problem of fraud, cannot avoid misrepresenting the client. As previously pointed out, those advocating for a family relational diagnosis and others have suggested including a sixth axis in which a diagnosis of the family system (or other factors) might be included as part of the multiaxial system. If such an axis existed, one could then determine a DSM diagnosis that was more accurate.

The first step in resolving this dilemma is to review with Pam, the client's mother, the risks and benefits of providing a diagnosis for her daughter. Although she may understand that a diagnosis will make insurance reimbursement possible, she may not understand the other ramifications of diagnosis. Because Pam was clear in the initial telephone contact that she wanted to use her health insurance to pay for services, it can be assumed that she will want to proceed with discovering and assigning a diagnosis. Because the clinician has agreed to work with this family with the understanding that medical insurance will be used for payment of services, a diagnosis will need to be made if services are to be provided. Of course, the clinician could not know ahead of time whether the daughter would meet criteria for a diagnosis. It may also be assumed that Pam will not pursue counseling for herself and her daughter should the clinician not assign a diagnosis. As illustrated in Max Hines's report above, this is, in fact, what happened. Frequently family therapists struggle with wanting to rescue children and being constrained by the parents' constantly fluctuating motivations for counseling. The ethical struggle becomes whether to assign a diagnosis just to ensure that Janelle receives services and is not further harmed by her mother's behavior.

Diagnosing Children

The second ethical quandary that this case illuminates is the problem in diagnosing children. Oftentimes, the diagnostic process is enhanced by collaboration with significant others and previous or other care providers. With children, parents are typically the primary source of information. However, as previously cited, Rosenhan's experiment (Rosenhan, 1973; Seligman, Walker, & Rosenhan, 2001) suggests that the setting influences the diagnosis and may become a self-fulfilling prophecy. In this case, Pam is part of the "setting" and may be contributing to and perpetuating the problem with Janelle, as well as shifting other's perceptions about whether Janelle has a problem. It is important to examine to what extent a diagnosis of depression for Janelle will help Pam. Frequently, we find that parents ascribe conditions to their children so that they can focus all of their attention on the problems of their children and not have to deal with their own problems. In this case, neither the client nor her teacher can substantiate the symptoms cited by the mother as indicative of a mental health problem. In fact, it is interesting to note that both Janelle and Pam indicated that when they have guests over to the house Janelle appropriately interacts with them and doesn't appear to have any problems. It would be helpful to ask Pam why she thinks Janelle is able to interact appropriately with her cousins whenever they visit and yet she thinks Janelle has no friends and lacks social skills.

However, even if Pam is not trying to refocus attention onto Janelle in an effort to distract from her own problems, even if a therapist found that neither Janelle nor Pam met the criteria for a DSM diagnosis, a therapist might consider treatment to be necessary to resolve family systems problems or to offer a child support when she is in a difficult situation. Frequently children are brought into counseling for various "acting out" behaviors that are not diagnosable with the DSM system, and yet, family therapists still see the families and play therapists still see the children. These therapists clearly use different criteria for deciding what is necessary treatment than might Pam or the insurance industry.

Assigning a diagnostic disorder to Janelle may also present an ethical dilemma solely because she is a child. The DSM is largely designed for the classification of adult disorders, with the few exceptions including attention and conduct problems. To what extent does Janelle, as a child, represent an "oppressed" minority? As Kutchins and Kirk (1997) suggest, we tend to make negative statements about those who have less power. Although considering the power imbalances in this case sheds little light on how to diagnose Janelle, it does raise the question of whether Janelle should be diagnosed at all. It is interesting to note that Pam demonstrated flat affect when she reported information about Janelle's father, which may suggest that she, in fact, has mental health issues of her own. If Janelle had equal power to her mother, would we still be trying to diagnose her? On the other hand, would we ascribe any different meaning if it was Janelle's father who maintained that Janelle was depressed, had no friends, lacked social skills, and was suicidal?

In examining possible solutions to these quandaries, solutions that take into account the above concerns, several ideas come to mind. First of all, assuming that Janelle still has contact with her father and that her mother would permit the counselor to contact him, it would be helpful to glean what information he has regarding his daughter's mental health. It might also be helpful to have a more in-depth discussion with Pam about how she feels about her own life, the dissolution of her marriage, and the number of friends Pam has contact with on a regular basis. Frequently taking the time to talk to parents about what is going on in their lives fosters a greater understanding of the nature of the situation and increases parental motivation to participate in working on their own problems. In this situation, we know that Pam has reported being in a relationship with an abusive alcoholic. One of the most important things to do in making a decision about a diagnosis in this case would be to complete an assessment of Pam to rule out the possibility that she has mental health problems. Although it is important not to engage in mother blaming, it is also important not to victimize the person with less power, who, in this case, is Janelle.

Family Therapy

Finally, another ethical quandary that this case presents relates to the principles underlying family therapy. Family therapists frequently view symptoms as an expression of the problems in the family system. For example, Janelle seems to be avoiding her mother because of the conflict that ensues when she interacts with Pam. Although an individual therapist may assess this as a problem for Janelle and may proceed to assist Janelle in coping with the situation, the family therapist views this as a problem in a family system that includes both Janelle and her mother. Ascribing an individual diagnosis serves little purpose for the family therapist because at present there aren't Axis I diagnostic codes relating to family interactions. In fact, as previously mentioned, Doherty & Simmons (1996) found that many family therapists ignore the issue of diagnosis altogether. This may in part be due to the family therapy objective of moving family members away from blaming any one person and of challenging each family member to recognize how they are perpetuating the problems within the system. Furthermore, in terms of accuracy versus misrepresentation, should an individual be diagnosed when it is the system that needs fixing? In the case of Janelle, is it appropriate to give her a diagnosis when her family has a history of alcoholism and verbal abuse, and when her mother may, intentionally or unintentionally, be creating symptoms to distract from her own struggles? On the other hand, is Janelle's behavior in the home a metaphor for the tensions and difficulties between her parents, despite the fact that her father is no longer in the home?

Summary

The case of Janelle highlights several of the ethical problems in making a diagnosis. First, because Pam will request insurance reimbursement, several issues arise. Specifically, because most insurance companies require an Axis I diagnosis prior to reimbursement, it becomes imperative that a diagnosis be made to receive payment from an insurance company. However, that diagnosis must reflect the clear and present symptoms of a disorder, and it is questionable whether Janelle is exhibiting those. Second, Janelle's minority position as a child poses several challenges to the diagnostic process. It is unclear whether Janelle is the victim and an oppressed minority or whether Pam is being disregarded because she is a mother. Completing an assessment with Pam and obtaining some more collateral information about Janelle may provide the answers to these questions. Finally, this case sheds light on some of the conflicts that family therapists must resolve between their systems approach to case conceptualization and the individualistic approach of the DSM.

Based on the information provided, I would be inclined not to give Janelle a diagnosis. Rather, I would spend time trying to develop an alliance with Pam and trying to determine the appropriateness of assessing her for a diagnosis so that the need to meet insurance requirements would be met and further intervention could be directed at changing the family system.

As illustrated in the actual case response by Max Hines, collateral information from the two physicians that Pam previously sought a diagnosis from confirms that assigning a diagnosis for Janelle is more about Pam than it is about Janelle. That is to say, knowing that Pam has sought a medical diagnosis for Janelle based on physical symptoms that were found to be unsubstantiated confirms the likelihood that in this case Pam is seeking a mental health diagnosis for something that is equally unsubstantiated. Pam and Janelle would be best served by a clear and direct confrontation with Pam about her need to have help for her daughter, as opposed to addressing the need that Pam has for assistance. At this point it is helpful for clinicians to remember that sometimes clients are not ready to engage in the therapeutic work necessary to effect change. Our responsibility lies in identifying the problem and presenting clients with a choice in dealing with it. As the previous author indicates in this case, Pam chose not to deal with it.

RESPONSE BY WENDY K. ENOCHS, COLLEEN A. ETZBACH, AND WILLIAM ETZBACH

We believe that the DSM-IV-TR diagnostic possibilities for this case study include parent–child relational problem (V61.20); depressive disorder NOS (311) for the daughter, based solely on the information that the mother has provided; and factitious disorder by proxy (300.19) for the mother. In choosing one or more of these diagnoses, several variables must be examined.

First, the mother is the only one who believes that Janelle has problems, and these problematic behaviors are apparent just in the home, where only the mother and Janelle reside. The home appears to be somewhat isolative, with only an aunt and two cousins coming to visit. Janelle does interact and play with the cousins when they visit, but otherwise isolates herself from her mother because Pam's accusations upset her. The mother apparently has no other situations in which she observes Janelle's interactions with others, and Janelle's teacher reports that she displays no problems at school. These situations, along with the increasing tension within the home setting and Janelle's continuing frustration with her mother, warrant a diagnosis of parent–child relational problem.

In addition, if the clinician were to rely solely on the mother's reports of Janelle isolating, lacking socialization, being depressed, and perhaps being suicidal, then potentially a diagnosis of depressive disorder NOS might fit Janelle's symptoms. With teacher's reports and clinician's observations that contradict the mother's reports, however, a clinician would certainly hesitate to diagnose Janelle with depression. Janelle may, should she continue to experience the negative attributions by the mother, very well become depressed as time goes on. But, given the mother's flat affect and lack of socialization, it might currently be more likely that the mother is the one experiencing a depressive disorder. Further information is necessary to assess this, however.

The more likely diagnosis for the mother, given the existing information, is factitious disorder by proxy. Pam has pursued multiple assessments for her daughter, constantly searching for a diagnosis, and seeking a new clinician when those consulted failed to provide a diagnosis. Pam reports mental health problems in her daughter that the daughter and her teacher do not believe exist. Instead, any problems that Janelle might have seem to stem from the mother's attributions that Janelle is experiencing depression, poor socialization, and suicidality.

More exploration into family and clinical history would be helpful in verifying such a diagnosis. For instance, the clinician would want to know whether Pam's fears for her daughter are grounded in a family history of depression that she is desperate to avoid for her daughter. If Pam continues to insist that her daughter has some type of mental health problem, it would be important to find out how many clinicians she has enlisted as well as how long she has been seeking help. Questions about whether Pam has received counseling in the past related to being verbally abused by Janelle's father ought to be explored. If she did not receive counseling, she may be seeing herself as a victim or be acting out her anger about his treatment. Pam clearly does not see herself as having a problem. However, her

continuous imposing of problems onto Janelle, despite other clinicians, the school teacher, and the current counselor failing to observe such mental health problems, provides some evidence that Pam's issues may need to be the focus of counseling. Pam's failed relationship with Janelle's father, the verbal abuse she evidently received from him, and her lack of social relations outside of her family raise concerns that she may be seeking attention from others. A counselor might question whether Pam initiates interactions with her daughter, or expects her daughter to do so. Does mom isolate herself? Does Janelle's father have any involvement in Pam's or Janelle's life currently? Whether he does or does not, does the situation perpetuate Pam's perception of herself as a victim? What stressors is Pam experiencing? For instance, she is a single parent and may struggle with having complete care of her daughter, or possibly, with financial difficulties. Answers to these questions should offer the clinician a greater understanding of Pam and should clarify the diagnostic picture.

Ethical Dilemmas

One of the primary ethical challenges in this case is deciding who really has the disorder or problem, and which diagnosis should be ascribed, particularly in light of the need for insurance reimbursement, of the potentially harmful effects of diagnosing a child, and of the shifts in motivation to pursue counseling that might occur depending on who is diagnosed. Because insurance reimbursement requires a diagnosis, and because the mother has assured the clinician that she will not pursue counseling without insurance reimbursement (perhaps she cannot afford counseling without the use of insurance), the clinician may face a mother who terminates counseling if the clinician determines that a diagnosis isn't warranted. For this child, at least a V Code is warranted, but this diagnosis alone will not result in insurance reimbursement. Furthermore, if Pam does not have insurance, but her daughter does, the clinician may struggle with whether to ascribe a diagnosis to the daughter, even if she does not have a disorder, to ensure that the family receives services and that Pam's difficulties are addressed, which, in turn, hopefully, ensures that Janelle escapes further harm. The clinician is thus faced with the ethical struggle of whether to give the child (or the mother) a reimbursable diagnosis without all of the criteria being met to ensure that the child will be protected from any further harm.

The system of relying primarily on insurance for reimbursement for services encourages the practice of giving diagnoses to clients who do not exhibit all of the criteria designated by the DSM for a disorder. This practice serves the interests of the clinician, in that the clinician will be reimbursed, and of the clients, in that they can receive necessary or desired services without paying out-of-pocket. Insurance companies are increasingly unwilling to pay for services unless treatment is a medically necessary response to a diagnosable problem, which many problems warranting counseling are not. To participate in the current insurance reimbursement system, clinicians must provide an accurate DSM diagnosis; not to do so is fraud. Of course, some would argue, as cited in this book, that the current DSM system of diagnosis makes accurate diagnosis impossible, so from this perspective, clinicians would always be misrepresenting themselves if they use the DSM system. In any case, with a family such as this one, the clinician must weigh the legal requirements to provide an accurate diagnosis against the ethical mandates to assure that children are not harmed. And the counselor must weigh the potential for preventing or interrupting the current and ongoing harm to the child against the possibility of future harm that may occur as a result of receiving a diagnostic label, accurate or not.

Janelle definitely needs some type of intervention to assist her in dealing with her mother's behavior. She has become very frustrated with her mother and does not have any other resources to assist her at this point. She has already tried persuading her mother that she does not have problems and has resorted to isolating herself from her mother to maintain her sanity. She will certainly come to harm, if she is not already being harmed, without receiving assistance, yet her mother has placed limits around the ways in which such assistance can be received. If the clinician doesn't provide the child with a diagnosis and the mother refuses counseling, the clinician is faced with knowing that the child will be negatively impacted because the family is not receiving the help that it needs. How does one weigh the potential benefits and risks of a diagnosis in such a situation?

Whether the clinician decided that a diagnosis was warranted for the child, or merely decided to ascribe a diagnosis, the clinician is still faced with weighing the benefits of that diagnosis (the child receives services) against the harm of so labeling the child. The long-term effects of a mental health disorder label may impact professionals' and others' perceptions of the child, for instance, the perceptions of her school teacher and school counselor. The child could bear the label for life, and being labeled with a mental illness can result in great stigma in our society. Ultimately, such a label may impact the way that others treat Janelle. For instance, Janelle's mother might refuse to address her own problems if Janelle was the only one receiving a diagnosis. If others' perceptions and treatment based on a diagnosis are helpful to Janelle, such a diagnosis may be warranted. However, because Janelle might be mistreated as a result of bearing a label, the clinician must carefully consider whether a diagnosis will be helpful enough to her to be warranted.

Also, the clinician must consider whether a diagnosis—warranted or not—will negatively impact Janelle's perceptions of herself and, in turn, her behavior. Might bearing a label drive her into isolation, even if she was not currently feeling isolated? Or might a label become a self-fulfilling prophecy; that is, might Janelle feel that if people already think I am not "normal," then why act "normal?" She might then use the diagnosis as an excuse for any of her difficulties with her mother or with other people, or as a means to avoid consequences for negative behavior.

Finally, if the clinician decides that diagnosing the mother with factitious disorder by proxy is the most warranted choice, a choice that is ethical and legal if the mother actually meets the criteria and a choice that addresses both the insurance needs and the problems with diagnosing a child, the clinician needs to carefully consider how the mother is likely to react. Would it be most helpful to speak with the mother straightforwardly about the belief that the problem stems from her behaviors and that her daughter displays no disorders? Might the mother then be offended and increase her accusations against her daughter? Might the mother immediately terminate counseling because the clinician is not concurring with her beliefs about her daughter's problems and is instead focusing on the mother's mental health problems? Might diagnosing the mother feed into her "victim" role? Might she again seek a different clinician who would validate her assertions that her daughter has mental health problems? Might the mother become depressed or suicidal when confronted with her behaviors, as is possible with individuals who are diagnosed with this disorder? Given the harm that is likely occurring to Janelle, would the clinician be within bounds to make a child abuse report regardless of whether the family does or does not pursue counseling?

However one answers these questions, it is clear that for Janelle and her mother to develop a productive parent–child relationship, the mother's problems will need to be addressed at some point. The clinician obviously needs to be cautious in how the diagnosis of factitious disorder by proxy is presented to

the mother. Some clinicians may hesitate to discuss the diagnosis for fear that the mother would become very angry and refuse any type of service. However, some options exist that may assist in minimizing Pam's resistance to treatment. The clinician might suggest to her that the only way to ensure insurance reimbursement would be to use the diagnoses Factitious Disorder by Proxy and the V code of Parent–Child Relational Problem. Informing the mother that the codes are solely for the purpose of ensuring insurance reimbursement might soften the impact of ascribing a diagnosis to the mother. The clinician could also validate to Pam that Janelle does have problems that need to be addressed in the hopes that if the counselor concurs with mom about Janelle having some issues, even if they aren't diagnosable using the DSM, mom may be more accepting of the diagnosis and of treatment. During this process the clinician can stress and validate the mother's need to have her daughter's issues addressed.

Other practitioners might question the helpfulness of discussing the specific DSM diagnosis, preferring, instead, a competency-based case conceptualization that might better motivate the mother to actively participate in improving the parent–child relationship. Pam sees her daughter as needing to be "fixed," and even if the counselor disagrees with her focus, the mother is actually correct in pursuing counseling for her daughter. Janelle is facing numerous challenges that emerge from her mother's reports of her depression, suicidality, and poor social skills. It is most likely that if the mother continues her negative ascriptions, Janelle will develop more serious problems. "Going with" the mother's insistence that Janelle has problems and needs counseling may help to solidify Pam's desire to pursue counseling. She may be more receptive to treatment if given the opportunity to help Janelle resolve her problems.

If the current reimbursement system could be changed, then many of the ethical dilemmas posed by this case would be resolved. For instance, if clinicians could use the V code parent–child relational problem for insurance purposes, Pam would have her diagnosis and insurance reimbursement, and might be more amenable to family treatment. The focus of the V code on treating the family as a whole, rather than singling out one person as "the problem," may increase each individual's motivations to work on problems, as no one has to "lose face" by admitting that she or he is the problem. Furthermore, because the counselor would not need to diagnose Janelle at all, the counselor would be relieved of the ethical struggle of whether to ascribe an inaccurate or potentially damaging diagnosis to Janelle.

Others might propose changing the reimbursement system so as to make diagnosis unnecessary, change it so that the clinician was only required to assess the situation and propose and carry out a treatment plan without ascribing a diagnostic label. In this case, Pam and Janelle's counselor, and Pam herself, would not inhabit a world in which Pam or the counselor would be constrained by diagnostic labels, and thus, perhaps, they would not face the dilemma of Pam refusing services or becoming angry regarding the ascription of a specific diagnosis. Furthermore, it is possible that Pam would not use the "weapon" of diagnosis against her daughter (although, realistically, she would most likely locate another sort of weapon).

Treatment Implications

If a practitioner chooses to diagnose the mother with factitious disorder by proxy, and the family is still willing to participate in ongoing counseling, a number of issues become prominent as counseling goals, and the clinician's theoretical framework would determine the best ways to meet these goals. The mother will need to reduce her negative attributions about the daughter, particularly in the daughter's

presence. The mother will need to explore and rectify the reasons for her behavior toward her daughter. The two will need to enhance their positive relating, a process that should probably be initiated by the mother. And the daughter would need to increase her activities with people other than her mother, cousins, and aunt, a shift that would also probably have to be initiated by the mother.

Counseling around a factitious disorder for the mother would most likely need to include both Pam and Janelle. Monthly sessions with Pam and Janelle would be important to allow the clinician the opportunity to observe interactions between the mother and daughter, as well as to discuss and work on any complications that developed as a result of the individual work with the mother. Weekly individual counseling for Pam would offer the opportunity to build a trusting relationship with Pam, to validate her concerns about her daughter, and to develop strategies for changing her behaviors. For instance, because Pam indicates that she is concerned about Janelle's lack of social skills, the mother could be encouraged to identify and pursue activities that they would enjoy together, activities that would also provide opportunities for Janelle to interact with others. It would then be important for the clinician to check with Janelle on how these activities were evolving for her and her mother. Individual sessions with Pam would also allow the clinician to address the mother's own issues, which might include the reasons for her behavior toward Janelle, her abusive relationship, or the absence of a sense of purpose for her life.

Because Pam doesn't see herself as "the problem," the clinician will need to invest a great deal of energy in motivating the mother to participate in the counseling process. The clinician may begin with "going with" on the chief complaints that the mother presents, which of course will focus on Janelle. The mother's motivation may also be increased if the counseling goal is to help her to "fix"

Janelle's problems. Further, her motivation may be enhanced if she receives validation about raising her daughter as a single parent and about any of the concerns that she reported during the initial intake. Although such strategies are fairly common with "resistant" clients, some practitioners may be concerned with the lack of straightforwardness (some might consider it dishonesty) in these strategies, and might wonder whether the mother would actually consent to participate were she fully informed about such strategies. An ethical counselor would thus need to carefully weigh the need for such strategies against the ethical mandates regarding informed consent.

If the clinician chose to diagnose Janelle with depressive disorder NOS, a number of ethical concerns arise. For instance, because of the common belief that medication is necessary to treat depressive disorders, Pam might push for medicating Janelle, which, given the paucity of true diagnostic criteria, would be contraindicated. In addition, this diagnosis and the ensuing treatment would probably focus more on Janelle, unless the clinician approached family treatment as described above, with the mother helping Janelle to resolve her depression. However, being so labeled might lead Janelle to view herself as being the problem, contradicting her internal sense that her mother is making up the problems, and challenging her inherent trust in herself.

As mentioned before, choosing the diagnosis of parent–child relational problem would focus both the mother and daughter during family sessions on improving their relationship. This diagnosis would encourage healthy attachments and interactions between Pam and Janelle, which are critical to a young child's mental health. But such a focus would not preclude work on any individual factors that might be hurting their relationship, even if these individual factors could not officially be considered diagnosable.

Decreasing negative attributions. If the mother continues to make negative attributions that Janelle has socialization problems and, even worse, that she is suicidal, Janelle may actually develop mental health problems. Therefore, treatment needs to focus on having the mother reduce the number of negative attributions that she makes about Janelle. In addition, Pam needs to focus on Janelle's positive qualities and be able to express her appreciation of these to Janelle.

Resolving reasons for mother's disorder. The clinician should also encourage Pam to participate in an assessment and counseling to address the issues of verbal abuse that she experienced when with Janelle's father. Perhaps, the only way that Pam feels good about herself is when she is focusing on Janelle's problems. What is it that she gains from the constant negative comments she makes about Janelle? Perhaps she does not even realize that she makes them or the potential impact that they may be having on her daughter. What is the etiology of this disorder for the mother? What needs to be resolved in order for her to change her behavior and/or have a life outside of her relationship with Janelle? The clinician could encourage Pam to participate in adult activities, cultivating adult relationships, decreasing her isolation, and thus reducing the amount of time she spends focusing solely on her daughter. In some ways, it appears that Pam is obsessing about her daughter and her daughter's behavior. The participation with other adults might give Pam an outlet for her concern about other people. The clinician might also tune in to Pam's positive qualities, encouraging her to identify her assets and to focus on the positives in her life rather than only on the negatives.

Increasing Janelle's activities away from home. Janelle is relatively isolated and only has her mother to communicate and interact with in the home most of the time. The only regular visitors are her aunt and two cousins. Her teacher reports that she is sociable at school. Rather than making negative comments about Janelle, if she is concerned about Janelle's lack of socialization, Pam could encourage Janelle to invite a friend to the house or to join friends in activities outside the home. Treatment may thus focus on having Janelle participate in activities outside of school so that she has the opportunity to interact with other peers. Perhaps Pam and Janelle could participate in activities together and meet other parents, which might take some of the pressure off of Pam and Janelle's relationship. Not only would Janelle interact with other peers, but Pam might make friends with whom to compare notes on normal childhood behavior.

Improving the Parent–Child Relationship. The parent–child relationship has become very poor because of Pam's destructive comments. Because Janelle cannot fight back, she is coping with the attributions that her mother makes in the most positive way she knows: by isolating herself and trying to ignore her mother as best as possible. However, this is not a feasible response over the long term. Therefore, treatment needs to focus on assisting Janelle and her mother to relate more effectively. Janelle will need assistance in expressing her feelings to her mother and ensuring that Pam hears what she is saying. For instance, Janelle has expressed frustration about her mother stating that Janelle has problems. Janelle doesn't want to have to prove that she doesn't have these problems. The clinician might encourage Janelle to express these feelings to her mother.

The clinician also needs to assist Pam in relating to Janelle in other positive ways. For instance, Pam might initiate activities with Janelle that would help mom to get to know her daughter. They might allot time each evening to discuss something fun that happened during the day, an accomplishment that Janelle was proud of, or an important thing that one of them learned that day. The mother might also initiate joint activities like cooking together, playing board games, or watching movies together. Focusing on pleasurable subjects, accomplishments, or activities may add to the positiveness of their relationship and may help Janelle to feel better about herself.

CONCLUSION

As in any case that includes a sweet, young child like Janelle, one's heart breaks at the possibility that the youngster will incur harm at the hands of a parent. And so one tries everything possible to ensure that the family receives help and that Janelle will have a brighter future. It is in the efforts to pursue everything possible that one may be tempted to "fudge" ethically and legally, by inaccurately representing the case for insurance purposes, or by holding the child's interests higher than the mother's, rather than discovering the ways in which the mother's hopes and desires and strengths can be turned around for the child's benefit. Some parents seem to constrict the possibility of hope impossibly. And often the current diagnostic and reimbursement system constricts the treatment process unnecessarily. It is for these reasons that ethical decision making is a lifelong process of discovery, rather than the mere opening of a rule book to find the answers. We hope that our discussion of this case has enhanced your discovery process and challenged the temptation to rely on simple rules where none really exist.

7

The Case of Ana and Mark

MONTSE CASADO, VICTORIA E.
KRESS, AND KAREN ERIKSEN

CASE BY MONTSE CASADO

Ana, a 26-year-old Hispanic female, and her fiancé, Mark, a 28-year-old White male, had been dating for 3 years and living together for 6 months when they decided, on the basis of a referral by Ana's individual counselor, to seek premarital counseling. Ana had lived in the southeast most of her life, although her parents had moved to the United States from Mexico. Ana came from a family of six: four boys and two girls. Ana's parents had moved to the United States as migrant workers when Ana was 4 years old. The two youngest children in the family were still living at home with the parents. Mark had grown up in the north and had moved to the south when entering his master's program in social work. Mark's parents and sister still lived in the Chicago area and his parents were divorced. The couple met during graduate school and began dating. When they entered counseling, Mark was working as a case manager in a children's home and Ana was working as a social worker for an agency.

Ana had previously been diagnosed with bipolar disorder, and she also struggled with bulimia. Ana's individual counselor had referred the couple for premarital counseling at the conclusion of a recent follow-up session with Ana a year after her last hospitalization. Ana had been psychiatrically hospitalized once 2 years previously for 2 weeks, and twice, later in that same year, for 1 week each time. Prior to being referred to couples counseling, Ana had participated in outpatient group counseling and individual counseling for a year, as well as being seen by a psychiatrist. During the initial couples session, Ana seemed to be stabilized. She reported taking her medication for the bipolar disorder and managing her eating disorder tendencies most of the time. However, during the period just prior to their first session, Ana had experienced a couple of episodes of purging when feeling relationship-related stress. Mark was concerned about

Ana's health, having supported her through her latest hospitalization.

During the initial interview, when I asked the couple what they wanted to get out of therapy, they both agreed that they needed help in learning how to handle conflict, intimacy, and their upcoming wedding. For example, since moving in together, the couple had experienced gender role conflict related to issues such as completion of household chores. Ana complained that Mark was not doing many chores around the house and that she felt exhausted by taking on too many responsibilities. They also experienced conflict about how much socializing they would do with friends and with one another. When I asked the couple about the last time that they had gone on a date, both agreed that it had been several months. Ana reported that she wanted to spend more time doing things together, particularly being romantic and planning the wedding. Ana felt that Mark was not contributing as much as he should to planning for the wedding, which made her doubt his love for her. Mark's response was that he felt that Ana's mother was domineering and that his opinion did not really count much in planning the wedding. The couple had also been experiencing pressure as a result of the differences between what each set of parents envisioned for the wedding and for their role in it.

In the service of determining goals for therapy, I asked both clients to rate their satisfaction with their relationship (0 being extremely dissatisfied and 10 being extremely satisfied). Mark ranked his satisfaction at 6 while Ana ranked hers at 7. I asked Mark to explain what 6 meant to him, and what needed to happen for him to move to a 7 or 8. Mark disclosed that part of his dissatisfaction in the relationship had to do with sexual frustration. He felt that their sex life was far too inactive for his satisfaction. In fact, he explained that the frequency of sex had declined consistently since living together. When I asked Ana how she felt about what Mark had said, she

reported that she felt very self-conscious about her body and that, as a result, she had a difficult time sharing herself sexually with Mark. She also admitted that it was very hard for her to be receptive sexually when she was upset with him about other issues.

I asked Ana the same question, what made her level of satisfaction a 7 and what needed to change to improve the relationship. Ana also expressed dissatisfaction with getting her sexual needs met. She wanted more romance with Mark and more opportunities to be intimate without it leading into sex.

The couple also felt discouraged with their increasing arguments, and wanted assistance in handling conflict. From their descriptions of the arguments, it seemed to me that Ana was the pursuer in the relationship and Mark was the distancer. I explained these terms to them and asked them if they felt those roles applied to them. Toward the end of the session, I asked the couple to define what things would be different in their lives by the time they finished premarital counseling; how would they know that they had been successful?

RESPONSE BY MONTSE CASADO

My general assessment, after the initial session, was that there were relational, communication, negotiation of differences, gender role, sexual need, and family dynamics issues to address during counseling. I worked with the couple to create a genogram during the second session in order to understand the context of patterns that this couple had inherited from their families. The genogram was also intended to increase the couple's insight about the new system that they had created as a couple living together. I planned to reevaluate Ana's depressive disorder and her eating disorder tendencies, and to assess how these previously existing difficulties might be impacting the current relationship. I also made plans to assist the couple in exploring such marital issues as personality differences; communication patterns; conflict resolution skills; intimacy and relational skills; financial management; gender role determination and distribution of power; and ways to affirm and encourage one another.

Assessment is a crucial element of the therapeutic process. It begins from the moment the couple contacts the therapist and is an ongoing process until treatment ends. According to Young and Long (1998), assessment of couples requires (a) definition of the problem from each partner's point of view; (b) exploration of family historical patterns; (c) consideration of the couple's developmental stage; and (d) review of how the couple has handled and solved problems in the past. From this information, the therapist forms an opinion about what is going on with the couple, including possible hypotheses that explain the presenting problem, desired goals and outcomes for therapy, and a treatment plan.

Clearly, this assessment process is more comprehensive than merely ascribing a diagnosis. It offers the therapist and client(s) greater understanding about the problem and the client system than might diagnosis. And it thus provides more guidance about how to proceed in counseling. However, during the assessment process, therapists will often also decide on a diagnosis for the client(s). Some therapists may find themselves challenged by the question of who knows best what is wrong with the client, the therapist or the couple. In most cases, therapists give diagnoses without involving the client. However, some professionals use a more collaborative approach and involve the couple in both the assessment process and in determining an appropriate diagnosis.

I work from a strength-based perspective when working with individuals. This means that although I attempt to understand people's deficits or ascribed diagnoses, I also try to identify the individuals' strengths as much as possible and how these may play a role in

helping them to overcome problems and challenges. A guiding principle of my work is my belief that people grow from their strengths, not from their weaknesses.

The Place of Diagnosis in This Case

As part of the assessment process, Ana's bipolar disorder and her eating disorder needed to be reevaluated. How much was the upcoming stress of the wedding bringing back some pathological tendencies for Ana? According to Mark, it seemed as if Ana's pathology was playing an important role in the relationship, that Mark felt overwhelmed at times in dealing with it. Explicitly processing the diagnoses during family counseling, and the ethical implications of continuing to use or focus on these diagnoses, would be essential.

Therefore, I asked the couple how much Ana's diagnosis had "ruled" the relationship, in what ways was she considering the diagnosis to "be" her personal identity, and what Mark's role might be in each of these processes. Because of my competency and strength-based approach to counseling, I wanted the couple to take as active a role as possible in assessing the previous diagnoses given and also in deciding the direction of counseling. As a marriage and family therapist, I wanted to be aware of Ana's previous history but not let her history be the guiding force in couples counseling. Disregarding her previous diagnoses would have been unethical, particularly if Ana was to deteriorate during treatment. If at any point I thought that Ana was feeling depressed or exhibiting old patterns, I planned to reevaluate her previous diagnoses and refer her to individual counseling.

I wanted to avoid focusing on Ana's previous diagnoses during couples work because of the potential for Ana alone to become the identified patient. Were this to happen, attention might be drawn away from systemic problems. I wanted to stay grounded in the couple's reasons for pursuing premarital counseling, which extended beyond Ana's previous diagnosis. So, in some ways, I wanted to keep the diagnosis in mind and help the couple understand the impact of it on their relationship, while helping to create boundaries around it so that the diagnosis did not rule their lives. Such goals are quite common in working with families in which one family member is dealing with an illness that challenges a couple or family's ways of being.

My goal then was to create an environment in which both Ana and Mark would feel like a team rather than an identified patient and caregiver. This required some balancing on my part. I needed to be aware of Ana's previous history and assess how her pathology had impacted her sense of self and the relationship. However, I also wanted to find a way to deconstruct her "pathological label," so she would feel more like an equal in relation to Mark. Part of my role in therapy was to help the couple co-construct some shared goals for therapy for the sake of the relationship, while also evaluating their individual needs. I also wanted to help the couple to understand the basic elements of couples counseling: I, You, and We. My focus was on helping the couple become better at defining "We" by identifying common, shared issues to address in counseling. But throughout this discussion, I encouraged them to hold on to, rather than losing, "I." I hoped that simultaneous attention to both "We" and "I" would help them feel safe enough to develop the ability to transcend their individual views in order to understand their partner's views and the relationship that they had created together.

Diagnostic Process

Accurate diagnosis is grounded in assessment, that is, the gathering of information about the couple as one tries to figure out what is going on in the relationship and the

individuals. As mentioned before, therapists err if they stop at merely ascribing a diagnostic label to one member of the couple because such a label fails to create a picture of the couple's experience or the reasons that they have reached such a troubled place or impasse. Therefore, with this couple, I used several assessment tools. The genogram, observation of the couple's interactions, and the Prepare–Enrich Inventory assisted me to gather specific information about the different areas that the couple wanted to focus on in therapy, to refine the definition of the problem (a relationship definition), and to gather knowledge about family historical influences. In couples counseling, it is crucial during the assessment phase that the therapist redefine individual attributions of fault in one member of the couple toward a more conjoint or systemic understanding of the problem (Young & Long, 1998). In couples counseling, the therapist looks at how each individual is affecting the other and looks more for relational than individual diagnoses. Although relational diagnoses do not preclude individual diagnoses, as individuals can experience diagnosable symptoms as a result of relational problems, the struggle for the therapist who may want to ascribe an individual diagnosis for insurance purposes is how to encourage a couple to think systemically about their difficulties even when an individual diagnosis is given to one member of the couple. The ethical struggle is whether one should really ascribe an individual diagnosis when such an action flies in the face of the grounding philosophies for one's profession. Therapists must wonder how they are to achieve a therapeutic relationship if they ignore congruence or genuineness, one of the three conditions for establishing such a relationship.

After the initial assessment of a couple, the therapist transforms the data collected during the assessment phase into explanations about what may be going on with the couple. The therapist may also explore various meanings for the data. This clinical interpretation of the case can also include diagnosis. During this process, the therapist finds a way to classify the gathered data into labels or categories that describe the couple and their functioning, individually and as a couple. Although couples therapists generally stay away from DSM diagnosing, a few of its systems-related diagnoses are used regularly by many marriage and family therapists, for instance, the "relational problems" described by the DSM-IV-TR's V codes (*Diagnostic and Statistical Manual of Mental Disorders,* 4th ed., Text Revision). Other types of labels that may describe unhealthy relationships include "fused," "enmeshed," "dysfunctional," or "co-dependent" (Young & Long, 1998).

In this case, I also needed to decide how much attention or weight to give to the diagnostic labels that Ana had been given prior to entering into premarital counseling. I needed to decide how my accepting these labels would affect the couple's dynamics in couples counseling. It was my opinion that although Ana's initial diagnoses should not be disregarded, they should not become an excuse to ignore family interactions and influences on her symptoms. As a marriage and family therapist, when symptoms are present I want to know to what degree the client's symptoms are the result of problems that are systemic in nature. When working systemically, the couple becomes the client and the focus of therapy, rather than focusing on one member of the couple who might be identified as the client because of a diagnosis. Therefore, my focus is more on diagnosing what was going on with the couple rather than each individual separately.

There were several reasons why I chose not to use individual diagnoses with this couple. Although I see the value of having labels that assess levels of pathology for individuals and believe that mental disorders are very real and do exist, I find the overuse of DSM-IV-TR labeling to be constraining in its focus on pathological processes. I tend to find an assessment that is broader in scope to be more helpful. That is, I use a theoretical model that is humanistic in nature, that emphasizes the individual's ability to grow and the individual's human potential. I prefer to work using a strength-based model and to understand the client through contextual and constructivist lenses. For instance, I want to know what works for clients, what successes they have had in their relationship, what they have discovered on their own about their relationship dynamics, how culture impacts their relationship in positive as well as negative ways. I want to participate in a dialogue with clients about their story and about what works and what doesn't in their story. Then I prefer to collaboratively decide how we might construct a story that works better for them. Thus, my model focuses more on promoting growth than on the pathological processes that are described in the DSM.

Ethical Considerations

Ethical considerations in this case include which family members ought to be included; whether to use a diagnosis in family counseling; how to actualize informed consent and confidentiality; how to be cognizant of inclusion of multicultural issues (in this case culture and gender specifically); and what effect all of these ethical considerations might have on treatment.

First, when clients contract for counseling, the therapist needs to decide whether the problem requires individual, couple, or family counseling, or another type of service. If the problem is not just experienced by an individual, the therapist needs to decide who to include in therapy. From a marriage and family therapy perspective, when couples counseling is the treatment of choice, the therapeutic responsibility is toward the couple as a system (Bobes & Rothman, 2002). In this particular case, the couple presented themselves as a system and wanted to work on premarital issues, and I wanted to respect their choice to do so. That meant that I chose not to focus directly on Ana's diagnoses, and I didn't look for an individual diagnosis for Mark. However, as is clear in this case, individual diagnoses rarely stay individual. Individual problems may be caused by relational difficulties, may themselves cause relational difficulties, and may require the support of relationships to resolve.

Second, therapists need to decide whether to provide a DSM diagnosis when working with families or couples and how to adequately provide information to the clients on the ramifications of doing so. The placement where I saw this couple focused more on wellness than on pathology. Therapists saw clients on a "sliding scale," rather than billing clients' insurance companies. Thus, DSM diagnostic labels were not always given to clients, and ethical dilemmas regarding giving DSM diagnoses rarely arose.

However, were this not the case, it would be important to consider, and to help the clients to consider, the potential problems of choosing to be diagnosed for the purpose of accessing insurance reimbursement. For instance, the required diagnostic label might follow them for life. What effect might this label have on the clients? Might the clients start thinking of themselves as having a mental disorder? Would the clients "have" such a mental disorder for life, or would the clients envision the possibility of becoming normal again? Many diagnoses seem to imply permanency. As a result, once assigned, the clients may not believe that they will ever overcome the diagnosis. The helplessness associated with such assumptions may result in difficulty learning how to manage the "disorder" with treatment and medication. Thus, to make an informed decision about payment methods, clients need to know about such potential problems.

If billing insurance for services were to be done, Ana's preexisting diagnosis would make it easy to bill the insurance company for treatment of her individual diagnosis. However, ethically, if a therapist espouses a systems orientation that considers the couple to be the client, diagnosing an individual would be wrong and perhaps countertherapeutic. If the marriage and family therapist ascribes only a relational diagnosis, the insurance company would probably not reimburse for services because most insurance companies do not pay for relational problems, and certainly not for preventive services such as premarital counseling.

Third, should clients choose to use an insurance plan, therapists need to determine how to maintain adequate confidentiality of therapeutic material, and how to inform the clients about the confidentiality of materials submitted to insurance companies. The therapist would certainly need to inform the clients about what specific information would be shared with the insurer about the diagnosis, the types of services received, and the length of treatment (Goldenberg & Goldenberg, 2004). But further, the marriage and family therapist would need to consider the impact on the therapeutic process of limiting confidentiality in this way. Might clients choose to disclose less-important information if they were made conscious of the involvement of a third party? Although certainly discussing these issues with clients is necessary during the informed consent process, therapists may also struggle with how much information to give to clients during an initial session because they do not want to discourage clients from participating in the counseling process when it is needed.

Fourth, all therapy is a multicultural encounter, because each client and each therapist is culturally unique and different. Thus, marriage and family therapists need to consider how multicultural issues, such as gender, age, language, ethnicity, race, and religion, among others, impact the diagnostic and therapeutic processes. In this case, the couple's diverse backgrounds needed to be explored in counseling. How does the blend of two ethnic backgrounds impact the relationship, and how will the blend impact the relationship in the future? Culture also influences our preconceived notions of health and illness. What may be seen as normal in one culture may be considered pathological in another. With this couple, I asked Ana how her culture would see her diagnostic label and what type of treatment she would have received if she had been treated by someone within her culture. An ethical therapist is one who gives consideration to questions about how cultural issues may impact the couple, their problem, and the diagnostic process.

Conclusion

Integrating DSM diagnosis into couples work can be challenging if one works from a systemic orientation. At the very least, one's genuineness or congruence faces challenges when trying to integrate an individualistic focus with a systems focus. Of greater concern, however, is the therapeutic challenge of achieving the desired systemic focus with a couple given the stigma associated with diagnostic labels, even if one considers DSM diagnosis to be only a small part of a comprehensive assessment process, one that draws attention to individual symptoms and possible needs for medication and/or referral. With this couple, in the setting in which I worked, I was not placed in a position that posed such challenges. However, counselors frequently work in settings that daily present such challenges. For that reason, I hope that the consideration of this case increases awareness and challenges practitioners toward improved ethical practice.

RESPONSE BY VICTORIA E. KRESS AND KAREN ERIKSEN

Many diagnostic and assessment complexities become apparent when considering this case. These complexities might be discussed in terms of (a) the benefits of incorporating a developmental perspective; (b) the advantages of understanding the impact of normal personality differences on the couple; (c) the importance of determining cultural and gender influences on the couple and on the counseling process; and (d) the intersection of ethical principles, such as competence, reimbursement, boundaries, values, and informed consent, with the diagnostic and reimbursement process. Treatment implications emerging from the above diagnostic complexities will also be considered throughout the following discussion.

Incorporating a Developmental Perspective

Human behavior is complex, and understanding pathology and abnormal behavior is sometimes important in understanding a person's behavior. Yet a comprehensive understanding of human behavior should also involve a consideration of normal growth and developmental transitions. The undergirding philosophies of a number of mental health disciplines incorporate a developmental perspective, one that urges therapists and clients to engage in movement toward optimal mental health and wellness. Such perspectives ask counselors to broaden their notions of diagnosis beyond the traditional applications of the number and name of a disorder to a more comprehensive understanding of the client(s). Thus, rather than thinking of Ana and Mark as a DSM "V code," such as a "Partner Relational Problem," which by definition, focuses on a "problem," developmental counselors might consider other assessment language to be more helpful to the client and to positive therapeutic movement.

Erikson. For instance, a number of developmental concepts might be used to describe this couple and their situation. Erik Erikson (1963) might say that because of Ana and Mark's age and their entrance into a lifelong committed relationship, they are engaged in the normal developmental stage of intimacy versus isolation. Successful achievement of the developmental task for this stage would mean succeeding at an intimate, love relationship. Leaving a "single lifestyle" and embracing the commitment and responsibility inherent in an impending marriage or other life or long-term partnership might be overwhelming for some, but is certainly a significant and expectable life transition for all. One of the pressures associated with this developmental transition includes learning how to deal with the new partner's family, a struggle with which Mark is currently contending. From a developmental perspective, these adjustments would be considered normal, not issues that would meet the DSM criteria for an adjustment disorder (unless they were significantly impacting the functioning of Mark and Ana). Counselors who include this Eriksonian perspective in their assessment of Ana and Mark would assist the couple with normal adjustments to living together, getting married, dealing with in-law interactions, and dividing household chores. Such counseling might center on improving communication and conflict resolution skills. However, if successful adjustment did not occur, Ana or Mark might eventually develop a DSM Adjustment Disorder. Accomplishing these goals so as to preclude the development of a DSM disorder makes such a developmental perspective preventative.

Super. Super's (1990) career development theory might focus the counselor on the normal career transitions that Mark and Ana are experiencing, and the impact that such transitions might have on an intimate relationship. Mark and Ana each recently finished graduate school and have taken on new roles and responsibilities in their careers. They are in what Super would call the "establishment" stage of career development. Normal tasks of this stage include encountering an actual work environment, becoming established in one's career and organization, adapting to career

and organizational demands, and performing career responsibilities in a satisfactory manner. The middle phase of this stage requires consolidating one's position by gaining experience and proficiency. The third phase, although not always evident or taken on by workers, is advancement to new levels of responsibility. Thus, counselors who focus on Ana and Mark from a career development perspective might assist the couple to explore the impact of their beginning careers on their relationship, might assist them to understand the differences in the ways that men and women balance career and family responsibilities, and might normalize the couple's career experiences and stresses and the impact of such experiences on their relationship.

Constructive development. From a constructive, cognitive, ego, or moral developmental perspective (Kegan, 1982; Loevinger, 1976; Perry, 1970; Kohlberg, 1981), Ana and Mark are developing their postformal operational reasoning skills, increasing their abilities to use relativistic thinking (understanding that knowledge depends on the subjective perspective of the knower), and emerging into the ability to think systemically. They may be engaged in the transition from conventional (or subjective, interpersonal, dualistic) ways of knowing about the world and relationships to postconventional (or procedural, institutional, autonomous) ways of knowing. Counselors who are knowledgeable about such transitions might help Mark and Ana move forward into less-limiting ways of knowing by optimally "matching" them—by holding them or relating to them at their current developmental stage—and "mismatching" them—or challenging them by relating to them from the stage one level above where they currently are.

There may be benefits to using the developmental perspectives described in this section in conjunction with or separate from the DSM diagnostic processes. If therapists only focus on what they perceive to be problematic or abnormal behavior, they may unknowingly send a message to clients that this is the most relevant aspect of clients' experiences, thus reinforcing a problem story or narrative. A focus on the normalization of human reactions and experiences, and a de-emphasizing of stigmatizing labels, may provide clients with a greater sense of resiliency and strength, which may, in turn, lead to a greater belief in their efficacy and to a greater motivation to make life changes. Theoretically, a client's sense of empowerment may be increased by framing problems in a developmental context, reinforcing the idea that the "problem" can and will change, and emphasizing that clients can facilitate this change.

Understanding Normal Personality Differences

Differences in styles of approaching life, career, and relationships may also challenge those in new relationships. These differences may fall within the "normal" range of personality, and may therefore be beyond the scope of a DSM diagnosis. Yet, they may be no less important in understanding the couple's struggles. Assessment instruments, such as the Myers Briggs Temperament Inventory (MBTI) or the NEO-Personality Inventory (NEO-PI; Costa & McCrae, 1992), that assess normal personality variables may increase the counselor's and the couple's understanding of the normal personality differences that are exacerbating the couple's relational struggles. The couple may then be encouraged to develop "normalizing" ways of thinking about these differences and to more productively engage in developing strategies for handling the differences.

Mark and Ana's presenting complaints point to the possibility of a number of personality differences. For example, Mark claims that he wants to be more social as a couple, and Ana indicates frustration with Mark's lack of planning for the wedding and failure to complete chores around the house. Ana and Mark also seem to feel misunderstood, a situation that could lead to their needs not being met. From an MBTI perspective, it may turn out that Mark is more extraverted and more of a perceiver than Ana. The NEO-PI may reveal that Mark is less conscientious than Ana. These and other personality differences would result in different needs and different ways of communicating these needs. By conceptualizing their problems in a manner that does not pathologize their differing needs and styles, Ana and Mark may become more open to learning about each other's different needs, and about how to meet these needs.

Although it is possible to perceive the couple's differences as a hindrance or obstacle, it is also possible to perceive their differences as a strength. One potential benefit of their differences is that they both bring unique characteristics to the relationship. These different contributions may illuminate areas for growth, may add interests to the other's life, and may result in higher functioning as a couple as each fills in the gaps left by the other. Ultimately, then, these differences may add new dimensions and depth to their individual lives. Furthermore, as they learn how to manage their differences, their relationship may grow stronger, and they may develop personal awareness (a person only knows who she or he is when relating to someone who is different) and an improved ability to interact with others.

Ana and Mark's personality differences might add to the other's life or their lives as a couple in a number of ways. For instance, acknowledging Mark's affinity for an increased social life might lead the couple to assign Mark the responsibility for planning social engagements in discussions about division of labor, and Ana might learn to feel more comfortable in social situations. To counterbalance Mark and Ana's needs socially, Mark also might take responsibility for planning one romantic evening for each social engagement that he planned. Ana might then assist Mark in becoming more comfortable with the emotional intimacy of such encounters. Recognition of the benefits of Ana's organizing skills around household chores might lead Mark to a greater awareness of what she was adding to the relationship and of areas in which he was less talented. He might ask Ana to discuss with him how she organizes the home, so that he could learn more in that area, and might, as a result of such discussions, relieve her of some of the overwork that she experiences.

Many other conceptualizations of "normal" personality differences can also be used to help Mark and Ana conceptualize their differences in a nonpathologizing fashion. Therapists can select the normal personality development model with which they are most familiar and apply it in helping the clients become respectful and appreciative of differences.

Tuning in to Ethnic and Gender Influences

One complaint about DSM diagnosis has been its failure to account for cultural differences, and this failure impacts diagnosis, treatment, research about abnormal behavior, perceptions of illness, and pursuit of treatment. Although cultural factors influence all counselors and clients and every therapeutic encounter, whether consciously or not, the cultural issues faced by this couple seem particularly obvious. A full understanding of this couple's struggles would clearly require more than a determination of their DSM diagnosis; it would require careful consideration of the ways in which ethnicity, religion, geographic heritage, gender, (dis)ability, and socioeconomic class impact the couple, the counselor, and the individuals' perceptions of the problem and the potential solutions.

For instance, consider some of the cultural differences that are experienced by this couple: Mark grew up in the northern United States and Ana grew up in the south. Ana is of Mexican American heritage, and Mark is White. Ana may be Catholic, given her ethnic heritage, and it would be important to explore any differences from Mark's religious heritage. If Ana's parents were immigrants, they may have experienced financial difficulties during Ana's childhood, and it would be important to explore how Mark's family was different or similar socioeconomically. Also, Ana enters counseling with an ascribed "disability," an experience that faces her with different obstacles than Mark will have knowledge of.

Religion. We can imagine a number of ways in which these cultural experiences might impact Mark and Ana's relationship. For example, if Ana is Catholic and from a rather traditional Hispanic home, what might her living with and having sexual relations with a man before marriage mean to her and to her family? Is it possible that she experiences pressure from her family or from inside of herself for challenging her culture's customs? How might her concerns about stepping outside of the "norms" affect her relationship with Mark? She may feel guilty, which may manifest in her having difficulties with feeling secure and intimate in the relationship, which may in turn affect their sexual relationship.

Ethnicity and class. Also, cultural issues may be impacting the degree to which Mark and Ana's families have become involved in their wedding plans and envision becoming involved in their future lives together. If Ana is considered a child in her family until she is wed, it would be understandable that her parents would consider it their responsibility to conduct the wedding, a stance that may be less understandable to Mark and his family. If her family struggles with her choice to live with Mark before marriage, they may feel great pressure to save face with their friends and relations by putting on a wedding that draws attention away from the "sin." If her family feels disadvantaged financially in comparison with Mark's, they may feel some need to prove themselves during the wedding to the other side of the family. Finally, because extended family seems to play a greater role in families of "other-than-Northern European" heritages, Ana's family may expect to continue to play a daily role in Mark and Ana's family life, an expectation that may trigger conflicts for the couple.

Disability. Ana's experience of disability may also impact both parties' perceptions of the problems in their relationship. Ana may worry about returning to bulimia or depression, and about how this might disadvantage her in her relationship with Mark or in her career. She may also worry that Mark might think less of her because of her history of disability, that he might consider her opinion on things to be "less than" his as a result. She may feel the need to "prove" herself repeatedly so as to persuade Mark, the counselor, and their families that she is "okay," and thus deserving of credit for her choices. Concurrently, Mark may worry about choosing a disabled person as a partner. He may feel the need to prove to his friends and relations that he has made a good choice in marrying Ana. He may wonder if he can fully be himself, or if being himself might tip her over the edge, back into disability. He may feel pressure to take care of both himself and her, financially and emotionally.

On the other hand, Mark and Ana's acceptance of the diagnosis as a medical problem (like diabetes) might decrease the tendency to blame either the self or the other. In fact, having a label for the problem might free them up and allow them to focus on managing and adjusting to the problem. For instance, Ana may continue to struggle with body image issues that are typically associated with bulimia survivors. Ana and Mark may need to process these types of body image issues and the possible impact that they have on their relationship, in particular, their sexual relationship. Mark may be able to play an important

role in supporting Ana in improving her body image. The counselor would need to assess what the impact of Ana's previously diagnosed disability might be on their relationship. Rather than making assumptions, the counselor could keep the range of possibilities listed above in mind during assessment.

Beyond the impact of the preexisting diagnosis on the clients, the counselor would need to stay aware of the impact on him-/herself of Ana entering counseling with a such a diagnosis. It may be tempting to assume, without reevaluating, that Ana "has" these diagnoses, that these diagnoses are permanent regardless of the current lack of symptomatology. The therapist may be tempted to allow her diagnoses to define not only her but her relationship. The diagnoses might make it easier for the counselor to see Ana as "different," as "sicker than," as "in a different class" from the therapist, thereby facilitating an increased distance from the client. Such distance might cause the counselor to align with Mark, hindering a systemic, couples focus.

Gender. Consciousness of gender socialization also seems key to fully understanding this couple. For example, with respect to household responsibilities, Mark may believe, as a result of certain cultural experiences, that household tasks are women's responsibility, and may not find himself well-trained to take on such responsibilities. Ana may also manifest internalized cultural expectations and may vacillate between wanting Mark to do more household chores and believing on some level that she should be doing these activities; she may, as a result, experience a state of dissonance that could lead to increased future frustrations.

Additionally, Ana and Mark may have internalized societal expectations about sexuality that complicate their emerging relationship. For instance, Ana may believe that "women should wait" until after marriage to become sexually active, and may thus feel guilty about living together and having sexual relations before marriage. She may also believe, again based on gender-related societal expectations, that women should be sexually passive and should resist sexual advances. Mark, in contrast, may have internalized societal expectations that indicate that men are entitled to sex from a partner, that sexual frequency is a measure of one's manhood. This belief may affect his ability to communicate effectively about sex and to have reasonable sexual expectations of Ana.

Counselors also need to consider how their own gender-related socialization influences their perceptions of the partners. Might the gender of the therapist and/or the gender-related values of the therapist influence the therapist's perceptions of Mark and Ana's situation? For example, if the therapist is male, might he find it harder to relate to bulimia and might he thus pathologize Ana's behavior more than a female therapist, who might relate to her food-, body image-, and eating-related struggles?

As with personality differences, it is possible to perceive the couple's cultural and gender differences both as a hindrance and as a resource or a strength. Their differences may provide different resources and strengths that strengthen them individually and as a couple/family. As they learn how to manage their differences, their self-awareness and relationship may grow stronger. For instance, were Mark of Scandinavian heritage (possible if raised in the north) in which independence and individualism are often values, he might not have experienced the full inclusion of an extended family in his family life. He might benefit from experiencing the involvement and support of an extended family that would be more likely to have been Ana's experience, given her Hispanic family upbringing. If our assumptions in the discussions above about religion are founded, Ana may learn from Mark how to free herself from guilt, particularly guilt about sexual involvement. If our assumptions about the intersection of ethnicity and class bear out, Ana might learn from

Mark how to stand up to her family, set limits around their involvement in the wedding, and feel happier about the choices that she and Mark make together. Or Ana might help Mark to be more understanding of her family's wishes and actions by explaining her culture. The therapist might help both Ana and Mark to understand normal gender differences, and to universalize the struggles that heterosexual couples experience when entering a marriage for the first time. They might, as a result, acknowledge the benefits of gender role socialization, while clearly defining those deficits that they would like to focus on managing.

Although the DSM helps to understand a piece of this couple's reality, it is not comprehensive enough to explain the whole of the clients' situation, and, similarly, does not provide direction for therapist-initiated interventions. A consideration of the clients' culture and gender contributes a more comprehensive understanding of the couple's dynamic and thus provides a starting place for hypothesizing about the clients' situation and how to best help them.

Specific Ethical Complications

Professional ethical codes require mental health practitioners to attend to such issues as competence, accuracy of reporting for reimbursement purposes, boundaries, values, and informed consent, among others. Each of these links to the diagnostic process when considering Ana and Mark's case.

Competence. In Ana and Mark's case, counselors need demonstrated competence in diagnosing and treating clients with bulimia and/or bipolar disorder, in couples work, and in counseling Hispanic and/or interracial couples. The accurate assessment, diagnosis, and treatment of clients with eating disorders and/or bipolar disorder requires specialized training, which would be necessary if the counselor was to adequately ensure Ana's continuing mental health and to appropriately address systemic issues that are likely to arise around such diagnoses. It asks a lot for a therapist to be specially trained in couples and/or family counseling *and* in assessing and monitoring eating disorders and/or bipolar disorder. Often, therapists who are trained in the systemic orientation of family counseling are not trained in treating those with individual mental illnesses. Furthermore, should Ana require a therapist who speaks Spanish, or should the inclusion of extended family members in counseling require such a therapist, the requirement for specialized training becomes even more complicated. A colleague once told me (Eriksen) that counselors who spoke Spanish (may also apply to other languages) treated Spanish speakers with every kind of disability—substance abuse, eating disorders, family violence, and the like—because they were the only ones available to do the work, specialized training or not. Therefore, should a Spanish-speaking therapist be necessary, it becomes less likely that the therapist would be adequately trained to treat clients with these special issues, and the therapist would thus require supervision by a counselor who had been adequately trained.

Accuracy of reporting for reimbursement. If the clients expect counseling services to be reimbursed by one of their insurance companies, the counselor will need to ascribe a DSM diagnosis. However, most insurance companies do not reimburse for a V code such as "V61.1 Partner Relational Problem," the only diagnosis that has yet been discussed for the couple. An Axis I diagnosis would have to be assigned to one of the members of the couple if the couple was to receive financial assistance in paying for the counseling sessions. We should probably assume that they will need such assistance given their status as recent graduates in human service fields.

But Axis I disorders only apply to individuals. If a counselor thinks systemically, and

considers the couple to be the "client," then the counselor would not ascribe an individual diagnosis. Instead, the assessments that have been discussed thus far would be considered the couple's "diagnosis." Yet, these assessments are not recognized by insurance companies for reimbursement purposes. It is likely, then, that a counselor would be tempted to give one member of the couple an individual diagnosis. Yet the couple is not pursuing counseling for individual problems; rather, they are interested in receiving couples counseling to work on relationship issues. The counselor may thus engage in a difficult dialogue between the part of him-/herself that wants to help the couple, if they were unable to pay out-of-pocket, and the part that fully believes in a systemic focus. The counselor might ask him- or herself whether an ethical counselor would refuse services to the couple rather than "find" an individual diagnosis that came close to fitting, despite the couple's stated counseling aims.

Some practitioners might consider applying one of Ana's previously ascribed diagnoses as a means of obtaining reimbursement. However, if Ana continues to be ascribed a diagnosis that she does not actively and currently demonstrate (i.e., bulimia and/or bipolar disorder), is this not a misrepresentation of her current situation and an unethical means of garnering financial reimbursement? If the therapist does choose to continue to use these diagnoses to receive reimbursement, what implications arise? Might continuing a diagnosis that Ana does not currently manifest negatively impact her, for instance by continuing stigmatization and presenting her as struggling with issues that are not still salient? Might continuing to use Ana's past diagnoses as a means of obtaining reimbursement inadvertently label Ana as the "sick one" or the person with the problem in the relationship? If so, what implications would this have for counseling? Continuing to ascribe a diagnosis to Ana that is not currently warranted may also have implications for her future. For example, what if Ana becomes involved in court proceedings or job-related issues (e.g., joining the military) in which the duration of counseling services and the prolonged diagnosis could negatively affect her opportunities?

On the other hand, some clinicians would argue that bulimia and bipolar disorder are lifetime (perhaps organic) disorders, and that lack of symptomatology merely means that the disorder is being medically managed, not that it is no longer present. If a counselor held such a belief, the counselor would still, however, have to ask whether using an individual diagnosis for reimbursement purposes is ethical for a counselor operating from a systemic perspective and being asked to treat relational issues.

Values. Personal values and perceptions about mental illness and mental health always impact the counseling process. Because Ana has in the past been given several diagnoses, the therapist might ask him-/herself what she or he believes about such diagnoses and about the people who bear them. For instance, might the counselor be biased toward Ana, wanting to coddle her a bit, because of her past mental health diagnoses and history? Or, in contrast, might the counselor view Ana as the "sick" one and wonder if Mark has some type of disorder that contributes to his staying with an ill partner. Some therapists might ask: What does Mark get out of being with someone who is mentally ill? Values of normal versus abnormal behavior are always involved in ascribing a DSM diagnosis, and it is important that any practitioner examine his or her meanings related to the various diagnoses (What does it mean to the therapist to be

bulimic? To be depressed? To have any DSM diagnosis? etc.). As therapists are to avoid imposing their values on clients (American Association for Marriage and Family Therapy [AAMFT], 2001, Standards 3.3, 3.4, 3.5; American Counseling Association [ACA], 1995, Standard A.5.b; American Psychological Association [APA], 1992, Standards 1.08, 1.09, 1.10; National Association of Social Workers [NASW], 1999, Preamble), they must ask themselves what they consider to be normal versus abnormal, mentally ill versus mentally healthy. Seeing Ana as dysfunctional or "ill" because of her past DSM diagnoses is a value-laden perspective more than a factual reality believed by all. Unfortunately, the perspective that Ana is ill fails to recognize all of the assets that Ana may bring to the relationship, assets that Mark may cherish and may believe himself unable to find in anyone else.

CONCLUSION

As with all human behavior, this couple's situation is multifaceted and complicated. A comprehensive and responsible understanding of their situation and of how to best help them involves an awareness of the DSM diagnostic process and abnormal behavior, but also requires an understanding of their developmental stages and transitions, normal personality characteristics, and culture and gender issues. Additionally, the ethical issues associated with competency, boundaries and values, and insurance reimbursement also need to be addressed in such a way that the couple receives the best services in the most ethical fashion possible.

8

The Case of Ellen

ROBYN TRIPPANY AND DEBRA PENDER

CASE BY ROBYN TRIPPANY

Ellen, a 22-year-old college sophomore, presented for counseling with issues related to childhood sexual abuse. She had been sexually abused by her biological father since the age of 5 years, as were her older and younger sisters. Her father was an evangelical minister, and he presented to his daughters verses in the Bible that he interpreted to support a father's right to engage in sexual intercourse with his offspring. In fact, he included in his plans that Ellen's older sister was to conceive and bear her father's child. Seemingly, the mother supported the father's decision, as she did not intervene on behalf of her daughters.

Ellen grew up thinking that this sexual relationship with her father was "normal." She was isolated from the world in many ways: She was home schooled, her family did not have a television, and because her father was a traveling evangelist, the family did not attend one particular church on a regular basis. Thus, Ellen and her sisters did not have the opportunity to obtain information regarding the inappropriateness of her father's activities.

Ellen reported that she never felt "right" about the sexual relationship with her father, although she did admit pleasure in some of the sexual activities. She reported that her father was a very loving man and even during the occurrence of abuse was gentle and interested in his daughter's pleasure. Nonetheless, at 15 years old she ran away from home. Her decision to run away came after the birth of her sister's child by her father. She reported that that event was a salient moment in her coming to believe that the sexual relationship with her father was wrong.

Ellen contacted a maternal aunt when she ran away from home. The aunt took her in and, after hearing Ellen's story, helped her to report her father. This aunt was a great support throughout the court proceedings, which ultimately culminated in Ellen's father being imprisoned, where he died a short time later. Ellen's mother and sisters did not support Ellen's decision and cut her off from the family. While living with her aunt, Ellen participated in 2 years of counseling.

After high school, Ellen joined the military. She was dishonorably discharged, although she would not give the reason why. After her dismissal from the military, she entered college. She left her first university after 2 semesters and transferred to a different university. She reported that she had left the first university because she was unhappy there due to conflicts with friends.

Ellen was in her second semester at the second university when she entered counseling. She reported wanting to work on resolving issues related to her childhood abuse. She signed a release for the counselor to talk with her previous therapist. The previous therapist discussed Ellen's treatment and pointed to Ellen's pattern of "rocky" relationships with friends and family, including her aunt. At the time of the counseling, the therapist had written down a diagnostic impression of Ellen that included borderline features (at the time of treatment, she was under the age to receive a diagnosis of borderline personality disorder).

Not long after entering the current counseling relationship, Ellen disclosed that she was a part-time prostitute. She reported that it was the best way to make a lot of money quickly and that she was able to decide with whom, when, and where she engaged in sexual relationships. Ellen lacked insight into the risks, both physical and emotional, that this profession held. She maintained the importance of supporting herself in this manner and saw no potential problems. She had also worked part-time as a waitress, but was fired after 2 months for getting into an argument with a customer. Because of her financial problems, she believed that she could not give up her earnings from prostitution.

Ellen reported no female friendships and only a few male friendships. She stated that she could not trust women and that men were much easier to get along with because she always knew where they were coming from:

"their pants." She reported that, after hanging out with any of her male friends, she usually ended up having intercourse with them. Ellen denied substance abuse and suicidal ideation. Although she began sessions in an upbeat manner, she cried a great deal as each session progressed. She often waited until sessions were almost over to process difficult material; she did so to such an extent that to avoid having to lengthen sessions, the counselor began setting limits related to the time when new material could be introduced.

RESPONSE BY ROBYN TRIPPANY

Because she demonstrates difficulty in interpersonal relationships, risk-taking behavior, and impulsivity, the most obvious diagnosis for Ellen would be borderline personality disorder (BPD). The diagnostic criteria for BPD are similar to some of the long-term consequences of and reactions to childhood sexual abuse. For instance, some noted long-term consequences of sexual abuse include impaired relationships with and distrust of others, preoccupation with sexual themes and promiscuity, sexual dysfunctions, impulsivity and risk-taking behaviors (e.g., substance abuse, prostitution, self-destructive behaviors), and suicidal ideation and depression (Murray, 1992). Owens and Chard (2001) suggested that cognitive distortions may also result from childhood sexual trauma. These distortions focus around five areas: safety, trust, power, self-esteem, and intimacy. The outcomes of such distortions can include anxiety, avoidant behavior, fear of betrayal, anger, passivity, and feelings of powerlessness and weakness. Briere and Runtz (1993) further indicated that childhood sexual trauma survivors may exaggerate the potential for danger.

Because of the similarity of symptoms in clients with BPD and clients who have been sexually abused, therapists may be tempted to diagnose sexual abuse survivors with BPD.

Ethically, however, such a decision poses several dilemmas. For instance, the stigma associated with borderline personality disorder may result in discrimination by insurers or retraumatization during therapy, both of which contradict mandates to promote the welfare and respect the dignity of clients (discussed further below) (American Association for Marriage and Family Therapy [AAMFT], 2001; American Counseling Association [ACA], 1995; American Psychological Association [APA], 1992; National Association of Social Workers [NASW], 1999). Instead, the symptoms that are displayed by sexual abuse survivors that so resemble BPD may more accurately reflect "trauma reenactment syndrome" (Miller, 1994). The benefits and difficulties with each diagnostic focus and the resulting implications for Ellen's treatment will be discussed later.

Janet, Freud, and van der Kolk (van der Kolk, 1989), offer explanations for symptoms such as Ellen's by pointing out that traumatic childhood experiences may impede normal developmental growth in individuals. Janet (as cited in van der Kolk, 1989), suggested that personality development is halted as a result of traumatic experiences and "cannot expand any more by the addition or assimilation of new elements" (p. 389). Thus, traumatic experiences, as a result of halting development, may disturb the ability of the individual to cope with future challenges and leave the individual unable to integrate the trauma material into existing cognitive schemas. Freud (1920) suggested that individuals who were unable to assimilate traumatic experiences into the memory system would repeat the repressed material as contemporary experiences. van der Kolk (1989) further indicated that the trauma survivor is not likely to make a conscious connection between past experiences and these current reenactments.

Doob (1992) suggested that the link between sexual trauma history and seeming borderline pathology is in the accommodation or coping process. Victims of chronic abuse accommodate to the abuse initially as an adaptive strategy for survival by denying the occurrence of the abuse, altering affective responses related to the abuse, and altering thought processes about those who are supposed to protect but instead harm the child. Ultimately these strategies result in redirected anger that often manifests itself as self-harming behaviors. These behaviors are essentially, in themselves, reenactments of the client's trauma history. The strategies allow the survivor to remain connected to family members during childhood. However, as adults these accommodations manifest themselves as dissociative symptoms, self-harm, irrational anxiety, interpersonal conflicts, paranoia, depression, and anxiety, and tend to be viewed as psychopathology rather than coping skills.

These explanations for the symptoms that may be experienced by a survivor of childhood sexual abuse make some sense in Ellen's case. Indeed, Ellen exhibits a great number of interpersonal conflicts, as evidenced by her limited friendships and difficulties in work and school. Furthermore, she demonstrates risk-taking behaviors (evidenced by her work as a prostitute) and impulsivity (evidenced by her financial problems and arguing with a customer). However, from a trauma framework rather than a characterological disorder perspective, her symptoms make sense. She was harmed not only by a parent who was supposed to protect her, but also by the family who sanctioned his behavior, and, misleadingly, by the Bible. She was not offered the opportunity to be involved in any supportive, honest relationships, as she was basically isolated from society. Then, when she advocated for herself by reporting her father, she was disowned by her family. In addition, she was taught by her father, an evangelical minister, that sex, even sex with children, was authorized by God. Although she eventually realized that the sexual relationship with her father was not right, she was still groomed during important years of cognitive and emotional development to believe that her purpose was to fulfill a man's sexual appetites.

Any person with Ellen's history would find it hard to trust others or to trust herself. Does this mean Ellen is pathological? A diagnosis of BPD would indicate that something is inherently wrong with Ellen's character, and that this "disorder" drives her to behave in such ways. However, considering her symptoms as trauma reenactments lessens such a stigma and allows the clinician to focus on the traumatic history that underlies those interpersonal difficulties.

The Stigma of Borderline Personality Disorder

The diagnosis of BPD often carries with it a stigma that makes BPD seem like a death sentence for a client (Gallop, Lancee, & Garfinkel, 1989; Nehls, 1998). Such a diagnosis could, in fact, lead to discrimination by the mental health community. For instance, mental health professionals report frustration with the cycle of manipulation and rejection by clients with BPD (Gallop et al., 1989). Lewis and Appleby (1988) also found that psychiatrists were pejorative, judgmental, and rejecting of the BPD patient. They used terms such as "manipulative" and "attention seeking" in describing these patients. Psychiatrists also implied that clients with BPD were not worthy of the same quality of care as other patients. Reiser and Levenson (1984) wrote that the term "borderline" creates a breakdown in empathy between the clinician and the client. Miller (1994) wrote the following about BPD:

> While I have found it [BPD] to be a useful means of briefly identifying a cluster of behaviors when I am consulting with other mental health professionals, I continue to have serious questions about whether the very existence of the diagnosis may cause us to mislabel patients and thus approach treatment in a damaging way. When I think about the need of the TRS [trauma reenactment

syndrome] woman to be understood from a perspective of exploring her self-harm, rages, and relational turbulence, I worry that the traditional treatment protocol of "containing" the borderline client will be used to silence the TRS woman as long as the diagnosis continues to be used. (p. 162)

Miller (1994) suggested instead that the characteristics demonstrated by sexual abuse survivors might, in fact, be a reexperiencing of the trauma, rather than a deficit in the personality. From this perspective, the stigma attached to BPD could actually lead to retraumatization of the adult survivor during therapy. That is, adult survivors often continue to "blame themselves for their victimization, explaining that they were abused because of their essential badness" (Doob, 1992, p. 246). The label of a personality disorder may confirm this notion for the adult survivor.

In the case of Ellen, as with most adult survivors of sexual trauma, a clinician who ascribed a diagnosis of BPD would essentially be saying, "You need to fix what is wrong with you in order to have more stable interpersonal relationships and to be less promiscuous." Such a belief would hold Ellen responsible, or blame her (revictimize her), rather than appreciate the only coping strategies that she could figure out in response to a traumatic childhood. It is possible that such revictimization would result in even greater reliance on the traumatic reenactments as coping strategies.

If the stigma that is associated with the BPD diagnosis can impact mental health professionals in these ways, it is conceivable that this stigma also impacts insurance company employees. Clients diagnosed with BPD may be red-flagged by insurance companies as cost risks because of the frequent number of suicide attempts and hospitalizations associated with the diagnosis. Thus, a diagnosis of BPD may also result in insurance discrimination in terms of higher premiums or even refusals to insure. Therapists might instead consider a diagnosis of post-traumatic stress disorder (PTSD) because it is both less stigmatizing and meets insurance reimbursement requirements. Conversations with other clinicians indicate that PTSD is often chosen as a diagnosis for sexual abuse survivors. Although Ellen certainly experienced trauma during which she felt helpless, she demonstrates none of the other required symptoms as described in the DSM (*Diagnostic and Statistical Manual of Mental Disorders*) for PTSD. Therefore, ascribing this diagnosis for insurance purposes would be fraud.

The potential problems, as cited, with ascribing a BPD diagnosis may thus retard the growth potential of Ellen even further. Thus the ascription of borderline personality disorder—particularly for survivors of sexual abuse—may conflict with the most fundamental ethical mandate for mental health professionals: to promote the welfare and respect the dignity of clients (AAMFT, 2001; ACA, 1995; APA, 1992; NASW, 1999). Throughout history, adult and child survivors of sexual trauma have at best been neglected, at worst retraumatized, by people with power, and, in general, have had their welfare and dignity disregarded (Lewis & Appleby, 1988). Giving a diagnosis of BPD to adult survivors may thus compromise the ability of a mental health provider to adequately promote the welfare and dignity of clients who have been sexually abused.

Trauma Reenactment Syndrome: A More Helpful "Diagnosis"

Miller (1994) suggests, instead, that the "borderline" symptoms displayed by survivors of sexual abuse be called "trauma reenactment syndrome" (TRS). Miller believes that the self-injurious and addictive behaviors in this syndrome, such as, self-mutilation, compulsive plastic surgeries, smoking, drinking, eating disorders, sexual promiscuity, and difficult relationships, are actually reenactments of

trauma that was suffered in childhood. "In the same way that . . . women reenact their trauma, they also reenact the relationships of their childhood" (Miller, 1994, p. 33). Victims of past trauma may respond to contemporary events as though the trauma has returned and reexperience the hyperarousal that accompanied the initial trauma. "As adults they hope to undo the past by love, competency, and exemplary behavior" (van der Kolk, 1989, p. 395). When they fail, they blame themselves and return to earlier, self-destructive coping mechanisms.

Arousal may be another impetus for trauma reenactment (Miller, 1994), because as a child the client may have been in a constant state of arousal resulting from fear, rage, hyperalertness, or anxiety. For survivors of childhood trauma, negative experiences, possibly violence, became synonymous with relationships. Arousal would have impacted the biochemistry of the child in such a way that the child could not return to a baseline of unarousal. Thus, as an adult, the individual may be "addicted" to excitement, which has become painful and pleasurable, as well as comfortable. van der Kolk (1989) suggested that individuals who are addicted to trauma have been observed to have feelings of boredom, apprehension, and anxiety when not experiencing some form of activity reminiscent of their trauma.

Miller (1994) suggested that a vital part of this self-abuse cycle is keeping others at a distance. That is, the self-harming behaviors of TRS have a self-protective function. Paradoxically, while these individuals are engaging in such destructive and distancing behaviors, they also want to be rescued and protected, which creates relational instability. This self-protection helps the adult survivor protect personal boundaries while leaving those boundaries vulnerable. The process of TRS is cyclical and includes thoughts, feelings, and behavior that can be interpreted differently, depending on what point in the cycle one observes the person so diagnosed. At one point in the cycle, feelings of rage, shame, or fear could be leading an individual to self-harm. At another juncture, self-harming could be causing disgust, which could, in turn, result in further self-punishment. At still another place in the cycle, interpersonal relationships might become too intimate, with self-harming behaviors being used to push others away (Miller, 1994).

Consistent with these descriptions of TRS, Ellen has kept others at a distance using sexual promiscuity, choosing only male friends with whom she eventually has sex, and working as a prostitute. In addition, her relational instability is demonstrated in her limited support system and impulsive behaviors (e.g., arguing with a customer). It is likely that Ellen never witnessed a healthy relationship, as the sexual abuse was part of her family system and she was isolated from children her age and other adults. Thus, Ellen's notion of relationships was based on these negative experiences limiting her ability to function "normally" and increasing her use of maladaptive coping mechanisms. However, this does not mean her character is disordered; rather that her cognitions or, as Adler would suggest, her subjective perceptions of reality, are disturbed (Adler, 1929).

Treatment Implications
Resulting from Diagnostic Choice

The beauty of thinking of adult survivors of sexual trauma, like Ellen, as having trauma reenactment syndrome rather than borderline personality disorder is the avoidance of a diagnosis with potentially harmful effects and the use of a label that acknowledges the client's attempts to cope. From the TRS perspective, the symptom pattern essentially indicates that the client is coping with the traumatic history in the best way he or she knows how.

Understanding a client from the TRS perspective also provides the clinician with more diverse intervention options, as well as the opportunity to educate clients regarding "the why" of their problematic symptoms. In this case, for instance, the therapist might frame Ellen's decision to become a prostitute as the re-creation of the trauma that she has experienced. Such a framework would steer the therapist away from seeing her prostitution as an occupational decision, and would thus preclude judgmental feelings on the part of the therapist. The therapist might also help Ellen to understand the reasons for her symptomatic behavior and, in turn, to become clear that her behavior is not meeting her underlying needs. They might then work together to discern more effective means of coping with Ellen's traumatic past. In addition, the therapist who operates within the TRS model does not view the client as deficient, but rather, to borrow from Carl Rogers (1961), as an individual who has the capacity to become a fully functioning person should she learn the skills necessary to move beyond the need for destructive behavior. Thus, therapists who "diagnose" Ellen with TRS focus counseling on insight gaining, skill building, and increasing understanding of a past as a victim. But more importantly, counseling also focuses on the client's "present" as an individual who has many opportunities ahead that are not defined by a past as a victim (Miller, 1994).

In contrast, few interventions demonstrate long-term success with clients diagnosed with BPD, and these interventions may be restrictive. For instance, BPD patients have historically been hospitalized psychiatrically, medicated, or treated with long-term psychoanalytic approaches (Mohan, 2002). However, many clinicians don't even believe that personality disorders *can* be successfully treated (Gallop et al., 1989; Nehls, 1998), which certainly restricts BPD clients' options even further.

Diagnosing a client with TRS rather than BPD is, thus, consistent with ethical standards of mental health disciplines in that it provides more hopeful options for the client, is less stigmatizing, and therefore causes less damage. TRS is not a diagnosis, but rather a conceptualization of client issues. Offering a diagnosis for reimbursement by an insurance company when that diagnosis is not the most accurate or helpful, and may in fact be damaging for the client, is not only unethical, it is illegal.

Although it is possible, and often likely, that the TRS client's symptoms are synonymous with the diagnostic criteria of BPD, it is imperative for the clinician to consider the underlying causes of such symptoms before offering such a diagnosis. It may be that the client does indeed fit the BPD diagnostic criteria; but it is important to judge whether it is more harmful to offer a BPD diagnosis when TRS is more reflective of the client's experiences. Furthermore, justice seems better served in not "criminalizing" or blaming the victim of trauma for maladaptive efforts at survival.

There are few negative ramifications of ascribing the TRS conceptualization in place of a diagnosis of BPD. The main problem is that because TRS is not a DSM diagnosis, insurance companies won't reimburse for services to treat it. In the age of managed care, in which every medical or mental health care visit must have a diagnosis, it thus seems unfeasible to have a thriving practice based on a conceptualization rather than a diagnosis. However, ethical guidelines dictate that clinicians diagnose only when clients meet criteria for a diagnosis (ACA, 1995; APA, 1992; AAMFT, 2001). Thus, this dilemma creates internal conflicts between typical standards of practice and optimal ethical behavior.

Considering Ellen's case from a trauma framework would allow the clinician to explain to her in a nonthreatening manner how the experiences of her past are being reenacted through her present choices. This would allow Ellen to acknowledge her understandable efforts to cope with the trauma, face the fact that the usual coping mechanisms that are chosen in these situations actually maintain her victim status, and provide an opportunity for her to learn more positive coping mechanisms that move her into survivor status, all without the blaming or revictimizing that is inherent in a personality disorder diagnosis and the resulting treatment strategies that are typically used.

Conclusion

At first glance, Ellen's symptoms seem similar to the diagnostic criteria of borderline personality disorder. On closer examination, however, her behaviors and thought processes seem to reflect a reenactment of the sexual trauma that she suffered as a child. Therapists need to carefully weigh the risks and benefits of offering a BPD diagnosis when symptomatology may be better explained by TRS. In particular, BPD is a powerful diagnosis that has the potential to create lifelong problems with insurance companies, as well as the potential for discrimination among mental health practitioners. As a result, this diagnosis may lead to revictimization of the client by validating the mistaken belief that survivors of childhood sexual abuse have a personal deficit that makes them inherently responsible for their own abuse. Such consequences of misdiagnosis are not in accordance with ethical professional practice.

RESPONSE BY DEBRA PENDER

Several central themes emerge in Ellen's story: early paternal betrayal and invasion of boundaries through sexual violation that was mixed with messages of nurture; early maternal abandonment; immersion in "group think" or ritual explanations for the violations; severe social isolation; lack of normative peer group experiences; and, at the core, knowledge that "what was happening was not right." She presents for counseling, self-identifying as having issues of childhood sexual abuse; reporting dysfunction and/or conflict in relational patterns in personal, academic, and career contexts; and demonstrating emotional dysregulation, poor self-care, depersonalization in sexual relationships, and identity problems. The information in the case study focuses primarily on the behavioral/relational challenges and provides minimal details on Ellen's affective and cognitive experiences.

Long-term exposure to traumatic experiences, coupled with a lack of mitigation of those experiences can lead to long-term changes in three primary areas: (a) psychological functioning, (b) relational/behavioral functioning, and (c) physiological functioning (Everly, 1995). In terms of the *Diagnostic and Statistical Manual of Mental Disorders,* 4th ed., Text Revision (DSM-IV-TR), these areas relate to Axis I, II, or III diagnoses. In Ellen's case, her current lack of self-care around sexual encounters could eventually lead to serious, if not life-threatening conditions, such as HIV and/or other sexually transmitted diseases. Axis I diagnosis could include post-traumatic stress disorder (PTSD), as she has experienced trauma and is exhibiting symptoms from the intrusion cluster (reexperiencing of the false nurture mixed with sexual exploitation in her current male–female relationships; although more common with young children, this history indicates an age of onset consistent with reenactment), the avoidance cluster (lack of meaningful connections with others and restricted range of affect), and the arousal cluster (anger outbursts and timing intense therapeutic work in a way that limits opportunities for resolution within the session). Although the details mention frequent crying, it is not known whether this is contextual to the topic at hand or reflects depressive symptoms. Because the primary details provided in the case study focus on Ellen's various relationship difficulties, further interview might yield more information about the symptoms within each of the clusters (e.g., nightmares, intrusive thoughts, anxiety reactions, insomnia).

An alternative Axis I diagnosis might be depersonalization disorder (American Psychiatric Association [APA], 2000, p. 530). Ellen seems detached from self, yet maintains her ability to reality test. Diagnostic criteria evident in Ellen for depersonalization disorder include her lack of awareness of choices related to her prostitution along with her reported disregard for current or future harm, and her general detachment in sexual relationships which results in significant impairment in her ability to address personal safety. Depersonalization is often a symptom that is subsumed in other diagnostic categories. This is probably true in Ellen's case as well.

However, it is the Axis II diagnosis of borderline personality disorder (BPD) that seems to capture most of the details reported in the case study. "A pervasive pattern of instability of interpersonal relationships, self-image, and marked impulsivity beginning by early adulthood and present in a variety of contexts. . ." (APA, 2000) provides a seemingly accurate template to describe her problems with living. Borderline personality disorder is a common diagnosis for females who have experienced pervasive intrafamilial sexual abuse and continue to experience the aftereffects of fragmented self-image, poor self-esteem, pronounced distrust, and pronounced difficulty in establishing safe healthy adult relationships (Courtois, 1997; McClean & Gallop, 2003; Messman-Moore & Resick, 2002).

Alternatively, the field of trauma stress research suggests a diagnosis of "complex PTSD" (CPTSD) (Herman, 1995). Although not a diagnosis as presented or accepted in the DSM-IV-TR, complex PTSD (also called disorders of extreme stress not otherwise specified [DESNOS]) is recognized by contemporary trauma stress authors when the traumatic experience has "an impact on the inner core of self-structure" (p. 8; see also Herman, 1992, 1993, 1995; McClean & Gallup, 2003; Wilson, Friedman, & Lindy, 2001). Contemporary diagnostic criteria for PTSD were developed largely through observation and description of reactions of people post singular events (Herman, 1995). For individuals like

Ellen, this conceptualization is too circumscriptive. Herman's conceptualization of the traumatic experience (level of captivity, degree of control, and age of onset), includes subsequent adaptation. This adaptation is often characterized by complex symptomatology (excessive somatization, dissociation, and changes of affect), by character traits (pathological relationships, pathological identity formation), and by vulnerability to repeated harm. Recent research seems to support early onset of sexual abuse as more prevalent within women who meet diagnostic criteria of both BPD and CPTSD, and that some women with this history can be extricated from the BPD diagnosis and subsumed under CPTSD (McClean & Gallop, 2003). Allen, Huntoon, & Evans (2000) have reported some success in developing psychometric profiles on standardized clinical personality measures such as the Millon Clinical Multiaxial Inventory, III (Millon, Millon, & Davis, 1994).

The CPTSD diagnosis offers a holistic view, encompassing cognitive, affective, behavioral, relational, and physical manifestations as acquired adaptations to long-term, unmitigated stress; it captures the long-term pervasive nature of the trauma. In the course of treatment for CPTSD, the clinician and client may work through a variety of diagnostic categories relevant to the current clinical manifestation of the trauma survivor's day–to-day needs. CPTSD allows for the consistent acknowledgement of a trauma-based etiology. The current patterns can be viewed as attempts to assimilate and accommodate abnormal experiences, not as pathology of the psyche or the personality. It may be useful to consider CPTSD as a subset of PSTD that offers both a quantitatively and qualitatively different presentation than that of the single event onset. This potentially frees the clinician from false expectations that dealing with the traumatic memory is necessary to resolve symptoms.

Ellen's case history offers a variety of diagnostic options that lead to potential ethical considerations. As her clinician, it would be important to assess what Ellen wants to accomplish in the current counseling relationship, establish her goals for treatment, define boundaries or parameters of the working alliance, develop resources beyond the therapeutic relationship, and plan for successful conclusion. It is very important that Ellen create a sense of being in control of her own treatment. This sense of self-directed treatment can be essential in her not becoming a victim to managed care rulings and policy limits.

Ethical Considerations

Even though researchers and clinicians in the fields of stress medicine and psychodynamic thought have long understood that traumatic experiences impact the way one thinks, feels, behaves, and reacts, the diagnosis of post-traumatic stress disorder was not included in the diagnostic classification system until the third edition of the *Diagnostic and Statistical Manual of Mental Disorders* (DSM-III) (American Psychiatric Association [APA], 1980). Some could argue that giving this diagnosis to Ellen based on her current presentation might not be warranted. The case history, while clearly containing traumatic experiences and some of the indicators of the three clusters, intrusion, avoidance, and arousal, lacks specifics often seen in a PSTD diagnosis (e.g., flashbacks, nightmares, recurring thoughts, or hypervigilance). The diagnosis of depersonalization disorder is also difficult to ascribe based on the descriptors provided. The proposed diagnostic construct of CPTSD is inviting because of its holistic focus and its ability to incorporate the less pathological notions of adaptation and assimilation; but as a concept, it is only present in research and theoretical literature, not in the DSM-IV-TR.

The Axis II BPD seems to be the most likely diagnostic label, given case information that is primarily relational and given the current DSM system. It is significant that Ellen does not report the self-mutilation, suicidal ideation, or substance abuse that is often associated with BPD, as well as with long-term pervasive childhood sexual abuse. This may indicate a measure of successful adaptation and/or a willingness to survive.

The language of the DSM, particularly the idea of pervasive patterns, goes to the core of the ethical problem. How reasonable is it to expect anyone who grew up in the circumstances of this young woman's life to have developed stable and enduring patterns of relating based on mutual self-care, self-respect, and well-being? It seems reasonable to expect serious problems in both identity formation and in relationships to self and others. Yet, the DSM does not include a diagnostic category for expected reactions to systems problems. In fact, it specifically indicates that expected reactions to external situations are not diagnosable.

The label of BPD, which in the absence of anything better seems the diagnosis that will most likely be chosen for Ellen, has become a catchall for difficult-to-reach, challenging clients, who present with multiple problems in living and often stretch the limits of stress for therapist and therapeutic resources. The label can predispose both the treatment provider and a health maintenance organization (HMO) or insurance company to assume that this client will require high service utilization, despite recent research on the longevity of BPD symptoms and relapse of symptoms after treatment that found that 73.5% of those diagnosed with BPD remain in remission for at least 6 years (Zanarini, Frankenburg, Hennen, & Silk, 2003). In Ellen's case, the diagnosis of BPD could carry more harm, in terms of future insurability and unnecessary labeling in a clinical record, than a diagnosis of PTSD. (Remember the premise: "once written, always there.") However, failing to accurately diagnose or avoiding the label could result in failure to obtain approval for treatments known to be successful.

The second ethical aspect in this case emerges in the assumptions that counselors

may make about the trauma and adaptation. When a client presents for treatment and self-labels the need for treatment in terms of working on past trauma, there can be an invitation to engage in support of the victim identity. Contemporary media, literature, and self-help psychology offer both a resource for people to understand sexual abuse, as well as a means to immerse oneself in the identity of "abused child." The victim mentality (Myss, 1994) can become a joint frame of reference that provides excuses for continuing patterns of self-harm. Ellen's childhood story and subsequent relationship patterns certainly fit the "expected" maladaptation. Her decision to financially support herself via prostitution presents at one level Ellen's right to self-determination, and yet it is grounded in the reality of substantial physical and emotional risks. The fact that social and psychological systems label the expected adaptations as pathology serve to support the notion that anyone who endured such a childhood would be damaged. This construct can provide blinders to the possibilities for healthy adaptive components in the client's history and current functioning.

It is essential that Ellen take an active role in the consumption and use of her mental health benefits. Her active role in deciding what strategies would help right now and for how long (treatment planning), controlling session frequency, charting successes, and identifying resources removes her from the role of victim to the limits of managed care and establishes her as an adult consumer of healing resources. Open, honest discussion of her diagnosis, potential implications of managed care influences, and her right to self direction as a consumer may help create a clearer picture of how to move forward with managed benefits.

Treatment Considerations

Ellen seems to have provided the counselor with a golden thread in her story of her life. Ellen knew that what was happening to her did not feel right. Ellen held onto this inner vision and sense until she gathered enough external evidence (sister's pregnancy) and age (15 years) to mobilize her own resources to leave. She looked for and found help, then survived the trial, alienation of mother and siblings, and possible guilt over her father's death. Finding this part of herself, the part that led to her survival, should be a key element in treatment. Helping her to recognize this self-aspect and use it to further guide her choices would follow. Traditional diagnostic categorization implies pathology; that is, you are ill/damaged from your life's experiences. When the internal message concurs with the social/psychological message, it can be very challenging to achieve growth. The philosophical difference in the suggested approach lies in the belief that the root of the problem was a maladaptive system and focusing instead on a solution grounded in discovering together how survival was attained. Treatment then asks the question, "What new skill do we add now?" instead of, "What else needs to be fixed?"

The therapist might incorporate such questions into initial goal setting. Ellen's reasons for coming in to therapy at this time seem a bit vague, at least as presented in the case above. Contracting for change and establishing her goals for counseling needs to go beyond "working on my sexual abuse history" and to be converted into the tangible changes that she desires. For instance, Wilson (2001) suggests that holistic treatment for PTSD requires understanding the impact of the trauma in terms of the memory (or story) of the trauma, the impact of the PTSD triad (intrusion, avoidance, and arousal), the impact upon self-structures (ego defenses, self-esteem, and self-concept), the impact upon interrelational skills, and the physiological processes. Subsequently, therapists plan for dealing with each of the areas in treatment.

In Ellen's case, she shares her memories of the abuse but often chooses to delay the deepest disclosures until the end of the session when there is little time for processing that experience. While that might be seem to be a way to avoid working through the affectively charged elements, it might also be reframed as making a choice to limit her openness to the end of the session and as a positive attempt on her part to check out the safety of the therapeutic relationship and to pace herself. If reframed in this way, she and the therapist could use her timing for disclosure as a means to determine whether the safety in the session was progressing; that is, her willingness to disclose earlier would indicate progress in her feelings of safety. If her sense of safety was not progressing, they could explicitly discuss what would help her to feel safe enough to disclose earlier. Ellen's management of when she chooses to disclose feelings could be linked to her childhood strength of "knowing what was right for her." Such reframing does not change the need for the therapist to maintain a health boundary by not extending the session time.

Although some might argue that Ellen has the right to choose prostitution, as her therapist I would want to consult that still small voice inside of her to see if that quieter part of herself concurs that her choice is "right for her." Safety concerns extend beyond her management of information and pace of exposure in the therapy. Here they include behavior that could result in her death. How does she plan for the risks of sexually transmitted disease, unwanted pregnancy, rape, assault, and/or murder? Within this part of the treatment contracting, it will be important to process the interpersonal reactions she has to such discussions about prostitution and safety.

CONCLUSION

Working with traumatized clients can be hindered by the notion that traumatized means damaged. Negative connotations in the relevant diagnostic categories can lead to therapeutic bias and even blinders to potential positive outcomes. Adopting a perspective that long-term trauma can lead to adaptive patterns that may no longer serve the client, yet provide cues for healing, can facilitate opportunities for empowerment and growth. Instead of seeing and defining challenging client behaviors as negative to the therapeutic process, they can be viewed as further attempts to employ survival skills. Clear contracting for what the client hopes to gain from the therapy and establishing a level of safety prior to engaging in deeper levels of work are vital to the process.

Practitioners could benefit from considering the diagnosis of CPTSD as a more accurate description of the clinical presentation for adults with complex, enduring exposure to trauma. It seems fitting that these efforts should focus on differentiation of the needs of those with severe levels of exposure from those who have circumscribed events, as well as of those who have enduring alterations in character traits.

9

A Developmental, Constructivist Model for Ethical Assessment (Which Includes Diagnosis, of Course)*

GARRETT MCAULIFFE, KAREN ERIKSEN, AND VICTORIA E. KRESS

The search for a developmental, health-focused, systemic approach to assessing and counseling clients has been part of many humanistically and systemically oriented mental health disciplines. However, in general, none of these disciplines have fulfilled their wellness-oriented, systemic, developmental promise with respect to diagnosis (Blocher, 1988; D'Andrea, 1988; Ivey & Rigazio-DiGilio, 1991). We have discussed many of the reasons for this failure throughout the book. There are two other factors that also help to explain this failure: First, despite the emergence of a plethora of developmental theories in the past 30 years (e.g., Belenky, Clinchy, Goldberger, & Tarule, 1986; Kegan, 1982; Kohlberg, 1981; Loevinger, 1976; Perry, 1970), actual methods for developmental assessment and counseling have been scarce and often vague (Darden, Ginter, & Gazda, 1996; Sprinthall & Thies-Sprinthall, 1983). Second, the dominant culture's emphasis on independent functioning often prevents individuals from asking for help. Thus, people frequently wait until a crisis or evidence of dysfunction forces them to seek help, rather than seeking assistance as they traverse a normal developmental transition. As a result of these trends, mental health diagnosis and treatment has increasingly inclined toward a remedial and pathological orientation (versus a personal growth and development orientation).

---

*Much of this chapter originally appeared in McAuliffe and Eriksen (1999) and is reproduced here with permission.

Reclaiming a commitment to universal development and its embrace of a strengths-oriented approach to assessment and diagnosis is in order at this time. Throughout the book, we have discussed in a piecemeal fashion ways that educators, students, supervisors, supervisees, and practitioners might become aware of the limitations of traditional diagnosis and work toward integrating other ways of making meaning into the diagnostic process. Here the developmental and constructivist meta-theories are brought together into a model for facilitating such a commitment. The proposed model is translated into four dimensions of human functioning: *context*, life *phase*, constructive *stage*, and personality *style* (CPSS) (McAuliffe & Eriksen, 1999). This CPSS approach to assessment, diagnosis, and intervention uses constructivist and developmental perspectives for the ultimate purposes of increasing clients' self-awareness and self-acceptance, promoting their determination to manage and maximize their so-called "natural" inclinations, and enhancing clients' capacities to address oppressive social conditions that contribute to their and others' distress. Such a shift in purposes will likely require many mental health practitioners to substantially rethink their own ways of knowing and their perspectives on the nature of reality (McAuliffe & Eriksen, 1999; Neukrug & McAuliffe, 1993).

In this chapter, the CPSS model (McAuliffe & Eriksen, 1999) is described and its relevance to DSM (*Diagnostic and Statistical Manual of Mental Disorders*) diagnosis is discussed. We present the theoretical groundings of the CPSS model, details of the model, applications of the model to a case, and, finally, a worksheet to ease practitioners' use of the model. It is hoped that this model will help to provide solutions to the difficult questions posed in this book. It is our belief that the CPSS model can be used to improve mental health practitioners' abilities to develop contextually sensitive diagnoses.

CONSTRUCTIVISM AND DEVELOPMENT: FOUNDATIONS FOR THE CPSS MODEL

"Constructivism" and "development" are the driving notions behind culturally sensitive, wellness-oriented assessment. Both evoke a world view that honors diversity, values equality among all individuals, recognizes the influence of social and physical context on lives, and emphasizes the conditions that enhance mental and emotional growth for all human beings.

Constructivism

From the constructivist perspective, all human beings are active creators of experience, not passive receptors of an objective reality. To know is to construct, not to find. To paraphrase Neimeyer (1993), constructivists view knowledge as an invented and constructed meaning system rather then as a free-standing, stable, external entity. Consequently, constructivists recognize that there are potentially, as Gergen and Kaye (1992) propose, a "multiplicity of accounts of reality" and recognize "the historical and cultural contingency of each" (pp. 179–180).

"Constructivism" has been used variously to refer to a number of traditions (e.g., Kelly, 1955; Piaget, 1963). For example, *social constructionism,* whose origins are in the field of social psychology, emphasizes that meaning is inevitably made within an interpersonal and cultural context (Olson, 1989). The "social constructionist" perspective relativizes meanings as socially derived creations, rather than references to already-existing essences (Anderson, 1990). Human beings are always "in the language" of their culture, time, and place in history, although they can also take a more or less critical stance toward those influences on their meaning making. Individuals are not necessarily passive "victims" of their social and physical context, as they can take increasing responsibility for the sense they make as they develop, according to the *constructive developmental* view (Kegan, 1994).

In this chapter, the term *constructivist* will be used as an umbrella term to incorporate all of these traditions, but a distinction will also be drawn between *social constructionism* and *developmental constructivism*. From the overall constructivist perspective, every mental health professional, like every client, is engaged in the act of making sense of experience. The mental health practitioner is not a passive receptor of client input, or an expert who interprets the "true" meaning of client behavior or who doles out curative prescriptions. Together, practitioners and clients co-construct "narratives" in counseling (White & Epston, 1990). All human explanations, then, including counseling theories, can be considered "stories," rather than essential truths.

Mental health professionals' awareness of the constructed nature of reality can reduce the distance between the practitioner and the client, making assessment a collaboration between two (or more) fundamentally equal partners. Constructivism, as it is used here, implies respect, multiple perspective taking, humility, willingness to reconstruct meaning, and a recognition that there is no "essential" diagnostic truth or theory that applies to all clients in all circumstances (Sexton, 1997). Constructivism has been translated into counseling practice by such writers as Hoyt (1996) and Monk, Winslade, Crocket, and Epston (1997).

Development

The second major foundation for the CPSS assessment model is that of development. Developmental theorists propose that humans evolve in regular ways through qualitatively different psychosocial phases (or "eras") and constructive stages (or "cognitive structures"). Developmental movement requires the performance of tasks of increasing complexity.

Developmental theories can be loosely divided into two branches (Rodgers, 1989):

(a) the so-called life span or psychosocial approaches, which in this article are called *phase* theories, and (b) the cognitive or constructive *stage* theories. The life-phase theories, in the Buehler (1933), Havighurst (1972), and Super (1963) traditions, pay attention to the culturally expected tasks of growing up and growing old, or the "when and what" of development. In contrast, cognitive, or, as Kegan (1982) has suggested, constructive, stage theories come from the Piagetian (Piaget, 1963) tradition of positing universal structures of knowing that can evolve based on a person's encounter with challenging and supporting environments, and the person's subsequent accommodations to new ways of knowing.

All developmental theories suggest that human beings can evolve in vital ways if the environment is sufficiently challenging and supportive. It is the developmentally oriented practitioner's task to (a) consider the client's *readiness* and (b) contribute to development-enhancing environmental conditions by adequately *supporting* (responding to clients with interventions that match their developmental stage) and *challenging* (presenting interventions that are one stage ahead of clients) clients.

The CPSS model, based on these constructivist and developmental theoretical perspectives, was developed for use as a counseling assessment tool (McAuliffe & Eriksen, 1999). Of course, assessment has clear implications for diagnosis and intervention as well. The following section describes in detail the CPSS model.

THE CPSS MODEL: ASSESSING CLIENT CONTEXT, PHASE, STAGE, AND STYLE

The CPSS model spans four strands of constructivist and developmental thinking. These four dimensions, like other organizing heuristics, can provide the mental health practitioner with a framework for applying the diverse constructivist and developmental theories to diagnostic practices and, in turn, to the counseling process. The key words *Where, When, How,* and *What* are added as a cue for each dimension of the model:

1. **C: context,** or **"Where?"**
   Key question: "*Where* is the client placed in the social or physical circumstances around him or her and how do these various contexts affect how he or she makes meaning?"

2. **P:** life **phase,** or **"When?"**
   Key question: "*When* will (or has) the client engage(d) in the sequence of age-related, psychosocial tasks that are expected of a person in this culture?"

3. **S:** constructive developmental **stage,** or, **"How?"**
   Key question: "*How* does the client currently make meaning; that is, what is his or her orientation toward sources of knowledge?"

4. **S:** personality **style,** or **"What?"**
   Key question: "*What* tendencies does the person show in his or her interests, abilities, values, and temperament?"

Context or "Where"

Context defined. The context element of the CPSS model is especially guided by the previously mentioned social constructionist notion that all human meaning-making is inextricable from the human communities in which we participate. Social constructionist-oriented thinkers (e.g., Gergen, 1991; Gergen & Kaye, 1992; Mead, 1934; Vygotsky, 1978) are characterized by Rorty (in Olson, 1989) in this way: "Social constructionists understand reality, thoughts, facts, texts, selves, and so on as community-generated and community-maintained linguistic entities . . . that define or 'constitute' the communities that generate them" (p. 3). From this perspective, the social dimension in human experiencing is so

pervasive that who we are at any given time cannot be separated from our past and present interactions with others. According to social constructionist thinkers, even when we are alone, our very thoughts and meanings are bound up in the language, social categories, and social values of our place and time. Social constructionist thinking can lead the mental health practitioner and client to appreciate a diversity of possible interpretations of events. Such awareness can be turned inward by practitioners as they reflect on the socially constructed lenses through which they themselves create reality, assess clients, and propose treatment options. Through this context dimension, practitioners and clients are asked to look through the specific lenses of family, community, and cultural influences on experiencing. Specific social identities of gender, ability (versus disability), race, religion, ethnicity, age, class, and sexual orientation (GAR-REACS) are highlighted as dimensions of "culture" in this model, although some authors have also added geographic region and a rural–suburban–urban dimension as cultural influences on individuals. Attention to these social identities sensitizes the mental health practitioner to the dual issues of "internalized" client assumptions based on these contexts and to "external" issues of power and oppression that clients encounter.

The physical dimension in human experiencing is also so pervasive that we cannot separate ourselves from its influence. It is referred to above as an *ability–disability* continuum because communities construct meanings about ability and disability, about illness and wellness, that profoundly impact individuals. In light of our discussions of diagnosis, we believe that this *ability–disability* continuum bears further mention as a critical aspect of a client's context. Perceptions about physical and psychological "dysfunctions" profoundly influence our perceptions of the world, our sense of hope or powerfulness in the world, and our ways of approaching problems.

Therefore, the CPSS model incorporates clients' physical and psychological systems, including their own and others' perceptions about varying diagnoses, as part of their context. As mentioned in other sections of this book, it is our belief that the clients' and their community's perceptions about their diagnoses profoundly impact clients' self-perceptions and personal narratives.

Assessing context. Through context assessment, the mental health practitioner considers the impacts of the physical and psychological situation, the family, the community, the nation, and the culture on clients' self-definitions and problem constructions, and considers how each of these systems might be accessed for effective interventions. Sample interview probes for assessing clients' social context are listed below.

"How would you describe your family's social class?"

"What were the messages to you about work, love, and play?"

"What religious tradition, if any, are you a part of? What role does religious faith play in your life?"

"How would you describe your ethnic heritage? What does it mean to you?"

"How does gender role influence your expectations, and your perceptions of opportunities?"

"What physical problems are you currently experiencing?"

"What resources can you draw on from those around you, or from the assumptions of and experiences in your cultural groups?" (Note that the practitioner might have to explain that "culture" includes all of the GARREACS dimensions mentioned above.)

"What perceptions of those around you help you to make sense of problems you are having, for example, of the diagnostic labels that you may have received (e.g., 'What do the people around you think of depression, substance abuse, attention-deficit hyperactivity disorder, etc.?')? What do those around you think of people who have a 'mental illness' or who receive psychological assistance?"

Practitioners should also ask about the client's experience of psychological and other physical symptoms.

Many clients will be naïve about social construction, because it is counterintuitive to the dominant Western ethos of "hyperindividualism" (Bellah, Madsen, Sullivan, Swider, & Tipton, 1985). Also, Western mental health practitioners themselves, in order to balance this individualistic bias, will need to proactively pursue awareness, knowledge, and skills related to social constructionism, multiculturalism, family and organizational systems, and social justice issues to increase their alertness to their own and clients' context issues.

In *context* assessment, issues of power, oppression, and current capacities can be investigated. The practitioner might probe racial or ethnic identity awareness levels in clients (e.g., Cross, 1991; Hardiman, 1982; Helms, 1990; Jackson, 1975; Sue & Sue, 1990). For example, in much of the Western world, a person of color's naïve status of racial identity may commonly be associated with internalized oppression and low self-esteem (Cross, 1991). In such a case, counseling might challenge a client's naïve understandings of culture; such challenges are common to feminist counseling (Chaplin, 1992) and the psychotherapy of liberation (Ivey, 1995).

Implications of context assessment for intervention. A primary reason for an in-depth discussion of diagnosis such as we have attempted in this book is diagnosis and/or assessment's primacy in laying a foundation for intervention. Many of the challenges that have been raised in this book emerge precisely because of the implications of traditional diagnosis for treatment. For instance, how does a family therapist glean much direction for treatment planning from a medical model version of what is "going on" with a client? How does a developmental practitioner promote the development of a client with a diagnosis that is by definition static or permanent and not considerate of the client's developmental phase/stage? Thus, as we discuss each part of the CPSS model, we will also demonstrate how such assessment can contribute to developmental, systemic, and wellness-oriented interventions.

We propose a three-step guide for constructive-developmental assessment and counseling that is summarized as "Explore–Know–Act." The following is an example of this model as applied to a client's ethnicity. While recognizing the risk of oversimplifying both ethnicity and the counseling process, we portray the sequence this way in the context domain:

1. *Explore* the situational, family, community, and cultural contexts, or the "facts" (e.g., "My German family and culture valued independence, achievement, and controlling emotions.").

2. *Know* the implicit socially derived assumptions that are embedded in their stories; that is, the "meanings" (e.g., "I have taken independence as 'the way to be.' While it serves me well at times, it hurts my ability to stay connected in discussions with my partner.").

3. *Act* (i.e., accept/manage/change) after deciding which social assumptions, values, manners, and conditions are helpful or unhelpful to them at this place and time (e.g., "I will try to balance the separate style I've learned with engaging in conversations with my partner, even when I feel tense.").

In general, context-oriented intervention directs the practitioner to assist clients in four ways: (a) to rewrite their socially embedded family, community, and cultural narratives into stories that are more useful to them at this time and place; (b) to understand physical and psychological problems within a social context; (c) to understand the resources that clients can draw on from their social surround or cultural beliefs, assumptions, and experiences; and (d) to engage in social actions in order to change oppressive systems of power.

In an example of assessing and intervening in a *context*-sensitive manner, one author found a Puerto Rican man's religious and cultural background to play a significant role in his understanding and construction of his presenting problems. The man met the DSM criteria for bipolar I disorder, had experienced repeated hospitalizations, and still refused to take a mood-stabilizing medication. Despite the hospital's, emergency service's, and psychiatrist's repeated attempts at education about bipolar disorder, the man was unable to fully integrate this medical model perspective into his reality. The client strongly believed that his problems originated as a message from God that he needed to become more involved in his church, that he was not active enough in his faith. This belief was shared by members of his family and church community. The counselor, upon discovering these beliefs, integrated the client's pastor and members of his family into the counseling process. With their support, the client was able to do what he thought he needed to do—attend church more and increase his faith. Because the counselor included his family and church in counseling, the client was also able to build a strong relationship with the counselor and see her as a messenger of God. Her "message" about taking a mood stabilizer thus became more palatable; he could now believe that this was what God wanted for him. Sensitivity to the client's contextual reality, and an appreciation and integration of this reality into the counseling process, made it possible for the client to take the steps necessary to improve his situation.

Life Phase or "When"

Phase defined. The notion of a psychosocial "phase" here represents an interval of time in the life span during which certain themes are ascendant. The assumption is that the individual who accomplishes the central tasks of that era is likely to function more effectively in society. A phase is marked by the coalescence of (a) internal physical, cognitive, and emotional *readiness* on the part of the individual and (b) societal *expectations*. The following is a summary of developmental phase principles based on Havighurst (1972), Erikson (1963), and Rodgers (1989).

1. Individual growth is continuous, but it can be divided into periods, or "life phases," for descriptive purposes.

2. Individuals in a given culture share certain general characteristics in each life phase.

3. Society makes certain relatively uniform demands on all individuals; these demands differ from phase to phase.

4. "Developmental crises" occur when individuals perceive the demand to alter their behavior and learn new things (e.g., establish intimate adult relationships, choose an occupation, go to school, reappraise career role).

5. While the crisis or task appears in its "purest form" at one phase, preparation for it occurs at earlier phases, and it may arise again during a later phase.

6. This task must be mastered (e.g., childhood autonomy) before the individual can successfully move on to related later-phase tasks (e.g., career growth, ability to be intimate in young adulthood).

7. Successfully meeting the crisis by learning the required task leads to societal approval, positive feelings, and success with later tasks.

8. Failure to adequately address a task leads to disapproval by society.

Thus, for example, the dominant groups in Western societies expect school-age children to be industrious at their schoolwork, adolescents to begin interacting romantically with others, adults to teach and mentor the younger generation, and elders to shift gears toward modified career and leisure pursuits. Cultural factors, such as gender, ethnicity, religion, and socioeconomic class, play important roles in these expectations. Some broad developmental tasks, such as "preparation for mating" can be concretized by particular subcultures into strict rules, such as "marriage to a heterosexual person." Phasic tasks will be viewed here as the more general imperatives, which are partly biologically driven and partly societal.

Mental health practitioners can be guided by the major psychosocial development theories such as (a) the life-span formulations of Erikson (1963) and the follow-up identity work of Josselson (1987), Marcia (1966), and Holland, Daiger, and Power (1980); (b) Havighurst's (1972) work on school-age youth; (c) both Levinson's (1978, 1996) and Sheehy's (1976) observations on life seasons and passages; (d) Vaillant's (1977) notion of mature defense mechanisms; (e) Super's (1963) model of career phases; and (f) Gould's (1979) adult transformations theory.

Assessing phase. Mental health practitioners might begin to assess phasic tasks by exploring clients' levels of engagement in the tasks of their life phase (as defined by the above theorists). Some phase-assessment questions might cover areas of body image and self-esteem (especially with adolescents), career match and discontent (e.g., with midlife adults), and the task versus relationship balances of any life phase. For example, the following practitioner probes can evoke responses to such life-phase themes as identity, competence, intimacy, career purpose, autonomy, achievement, and nurturing:

"At this time in your life, how is the balance of work, family, and leisure going for you?"

"Name some skills you have or things that you are good at. How do you express these skills?"

"How are you doing in school? How do you get along with your classmates?"

"How do you feel about how you look?"

"At this time in your life (e.g., older adulthood) what do you see as important?"

"How important is the idea of a career to you?"

"How satisfied have you been with your occupation? What might need to change, if anything? Have you been considering alternatives?"

"As you look back over your life so far, what are you proud of?"

If clients are unprepared to address such issues, practitioners can help them to become aware of societal expectations and together they can construct responses to these demands.

Formal and informal assessment tools can be used to determine task engagement. Such tools include Super, Thompson, and Lindeman's (1988) measure of career development; Holland et al.'s (1980) vocational identity measure; Goldman's (1992) trust and friendship inventories; Winston, Miller, and Prince's (1987) measure of young adult tasks; and Darden et al.'s (1996) measures of four generic life-skills dimensions.

Whether or not an instrument is used, the practitioner who is assessing phase can seek out and honor the client's own constructions of developmental tasks during the interview. The practitioner might especially note gaps between client readiness and societal expectations. If clients themselves are unaware of phasic expectations, practitioners can use their knowledge of life-phase issues to ask questions and to anticipate client struggles. Practitioners might note whether the client is alert to the issues of a particular life phase or is avoiding the challenge. For example, a young adult who is floundering in his or her career (Super, 1963) can be helped to understand and to actively engage in the "exploration" task. Other examples of phase alertness include the practitioner's assessing how an adolescent constructs the "dating" task, how a young adult envisions relationship commitments, and how the mid-life adult reappraises earlier life role choices.

With regard to DSM diagnostic applications, practitioners might consider how the client's current life phase relates to the presenting problem and possible DSM diagnoses. A consideration of life phase has significant implications for how clients and counselors conceptualize presenting problems. For example, might an older adult transitioning to (and therefore experiencing some struggle with) retirement be experiencing mild depression as a "normal" life-phase transition reaction? Perhaps a sensitivity to this life-phase transition might affect the diagnosis one chooses (e.g., adjustment disorder versus a mood disorder), which would then affect intervention (e.g., facilitating life-phase transition and finding new sources of meaning in one's life versus using a psychotropic medication). As another example, might a first-generation college student beginning college at an out-of-state school experience anxiety as a normal reaction to life transition and phasic changes?

Implications of phase for intervention. Becoming aware of psychosocial phase tasks sets the stage for clients to engage in activities such as studying, dating, exploring occupations, becoming assertive, increasing intimacy, and reappraising life roles, to name a few examples. Mental health practitioners can help clients to anticipate and prepare for upcoming phases and transitions through one-to-one guidance, bibliotherapy, and psychoeducational programs. Practitioners can also stay aware of the typical "coping" strategies used during the various life stage transitions, so as to incorporate prevention strategies into their work. Examples of phase-related interventions include assertiveness and social relations workshops in college; instruction in handling peer pressure in high schools; substance abuse, rape, sexually transmitted disease, and eating disorder prevention courses in high schools and colleges; career exploration in early adulthood; readings on gender and career for women about to have children; career reentry groups for homemakers; marriage enrichment seminars for couples who are launching children; midcareer reappraisal programs for adults; and "deceleration" planning for older adults. Each of these education efforts may prevent the development of depression, anxiety, substance use disorders, or other DSM disorders.

In individual work, practitioners might challenge clients to accept "expected" transitional struggles and might "normalize" the distress that accompanies such transitions. Practitioners might also assist some clients to accept that they are "off-time" from the norm on some life-phase tasks, such as having offspring in young adulthood or middle age, or advancing in career during middle adulthood, and to carefully weigh the difficulties and the satisfactions of alternative, less-conventional paths. Practitioners can also help clients to deconstruct rigid interpretations of phasic tasks (e.g., "I must be successful in my occupation and I must raise children at the same time" or "I must marry and have children in young adulthood"). Such deconstruction may free clients of rigid, internalized expectations, and prevent the experience of unnecessary depression or anxiety. Finally, clients who are resistant to act on a phasic task because of fears or other obstacles might be challenged or encouraged (with substantial support) to do so (e.g., "I'm scared to move out from my parents' home and go away to college").

Overall, the practitioner might use the same Explore–Know–Act approach to actualize constructivist-developmental assessment and intervention when addressing phase. Clients can be helped to (a) *explore* their life phase, (b) increase their *knowledge* of phasic tasks, and (c) *act* on those tasks.

Stage or "How"

Stage defined. Stage theory might be called "developmental constructivism" because it is concerned with progressive changes in how individuals make meaning, or develop cognitively. A stage represents the set of common organizing principles (Kegan, 1994) that individuals use in constructing experience. Stage theory is developmental in that it posits regular, progressive change in how those meaning-making principles evolve.

As meaning-making evolves, thinking becomes less rigid, exclusive, simple, and dogmatic, and more flexible, open, complex, and tolerant of differences. It is assumed in stage theory that increased constructive capacity is generally *more adaptive* and gives the individual more meaning-making options or provides them with a broader range of "ways of knowing" (Belenky et al., 1986).

The limitations of the stage construct include the risk of rigidly stereotyping and "totalizing" a person's constructive tendencies. Practitioners must remind themselves that the notion of "stage" is itself an artifact, or a construction, and it cannot represent any individual's total way of making meaning. It is likely that much meaning-making is situational and contextual and that stage refers to a "more or less" tendency to use certain constructive capacities in specific situations. This fluid notion has been called the "soft-stage" approach to constructive development.

Some of the stage theories that can be useful to mental health practitioners in assessing the client's meaning-making orientation include Piaget's (1963) cognitive development; Loevinger's (1976) ego development; Perry's (1970) ethical and intellectual development; Belenky et al.'s (1986) women's ways of knowing; Kohlberg (1981) and Gilligan's (1982) moral development; and Kegan's (1982) subject–object development.

Assessing stage. Both formal and informal methods might be used to assess a client's general stage tendency. During a session, a practitioner can use a semi-structured interview approach (Vacc & Juhnke, 1997) to probe a client's general meaning-making orientation. A key stage-evoking question is, "How did you come to decide or know . . . (e.g., that this gender role in necessary, or that a person cannot marry someone of another ethnic group, or that you must follow the career path that your parents prefer)?" Other constructive development-evoking questions (Lahey, Souvaine, Kegan, Goodman, & Felix, 1985), that are meant to evoke how the client comes to know in general, might include:

"What lets you know that something is good (right, important)?"

"Why is that important to you?"

"What's at stake here?"

"What makes you most nervous (angry, etc.) about that?"

"If it were to turn out another way, what would be the cost for you?"

"How would you have liked this to turn out? Why?"

Related to diagnosis, a person might be asked:

"How did you come to know that you are depressed (that you are a 'borderline,' etc.)?"

"How did you come to perceive that this issue was a problem for you?"

"What does it mean to you to have this problem?"

"What worries you the most about this problem?"

"How would you like this situation/problem to evolve and change?"

Following the client's initial response, the practitioner might then probe the assumptions used to construct a particular meaning via a "spiraling downward" technique, in which the practitioner continues to ask epistemology-evoking questions until the client reaches the ultimate ground of her or his knowing.

An inexact cue to epistemology might be the brevity of a client's response: Those who generally rely on "outside" sources of knowing (e.g., conventions, parents, religious tradition, peers, or authorities) seem to provide brief, minimal responses to such epistemology-evoking probes (Lahey et al., 1985). More "internal" or "self-authoring" knowers tend to offer a method of considering pros and cons to come to a decision. They may weigh others' (such as parents', teachers', and practitioners') suggestions, but they hold their own internal weighing procedure—whether it be logic or intuition—as the ultimate criterion for making life decisions. If they take others' suggestions, it is with the awareness that they have a choice not to do so.

Stage-evoking interview methods are elaborated in the *Ways of Knowing Interview Schedule* (Belenky et al., 1986) and the *Subject–Object Interview* (Lahey et al., 1985). More formal stage assessment methods include recognition tasks, in which the client must choose responses from options on an inventory (e.g., Moore, 1987; Erwin, 1983; Kitchener & King, 1981). Each assesses a person's view of how knowledge is gained, progressing from a more external or authoritarian position through a more relativistic orientation. A more intensive and time-consuming measure of Perry's theory is Baxter-Magolda and Porterfield's (1988) *Measure of Epistemological Reflection*. Rest's (1979) *Defining Issues Test* determines moral reasoning via the Kohlberg scheme. Loevinger's (1976) stage theory of ego development can be measured by the *Washington University Sentence Completion Test*.

With regard to diagnostic applications, practitioners might assess a client's stage in relation to his or her perceived problem. For example, Christina is a client who recently indicated to one author that she thought she had social anxiety. In exploring the client's meaning of this problem (using the aforementioned questioning), the client, a college campus resident, indicated that she believed that she had social anxiety, a belief based on commercials she had seen advertising the antidepressant Paxil (paroxetine hydrochloride). Probing further, it became evident that Christina had come to believe that she was somehow abnormal because she didn't always enjoy the myriad of social activities involved in her sorority and in the college campus community. She reported that sometimes she felt overstimulated and wanted to be alone and have "down time." Without such probing about Christina's understanding of her problem, a practitioner might have concluded that the client had "social phobia." However, the probing allowed the counselor to frame the problem differently; that is, as being in transition from one stage to another, from a more externally focused to a more internally defined stage.

Implications of stage for intervention. In general, mental health practitioners can selectively "match" (support) or "mismatch" (challenge) client assumptions during the course of counseling (Sanford, 1962). Thus, developmental constructivist counseling consists of providing an optimal mismatch between the client's current dominant ways of knowing and the client's next potential way of knowing. This "stretching" of constructive capacity toward the next viable way of knowing parallels Vygotsky's (1978) notion of movement through the "zone of proximal development." The practitioner can thus be part of the development-enhancing environment. For instance, in Christina's case, the counselor could promote her constructive development by supporting (recognizing) her ability to tune in to, be aware of, or be sensitive to external authorities (Paxil commercials, sorority leaders) and their definitions of what is right for her or what is normal, while at the same time challenging her to carefully consider her own experiences of her needs (for quiet and down time). Supporting her current stage (being defined by others) will provide scaffolding or a holding environment for the challenge to move toward a stage ahead (being self-defined). As another example, a 52-year-old client who was concerned about his family

proscriptions against leaving the family business was helped by the first author's offering both "support," in acknowledging his love of his family and sensitivity to their needs and desires, and "challenge," in asking "What would *you* want?" The client discovered "his own" interests and preferences and began to move toward a more self-authored way of knowing. Other stage-challenging counseling strategies are described by Ivey (1991), Kegan (1982), Knefelkamp and Slepitza (1976), McAuliffe (1993), and McAuliffe and Strand (1994).

Style or "What"

Style defined. The notion of "style" is defined here as an individual's relatively consistent inclinations and preferences across contexts. Sometimes the words "personality traits" and "types" are used to represent the person's consistent orientations toward constructing meaning and acting. The more biological notion of "temperament" (e.g., Kagan, 1995) may be another useful construct for helping clients to know, accept, and manage their inclinations. Such terms as "artistic," "energetic," "even-tempered," "field independent," "investigative," "compulsive," "reactive," and "extroverted" are common descriptors of what we here call style. Personality styles originate in some combination of genetic inheritance and environmental influence (Holland, 1985; Kagan, 1995; Krumboltz, Mitchell, & Jones, 1976). Like stage inclinations, personality styles should be recognized as constructed approximations of human experience and should be arrayed on a continuum rather than being reified or totalized in all-or-nothing terms. Practitioners must be vigilant to deconstruct their and others' uses of style constructs in favor of an ongoing reflexivity about the use and misuse of such labels (Parker, Georgaca, Harper, McLaughlin, & Stowell-Smith, 1995).

The notion of style contrasts to that of stage in that style represents long-term constructive *preferences,* whereas stage represents current constructive *capacity* (Kegan, 1994). A second distinction between the two is that personality style is relatively long-term and consistent over time, whereas stage tendencies are mutable—they evolve under development-enhancing conditions. Both notions, however, share a constructivist dimension in that each calls attention to the lenses that humans use to create experience. Both stage and style theories are also similar in that they concern themselves with individuals' consistent tendencies across life contexts, either in *how* the person knows (i.e., stage) or in *what* (environments, people, interests, values) the person prefers (i.e., style).

A central value of style assessment is that it helps practitioners and clients to appreciate human diversity, or, in Myers's (1980) paraphrase of a biblical passage, respect for "gifts differing." Style assessment can help practitioners and clients to celebrate the range of assets, interests, and inclinations that are represented in the human community. Such a celebration may result in a more non-judgmental stance—the recognition within individuals, families, and communities that styles can often be constructed as merely varying, neither wrong nor right, neither ill nor healthy. The range of normal variation in styles can explain much human behavior without reference to notions of pathology. Ivey, Ivey, and Simek-Morgan (1997) even suggested that personality disorders be reconceptualized as being on a continuum, with one end being a more adaptive inclination. Style assessment can also complement the search for personality "disorder." All notions of style and disorder are, of course, socially constructed and are therefore subject to probing deconstruction of their historical origins and their place within current social relationships among class, gender, and other identities (Parker et al., 1995).

Specific style theories that might be useful for the mental health practitioner include person-environment matching theory (Holland, 1985), personality type theory (Myers, 1980), and Ivey's reconceptualization of the DSM personality disorders as a continuum of personality styles (Ivey et al., 1997).

Assessing style. The practitioner can informally assess style by asking key questions during the counseling interview. Examples of style probes include the following:

> "What work environments do you prefer (or have you preferred)?"
>
> "Name some of your interests and/or favorite school subjects."
>
> "How do you prefer to socialize?"
>
> "Where do you tend to get your energy?"
>
> "How do you tend to make decisions: carefully, by considering much data, or quickly, or somewhere in-between?"
>
> "Are you easily distracted by events and persons in the environment, or can you easily 'tune out' such potential stimuli?"
>
> "Tell me about your relative preference for details? creative activity? hands-on work? influencing others? analyzing information? teaching and helping people?

A sound knowledge of current trait and personality theories is clearly required for such an assessment.

Style can also be assessed by formal instruments or brief questionnaires (e.g., the *Self-Directed Search,* Holland, 1990; the *Myers Briggs Type Indicator,* Myers, 1980; the *Personality Style Inventory,* Ivey et al., 1997). Regardless of assessment method used, it is paramount from the constructivist perspective that the client's own meanings be evoked by the mental health practitioner and reflected upon by the client. Goldman's (1972) method of demystifying tests by referring the client back from the inventoried summary to the original items and responses on the questionnaires themselves can assist with such reflections.

Implications of style for intervention. Knowledge of clients' styles lays the foundation for helping them to (a) explore, (b) know, and (c) act on (accept, manage and/or compensate for) such tendencies. Such knowledge also allows practitioners to consider interventions that match client style (e.g., journaling for more introverted depressed clients versus social interactions for more extraverted depressed clients). Clients can be helped to recognize and value the assets of certain styles and to match those preferences with congruent work settings, tasks, friends, and partners. They can also be encouraged to recognize the problems with certain styles, and to achieve greater balance, thereby reducing the consequences of these problems, by developing the opposite end of the continuum. Furthermore, when there is a mismatch between clients' styles and environments (e.g., work activities), practitioners can encourage clients to compensate for or avoid those activities that require styles that are not natural to them. For, example, the non–detail-oriented client might find an assistant to help her keep financial records for her organization. Similarly, the extrovert who must study or perform other isolated tasks can be encouraged to compensate for his strong social needs by learning to resist social engagements until tasks are accomplished. Each of these interventions may prevent the development of DSM disorders or other life problems, or may reduce client experiences of depression and anxiety.

The case of Christina, mentioned under the discussion of client stage of development, provides a good example of the importance of considering a client's style. Christina would be considered more intraverted, according to the five-factor model of personality and the Myers Briggs Typology. Her "problem" of not wanting to be continually involved in social activities on campus and needing time to herself may not be a diagnosable problem when considered from a style perspective. Instead, the problem might be defined as a conflict between her temperament or personality and the demands of her social surround. The counselor was able, as

a result of doing a style assessment, to reframe Christina's "problem" in less pathological and more systemic terms. She was also able to help Christina to see herself as normal by explaining extraversion and intraversion as different ends of a continuum of normal functioning. This freed Christina from labeling herself as "ill" and allowed her, from a position of greater self-acceptance, to consider the possible choices for managing the conflict between her natural inclinations and her current environment. Thus, including style assessment resulted in a very different story than her initial construction of her problem as an anxiety disorder.

Another author's client stated in counseling that he was afraid that there was something wrong with him because he wanted to do "everything" and had many varied interests. The client, a musical theater major, indicated that during his college program the director frequently stated that to be successful in musical theater you had to "eat, breathe, and sleep the theater." The director frequently communicated that commitments to and interests in other activities would only cause one to become side-tracked and weak, and that such interests demonstrated a lack of commitment to theater. After 2 years in the program, the client had unquestioningly internalized this message and now believed that his lack of focus reflected a lack of commitment to the theater. Despite his love of his program and his field of study, he was considering changing majors—he feared that he might not be successful in theater because he wanted to pursue other interests as well.

During counseling, the client and counselor discussed different realities related to his situation, one of which was that differences in styles or interests did not mean that one was abnormal. The client took the NEO-Personality Inventory (NEO-PI), an assessment of the big-five personality factors, and scored very high on the openness to experience scale. The client also took several career inventories, and although he clearly scored high on interests related to theater, his results reflected many other interests as well. The client was able to create new meanings about his problem as a result of greater self-awareness. He now could accept that he had many varied interests and that he enjoyed having new experiences, rather than buying into his director's implication that there was something inherently wrong with him that would preclude his being successful in his chosen occupation. From this position of strength, he was able to consider how to manage his competing interests and ward off further depression and anxiety.

WORKSHEET FOR CONSTRUCTIVE-DEVELOPMENTAL ASSESSMENT

A worksheet for constructive developmental assessment is provided in Table 9.1. It might serve as a guide to assessing clients' constructions and developmental tasks and capacities. Additionally, in the self-reflective constructivist tradition, the worksheet asks mental health practitioners to "foreground" their own constructs by reflecting on their own social contexts, life-phase issues, constructive stage tendencies, and personality style inclinations.

ILLUSTRATION OF CONSTRUCTIVE-DEVELOPMENTAL ASSESSMENT: THE CASE OF JANINE

Janine is a 55-year-old woman who decided to pursue counseling after an incident with her 27-year-old daughter, Sarah. Sarah's friend had called Janine from Minnesota, where her daughter lives, and had indicated that he was afraid for Sarah's life, that he thought she was a danger to herself. Janine and her husband flew to Minnesota in response to the crisis and got Sarah into treatment. During the intake process, Janine realized that she also had experienced many of the struggles and depressive symptoms that her daughter had been experiencing. Janine began to believe that perhaps she had been

experiencing depression throughout much of her adult life.

Janine is a slim, attractive, beautifully groomed and dressed woman who presented as cheerful, intelligent, and very articulate. Her depression was not evident, although she did describe many days in which she could not get up in the morning, spent the day watching television, and then rushed around to get dinner on the table by the time her husband came home. She indicated that she usually felt better when talking with other people, if she had the energy or motivation to get out of the house.

Context

Janine is an American of Danish heritage and is an unemployed wife of a military chaplain. As the practitioner began to ask her about her heritage and about her life in the military, it became clear that, for her, being of Danish heritage meant being Protestant, being cheerful and hardworking, never letting anyone know how she felt, and expecting that if she did feel badly it was her responsibility to fix it herself. She had been very involved in the church, and found her faith to be an important part of her life. Being a military wife had meant a history of moving often, and of fitting into her husband's career. She had found, as do many military wives, that her satisfactory participation in the wives' activities was necessary to her husband's success as a military officer. Therefore, she had often felt pressured to do social and service activities to promote his career, activities that she might not otherwise have chosen to do.

Finally, Janine characterized her husband as a "mighty ox," a large, blustery man, very extroverted and gregarious, forceful and determined, whom everyone liked. She had frequently felt like a "little bunny" being dragged along by the force of his personality. Furthermore, his success in his work life, paired with her unemployment, or sometimes underemployment, often resulted in her discounting her own opinions

Table 9.1

WORKSHEET FOR CONSTRUCTIVIST-DEVELOPMENTAL ASSESSMENT

The CPSS Model: Assessing Client Context, Phase, Stage, and Style

Client Name: _____   Age: _____

CONTEXT = "Where"

Situation (urgency, external barriers, similar past experiences, physical and/or psychological diagnosis):

Family (stage, support/dissonance, enmeshment/distance, etc.):

Community/Culture (pertinent characteristics of/client's cultural identity re: gender, ability, race, religion, ethnicity, age, class, sexual orientation, etc.):

Counselor's construction of his/her own situation, family, community/culture as it affects this case:

Plan to deal with situation, family, or culture: embrace, modify, etc.

PHASE = "When"	Overall Phase	Recycling of Previous Life Phase Issue(s)	Task(s)	Intervention(s) (Individual & Network)	Questions

General:
Eriksonian:
Career:
Counselor's own current phase issues:
Plan to accomplish developmental tasks:

STAGE = "How"	General C.D. Stage (from Integrated Theory)	and/or	Specific C.D. Theory Stage (e.g., from Kegan, BCGT)	Do, to match:	Do, to mismatch:

Counselor's own preferred meaning-making orientation:

Plan to enhance client developmental capacity:

STYLE = "What"	MBTI Types	Career (e.g., Holland)	Personality Style/Disorder (including ruling out)	Core Values/Other

Advantage of this style:

Plan to manage problems w/ style:

Counselor's own personality/learning styles and how they might impact:

OTHER CONSIDERATIONS: (e.g., maladaptive thinking, self-efficacy issues, psychodynamic possibilities) about her life choices and believing his negative evaluations of her choices. She found herself trying to "do it his way," and evaluating herself negatively when she did not succeed. Janine voiced these things about her husband very reluctantly, and was quick to assure the practitioner that she and her husband had a great marriage and that he was a very good man. In summary, context may be relevant to Janine's depression in a number of ways:

1. She may not have availed herself of the nurturing of friends and family, because her heritage has persuaded her to "keep a stiff upper lip" and never let anyone know she is hurt or struggling.

2. Her experience as a military wife and the wife of a very popular, successful, dominant husband may have led her to deny her own inner leading, ignoring her feelings and needs, which, by going unmet, contributed to emotional deprivation. Such emotional deprivation may have altered her body chemistry as well, which may contribute to the depression.

3. Her husband's and her ongoing negative evaluation of her life choices or methods of approaching life may have depleted her self-esteem, made her reluctant to make choices, and resulted in hopeless or helpless feelings.

4. The possible context of being around people who consider help-seeking and admittance of problems as weak may have resulted in further denial of personal experiences.

5. Her daughter's problems provided a context of personal self-reflection and increased self-awareness that may be leading her to seek help, rather than her help-seeking resulting from an increase in depressive symptoms, as many practitioners might assume when a client presents for services.

6. Her daughter's diagnosis of depression also contributes to Janine's context of believing that she may also be depressed; this experience may have opened up a reality for her that she may have otherwise not considered when making meaning of her own situation.

Janine's context also contributes to her life in ways that may foster successes during counseling. For instance, her context includes:

1. Financial stability and the ability to take time to decide what she wants to do with her time and her life.

2. Marital stability and support.

3. Loving feelings within the marriage; a relatively conflict-free marriage.

4. Faith that is real and can be depended upon in difficult circumstances.

5. Genuine caring about her daughter and her daughter's well-being.

6. Value placed on independence that contributes to a belief that she can be efficacious and is able to make changes in her life if she works hard.

A practitioner should not, however, neglect to assess Janine for the existence of DSM criteria for depression, despite the clear influences of Janine's social contexts on her life. Long-standing depression may indicate organicity, and without medical treatment, may interfere with her ability to shift or make changes in her life contexts. It would, in turn, be important for the practitioner to address and consider Janine's current life circumstances in ascribing a diagnosis. Many practitioners assume that when a client requests services, the client has experienced an escalation in symptoms. In Janine's case, her context (mainly her daughter's situation) led her to seek service and her symptoms may not have necessarily escalated. A thorough assessment that takes all of these historical and recent experiences into consideration is critical in selecting a diagnosis that best describes Janine's experiences. Failing to assess Janine's context might lead some practitioners to assume the presence of organic depression and to apply oversimplified interventions (e.g., medication management and cognitive behavioral therapy) that may disregard her context.

Phase

Janine's children recently finished college and began living on their own. Only recently has Janine thought about what she "wants to do when she grows up," about what will give her life meaning now that the children no longer play a central role in her life. She has made several attempts to try out different "lives," but finds that she starts and doesn't finish many of the choices that she begins. Janine may benefit from knowing that many women struggle with similar concerns about life's purpose once raising children is no longer their primary function. Not only does she need to find new activities that will give her life meaning at this stage of life, she also needs to regain, in the process, some knowledge of herself, her own desires, her own talents, and her own interests. While her husband is at the peak of his career, feeling successful and confident, she is experiencing uncertainty and a lack of confidence about her abilities and interests. This contrast in life experiences may be serving to further accentuate the feelings she has about her husband's way being "right," and her way being wrong. Janine's phase of life may thus contribute to her feelings of depression in the following ways:

1. She feels rudderless and without purpose or value, because she has not yet successfully redefined herself as a "woman beyond children."

2. She has just finished a phase of life in which her focus was on her children's needs, and is finding it difficult now to refocus on or to even know her own needs. This lack of self-knowledge contributes further to her feelings of rudderlessness or purposelessness.

3. The contrast between her stage of life and career and that of her husband may further her sense of being of less value, and further her dependence on her husband's evaluations of her.

The DSM system lists hopelessness, feelings of low self-worth, indecisiveness, and feelings of emptiness as several of the symptoms of depression. However, all of these symptoms might also be partly understood as normal reactions to Janine's phase-of-life adjustments. Although a DSM diagnosis should be applied if she meets the criteria for depression, certainly a diagnosis cannot by itself provide enough understanding of the problem without including the influences of her life phase. Additionally, the V code "phase-of-life adjustment" might also be added to her DSM multiaxial assessment to indicate that she is struggling with life transitions.

Janine's life stage, in concert with that of her husband, also comes with certain strengths; that is, her phase of life and her husband's career success also afford her relative stability and financial security in which to explore herself, her interests, and her talents. She has relatively few competing demands on her life to serve as distractions from her quest.

Stage

Janine has accepted the evaluations of and needs of others, particularly her husband's, as the way she knows the truth about herself and the way she constructs her reality. This places her in Kegan's (1982) interpersonal order of consciousness. She approached counseling as a place for an expert to give her answers about why she can't seem to make anything work in her life. Her way of expressing herself in the counseling session is, while complimentary, rather pressuring; that is, unless the practitioner can fill up the session with direction, there is likely to be great deal of silence and floundering around. Janine seems to be looking outside of herself for direction and for definition.

Janine has found herself getting started on various projects of interest; however, when she talks with her husband about them, he, with his usual enthusiasm and dominance, begins talking with her about all the things she "should" do to handle the projects in the best way. She either becomes overwhelmed by the sheer volume of what he suggests or deflated because what "should be done" doesn't seem to fit who she is or what she wants to do. If she does get started on a project, and tries to do it as he has suggested, she usually quits. There is a healthy element to this quitting, in that it is almost a declaration of her refusal to succeed by doing it his way. In fact, she would not tell him about coming in for counseling because she felt that he might not support her decision. So there is an element in Janine that is ready to transition to a new stage of knowing.

During the recent crisis with her daughter, Janine found that her depression lifted. Further explorations revealed that, in fact, Janine functions very well in crises, feels most alive, and lifts out of the depression. From the interpersonal stage perspective, it seems that Janine needs a lot of external stimulation and definition—initially from her children, and now perhaps from crises—to make meaning of her life or to know what to do and how to do it. Thus, time at home, without children and between crises, may feel like a void, like a hole she doesn't know how to fill.

From a stage perspective, Janine's depression could result from a temporary inability to conceptualize other life options and other ways of being and knowing. That is, she has been boxed into a singular reality, a singular way of functioning, for so long that she is currently unable to envision other possibilities and options for her life and experiences. It is possible that such other ways of being might facilitate an increased level of happiness and a less-depressed experience. Janine, as a result of the questions indicated in previous sections, might come to see that her past reality does not have to be her future reality. Facilitating her cognitive development away from a rigid to a more flexible reality that has varied behavioral, cognitive, and affective possibilities should change her current life experiences. Additionally, a focus on multiplistic thinking and alternative realities might help Janine to develop a strength-based identity, whereas a

focus on Janine as "depressed," apart from her stage, might continue to feed into her self-story of being helpless and needing to follow the directives of the "expert" mental health practitioner (or husband).

Style

The Myers Briggs Temperament Inventory revealed Janine to be an ESFP (Extraverted, Sensing, Feeling, Perceiving) and the Holland revealed Janine to be an ASR (Artistic, Social, Realistic). As the practitioner began discussing what these acronyms meant, Janine revealed how she tends to operate in the here and now, how she makes the best decisions when she pays attention to her intuitive feelings, and how she tends to float through her day without a schedule or plan. She finds that she is much happier when she is around people, but has enough intraverted characteristics to enjoy doing crafts by herself. In the past, she frequently found herself beginning a project and becoming so absorbed in it that she lost all track of time. She makes resolutions to exercise regularly and to get up at a regular time and finds it impossible to keep these resolutions. She is very tuned in to her own feelings and those of others, although she finds it very difficult to make clear decisions about how to act on these.

Her husband, in contrast, is an ENTJ (Extravert, Intuiting, Thinking, Judging), and because she believes his opinions are most often "right," she also evaluates his style of operating as right. She thus tends to consider it wrong not to have a schedule, not to get up and go to bed at regular times, not to have a list of activities for the day, week, or year to cross off as she accomplishes them. She evaluates herself negatively for not being organized, for not having a stepwise plan for accomplishing her objectives; she considers this the reason that she doesn't accomplish enough, or at least as much as he does. She often wants to just start doing a project, and finds that it works well for her that way, instead of spending a great deal of time planning all the ins and outs of the project. She seems to rely on her husband's organizing ability, and while often sabotaging it, she does consciously evaluate his method as right.

Janine is very artistic, enjoys crafts and creative endeavors, and found great pleasure in a former job as a graphic designer (before the profession was computerized). She also enjoys being with people and has plans (although planning doesn't work too well for her) to get a group of ladies together to work on "artsy" things. However, she tends to agree with her husband about the limited value of this type of endeavor.

From a style perspective, Janine's depression could result from her failure to acknowledge and value her natural temperament. Metaphorically, she has been failing to physically feed herself nourishing food; she seems to have been trying to survive emotionally and vocationally on food better suited to her husband than to herself. Furthermore, her husband's devaluing who she feels naturally inclined to be may result from his own style, and may be further encouraged by his observation of her own self-denigration.

Janine's style is one often found in artists, musicians, and professional athletes. Her recognition and acceptance of the value of her temperament to some professions may free her to act more in accordance with her natural temperament, to expect greater respect from her husband for who she is, and to succeed more often by pursuing projects that are more suited to who she is.

When considering a diagnosis for Janine, a clinician might want to ascribe "depression," given her symptoms. However, as indicated above, Janine's indecisiveness (one symptom she is experiencing that might indicate depression) might alternatively be conceptualized as "normal" and part of her personality style. Either way, the indecisiveness may be something for Janine to work at managing. It is possible,

though, that conceptualizing the indecisiveness as part of a normal personality style could decrease its stigma and increase her sense of powerfulness to make changes should she choose to.

Additionally, many practitioners might diagnose Janine's behaviors and her personality style to mean that she is "dependent"; some might even apply a diagnosis of "dependent personality disorder," which implies that her behavior is pathological and maladaptive. However, such a diagnosis reflects inherent value judgments. A clinician could just as easily consider her "symptoms" to be a normal personality style that is simply devalued by Western culture; a normal reaction to expectations and pressures placed on women in Western society; or a reaction to her life context and life stage.

CONCLUSION

Constructivist-developmental assessment in general, and the CPSS model in particular, might be part of the roadmap for beginning a new century in counseling diagnosis, assessment, and intervention. It now becomes the task of mental health practitioners to determine how to apply these principles to their work. It is hoped that mental health trainers will use this umbrella for constructive developmental human understanding to spur efforts to create and test methods for wellness-oriented, developmental diagnosis, assessment, and counseling. Together, practitioners and educators can further ground the work of such pioneers as Blocher (1982), D'Andrea (1988), Ivey (1991), and Knefelkamp, Widick, and Parker (1978). Only through such an evolution will mental health practice counter the potential harm of traditional diagnosis, encourage a rethinking and restructuring of the DSM diagnostic system or the development of a completely new sort of diagnostic system, and promote active social responsibility, individual development, and strength-enhancement for all populations. The CPSS model is perhaps a step in that direction.

Afterword

Now that we have reached the end of this journey together, I have been thinking about how the journey began. It ostensibly began at the suggestion of a colleague who indicated that he tried to write an article each semester related to what he was teaching. This sounded like a good idea to me. I was teaching diagnosis and treatment planning that semester and was using a standard psychopathology textbook along with the then current *Diagnostic and Statistical Manual of Mental Disorders* (DSM) and DSM casebook. I had also collected a large number of articles about challenges to the DSM system of diagnosis; however, I was struggling with how to decide which ones to give to students who were already overloaded with reading. I decided to write an article so that they could encounter these challenges without being overburdened with reading many articles. At that point, I was unfamiliar with any literature that comprehensively presented the challenges to DSM diagnosis, or that investigated the ethical use of the DSM.

However, the project really began 20 years before that, as I chose to practice family therapy and to, for many of the reasons cited in this book, minimize the importance of diagnosing in my clinical work. It continued through those years of clinical practice as I associated with practitioners in professional associations, primarily those in private practice, and became familiar with standards of practice in insurance billing and diagnosis,

standards that would certainly be considered unethical if not directly fraudulent. The journey included the years of making my own decisions about insurance billing and diagnosis. So, by the time I finished with the initial literature review for this book and added my own and my colleagues' experiences from 20 years of clinical practice and professional associations, the manuscript had reached 60 pages. Its length now precluded publication as a mere article. So, I began exploring the possibilities of a monograph or very short book.

At this point, my energy for the project was waning, so I also asked Victoria Kress to join me in authoring the book. I knew and was impressed with her work and perspectives as a result of her authoring a chapter on teaching diagnosis and treatment planning for a previous book of mine, and after I heard her speak on challenges to the DSM at the American Counseling Association Convention. I discovered that she also brought to the work years of clinical practice and a strong feminist perspective on diagnosis and practice. Together, we reworked the initial literature and constructed Chapter 5 in our attempts to exhaustively present possible solutions to DSM quandaries and awareness-building exercises. At this point, the book had grown to 150 pages. We were pretty proud of ourselves. Who had known that we had so much to say?

However, when the editor reviewed the book, he indicated that it needed to be almost twice as long for the publisher to consider contracting for the book. We wondered how we could possibly do this. We told him, "But we don't know anything more. We have exhausted all of our ideas." After a week or so of thinking about it and talking with other colleagues, I realized that I had already coauthored an article that would serve as a great conclusion to the book. We also took a lesson from a previous book that I had contributed to that presented cases to various authors and asked them to respond based on the model presented in the first chapter of the book. So during the period that the book was sent out for review, we found authors, asked them to submit case studies and responses, and coached them through the writing process into what are now Chapters 6 through 8. We found that including these other clinicians' experiences and perspectives greatly enriched the book.

As perhaps happens many times in writers' lives, the most difficult point arrived when, 2 years into the project, we received the reviewers' comments. We struggled with what the reviewers meant; with whether we could actually respond to their questions and suggestions; with whether we had the energy to continue; with whether we could actually do enough or respond well enough that the publisher would publish the book when we were finished. After a month or so of *sturm und drang*, again with reflecting and conversing with peers, we decided that the message was far too important to let go of, that practitioners everywhere really needed to hear what we were proposing. We decided that the reviewers were right—we had merely included what we wanted to include, rather than exhaustively searching the literature, becoming experts in the content area, and engaging in a scholarly rather than merely a political discourse. We clearly needed to know more and give evidence for our positions. So, we set specific goals and dove in.

And the rewards have been great. I have reaffirmed my understanding that writing is learning, and have passionately enjoyed learning more about diagnosis, challenges to the DSM, women's issues in psychology, and multicultural issues in mental health work. I have found my knowledge base deepened. I find that I have more to add to my courses, deeper learning experiences to offer my students, and a commitment to helping the students to make better decisions about these issues than I did as a practitioner and to develop better decision-making skills than I had when practicing. I have a wealth of information to offer to the faculty members who I mentor as they attempt to add dialogue to their multicultural and diagnostic courses and to deepen their students' abilities to think critically about issues that powerfully affect clients' lives. The faculty and students' deeper understandings enhance our counseling training program and the parallel clinical psychology program.

But most of all, awareness of multicultural and feminist challenges to the DSM (and other mental health standards and practices) has deepened my belief that the personal is the political; that scholars and practitioners cannot live in a value-free environment or engage in value-free teaching, research, or practice; if we pretend that we can, we cannot help but impose our own values on those who would perhaps not choose such values, and we also fail to counter societal conditions that cause more pain and distress than biologically based mental conditions will ever cause. I have also wondered how psychologists, psychiatrists, professional counselors, psychiatric nurses, or social workers can afford *not* to be feminist, multicultural activists if they are truly committed to healing human emotional suffering. I have wondered how these professionals can fail to have such commitments after they have graduated from training programs that usually, at a minimum, have a multicultural course, and when they participate in professional associations with clear ethical mandates about bias and discrimination.

Where is the message getting hung up? What keeps mental health professionals from fully embracing such knowledge? Is the information too new? Is it merely that these changes take time, and that those of us who think about the issues regularly have said "of course" to things that others haven't had time to truly consider? Is it fear? Although I cannot really answer these questions (perhaps feminists and multicultural practitioners who have been considering these issues longer than I have can more fully answer them), I now find myself more fully committed to activism and to creating change, to learning how to advocate more effectively about these issues. I find myself glad that I am now living in a very diverse community with very diverse students, whose very presence continually faces me with the questions and asks me to find solutions in a more consistent way. May our commitments enhance your commitments.

Karen Eriksen
keriksen@argosyu.edu

As a feminist, postmodern counselor, I was trained to be aware of how my values and experiences bias my belief system. I hope that by explaining a bit about my history, how I came to be interested in the DSM, and how mental health professionals use the DSM, readers will understand my context and my goal in writing this book.

During my sophomore year of college, I can recall taking an abnormal psychology course where we learned about the DSM. For me, DSM diagnoses were equitable with physical illnesses and I thought that all DSM mental disorders were mysterious diseases that very educated and smart people "knew" existed. At that time, I did not question the DSM, its veracity, or how people used the DSM.

As I finished my master's in counseling and entered my doctoral program, I can recall sitting in another DSM class and for the first time wondering about the DSM's validity; the values associated with what constituted a mental disorder; the links between environmental, cultural, socioeconomic conditions and mental disorders; and so on. By this point in my professional training, I had come to consider issues such as peoples' developmental levels and environmental and cultural contexts when considering human behavior, and I knew enough about the research process and the politics associated with research to question and critique various findings.

As I entered the clinical world, I had many negative experiences related to the DSM and, more importantly, the DSM's use by professionals. For instance, at one job I was instructed to provide a DSM multiaxial assessment after meeting with patients for only 15 minutes. At another job, the psychiatrist I worked with diagnosed every one of our patients with a personality disorder. In numerous situations, women in domestic violence situations were not granted their children in custody hearings primarily because they had been diagnosed with disorders such as major depression or post-traumatic stress disorder. Many clients had been diagnosed with innumerable different DSM diagnoses, yet no one had ever asked them about trauma histories or ruled out trauma reactions. It was during this time that I became truly aware of the complexity associated with the DSM and its use. Unfortunately, none of my instructors had ever taught me about these complex issues or how to mange them. The DSM and its use had always been presented to me in a cookbook, perfunctory fashion; the gray issues had never been addressed in my training and were rarely addressed in the literature, thus leaving me to develop my own theories as to how to use it in the least-harmful fashion.

Thus, I was delighted to be a part of this important project and to have a chance to share some of the "gray" areas I have found to be inherent in the DSM ascription process.

This book has been a significant project spanning almost 4 years, and one goal has helped me persevere: the hope that this book will help some mental health professionals better understand the implications of DSM diagnoses and ultimately use the DSM in the most contextually sensitive way possible.

In writing this book, I was very aware that passion can be a very powerful motivator when seeing a difficult task through to completion.

My contributions to this book would not have been a reality were it not for my clients, all they have taught me, and the passion they have evoked in me. I would like to thank all of my former, current, and future clients who teach me so much about the struggles and successes inherent in the human experience.

Victoria E. Kress
vewhite@ysu.edu

References

Abas, M., Baingana, F., Broadhead, J., Iacoponi, E., & Vanderpyl, J. (2003). Common mental disorders and primary health care: Current practice in low-income countries. *Harvard Review of Psychiatry, 11*(3), 166–174.

Abramowitz, S. (1973). The politics of clinical judgment. *Journal of Consulting and Clinical Psychology, 41*, 385–391.

Acierno, R., Hersen, M., & Van Hasselt, V. B. (1997). DSM-IV and multidimensional assessment strategies. In S. M. Turner & M. Hersen (Eds.), *Adult psychopathology and diagnosis* (3rd ed., pp. 578–594). Hoboken, NJ: John Wiley & Sons.

Ackley, D. C. (1997). *Breaking free of managed care.* New York: Guilford Press.

Acton, D. (2001). The "color blind" therapist. *Art Therapy, 18,* 109–112.

Ader, R., Felten, D. L., & Cohen, N. (Eds.). (2001). *Psychoneuroimmunology* (3rd ed). Burlington, MA: Academic Press.

Adler, A. (1929). *The practice and theory of individual psychology.* Paterson, NJ: Littlefield Adams.

Akhtar, S., Byrne, J. P., & Doghramji, K. (1986). The demographic profile of borderline personality disorder. *Journal of Clinical Psychiatry, 47*(4), 196–198.

Albee, G. W. (1999). Prevention, not treatment, is the only hope. *Counselling Psychology Quarterly, 12*(2), 133–147.

Allen, J. G., Huntoon, J., & Evans, R. B. (2000). Complexities in complex posttraumatic stress disorder in inpatient women's evidence from cluster analysis of MCMI-III personality disorder scales. *Journal of Personality Assessment, 73,* 449–471.

Allwood, M. A. (2002). Children's trauma and adjustment reactions to violent and nonviolent war experiences. *Journal of the American Academy of Child and Adolescent Psychiatry, 41*(4), 450–457.

Althen, G. (Ed.). (1981). *Learning across cultures.* Washington, DC: National Association for Foreign Student Affairs.

American Association for Marriage and Family Therapy (AAMFT). (2001). *AAMFT code of ethics.* Washington, DC: Author.

American Counseling Association (ACA). (1995). *ACA code of ethics and standards of practice.* Alexandria, VA: Author.

American Psychiatric Association (APA). (1980). *Diagnostic and statistical manual of mental disorders* (3rd ed. [DSM-III]). Washington, DC: Author.

American Psychiatric Association (APA). (1994). *Diagnostic and statistical manual of mental disorders* (4th ed. [DSM-IV]). Washington, DC: Author.

American Psychiatric Association (APA). (2000). *Diagnostic and statistical manual of mental disorders* 4th ed., text revision [DSM-IV-TR]). Washington, DC: Author.

American Psychological Association (APA). (1992). *Ethical principles of psychologists and code of conduct.* Washington, DC: Author.

American Psychological Association (APA). (2003). Guidelines on multicultural education, training, research, practice, and organizational change for psychologists. *American Psychologist, 58*(5), 337–402.

American Psychological Association (APA) Committee on Accreditation. (2002). *Self-study directions for doctoral programs.* Washington, DC: Author.

Anderson, C. E. (2000). Dealing constructively with managed care: Suggestions from an insider. *Journal of Mental Health Counseling, 22*(4), 343–354.

Anderson, C. E. (2001). The role of managed mental health care in counseling gifted children and families. *Roeper Review, 24*(1), 26–32.

Anderson, C. M., Reiss, D. J., & Hogarty, G. E. (1986). *Schizophrenia and the family.* New York: Guilford Press.

Anderson, H., & Goolishian, H. (1992). The client is the expert: A not-knowing approach to therapy. In S. McNamee & K. Gergen (Eds.), *Therapy as social construction* (pp. 25–39). London: Sage.

Anderson, T. (1996). Language is not innocent. In F. Kaslow (Ed.), *Handbook of relational diagnosis and dysfunctional family patterns* (pp. 119–125). New York: John Wiley & Sons.

Anderson, W. T. (1990). *Reality isn't what it used to be.* New York: HarperCollins.

Angermeyer, M., Matschinger, H., & Holzinger, A. (1998). Gender and attitudes towards people with schizophrenia. *International Journal of Social Psychiatry, 44*(2), 107–116.

Armsworth, M. W., & Holaday, M. (1993). The effects of psychological trauma on children and adolescents. *Journal of Counseling and Development, 72,* 49–56.

Arredondo, P., Toporek, R., Brown, S. P., Jones, J., Locke, D. C., Sanchez, J., et al. (1996). Operationalization of the multicultural counseling competencies. *Journal of Multicultural Counseling and Development, 24,* 42–78.

Arroyo, J. A., Westerberg, V. S., & Tonigan, J. S. (1998). Comparison of treatment utilization and outcome for Hispanics and non-Hispanic Whites. *Journal of Studies on Alcohol, 59,* 286–291.

Australian Bureau of Statistics (ABS). (1998). *Mental health and well-being. Profile of adults: Australia, 1997.* Canberra: Australian Government Publishing Service.

Avery, A. K. C. (2002). What have you been told about your illness? Information about diagnosis among psychiatric inpatients. *International Journal of Psychiatry in Clinical Practice, 6*(2), 103–107.

Bacon, S. F., Collins, M. J., & Plake, E. V. (2002). Does the Global Assessment of Functioning assess functioning? *Journal of Mental Health Counseling, 24*(3), 202–213.

Bahr, M., & Sinacore-Guinn, A. L. (1993, April). *Assessment of attention deficit hyperactivity disorder: Integrating a cultural framework.* Paper presented at the annual convention of the National Association of School Psychologists, Washington DC.

Bailey, C. (2002). Is it really our chemicals that need balancing? *Journal of American College Health, 51*(1), 42–48.

Bakan, D. (1966). *The duality of human existence.* Chicago: Rand McNally.

Baker, F. M. (2001). Diagnosing depression in African Americans. *Community Mental Health Journal, 37*(1), 31–38.

Barnard, C. P., & Hirsch, C. (1985). Borderline personality and victims of incest. *Psychological Reports, 57,* 715–718.

Barstow, A. L. (1994). *Witchcraze: A new history of the European witch hunts.* San Francisco, CA: HarperCollins.

Baskin, D. (1984). Cross-cultural conceptions of mental illness. *Psychiatric Quarterly, 56,* 45–53.

Bass, E., & Davis, L. (1988). *The courage to heal.* New York: Harper & Row.

Beck, A. T., Rush, A. J., Shaw, B. F., & Emery, G. (1979). *Cognitive therapy of depression.* New York: Guilford Press.

Becker, D., & Lamb, S. (1994). Sex bias in the diagnosis of borderline personality disorder and posttraumatic stress disorder. *Professional Psychology: Research and Practice, 25*(1), 55–61.

Belenky, M. F., Clinchy, B. M., Goldberger, N. R., & Tarule, J. M. (1986). *Women's ways of knowing.* New York: Basic Books.

Bellah, R. N., Madsen, R., Sullivan, W. M., Swider, A., & Tipton, S. M. (1985). *Habits of the heart: Individualism and commitment in American life.* New York: Harper & Row.

Belle, D., & Doucet, J. (2003). Poverty, inequality, and discrimination as sources of depression among U.S. women. *Psychology of Women Quarterly, 27*(2), 101–114.

Bem, S. (1974). The measurement of psychological androgyny. *Journal of Cognitive Psychotherapy, 1,* 2–27.

Benjamin, L. S. (1986). Adding social and intrapsychic descriptors of Axis I of the DSM-III. In T. Millon & G. Klerman (Eds.), *Contemporary directions in psychopathology: Toward the DSM-IV* (pp. 599–638). New York: Guilford Press.

Benjamin, L. S. (2002). *Interpersonal diagnosis and treatment of personality disorders* (2nd ed.). New York: Guilford Press.

Benson, M. J., Long, J. K., & Spokowski, M. J. (1992). Teaching psychopathology and the DSM-III-R from a family systems perspective. *Family Relations, 41,* 135–140.

Bever, E. (2002). Witchcraft, female aggression, and power in the early modern community. *Journal of Social History, 35,* 955–989.

Bhugra, D., & Bhui, K. (1999). Racism in psychiatry: Paradigm lost—paradigm regained. *International Review of Psychiatry, 11*(2/3), 236–244.

Bijl, R. V., deGraaf, R., Ravelli, A., Smit, F., & Vollebergh, W. A. M. (2002). Gender and age-specific first incidence of DSM-III-R psychiatric disorders in the general population: Results from the Netherlands Mental Health Survey and Incidence Study (NEMESIS). *Social Psychiatry and Psychiatric Epidemiology, 37,* 372–379.

Bilsbury, C. D., & Richman, A. (2002). A staging approach to measuring patient-centered subjective outcomes. *Acta Psychiatrica Scandinavica, 106*(4), 5–41.

Bischoff, R. J., & Barton, M. (2002). The pathway toward clinical self confidence. *American Journal of Family Therapy, 30*(3), 231–243.

Blankfield, A. (1987). The concept of dependence. *The International Journal of the Addictions, 22*(11), 1069–1081.

Blashfield, R. K., & Breen, M. S. (1989). Face validity of the DSM-III-R personality disorders. *American Journal of Psychiatry, 146,* 1575–1579.

Blocher, D. H. (1982). Human ecology and the future of counseling psychology. *The Counseling Psychologist, 9,* 69–77.

Blocher, D. H. (1988). Developmental counseling revisited. In R. Hayes & R. Aubrey (Eds.), *New directions for counseling and human development* (pp. 13–21). Denver, CO: Love.

Block, C. B. (1984). Diagnostic and treatment issues for black patients. *The Clinical Psychologist, 37,* 51–54.

Blum, J. D. (1978). On changes in psychiatric diagnosis over time. *American Psychologist, 33*(11), 1017–1031.

Bobes, T., & Rothman, B. (2002). *Doing couple therapy: Integrating theory with practice.* New York: W. W. Norton.

Bohan, J. S. (Ed.). (1995). *Re-placing women in psychology: Readings toward a more inclusive history.* Dubuque, IA: Kendall/Hunt.

Boy, A. V. (1989). Psychodiagnosis: A person-centered perspective. *Person-Centered Review, 4*(2), 132–151.

Boyd, M., & Mackey, M. (2000). Alienation from self and others: The psychosocial problem of rural alcoholic women. *Archives of Psychiatric Nursing, 14*(3), 134–141.

Bracken, P., & Thomas, P. (2001). Postpsychiatry: A new direction for mental health. *British Medical Journal, 322*(7288), 724–728.

Bracken, T. (2002). *Trauma: Culture, meaning and philosophy.* London: Whurr Publishers.

Bradley, L. J., & Ladany, N. (2001). *Counselor supervision: Principles, process, and practice* (3rd ed.). Philadelphia: Brunner-Routledge.

Breggin, P. (1995). *Talking back to Prozac: What doctors won't tell you about today's most controversial drugs.* New York: St. Martin's Press.

Briere, J., & Runtz, M. (1993). Childhood sexual abuse: Long-term sequelae and implications for psychological assessment. *Journal of Interpersonal Violence, 8,* 312–330.

Brodsky, A. M., & Hare-Mustin, R. T. (Eds.) (1980). *Women and psychotherapy: An assessment of research and practice.* New York: Guilford Press.

Brodsky, A. M., & Holroyd, J. (1975). Report of the Task Force on Sex Bias and Sex-Role Stereotyping in Psychotherapeutic Practice. *American Psychologist, 30,* 1169–1175.

Broverman, I. K., Broverman, D. M., Clarkson, F. E., Rosenkrantz, P. S., & Vogel, S. R. (1970). Sex-role stereotypes and clinical judgments of mental health. *Journal of Consulting and Clinical Psychology, 34*(1), 1–7.

Broverman, I. K., Vogel, S. R., Broverman, D. M., Clarkson, F. E., & Rosenkrantz, P. S. (1972). Sex-role stereotypes: A current appraisal. *Journal of Social Issues, 28*(2), 59–78.

Brown, J. E. (2002). Epistemological differences within psychological science: A philosophical perspective on the validity of psychiatric diagnoses. *Psychology and Psychotherapy: Theory, Research & Practice, 75*(3), 239–251.

Brown, L. S. (1986, August). Diagnosis and the zeitgeist: The politics of masochism in the DSM-III-R. In R. Garfinkel (Chair), *The politics of diagnosis: Feminist psychology and the DSM-III-R.* Symposium presented at the Convention of the American Psychological Association, New York.

Brown, L. S. (1990a). Taking account of gender in the clinical assessment interview. *Professional Psychology: Research and Practice, 21,* 12–17.

Brown, L. S. (1990b). Feminist therapy perspectives on psychodiagnosis: Beyond the DSM and ICD. In *Feminist diagnosis and therapy* (pp. 45–66). Amsterdam: Stichting de Maan.

Brown, L. S. (1991a). Diagnosis and dialogue. *Canadian Psychology, 2,* 142–144.

Brown, L. S. (1991b). Not outside the range: One feminist perspective on psychic trauma. *American Imago, 48,* 119–133.

Brown, L. S. (1992). A feminist critique of the personality disorders. In L. S. Brown & M. Ballou (Eds.), *Personality and psychopathology: Feminist reappraisals* (pp. 206–228). New York: Guilford Press.

Brown, L. S., & Gilligan, C. (1992). *Meeting at the crossroads.* Cambridge, MA: Harvard University Press.

Brunette, M., & Drake, R. E. (1998). Gender differences in homeless persons with schizophrenia and substance abuse. *Community Mental Health Journal, 34*(6), 627–642.

Bryer, J. B., Nelson, B. A., Miller, J. B., & Krol, P. A. (1987). Childhood sexual and physical abuse as factors in adult psychiatric illness. *American Journal of Psychiatry, 144,* 1426–1430.

Buehler, C. (1933). *Der menschliche Lebenslauf als psychologisches Problem* [The human life course as a psychological subject]. Leipzig: Hirzel.

Burgess-Watson, I. P., Hoffman, L., & Wilson, G. V. (1988). The neuropsychiatry of post-traumatic stress disorder. *British Journal of Psychiatry, 152,* 164–173.

Burns, D. D. (1980). *Feeling good: The new mood therapy.* New York: William Morrow.

Burr, V., & Butt, T. (2000). Psychological distress and postmodern thought. In F. Fee (Ed.), *Pathology and the postmodern* (pp. 186–206). London: Sage.

Busfield, J. (1989). Sexism and psychiatry. *Sociology, 23,* 343–364.

Busfield, J. (1996). *Men, women, and madness. Understanding gender and mental disorder.* London: Macmillan.

Butler, P. V. (1999). Diagnostic line-drawing, professional boundaries, and the rhetoric of scientific justification: A critical appraisal of the American Psychiatric Association's DSM project. *Australian Psychologist, 34*(1), 20–29.

Buysse, D. J., Reynolds, C. F., Hauri, P. J., Roth, T., Stepanski, E. J., Thorpy, M. J., et al. (1994). Diagnostic concordance for DSM-IV Sleep Disorders: A report from the APA/NIMH DSM-IV field trial. *American Journal of Psychiatry, 151*(9), 1351–1360.

Cahn, S. K. (2003). Come out, come out whatever you've got! or, still crazy after all these years. *Feminist Studies, 29*(1), 7–19.

Cameron, S., & Turtle-Song, I. (2002). Learning to write case notes using the SOAP format. *Journal of Counseling & Development, 80,* 286–293.

Campbell, J. (2000). Consumers' perspective of confidentiality and health records. In J. J. Gates & B. S. Arons (Eds.), *Privacy and confidentiality in mental health care* (pp. 5–32). Baltimore, MD: Brooks.

Caplan, P. J. (1973). The role of classroom conduct in the promotion and retention of elementary school children. *Journal of Experimental Education, 41,* 45–51.

Caplan, P. J. (1977). Sex, age, behavior, and subject as determinants of reporting of learning problems. *Journal of Learning Disabilities, 10,* 314–316.

Caplan, P. J. (1989). *Don't blame mother: Mending the mother–daughter relationship.* New York: Harper & Row.

Caplan, P. J. (1992). Gender issues in the diagnosis of mental disorder. *Women & Therapy, 12*(4), 71–82.

Caplan, P. J. (1995). *They say you're crazy: How the world's most powerful psychiatrists decide who's normal.* Reading, MA: Addison-Wesley.

Caplan, P. J., & Kinsbourne, M. (1974). Sex differences in response to school failure. *Journal of Learning Disabilities, 7,* 232–235.

Caplan, P. J., McCurdy-Myers, J., & Gans, M. (1992). Should "'Premenstrual Syndrome" be called a psychiatric abnormality? *Feminism and Psychology, 2*(1), 27–44.

Carden, A. (1994). Wife abuse and wife abuser: Review and recommendations. *The Counseling Psychologist, 22, 539–582.*

Carelock, J., & Innerarity, S. (2001). Critical incidents: Effective communication and documentation. *Critical Care Nursing Quarterly, 23*(4), 59–67.

Carlson, J., Hinkle, J. S., & Sperry, L. (1993). Using diagnosis and DSM-III-R and IV in marriage and family counseling and therapy: Increasing treatment outcomes without losing heart and soul. *The Family Journal, 1,* 308–312.

Carmen, E. H., Reiker, P. P., & Mills, T. (1984). Victims of violence and psychiatric illness. *American Journal of Psychiatry, 14,* 378–383.

Carmen, E. H., Russo, N. F., & Miller, J. B. (1981). Inequality and women's mental health: An overview. *American Journal of Psychiatry, 138,* 1319–1330.

Casey, B., & Long, A. (2003). Meanings of madness: A literature review. *Journal of Psychiatric and Mental Health Nursing, 10*(1), 89–100.

Castaneda, R., & Franco, H. (1985). Sex and ethnic distribution of borderline personality disorder in an inpatient sample. *American Journal of Psychiatry, 142,* 1202–1203.

Castillo, R. J. (1997). *Culture and mental illness: A client centered approach.* Pacific Grove, CA: Brooks/Cole.

Catalano, R., Libby, A., Snowden, L., & Cuellar, A. E. (2000). The effect of capitated financing on mental health services for children and youth: The Colorado experience. *American Journal of Public Health, 90*(12), 1861–1866.

Caws, P. (2003). Psychoanalysis as the idiosyncratic science of the individual subject. *Psychoanalytic Psychology, 20*(4), 618–634.

Cermele, J. A., Daniels, S., & Anderson, K. L. (2001). Defining normal: Constructions of race and gender in the DSM-IV casebook. *Feminism and Psychology, 11*(2), 229–248.

Cerullo, J. J. (1992). From epistemological critique to moral discourse: Reflections on the social constructionist movement in social psychology. *Canadian Psychology, 33*(3), 554–562.

Chambliss, C. H. (2000). *Psychotherapy and managed care.* Boston, MA: Allyn & Bacon.

Chaplin, J. (1992). *Feminist counselling in action.* London: Sage.

Charman, D. P. (2004). Effective psychotherapy and effective psychotherapists. In D. P. Charman (Ed.), *Core processes in brief psychodynamic psychotherapy: Advancing effective practice* (pp. 3–22). Mahwah, NJ: Erlbaum.

Chesler, P. (1972). *Women and madness.* New York: Doubleday.

Choi, H. (2002). Understanding adolescent depression in ethnocultural context. *Advances in Nursing Science, 25*(2), 71–85.

Chrisler, J. C., & Caplan, P. (2002). The strange case of Dr. Jekyll and Ms. Hyde: How PMS became a cultural phenomenon and a psychiatric disorder. *Annual Review of Sex Research, 13,* 274–307.

Christian, B. C. (2002). Notes for a cultural history of family therapy. *Family Process, 41*(1), 67–82.

Clark, L. A. (1995). The challenge of alternative perspectives in classification: A discussion of basic issues. In W. J. Livesley (Ed.), *The DSM-IV personality disorders* (pp. 482–496). New York: Guilford Press.

Clark, L. A., Watson, D., & Reynolds, S. (1995). Diagnosis and classification of psycho-pathology: Challenges to the current system and future directions. *Annual Review of Psychology, 46,* 121–153.

Clarkin, J. F., Kernberg, O. F., & Somavia, J. (1998). Assessment of the patient with borderline personality disorder for psychodynamic treatment. In J. W. (Ed.), *Making diagnosis meaningful: Enhancing evaluation and treatment of psychological disorders* (pp. 299–318). Washington, DC: American Psychological Association.

Clasen, C., Meyer, C., Brum, C., Mase, W., & Cauley, K. (2003). Development of the competency assessment tool to assess core competencies for mental health care workers. *Psychiatric Rehabilitation Journal, 27*(1), 10–18.

Cohen, J. A. (2003). Managed care and the evolving role of the clinical social worker in mental health. *Social Work, 48*(1), 34–44.

Cohen, P. N., & Casper, L. M. (2002). Stigma management among the voluntarily childless. *Sociological Perspectives, 45,* 21–46.

Cohler, B. J., Stott, F. M., & Musick, J. (1995). Adversity, vulnerability, and resilience: Cultural and developmental perspectives. In D. Cicchetti & D. J. Cohen (Eds.), *Developmental psychopathology: Vol. 2* (pp. 753–800). New York: John Wiley & Sons.

Cole, M., & Cole, S. R. (1996). *The development of children* (3rd ed.). New York: Freeman.

Collins, L. H. (1998). Illustrating feminist theory: Power and psychopathology. *Psychology of Women Quarterly, 22,* 97–112.

Collins, S., & Cutcliffe, J. R. (2003). Addressing hopelessness in people with suicidal ideation: Building upon the therapeutic relationship utilizing a cognitive behavioural approach. *Journal of Psychiatric and Mental Health Nursing, 10*(2), 175–186.

Comer, R. L. (2001). *Abnormal psychology* (4th ed.). New York: Worth Publishers.

Commission on Accreditation for Marriage and Family Therapy Education (COAMFTE). (1997). *Manual on accreditation.* Washington, DC: Author.

Committee on Women in Psychology. (1985). *Critique of proposed new diagnoses for the DSM-III-R.* Unpublished manuscript.

Conroy, R. M., Siriwardena, R., Smyth, O., & Fernandez, P. (2000). The relationship of health anxiety and attitudes to doctors and medicine to use of nontraditional and complementary treatments in general practice patients. *Psychology Health and Medicine, 5,* 203–212.

Cook, E. P. (1992a). Gender and psychological distress. *Journal of Counseling and Development, 68,* 371–380.

Cook, E. P. (Ed.). (1992b). *Women, relationships, and power: Implications for counseling.* Alexandria, VA: American Counseling Association.

Cook, E. P., Warnke, M., & Dupuy, P. (1993). Gender bias and the DSM-III-R. *Counselor Education and Supervision, 32,* 311–322.

Cooper, C. C., & Gottlieb, M. C. (2000). Ethical issues with managed care: Challenges facing counseling psychology. *Counseling Psychologist, 28*(2), 179–236.

Cooper, F. A. (1981). Descriptive and dynamic psychiatry: A perspective on DSM-III. *American Journal of Psychiatry, 138*(9), 1198–1202.

Cooper, J. E., Kendall, R. E., Gurland, B. J., Sartorius, N., & Farkas, T. (1969). Cross-national study of diagnosis of the mental disorders: Some results from the first comparative investigation. *American Journal of Psychiatry, 125,* 21–29.

Corey, G. (2001). *Theory and practice of counseling and psychotherapy* (6th ed.). Belmont, CA: Brooks/Cole.

Corey, G., Corey, M., & Callanan, P. (2003) *Issues and ethics in the helping professions* (6th ed.). Pacific Grove, CA: Brooks/Cole.

Cormack, S., & Furnham, A. (1998). Psychiatric labeling, sex role stereotypes and beliefs about the mentally ill. *International Journal of Social Psychiatry, 44(4),* 235–247.

Corrigan, P. (2003). Perceptions of discrimination among persons with serious mental illness. *Psychiatric Services, 54*(8), 1105–1110.

Costa, P. T., & McCrae, R. R. (1992). *The revised NEO Personality Inventory (NEO-PI-R) and NEO five-factor-inventory (NEO-FFI). Professional manual.* Odessa, FL: Psychological Assessment Resources.

Council for Accreditation of Counseling and Related Educational Programs (CACREP). (2001). *Accreditation manual and application.* Alexandria, VA: Author.

Courtois, C. A. (1988). *Healing the incest wound: Adult survivors in therapy.* New York: Norton.

Courtois, C. A. (1997). Healing the incest wound: A treatment update with attention to recovered memory issues. *American Journal of Psychotherapy, 51,* 25–32.

Couture, S., & Penn, D. (2003). Interpersonal contact and the stigma of mental illness: A review of the literature. *Journal of Mental Health, 12*(3), 291–306.

Cross, W. (1991). *Shades of black.* Philadelphia: Temple University Press.

Crossley, M. (2000). *Introducing narrative psychology: Self, trauma, and the construction of meaning.* Philadelphia, PA: Open University Press.

Crowe, M. (2000). Psychiatric diagnosis: Some implications for mental health nursing care. *Journal of Advanced Nursing, 31*(3), 583–590.

Crowe, M. (2002). Reflexivity and detachment: A discursive approach to women's depression. *Nursing Inquiry, 9*(2), 126–133.

Dana, R. H. (1998). *Understanding cultural identity in intervention and assessment.* Thousand Oaks, CA: Sage.

Daniels, J. A. (2001). Managed care, ethics, and counseling. *Journal of Counseling and Development, 79,* 119–123.

Danzinger, P. R., & Welfel, E. R. (2001). The impact of managed care on mental health counselors: A survey of perceptions, practices, and compliance with ethical standards. *Journal of Mental Health Counseling, 23*(2), 137–151.

Darden, C. A., Ginter, E. J., & Gazda, G. M. (1996). Life-Skills Development Scale–Adolescent Form: The theoretical and therapeutic relevance of life-skills. *Journal of Mental Health Counseling, 18,* 134–141.

Davanloo, H. (1990). *Unlocking the unconscious: Selected papers of Habib Davanloo, MD.* Chichester, England: John Wiley & Sons.

D'Andrea, M. (1988). The counselor as pacer: A model for revitalization of the counseling profession. In R. Hayes & R. Aubrey (Eds.), *New directions for counseling and human development* (pp. 22–44). Denver, CO: Love.

DeJulio, L. M., & Berkman, C. S. (2003). Nonsexual multiple role relationships: Attitudes and behaviors of social workers. *Ethics and Behavior, 13*(1), 61–79.

Demmitt, A., & Oldenski, T. (1999). The diagnostic process from a Freirean perspective. *Journal of Humanistic Counseling, Education and Development, 37*(4), 232–240.

Denton, W. H. (1989). DSM-II-R and the family therapist: Ethical considerations. *Journal of Marital and Family Therapy, 15*(4), 367–377.

Denton, W. H. (1990). A family systems analysis of DSM-III-R. *Journal of Marital and Family Therapy, 16*(2), 113–125.

Denton, W. H., Patterson, J., & Van Meir, E. (1997). Use of the DSM in marriage and family therapy programs: Current practices and attitudes. *Journal of Marital and Family Therapy, 23*, 81–86.

Desjarlais, R., Eisenberg, L., Good, B., & Kleinman, A. (1995). *World mental health: Problems and priorities in low-income countries.* New York: Oxford University Press.

Dewa, C. S. (2001). Using financial incentives to promote shared mental health care. *Canadian Journal of Psychiatry, 46*(6), 488–496.

Diaz, R. M., Ayala, G., Bein, E., Henne, J., & Marin, B. V. (2001). The impact of homophobia, poverty, and racism on the mental health of gay and bisexual Latino men: Findings from 3 US cities. *American Journal of Public Health, 91*(6), 927–933.

Dick, L. (1995). ""Plibloktoq"" (arctic hysteria): A construction of European-Inuit relations? *Arctic Anthropology, 32* (2), 1–42.

Dickerson, V. C., & Zimmerman, J. L. (1995). A constructionist exercise in anti-pathologizing. *Journal of Systemic Therapies, 14*(1), 33–45.

Dietz, C. A. (2000). Reshaping clinical practice for the new millennium. *Journal of Social Work Education, 36*(3), 503–521.

Dollarhide, C. T. (1997). Counseling for meaning in work and life: An integrated approach. *Journal of Humanistic Education and Development, 35*(4), 178–188.

Donzelot, J. (1979). *The policing of families.* London: Hutchinson.

Doob, D. (1992). Female sexual abuse survivors as patients: Avoiding retraumatization. *Archives of Psychiatric Nursing, 6*, 245–251.

Double, D. (2002). The limits of psychiatry. *British Medical Journal, 324*(7342), 900–905.

Double, D. (2003). Can a biomedical approach to psychiatric practice be justified? *Journal of Child and Family Studies, 12*(4), 379–384.

Draguns, J. (1985). Psychological disorders across cultures. In P. Pedersen (Ed.), *Handbook of cross-cultural counseling and therapy* (pp. 55–62). Westport, CT: Greenwood.

Dudley, M., & Gale, F. (2002). Psychiatrists as a moral community? Psychiatry under the Nazis and its contemporary relevance. *Australian and New Zealand Journal of Psychiatry, 36*(5), 585–595.

Duffy, M., Gillig, S. E., Tureen, R. M., & Ybarra, M. A. (2002). A critical look at the DSM-IV. *Journal of Individual Psychology, 58*(4), 363–374.

Durrheim, K. (1997). Social constructionism, discourse, and psychology. *South African Journal of Psychology, 27*(3), 175–183.

Edgerton, R. B. (1966). Conceptions of psychosis in four East African societies. *American Anthropology, 68*, 408–425.

Ellis, K., & Eriksen, K. P. (July 2002). Transsexual and transgenderist experiences and treatment options. *The Family Journal, 10*(3), 289–299.

Elstein, A. S., Shulman, A. S., & Sprafka, S. A. (1978). *Medical problem solving: An analysis of clinical reasoning.* Cambridge, MA: Harvard University Press.

Ely, M., Hardy, R., Longford, N., & Wadsworth, M. E. J. (1999) Gender differences in the relationship between alcohol consumption and drink problems are largely accounted for by body water. *Alcohol and Alcoholism, 34,* 894–902.

Endicott, J., Halbreich, A., Schacht, S., & Nee, J. (1981). Premenstrual changes and affective disorders. *Psychosomatic Medicine, 53,* 519–529.

Engelsmann, F. F. (2000). Transcultural psychiatry: Goals and challenges. *Canadian Journal of Psychiatry, 45*(5), 429–430.

Enns, C. (1993). Twenty years of feminist counseling and therapy: From naming biases to implementing multifaceted practice. *The Counseling Psychologist, 21,* 3–87.

Eriksen, K. (1997). *Making an impact: A handbook on counselor advocacy.* Muncie, IN: Accelerated Development.

Eriksen, K. P. (1999). Marriage and family licensing, state by state. *The Family Journal, 7*(1), 7–17.

Erikson, E. H. (1963). *Childhood and society.* New York: Norton.

Erwin, T. D. (1983). The scale on intellectual development: Measuring Perry's scheme. *Journal of College Student Personnel, 24,* 6–12.

Etchison, M., & Kleist, D. M. (2000). Review of narrative therapy: Research and utility. *The Family Journal: Counseling and Therapy for Couples and Families, 8,* 61–66.

Everly, G. S., Jr. (1995). An integrative two-factor model of posttraumatic stress. In G. S. Everly, Jr. & J. Lating (Eds.), *Psychotraumatology: Key papers & core concepts in post-traumatic stress* (pp. 27–48). New York: Plenum Press.

Eysenck, H. J. (1986). A critique of classification and diagnosis. In: T. Millon & G. L. Klerman (Eds.), *Contemporary directions in psychopathology* (pp. 73–98). New York: Guilford Press.

Eysenck, H. J., Wakefield, J. A., & Friedman, A. F. (1983). Diagnosis and clinical assessment: The DSM III. *Annual Review of Psychology, 34,* 167–193.

Fabrega, H. (1989). Cultural relativism and psychiatric illness. *The Journal of Nervous and Mental Disease, 177*(7), 415–425.

Fabrega, H. (1996). Cultural and historical foundations of psychiatric diagnosis. In J. E. Mezzich, A. Kleinman, H. Fabrega, & D. L. Parron (Eds.), *Culture and psychiatric diagnosis: A DSM-IV perspective* (pp. 3–14). Washington, DC: American Psychiatric Press.

Fabrikant, B. (1974). The psychotherapist and the female patient: Perceptions, misperceptions, and change. In V. Franks & V. Burtle (Eds.), *Women & therapy* (pp. 83–110). New York: Brunner/Mazel.

Fee, D. (2000). *Pathology and the postmodern.* London: Sage.

Fernald, P. S. (2000). Carl Rogers: Body-centered counselor. *Journal of Counseling and Development, 78,* 172–180.

Ferrara, F. F. (2002). *Childhood sexual abuse: Developmental effects across lifespan.* Pacific Grove, CA: Brooks/Cole.

Fewster, G. (2002). The DSM IV you, but not IV me. *Child and Youth Care Forum, 31*(6), 365–380.

Figert, A. E. (1995). The three faces of PMS: The professional, gendered, and scientific structuring of a psychiatric disorder. *Social Problems, 42*(1), 56–74.

Finkelhor, D. (1984). *Child sexual abuse: New theory and research.* New York: Free Press.

Fireman, G. D. (2002). Approaching accountability in psychotherapy. *Journal of Constructivist Psychology, 15*(3), 219–232.

Firsten, T. (1991). Violence in the lives of women on psych wards. *Canadian Woman's Studies, 11*(4), 45–48.

Fisher, C. B. (2002). A goodness-of-fit ethic of informed consent. *Urban Law Journal, 30,* 159–171.

Fisher, C. B. (2003). *Decoding the ethics code: A practical guide for psychologists.* Thousand Oaks, CA: Sage.

Fisher, P. A., Storck, M., & Bacon, J. G. (1998). Teacher, parent, and youth report of problem behaviors among rural American Indian and White adolescents. *American Indian and Alaska Native Mental Health Research, 8*(2), 1–27.

Fisher, P. A., Storck, M., & Bacon, J. G. (1999). In the eye of the beholder: Risk and protective factors in rural American Indian and Caucasian adolescents. *American Journal of Orthopsychiatry 69*(3), 294–304.

Fishman, D. B. (2003). Dual relationships and psychotherapy. *Psychotherapy Research, 13*(3), 395–397.

Fiske, S. T. (1993). Controlling other people: The impact of power on stereotyping. *American Psychologist, 48,* 621–628.

Fitzsimons, S., & Fuller, R. (2002). Empowerment and its implications for clinical practice in mental health: A review. *Journal of Mental Health, 11*(5), 481–490.

Flaskerud, J. H., & Liu, P. Y. (1991). Effects of an Asian client-therapist language, ethnicity, and gender match on utilization and outcome of therapy. *Community Mental Health Journal, 27,* 31–41.

Forsythe, B., & Melling, J. (1999). *Insanity, institutions and society, 1800–1914: A social history of madness in comparative perspective.* New York: Routledge.

Foucault, M. (1973). *Madness and civilization: A history of insanity in the age of reason.* New York: Vintage Books.

Frances, A., Clarkin, J. F., & Perry, S. (1984). DSM-III and family therapy. *American Journal of Psychiatry, 141*(3), 406–409.

Frances, A., & Widiger, T. A. (1986). Methodological issues in personality disorder diagnosis. In T. Millon & G. L. Klerman (Eds.), *Contemporary directions in psychopathology: Toward the DSM-IV* (pp. 381–402). New York: Guilford Press.

Frankl, V. E. (1969). *The will to meaning: Foundations and application to logotherapy.* New York: New American Library.

Freedman, J., & Combs, G. (1996). *Narrative therapy: The social construction of preferred realities.* New York: Norton.

Freud, S. (1920). Beyond the pleasure principle. In J. Starchey (Ed.), *Complete psychological works* (3rd ed., pp. 77–95). London: Hogarth Press.

Frisch, N. C., & Frisch, L. E. (1998). *Psychiatric mental health nursing.* New York: Delmar.

Fristad, M. A., Gavazzi, S. M., & Soldano, K. W. (1999). Naming the enemy: Learning to differentiate mood disorder "symptoms" from the "self" that experiences them. *Journal of Family Psychotherapy, 10,* 81–88.

Fugita, S. (1990). Asian/Pacific-American mental health: Some needed research in epidemiology and service utilization. In F. C. Serafica, A. I. Schwebel, R. K. Russell, P. D. Isaac, & L. B. Myers (Eds.), *Mental health of ethnic minorities* (pp. 66–84). New York: Praeger.

Gaines, A. D. (1992). From DSM-I to II-R: Voices of self, mastery, and the others: A cultural constructivist reading of the U.S. psychiatric classification. *Social Science and Medicine, 35,* 3–24.

Galambos, C. (1999). Resolving ethical conflicts in a managed care environment. *Health and Social Work, 24*(3), 191–198.

Gallant, S. J., & Hamilton, J. A. (1988). On a premenstrual psychiatric diagnosis: What's in a name? *Professional Psychology: Research and Practice, 19*(3), 271–278.

Gallop, R., Lancee, W. J., & Garfinkel, P. (1989). How nursing staff respond to the label "Borderline Personality Disorder." *Hospital and Community Psychiatry, 40,* 815–819.

Gallop, R., McKeever, P., Toner, B., Lancee, W., & Lueck, M. (1995). Inquiring about childhood sexual abuse as part of the nursing history: Opinions of abused and non-abused nurses. *Archives of Psychiatric Nursing, 9*(3), 146–151.

Gambrill, E. (2003). Evidence-based practice: Sea change or the emperor's new clothes? *Journal of Social Work Education, 39*(1), 3–24.

Gana K., Martin B., & Canouet, M. D. (2001). Worry and anxiety: Is there a causal relationship? *Psychopathology, 34*(5), 221–229.

Ganley, A. L. (1987). Perpetrators of domestic violence: An overview of counseling the court-mandated client. In D. J. Sonkin (Ed.), *Domestic violence on trial: Psychological and legal dimensions of family violence* (pp. 155–173). New York: Springer.

Gannon, L., Luchetta, T., Rhodes, K., Pardie, L., & Segrist, D. (1992). Sex bias in psychological research: Progress or complacency? *American Psychologist, 47*, 389–396.

Garcia, J. G., Cartwright, B., Winston, S. M., & Borzuchowska, B. (2003). A transcultural integrative model for ethical decision making in counseling. *Journal of Counseling and Development, 81*, 268–277.

Gergen, K. J. (1985). The social constructionist movement in psychology. *American Psychologist, 40*, 266–275.

Gergen, K. J. (1990). Therapeutic professions and the diffusion of deficit. *The Journal of Mind and Behavior, 11*, 353–368.

Gergen, K. J. (1991). *The saturated self*. New York: Basic Books.

Gergen, K. J., Hoffman, L., & Anderson, H. (1996). Is diagnosis a disaster? A constructionist trilogue. In F. Kaslow (Ed.), *Handbook of relational diagnosis and dysfunctional family patterns* (pp. 102–118). New York: John Wiley & Sons.

Gergen, K. J., & Kaye, J. (1992). Beyond narrative in the negotiation of therapeutic meaning. In S. McNamee & K. J. Gergen (Eds.), *Inquiries in social construction* (pp. 166–185). London: Sage.

Gilbertson, A. D., McGraw, L. K., & Brown, N. E. (1986). A different empirical perspective on sex bias in the diagnosis of DSM-III Axis II disorders. *Psychiatric Quarterly, 58*, 144–147.

Giles, J. (2002). Electroconvulsive therapy and the fear of deviance. *Journal for the Theory of Social Behavior, 32*, 61–87.

Gilligan, C. (1982). *In a different voice*. Cambridge, MA: Harvard University Press.

Gjerde, P. (1996). Alternative pathways to chronic depressive symptoms in young adults: Gender differences in developmental trajectories. *Child Development, 66*, 1277–1300.

Gladding, S. T. (2002). *Family therapy: History, theory, and practice* (3rd ed.). Upper Saddle River, NJ: Prentice Hall.

Glasser, W. (1984). *Control theory*. New York: Harper & Row.

Gleaves, D. H., & Hernandez, E. (1999). Recent reformulations of Freud's development and abandonment of his seduction theory: Historical/scientific clarification or a continued assault on truth? *History of Psychology, 2*, 324–354.

Glosoff, H. L., Garcia, J., Herlihy, B., & Remley, T. P. (1999). Managed care: Ethical considerations for counselors. *Counseling and Values, 44*(1), 8–17.

Goldenberg, I., & Goldenberg, H. (2004). *Family therapy: An overview* (6th ed.). Pacific Grove, CA: Brooks/Cole.

Goldman, L. (1972). It's time to put up or shut up. *Measurement and Evaluation in Guidance, 5*, 420–423.

Goldman, L. (1992). Qualitative assessment: An approach for counselors. *Journal of Counseling and Development, 70*, 616–621.

Golier, J. A., Yehuda, R., Bierer, L. M., Mitropoulou, V., New, A. S., Schmeidler, J., et al. (2003). The relationship of borderline personality disorder to posttraumatic stress disorder and traumatic events. *American Journal of Psychiatry, 160*(11), 2018–2025.

Good, B. J. (1993). Culture, diagnosis, and comorbidity. *Culture, Medicine and Psychiatry, 16*, 427–446.

Good, B. J. (1996). Culture and DSM-IV: Diagnosis, knowledge and power. *Culture, Medicine and Psychiatry, 20,* 127–132.

Good, G., & Mintz, L. (1990). Gender role conflict and depression in college men: Evidence for compounded risk. *Journal of Counseling and Development, 69,* 17–21.

Gordon, P. A. (2003). The decision to remain single: Implications for women across cultures. *Journal of Mental Health Counseling, 25,* 33–45.

Gottschalk, S. (2000). Escape from insanity. In D. Fee (Ed), *Pathology and the postmodern: Mental illness as discourse and experience* (pp. 18–48). London: Sage.

Gould, R. (1979). *Transformations: Growth and change in adult life.* New York: Simon & Schuster.

Gove, W. R. (1980). Mental illness and psychiatric treatment among women. *Psychology of Women Quarterly, 4*(3), 345–362.

Gove, W. R., & Tudor, J. F. (1972). Adult sex roles and mental illness. *American Journal of Sociology, 78,* 812–835.

Graham, I. W. (2001). Seeking a clarification of meaning: A phenomenological interpretation of the craft of mental health nursing. *Journal of Psychiatric and Mental Health Nursing, 8*(4), 335–346.

Graham, S. (1992). Most of the subjects were white and middle-class: Trends in published research on African Americans in selected APA journals, 1970–1989. *American Psychologist, 47,* 629–639.

Graybeal, C. (2001). Strengths-based social work assessment: Transforming the dominant paradigm. *Families in Society, 82*(3), 233–242.

Griffith, E. E. H. (1996). African American perspectives. In J. E. Mezzich, A. Kleinman, H. Fabrega, & D. L. Parron (Eds.), *Culture and psychiatric diagnosis: A DSM-IV perspective* (pp. 27–29). Washington, DC: American Psychiatric Press.

Group for the Advancement of Psychiatry, Committee on the Family. (1989). The challenge to relational diagnoses: Applying the biopsychosocial model in DSM-IV. *American Journal of Psychiatry, 146,* 1492–1494.

Group for the Advancement of Psychiatry, Committee on the Family. (1995). A model for the classification and diagnosis of relational disorders. *Psychiatric Services, 46,* 926–931.

Guarnaccia, P. J., Rubio-Stipec, M., & Canino, G. (1989). Ataques de nervios in the Puerto Rican Diagnostic Interview Schedule: The impact of cultural categories on psychiatric epidemiology. *Culture, Medicine and Psychiatry, 13,* 275–295.

Gunderson, J. G. (1992). Diagnostic controversies. *American Psychiatric Press Review of Psychiatry, 11,* 9–24.

Gunderson, J. G., & Gabbard, G. O. (Eds.). (2000). *Psychotherapy for personality disorders.* Washington, DC: American Psychiatric Press.

Guterman, J. T. (1994). A social constructionist position for mental health counseling. *Journal of Mental Health Counseling, 16*(2), 226–245.

Guterman, J. T. (1996). Doing mental health counseling: A social constructionist re-vision. *Journal of Mental Health Counseling, 18*(3), 228–253.

Guthrie, R. V. (1976). *Even the rat was white: A historical view of psychology.* San Francisco: Harper & Row.

Halasz, G. (2002). An ethical perspective. *Australian & New Zealand Journal of Psychiatry, 36,* 472–475.

Haley, J. (1987). *Problem-solving therapy: New strategies for effective family therapy* (2nd ed.). San Francisco: Jossey-Bass.

Halling, S., & Goldfarb, M. (1996). The new generation of diagnostic manuals (DSM-III, DSM-III-R and DSM-IV): An overview and a phenomenologically based critique. *Journal of Phenomenological Psychology, 27*(1), 49–70.

Hamilton, S., Rothbart, M., & Dawes, R. M. (1986). Sex bias, diagnosis, and DSM-III. *Sex Roles, 15,* 269–274.

Hansen, J. T. (2000). Psychoanalysis and humanism: A review and critical examination of integrationist efforts with some proposed resolutions. *Journal of Counseling and Development, 78,* 21–29.

Harari, E. (2001). Whose evidence? Lessons from the philosophy of science and the epistemology of medicine. *Australian and New Zealand Journal of Psychiatry, 35*(6), 724–731.

Hardiman, R. (1982). *White identity development.* Unpublished doctoral dissertation. University of Massachusetts, Amherst.

Hare-Mustin, R. T., & Marecek, J. (1990). *Making a difference: Psychology and the construction of gender.* New Haven, CT: Yale University Press.

Hare-Mustin, R., & Marecek, J. (1997). Abnormal and clinical psychology: The politics of madness. In D. Fox & I. Prilleltensky (Eds.), *Critical psychology: An introduction* (pp. 104–120). Thousand Oaks, CA: Sage.

Harkness, S., & Super, C. M. (1990). Culture and psychopathology. In M. Lewis & S. Miller (Eds.), *Handbook of developmental psychopathology* (pp. 41–52). New York: Plenum.

Harman, J. S., Crystal, S., Walkup, J., & Olfson, M. (2003). Trends in elderly patients' office visits for treatment of depression according to physician specialty: 1985–1999. *Journal of Behavioral Health Services and Research, 30*(3), 332–342.

Harrison, A., Serafica, F. C., & McAdoo, H. (1984). Ethnic families of color. In R. Parke, R. O. Emde, H. McAdoo, & G. Sackett (Eds.), *Review of research in child development: Vol. 7* (pp. 329–371). Chicago: University of Chicago Press.

Hartung, C. M., & Widiger, T. A. (1998). Gender differences in the diagnosis of mental disorders: Conclusions and controversies of the DSM-IV. *Psychological Bulletin, 123,* 260–278.

Haug, I. E. (1999). Boundaries and the use and misuse of power and authority: Ethical complexities for clergy psychotherapists. *Journal of Counseling and Development, 77,* 411–418.

Havighurst, R. J. (1972). *Human development and education.* New York: Longman.

Hawley, D. R. (2000). Clinical implications of family resilience. *American Journal of Family Therapy, 28*(2), 101–117.

Haynes, R., Corey, G., & Moulton, P. (2003). *Clinical supervision in the helping professions: A practical guide.* Pacific Grove, CA: Brooks/Cole.

Hayward, P., & Bright, J. A. (1997). Stigma and mental illness: A review and critique. *Journal of Mental Health, 6*(4), 345–355.

Heath, G. (2002a). Does a theory of mind matter? The myth of totalitarian scientism. *International Journal of Psychotherapy, 7*(3), 185–221.

Heath, G. (2002b). Philosophy and psychotherapy: Conflict or co-operation? *International Journal of Psychotherapy, 7*(1), 13–53.

Hegarty, J. D., & Baldessarini, R. J. (1994). One hundred years of schizophrenia: A meta-analysis of the outcome literature. *American Journal of Psychiatry, 151*(10), 1409–1417.

Helgeson, V. S. (1994). Relation of agency and communion to well-being: Evidence and potential explanations. *Psychological Bulletin, 116,* 412–428.

Helgeson, V. S., & Fritz, H. L. (1998). A theory of unmitigated communion. *Personality and Social Psychology Review, 2*(3), 173–183.

Helms, J. (1990). *Black and White racial identity.* Westport, CT: Greenwood Press.

Henry, K. A., & Cohen, C. I. (1983). The role of labeling processes in diagnosing borderline personality disorder. *American Journal of Psychiatry, 140,* 1527–1529.

Heppner, M. J., Good, G. E., Hillenbrand-Gunn, T. L., Hawkins, A. K., Hacquard, L. L., Nichols, R. K., et al. (1995). Examining sex differences in altering attitudes about rape:

A test of the elaboration likelihood model. *Journal of Counseling and Development, 73,* 640–747.

Herman, J. (1992). *Trauma and recovery.* New York: Basic Books.

Herman, J. (1993) Sequelae of prolonged and repeated trauma: Evidence for complex post-traumatic syndrome (DESNOS). In J. P. T. Davidson & E. B. Foa (Eds.), *Posttraumatic stress disorder: DSM-IV and beyond* (1st ed., pp. 213–228). Washington, DC: American Psychiatric Press.

Herman, J. (1995). Complex PTSD: A syndrome in survivors of prolonged and repeated trauma. In G. S. Everly, Jr., & J. Lating (Eds.), *Psychotraumatology: Key papers & core concepts in post-traumatic stress* (pp. 87–102). New York: Plenum Press.

Herman, J. L., Perry, J. C., & van der Kolk, B. A. (1989). Childhood trauma in borderline personality disorder. *American Journal of Psychiatry, 146,* 1527–1529.

Hermans, H. J. M., Kempen, H. J. G., & van Loon, R. J. P. (1992). The dialogical self: Beyond individualism and rationalism. *American Psychologist, 47,* 23–33.

Hermon, D. A., & Hazler, R. J. (1999). Adherence to a wellness model and perceptions of psychological well-being. *Journal of Counseling and Development, 77,* 339–344.

Herring, M., & Kaslow, N. J. (2002). Depression and attachment in families: A child-focused perspective. *Family Process, 41*(3), 494–519.

Hershenson, D. B., Power, P. W., & Waldo, M. (1996). *Community counseling: Contemporary theory and practice.* Boston: Allyn & Bacon.

Hill, C. L., & Ridley, C. R. (2001). Diagnostic decision making: Do counselors delay final judgments? *Journal of Counseling and Development, 79,* 98–104.

Hines-Martin, V., Malone, M., Kim, S., & Brown-Piper, A. (2003). Barriers to mental health care access in an African American population. *Issues in Mental Health Nursing, 24*(3), 237–257.

Hinkle, J. S. (1999). A voice from the trenches: A reaction to Ivey and Ivey. *Journal of Counseling and Development, 77,* 474–483.

Hinshaw, S. P., & Cicchetti, D. (2000). Stigma and mental disorder: Conceptions of illness, public attitudes, personal disclosure, and social policy. *Development and Psycho-pathology, 12,* 555–598.

Hirst, I. S. (2003). Perspectives of mindfulness. *Journal of Psychiatric and Mental Health Nursing, 10*(3), 359–366.

Hoagwood, K., & Jensen, P. S. (1997). Developmental psychopathology and the notion of culture: Introduction to the special section on "The fusion of cultural horizons: Cultural influences on the assessment of psychopathology in children and adolescents." *Applied Developmental Science, 1*(3), 108–112.

Hodges, S. (2003). Borderline personality disorder and posttraumatic stress disorder: Time for integration? *Journal of Counseling and Development, 81,* 409–418.

Hohenshil, T. H. (1993). Teaching the DSM-III-R in counselor education. *Counselor Education and Supervision, 32,* 267–275.

Holden, E. W., Santiago, R. L., & Manteuffel, B. A. (2003). Systems of care demonstration projects: Innovation, evaluation, and sustainability. In A. J. Pumariega & N. C. Winters (Eds.), *The handbook of child and adolescent systems of care: The new community psychiatry* (pp. 432–458). San Francisco: Jossey-Bass.

Holland, J. L. (1985). *Making vocational choices.* Englewood Cliffs, NJ: Prentice Hall.

Holland, J. L. (1990). *The Self-Directed Search.* Odessa, FL: Psychological Assessment Resources.

Holland, J. L., Daiger, D. C., & Power, P. G. (1980). *My vocational situation.* Palo Alto, CA: Consulting Psychologists Press.

Honos-Webb, L., & Leitner, L. M. (2001). How using the DSM causes damage: A client's report. *Journal of Humanistic Psychology, 41*(4), 36–57.

Hopper, K. (1991). Some old questions for the new cross-cultural psychiatry. *Medical Anthropology, 5,* 299–330.

Hornstein, G. A. (2002, January). Narratives of madness, as told from within. *Chronicle of Higher Education,* pp. B7+.

Horsfall, J. (1998). Mainstream approaches to mental health and illness: An emphasis on individuals and a de-emphasis of inequalities. *Health: An Interdisciplinary Journal for the Social Study of Health, Illness, and Medicine, 2*(2), 217–231.

Horsfall, J. (2001). Gender and mental illness: An Australian overview. *Issues in Mental Health Nursing, 22,* 421–438.

Howard, G. S. (1991). Culture tales: A narrative approach to thinking, cross-cultural psychology, and psychotherapy. *American Psychologist, 46*(3), 187–197.

Howell, E. (1981). The influence of gender on diagnosis and psychopathology. In E. Howell & M. Bayes (Eds.), *Women and mental health* (pp. 153–159). New York: Basic.

Hoyt, M. (1996). *Constructive therapies.* New York: Guilford Press.

Hughes, C. C. (1996). The culture-bound syndromes and psychiatric diagnosis. In J. E. Mezzich, A. Kleinman, H. Fabrega, & D. L. Parron (Eds.), *Culture and psychiatric diagnosis: A DSM-IV perspective* (pp. 289–305). Washington, DC: American Psychiatric Press.

Hunt, B., Niles, S. G., Jaques, J., Wierzalis, E. (2003). Career concerns for people living with HIV/AIDS. *Journal of Counseling and Development, 81,* 55–61.

Hyler, S. E., Williams, J. B., & Spitzer, R. L. (1982). Reliability in the DSM-III field trials: Interview v case summary. *Archives of General Psychiatry, 39,* 1275–1278.

Ivey, A. E. (1991). *Developmental strategies for helpers.* Pacific Grove, CA: Brooks/Cole.

Ivey, A. E. (1995). Psychotherapy as liberation. In J. G. Ponterotto, J. M. Casas, L.A. Suzuki, & C. M. Alexander (Eds.), *Handbook of multicultural counseling* (pp. 53–72). Thousand Oaks, CA: Sage.

Ivey, A. E., & Ivey, B. B. (1999). Toward a developmental diagnostic and statistical manual: The vitality of a contextual framework. *Journal of Counseling and Development, 77,* 484–491.

Ivey, A. E., & Ivey, M. B. (1998). Reframing DSM-IV: Positive strategies from developmental counseling and therapy. *Journal of Counseling and Development, 76,* 334–350.

Ivey, A. E., & Ivey, M. B. (2001). Developmental counseling and therapy and multicultural counseling and therapy. In D. C. Locke, J. E. Myers, & E. L. Herr (Eds.), *The handbook of counseling* (pp. 219–236). Thousand Oaks, CA: Sage.

Ivey, A. E., Ivey, M. B., & Simek-Morgan, L. (1997). *Counseling and psychotherapy: A multicultural perspective.* Boston: Allyn & Bacon.

Ivey, A. E., & Rigazio-DiGilio, S. A. (1991). Toward a developmental practice of mental health counseling. *Journal of Mental Health Counseling, 13,* 21–36.

Ivey, D. C., Jankowski, P. J., & Scheel, M. J. (1999). Relational diagnosis: Potential advantages and drawbacks associated with a universal system for the classification of couple and family difficulties. *The Family Journal, 7*(4), 335–342.

Jablensky, A., Sartorius, N., Ankar, M., Korten, A. (1992). Schizophrenia: Manifestations, incidence, and course in different cultures. *Psychology and Medicine, 26,* 1–97.

Jackson, B. (1975). Black identity development. *Journal of Educational Diversity and Innovation, 2,* 19–25.

Jacobson, A., & Herald, C. (1990). The relevance of childhood sexual abuse to adult psychiatric inpatient care. *Hospital and Community Psychiatry, 41,* 154–158.

Jacobson, A., & Richardson, B. (1987). Assault experiences of 100 psychiatric inpatients: Evidence of the need for routine inquiry. *American Journal of Psychiatry, 144,* 908–913.

James, R. K., & Gilliland, B. E. (2001). *Crisis intervention strategies* (4th ed.). Belmont, CA: Brooks/Cole.

Jenkins, J. H. (1991). Anthropology, expressed emotion, and schizophrenia. *Ethos, 19,* 387–431.

Jenkins, J. H. (1993). Too close for comfort: Schizophrenia and emotional overinvolvement among Mexicano families. In A. D. Gaines (Ed.), *Ethnopsychiatry* (pp. 203–221). Albany, NY: State University of New York Press.

Jenkins, J. H., & Karno, M. (1992). The meaning of expressed emotion: Theoretical issues raised by cross-cultural research. *American Journal of Psychiatry, 149,* 9–21.

Jenkins, P. (2002). Transparent recording: Therapists and the Data Protection Act of 1998. In P. Jenkins (Ed.), *Legal issues in counseling and psychotherapy* (pp. 45–56). Thousand Oaks, CA: Sage.

Jensen, P. S., & Hoagwood, K. (1997). The book of names: DSM-IV in context. *Development and Psychopathology, 9,* 231–249.

Jepson, R. G., & Robertson, R. (2003). Difficulties in giving fully informed consent. *British Medical Journal, 326*(7397), 1038.

Johnson, M. (1980). Mental illness and psychiatric treatment among women: A response. *Psychology of Women Quarterly, 4*(3), 363–371.

Johnson, S. S., & Kushner, R. F. (2001). Mind/body medicine: An introduction for the generalist physician and nutritionist. *Nutrition in Clinical Care, 4*(5), 256–265.

Jones, A. C. (2003). Reconstructing the stepfamily: Old myths, new stories. *Social Work, 48*(2), 228–237.

Jones, B. E., & Gray, B. A. (1986). Problems in diagnosing schizophrenia and affective disorders among blacks. *Hospital and Community Psychiatry, 37,* 61–65.

Jordanova, L. J. (1981). Mental illness, mental health: Changing norms and expectations. In Cambridge Women's Studies Group (Eds.), *Women and society* (pp. 95–114). London: Virago.

Josselson, R. (1987). *Finding herself: Pathways to identity development in women.* San Francisco: Jossey-Bass.

Jussim, L., Palumbo, P., Chatman, C., Madon, S., & Smith, A. (2000). Stigma and self-fulfilling prophecies. In T. Heatherton, R. Kleck, J. Hull, & D. Cioffi (Eds.), *The social psychology of stigma* (pp. 374–418). New York: Guilford Press.

Kaas, M. J., Suzanne, L., & Peitzinan, C. (2003). Barriers to collaboration between mental health professionals and families in the care of persons with serious mental illness. *Issues in Mental Health Nursing, 24*(8), 741–757.

Kagan, J. (1995, August). *Temperament and development.* Paper presented to the meeting of the American Psychological Association, New York.

Kagan, N. (1980). *Interpersonal process recall.* East Lansing, MI: Author.

Kanapaux, W. (2003). Managing in a managed care world. *Psychiatric Times, 20*(8), 1–4.

Kaplan, A. (1987). Reflections on gender and psychotherapy. *Women and Therapy, 6,* 11–24.

Kaplan, M. (1983a). A woman's view of the DSM-III. *American Psychologist, 38,* 786–792.

Kaplan, M. (1983b). The issue of sex bias in the DSM-III: Comments on articles by Spitzer, Williams, and Kass. *American Psychologist, July,* 802–803.

Kaslow, F. (1993). Relational diagnosis: Past, present and future. *The American Journal of Family Therapy, 21*(3), 195–204.

Kaslow, F. W. (Ed.). (1996). *Handbook of relational diagnosis and dysfunctional family patterns.* New York: John Wiley & Sons.

Kaslow, F. W. (2001). Families and family psychology at the millennium. Intersecting crossroads. *American Psychologist, 56*(1), 37–46.

Kass, F., Mackinnon, R. A., & Spitzer, R. L. (1986). Masochistic personality: An empirical study. *American Journal of Psychiatry, 143,* 216–218.

Kass, F., Spitzer, R. L., & Williams, J. B. W. (1983). An empirical study of the issue of sex bias in the diagnostic criteria of DSM-III Axis II personality disorders. *American Psychologist, July,* 799–801.

Kastrup, M. (2002). Experience with current multiaxial diagnostic systems: A critical review. *Psychopathology, 35*(2–3), 122–126.

Keenan, K., & Shaw, D. (1997). Developmental and social influences on young girls' early problem behavior. *Psychological Bulletin, 121,* 95–113.

Kegan, R. (1982). *The evolving self.* Cambridge, MA: Harvard University Press.

Kegan, R. (1994). *In over our heads: The mental demands of modern life.* Cambridge, MA: Harvard University Press.

Keisling, R. (1981). Under diagnosis of manic-depressive illness in a hospital unit. *American Journal of Psychiatry, 138,* 672–673.

Keller, M. B., Klein, D. N., Hirschfeld, R. M. A., Kocsis, J. H., McCullough, J. P., Miller, I., et al. (1995). Results of the DSM-IV mood disorders field trial. *American Journal of Psychiatry, 152*(6), 843–849.

Kelly, G. (1990). The cultural family of origin: A description of a training strategy. *Counselor Education and Supervision, 30,* 77–84.

Kelly, G. A. (1955). *A theory of personality: The psychology of personal constructs.* New York: W. W. Norton.

Kiecolt-Glaser, J. K., McGuire, L., Robles, T. F., & Glaser, R. (2002). Emotions, morbidity, and mortality: New perspectives from psychoneuroimmunology. *Annual Review of Psychology, 53,* 83–107.

Kimball, M. (1981). Women and science: A critique of biological theories. *International Journal of Women's Studies, 4,* 318–335.

Kimmel, D. C. (1990). Personality and psychopathology. *Adulthood and aging* (pp. 395–448). New York: John Wiley & Sons.

King, M., Coker, E., Leavey, G., Hoare, A., & Johnson-Sabine, E. (1994). Incidence of psychotic illness in London: A comparison of ethnic groups. *British Medical Journal, 309,* 1115–1119.

Kirk, S. A., & Kutchins, H. (1994). The myth of the reliability of the DSM. *The Journal of Mind and Behavior, 15,* 71–86.

Kirmayer, L. J., & Minas, H. (2000). The future of cultural psychiatry: An international perspective. *Canadian Journal of Psychiatry, 45*(5), 438–446.

Kirsh, G. A., & Kuiper, N. A. (2002). Individualism and relatedness themes in the context of depression, gender, and a self-schema model of emotion. *Canadian Psychology, 4*(2), 76–90.

Kirshner, L. A., & Johnston, L. (1983). Effects of gender on inpatient hospitalization. *Journal of Nervous and Mental Disease, 171,* 651–657.

Kitchener, K. S. (1984). Intuition, critical evaluation and ethical principles: The foundation for ethical decisions in counseling psychology. *The Counseling Psychologist, 12*(3), 43–55.

Kitchener, K. S., & King, P. M. (1981). Reflective judgment: Concepts of justification and their relationship to age and education. *Journal of Applied Developmental Psychology, 2,* 89–116.

Kjorstad, M. C. (2003). The current and future state of mental health insurance parity legislation. *Psychiatric Rehabilitation Journal, 27*(1), 34–43.

Kleinman, A. (1986). *Social origins of distress and disease: Depression, neurasthenia and pain in modern China.* New Haven, CT: Yale University Press.

Kleinman, A. (1988). *Rethinking psychiatry: From cultural category to personal experience.* New York: Free Press.

Kleinman, A. (1996). How is culture important for DSM-IV? In J. E. Mezzich, A. Kleinman, H. Fabrega, & D. L. Parron (Eds.), *Culture and psychiatric diagnosis: A DSM-IV perspective* (pp. 15–25). Washington, DC: American Psychiatric Press.

Kleinman, A. M. (1977). Depression, somatization and the "New Cross-Cultural Psychiatry." *Social Science and Medicine, 11,* 3–10.

Knaudt, P. R., Connor, K. M., Weisler, R. H., Churchill, E. L., & Davidson, J. R. T. (1999). Alternative therapy use by psychiatric outpatients. *Journal of Nervous and Mental Disease, 187,* 692–695.

Knefelkamp, L., & Slepitza, R. (1976). A cognitive-developmental model of career development: An adaptation of the Perry Scheme. *The Counseling Psychologist, 6,* 53–58.

Knefelkamp, L., Widick, C., & Parker, C. A. (1978). *Applying new developmental findings.* San Francisco: Jossey-Bass.

Knight, M., Wykes, T., & Hayward, P. (2003). "People don't understand": An investigation of stigma in schizophrenia using Interpretative Phenomenological Analysis (IPA). *Journal of Mental Health, 12*(3), 209–223.

Kocarek, C. E., & Pelling, N. J. (2003). Beyond knowledge and awareness: Enhancing counselor skills for work with gay, lesbian, and bisexual clients. *Journal of Multicultural Counseling & Development, 31,* 99–112.

Kohlberg, L. (1981). *The philosophy of moral development.* San Francisco: Harper & Row.

Kohlberg, L., & Wasserman, E. R. (1980). The cognitive-developmental approach and the practicing counselor: An opportunity for counselors to rethink their roles. *Personnel and Guidance Journal, 58*(9), 559–568.

Kolb, B., & Whishaw, I. Q. (1990). *Fundamentals of human neuropsychology* (3rd ed.). New York: W. H. Freeman.

Kondo, D. (1990). *Crafting selves: Power, gender, and discourses of identity in a Japanese workplace.* Chicago: University of Chicago Press.

Koocher, G., & Keith-Spiegel, P. S. (1990). *Children, ethics, and the law.* Lincoln, NE: University of Nebraska Press.

Koss, M. (1990). The women's mental health research agenda: Violence against women. *American Psychologist, 45,* 374–380.

Kovel, J. (1982). Book review: Diagnostic and statistical manual of mental disorders, edition III. *Einstein Quarterly of Biology and Medicine, 1–2,* 103–104.

Krener, P. G., & Sabin, C. (1985). Indochinese immigrant children: Problems in psychiatric diagnosis. *Journal of the American Academy of Child Psychiatry, 24,* 453–458.

Kroll, J. K. (1988). *The challenge of the borderline patient: Competency in diagnosis and treatment.* New York: W. W. Norton.

Krumboltz, J. D., Mitchell, A. M., & Jones, G. B. (1976). A social learning theory of career selection. *The Counseling Psychologist, 6,* 71–81.

Kunik, M. E. (2002). Obtaining age-related mental health competency: What is needed? *Educational Gerontology, 28*(1), 73–83.

Kurpius, S. E., & Gross, D. R. (1996). Professional ethics and the mental health counselor. In W. J. Weikel & A. J. Palmo (Eds.), *Foundations of mental health counseling* (2nd ed., pp. 353–377). Springfield, IL: Charles C. Thomas.

Kutchins, H., & Kirk, S. A. (1997). *Making us crazy: DSM: The psychiatric bible and the creating of mental disorders.* New York: Free Press.

Lahey, L., Souvaine, E., Kegan, R., Goodman, R., & Felix, S. (1985). *A guide to the subject–object interview.* Cambridge, MA: The Subject-Object Research Group.

Lain-Entralgo, P. (1982). *El Diagnostico Medico: Historia y Teoria.* Barcelona, Spain: Salvat.

Landrine, H. (1989). The politics of personality disorder. *Psychology of Women, 13,* 324–339.

Lambert, M. C., Weisz, J. R., Knight, F., Desroisiers, M., Overly, K., & Thesiger, C. (1992). Jamaican and American adult perspectives on child psychopathology: Further exploration of the threshold model. *Journal of Consulting and Clinical Psychology, 60,* 146–149.

Lammers, J. C., & Geist, P. (1997). The transformation of caring in the light and shadow of managed care. *Health Communication, 9*(1), 45–61.

Larkin, J., & Caplan, P. J. (1992). The gatekeeping process of the DSM. *Canadian Journal of Community Mental Health, 11*(1), 17–28.

Larner, G. (2000). Towards a common ground in psychoanalysis and family therapy: On knowing not to know. *Journal of Family Therapy, 22*(1), 61–83.

Laungani, P. (2002). Mindless psychiatry and dubious ethics. *Counselling Psychology Quarterly, 15*(1), 23–34.

Lego, S. (1996). The client with borderline personality disorder. In S. Lego (Ed.), *Psychiatric nursing. A comprehensive reference* (pp. 234–245). Philadelphia: Lippincott.

Lependorf-Palmer, M., & Healey, K. (2002). Family consulting: A new role for therapists. *American Journal of Family Therapy, 30*(3), 203–214.

Leslie, L. A., & Clossick, M. L. (1996). Sexism in family therapy: Does training in gender make a difference? *Journal of Marital and Family Therapy, 22*, 253–269.

Levin, B. L., Beauchamp, B. T., & Henry-Beauchamp, L. A. (1997). Education and training of children's mental health professionals: The existing and potential role. *Journal of Child and Family Studies, 6*(1), 131–137.

Levinson, D. (1978). *The seasons of a man's life.* New York: Knopf.

Levinson, D. (1996). *The seasons of a woman's life.* New York: Knopf.

Lewis, G., & Appleby, L. (1988). Personality disorder: The patients psychiatrists dislike. *British Journal of Psychiatry, 153*, 44–49.

Lewis, G., Croft-Jeffreys, C., & David, A. (1990). Are British psychiatrists racist? *British Journal of Psychiatry, 157*, 410–415.

Lewis, J. A., Lewis, M. D., Daniels, J. A., & D'Andrea, M. J. (1998/2003). *Community counseling: Empowerment strategies for a diverse society.* Belmont, CA: Brooks/Cole.

Lewis-Fernandez, R., & Kleinman, A. (1994). Culture, personality, and psychopathology. *Journal of Abnormal Psychology, 103*(1), 67–71.

Libbus, M. K. (1996). Women's beliefs regarding persistent fatigue. *Issues in Mental Health Nursing, 17*, 589–600.

Liebowitz, M. R., Salman, E., Jusino, C. M., Garfinkel, R., Street, L. (1994). Ataque de nervios and panic disorder. *American Journal of Psychiatry, 151*, 871–875.

Lin, K. M. (1990). Assessment and diagnostic issues in the psychiatric care of refugee patients. In W. H. Holzman (Ed.), *Mental health of immigrants and refugees.* Austin: University of Texas Press.

Lin, K. M. (1996). Asian American perspectives. In J. E. Mezzich, A. Kleinman, H. Fabrega, & D. L. Parron (Eds.), *Culture and psychiatric diagnosis: A DSM-IV perspective* (pp. 35–38). Washington, DC: American Psychiatric Press.

Lipschitz, D. S., Kaplan, M. L., Sorkenn, J. B., Faedda, G. L., Chorney, P., & Asnis, G. M. (1996). Prevalence and characteristics of physical and sexual abuse among psychiatric outpatients. *Psychiatric Services, 47*, 189–191.

Littlewood, R., & Lipsedge, M. (1989). *Aliens and alienists: Ethnic minorities and psychiatry* (2nd ed.). London: Unwin Hyman.

Liu, W. M., & Clay, D. L. (2002). Multicultural counseling competencies: Guidelines in working with children and adolescents. *Journal of Mental Health Counseling, 24*, 177–187.

Livesley, W. J., Jang, K. L., & Vernon, P. A. (1998). Phenotypic and genotypic structure of traits delineating personality disorders. *Archives of General Psychiatry, 55*, 371–410.

Ljunggren, B., & Sjoden, P. (2001). Patient reported quality of care before vs. after the implementation of a diagnosis related groups (DRG) classification and payment system in one Swedish country. *Scandinavian Journal of Caring Sciences, 15*(4), 283–295.

Lo, H., & Fung, K. P. (2003). Cultural competent psychotherapy. *Canadian Journal of Psychiatry, 48*(3), 161–171.

Loevinger, J. (1976). *Ego development.* San Francisco: Jossey-Bass.

Longo, D. A., & Peterson, S. M. (2002). The role of spirituality in psychosocial rehabilitation. *Psychiatric Rehabilitation Journal, 25*(4), 333–341.

Lopez, S. J., & Snyder, C. R. (2003). *Positive psychological assessment: A handbook of models and measures.* Washington, DC: American Psychological Association.

Lopez, S. R. (1989). Patient variable biases in clinical judgment: Conceptual overview and methodological considerations. *Psychological Bulletin, 106,* 184–203.

Lopez, S. R. (1997). Cultural competence in psychotherapy: A guide for clinicians and their supervisors. In C. E. Watkins Jr. (Ed.), *Handbook of psychotherapy supervision* (pp. 570–588). New York: John Wiley & Sons.

Lopez, S. R., & Guarnaccia, P. J. J. (2000). Cultural psychopathology: Uncovering the social world of mental illness. *Annual Review of Psychology, 51,* 571–598.

Lopez, S. R., Nelson, K., Polo, A., Jenkins, J. H., Karno, M., & Snyder, K. (1998). *Family warmth, attributions, and relapse in Mexican American and Anglo American patients with schizophrenia.* Paper Presented at the Applied Psychology Meeting, San Francisco, CA.

Lopez, S. R., & Nunez, J. A. (1987). Cultural factors considered in the selected diagnostic criteria and interview schedules. *Journal of Abnormal Psychology, 96,* 270–272.

López-Ibor, J. J. (2003). Cultural adaptations of current psychiatric classifications: Are they the solution? *Psychopathology, 36*(3), 114–123.

Loring, M., & Powell, B. (1988). Gender, race, and DSM-III: A study of the objectivity of psychiatric diagnostic behavior. *Journal of Health and Social Behavior, 29,* 1–22.

Luepker, E. T. (2003). *Record keeping in psychotherapy and counseling: Protecting confidentiality and the professional relationship.* New York: Brunner-Routledge.

Mahoney, M. J., & Marquis, A. (2002). Integral constructivism and dynamic systems in psychotherapy processes. *Psychoanalytic Inquiry, 22*(5), 794–814.

Maniacci, M. P. (2002). The DSM and individual psychology: A general comparison. *Journal of Individual Psychology, 58*(4), 356–363.

Mannuzza, S., Fyer, A. J., Martin, L. Y., Gallops, M. S., Endicott, J., Gorman, J., et al. (1989). Reliability of anxiety assessment. *Archives of General Psychiatry, 46,* 1093–1101.

Mansfield, E., & McAdams, D. (1996). Generativity and themes of agency and communion in adult autobiography. *Personality and Social Psychology Bulletin, 22,* 721–731.

Manson, S., Shore, J. H., & Bloom, J. D. (1985). The depressive experience in American Indian communities: A challenge for psychiatric theory and diagnosis. In A. Kleinman & B. Good (Eds.), *Culture and depression.* Berkeley: University of California Press.

Mappes, D. C., Robb, G. P., & Engles, D. W. (1985). Conflicts between ethics and law in counseling and psychotherapy. *Journal of Counseling and Development, 64,* 283–290.

Marcia, J. (1966). Development and validation of ego-identity status. *Journal of Personality and Social Psychology, 3,* 551–559.

Marecek, J. (1993). Disappearance, silences, and anxious rhetoric: Gender in abnormal psychology textbooks. *Journal of Theoretical and Philosophical Psychology: Journal of Division 24*(13), 115–123.

Markus, H. R., & Kitayama, S. (1991). Culture and the self: Implications for cognition, emotion, and motivation. *Psychological Review, 98,* 224–253.

Martin, J. (1993). The problem with therapeutic science. *Journal of Psychology, 127*(4), 365–375.

Mash, E. J., & Johnston, C. (1996). Family relational problems: Their place in the study of psychopathology. *Journal of Emotional and Behavioral Disorders, 4*(4), 240–254.

Maslin, A., & Davis, J. (1975). Sex-role stereotyping as a factor in mental health standards among counselors-in-training. *Journal of Counseling Psychology, 22,* 87–91.

May, R. (1981). *Freedom and destiny.* New York: W. W. Norton.

McAuliffe, G. J. (1993). Constructive development and career transition: Implications for counseling. *Journal of Counseling and Development, 72,* 23–28.

McAuliffe, G. J. (1999, Summer). Is there a liberal bias in multicultural counseling? Becoming a "multicultural liberal." *Association for Counselor Education and Supervision Spectrum, 60,* 9, 12.

McAuliffe, G. J., & Eriksen, K. P. (1999). Toward a constructivist and developmental identity for the counseling profession: The context-phase-stage-style model. *Journal of Counseling and Development, 77*(3), 267–280.

McAuliffe, G. J., & Strand, R. F. (1994). Advising from a constructive developmental perspective. *NACADA Journal, 14,* 25–31.

McClean, L. M., & Gallop, P. (2003). Implications of childhood sexual abuse for adult borderline personality disorder and complex posttraumatic stress disorder. *American Journal of Psychiatry, 160,* 369–372.

McDermott, P. A. (1996). A nationwide study of developmental and gender prevalence for psychopathology in childhood and adolescence. *Journal of Abnormal Child Psychology, 24*(1), 53–67.

McGivern, J. E., & Marquart, A. M. (2000). Legal and ethical issues in child and adolescent assessment. In E. S. Shapiro & T. R. Kratochwill (Eds.), *Behavioral assessment in schools: Theory, research, and clinical foundations* (2nd ed., pp. 387–434). New York: Guilford Press.

McGoldrick, M., Giordano, J., & Pearce, J. K. (1996). *Ethnicity and family therapy* (2nd ed.). New York: Guilford Press.

McLaughlin, J. E. (2002). Reducing diagnostic bias. *Journal of Mental Health Counseling, 24*(3), 256–270.

McLemore, C. W., & Benjamin, L. S. (1979). Whatever happened to interpersonal diagnosis? A psychosocial alternative to DSM-III. *American Psychologist, 34,* 17–34.

McMullen, L. M. (1999). Metaphors in the talk of "depressed" women in psychotherapy. *Canadian Psychology, 40* (3), 102–111.

McWilliams, N. (1998). Relationship, subjectivity, and inference in diagnosis. In J. W. Barron (Ed.), *Making diagnosis meaningful: Enhancing evaluation and treatment of psychological disorders* (pp. 197–226). Washington DC: American Psychological Association.

Mead, G. H. (1934). *Mind, self, and society.* Chicago: University of Chicago Press.

Mead, M. A., Hohenshil, T. H., & Singh, K. (1997). How the DSM system is used by clinical counselors: A national study. *Journal of Mental Health Counseling, 19,* 383–401.

Meara, N. M., Schmidt, L. D., & Day, J. D. (1996). Principles and virtues: A foundation for ethical decisions, policies, and character. *The Counseling Psychologist, 24*(1), 4–77.

Mellor-Clark, J., Connell, J., Barkham, M., & Cummins, P. (2001). Counselling outcomes in primary health care: A CORE system data profile. *European Journal of Psychotherapy, Counselling, and Health, 4*(1), 65–87.

Merriam-Webster's collegiate dictionary (10th ed). (2001). Springfield, MA: Merriam-Webster.

Messman-Moore, T. L., & Resick, P. A. (2002). Brief treatment of complicated PTSD and peritraumatic responses in a client with repeated sexual victimization. *Cognitive & Behavioral Practice, 9,* 89–99.

Mezzich, J. E. (1995). International perspectives on psychiatric diagnosis. In H. I. Kaplan & B. J. Sadock (Eds.), *Comprehensive textbook of psychiatry* (6th ed.). Baltimore. MD: Williams and Wilkins.

Mezzich, J. E. (1999a). Ethics and comprehensive diagnosis. *Psychopathology, 32,* 135–140.

Mezzich, J. E. (1999b). The place of culture in DSM-IV. *Journal of Nervous and Mental Disease, 187*(18), 457–464.

Mezzich, J. E. (2002). Comprehensive diagnosis: A conceptual basis for future diagnostic systems. *Psychopathology, 35*(2–3), 162–165.

Mezzich J. E., Kirmayer, L. J., Kleinman, A., Fabrega, H. Jr., Parron, D.L., Good, B. J., et al. (1999). The place of culture in DSM-IV. *Journal of Nervous and Mental Disorders, 187*(8), 457–464.

Mezzich, J. E., Kleinman, A., Fabrega, H., & Parron, D. L. (1996a). *Culture and psychiatric diagnosis: A DSM-IV perspective.* Washington, DC: American Psychiatric Press.

Mezzich, J. E., Kleinman, A., Fabrega, H., & Parron, D. L. (1996b). Introduction. In J. E. Mezzich, A. Kleinman, H. Fabrega, & D. L. Parron (Eds.), *Culture and psychiatric diagnosis: A DSM-IV perspective (pp. xvii–xxiii).* Washington, DC: American Psychiatric Press.

Mezzich, J. E., Kleinman, A., Fabrega, H., Good, B., Johnson-Powell, G., Lin, K. M., et al. (1993). *Cultural proposals and supporting papers for DSM-IV* (3rd rev.). Internal document of the National Institute of Mental Health Culture and Diagnosis Committee.

Miller, A. (1984). *For your own good: Hidden cruelty in child-rearing and the roots of violence.* New York: Farrar, Strauss, & Giroux.

Miller, D. (1994). *Women who hurt themselves: A book of hope and understanding.* New York: Basic Books.

Miller, J. B. (1976/1991). *Toward a new psychology of women.* Harmondsworth: Penguin.

Miller, M. J. (1990). Responding to diagnosis-expected clients: One counselor's alternative to the DSM-III. *Journal of Human Behavior and Learning, 7,* 19–27.

Miller, P. (2002). Inpatient diagnostic assessments: 2. Interrater reliability and outcomes of structured vs. unstructured interviews. *Psychiatry Research, 105*(3), 265–267.

Miller, R. D. (2003). Chemical castration of sex offenders: Treatment or punishment? In B. J. Winick & J. Q. La Fond (Eds.), *Protecting society from sexually dangerous offenders: Law, justice, and therapy* (pp. 72–95). Washington, DC: American Psychological Association.

Millon, T., Millon, C., & Davis, R. (1994). *Millon clinical multiaxial inventory–III.* Minneapolis, MN: Pearson.

Minsky, S., Vega, W., Miskimen, T., Gara, M., & Escobar, J. (2003). Diagnostic patterns in Latin, African American, and European American psychiatric patients. *Archive of General Psychiatry, 60*(6), 637–644.

Mintz, L. B., & Wright, D. (1992). Women and their bodies: Eating disorders and addiction. In E. P. Cook (Ed.), *Women, relationships, and power: Implications for counseling* (pp. 211–246). Alexandria, VA: American Counseling Association.

Mitchell, P. B., Parker, G. B., Gladstone, G. L., Wilhelm, K., & Austin, M. V. (2003). Severity of stressful life events in first and subsequent episodes of depression: The relevance of depressive subtype. *Journal of Affective Disorders, 73*(3), 245–252.

Mohan, R. (2002). Treatments for borderline personality disorder: Integrating evidence into practice. *International Review of Psychiatry, 14,* 42–51.

Mohar, W. K. (2003). Discarding ideology: The nature/nurture endgame. *Perspectives in Psychiatric Care, 39*(3), 113–122.

Moline, M. E., Williams, G. T., & Austin, K. M. (1998). *Documenting psychotherapy: Essentials for mental health practitioners.* Thousand Oaks, CA: Sage.

Monk, G., Winslade, J., Crocket, K., & Epston, D. (Eds.). (1997). *Narrative therapy in practice: The archeology of hope.* San Francisco: Jossey-Bass.

Moore, W. S. (1987). *Learning environment preferences.* Olympia, WA: Center for the Study of Intellectual Development.

Moos, R. H., McCoy, L., & Moos, B. S. (2000). Global assessment of functioning (GAF) Ratings: Determinants and role as predictors of one-year treatment outcomes. *Journal of Clinical Psychology, 56,* 449–461.

Morrow, K. A., & Deidan, C. T. (1992). Bias in the counseling process: How to recognize it and avoid it. *Journal of Counseling and Development, 70,* 571–577.

Mosak, H. (1991). Where have all the normal people gone? *Individual Psychology: The Journal of Adlerian Theory, Research and Practice, 47*(4), 437–447.

Mottarella, K. E., Philpot, C. L., & Fritzsche, B. A. (2001). Don't take out this appendix! Generalizability of the global assessment of relational functioning scale. *American Journal of Family Therapy, 29*(4), 271–279.

Mulvany, J. (2000). Disability, impairment or illness? The relevance of the social model of disability to the study of mental disorder. *Sociology of Health and Illness, 22*(5) 582–602.

Mundt, C. (2002). Psychological perspectives for the development of future diagnostic systems. *Psychopathology, 35,* 145–151.

Murnen, S., & Smolak, L. (1998). Femininity, masculinity, and disordered eating: A meta-analytic approach. *International Journal of Eating Disorders, 22,* 231–242.

Murray, J. B. (1992). Relationship of childhood sexual abuse to borderline personality disorder, posttraumatic stress disorder and multiple personality disorder. *Journal of Psychology, 127,* 657–676.

Musen, K. [Producer]. (1992). *Quiet rage: The Stanford prison experiment* [videotape]. New York: HarperCollins.

Mwaba, K., & Pedersen, P. (1990). Relative importance of intercultural, interpersonal, and psychopathological attributions in judging critical incidents by multicultural counselors. *Journal of Multicultural Counseling and Development, 18,* 107–117.

Myers, I. (1980). *Introduction to type.* Palo Alto, CA: Consulting Psychologists Press.

Myers, J. E., Sweeney, T. J., & Witmer, J. M. (2000). The wheel of wellness counseling for wellness: A holistic model for treatment planning. *Journal of Counseling and Development, 78,* 251–267.

Myers, J. E., Sweeney, T. J., & Witmer, J. M. (2001). Optimization of behavior: Promotion of wellness. In D. C. Locke, J. E. Myers, E. L. Herr (Eds.), *The handbook of counseling* (pp. 641–652). Thousand Oaks, CA: Sage.

Myss, C. (1994). *Why people don't heal.* Cassette recording, ISBN 56455–240–3.

Nakkab, S., & Hernandez, M. (1998). Group psychotherapy in the context of cultural diversity. *Group, 22,* 95–103.

Napier, A. Y., & Whitaker, C. A. (1988). *The family crucible: The intense experience of family therapy.* New York: HarperCollins.

Nathan, P. E., & Langenbucher, J. (2003). Diagnosis and classification. In G. Stricker, T. A. Widiger, & I. B. Weiner (Eds.), *Handbook of psychology: Clinical psychology, Vol. 8* (pp. 3–26). New York: John Wiley & Sons.

National Association of Social Workers (NASW). (1999). *Code of ethics of the National Association of Social Workers.* Washington, DC: Author.

National Institutes of Health (NIH). (1994). NIH guidelines on the inclusion of women and minorities as subjects in clinical research. *NIH Guide, 23* (10), 1–34.

Nehls, N. (1998). Borderline personality disorder: Gender stereotypes, stigma, and limited system of care. *Issues in Mental Health Nursing, 19,* 97–112.

Neill, J. (1990). Whatever became of the schizophrenogenic mother? *American Journal of Psychotherapy, 44*(4), 499–505.

Neimeyer, G. J. (1993). *Constructivist assessment: A casebook.* Thousand Oaks, CA: Sage.

Neimeyer, R. A. (1998). Social constructionism in the counselling context. *Counselling Psychology Quarterly, 11*(2), 135–150.

Neimeyer, R. A., & Raskin, J. D. (2000). *Constructions of disorder: Meaning-making frameworks for psychotherapy.* Washington, DC: American Psychological Association.

Nelson, M. L. (2002). An assessment-based model for counseling strategy selection. *Journal of Counseling and Development, 80,* 416–423.

Nelson, M. L., & Neufeldt, S. A. (1996). Building on an empirical foundation: Strategies to enhance good practice. *Journal of Counseling and Development, 72,* 609–616.

Neukrug, E. (2003). *The world of the counselor: An introduction to the counseling profession.* Pacific Grove, CA: Thompson–Brooks/Cole.

Neukrug, E. S., & McAuliffe, G. J. (1993). Cognitive development and human service education. *Human Service Education, 13,* 13–26.

Nigro, T. (2003). Dual relationship activities: Principal component analysis of counselors' attitudes. *Ethics and Behavior, 13*(2), 191–201.

Nolen-Hoeksema, S. (1995). Epidemiology and theories of gender differences in unipolar depression. In M. Seeman (Ed.), *Gender and psychopathology* (pp. 63–87). Washington, DC: American Psychiatric Press.

Nuckolls, C. W. (1992). Toward a cultural history of the personality disorders. *Social Science and Medicine, 35,* 37–47.

Ogata, S. N., Silk, K. R., Goodrich, S., Lohr, N. E., Westen, D., & Hill, E. M. (1990). Childhood sexual and physical abuse in adult patients with borderline personality disorder. *American Journal of Psychiatry, 147,* 1008–1013.

Ogrodniczuk, J. S., Piper, W. E., & Joyce, A. S. (2001). Using DSM Axis II information to predict outcome in short-term individual psychotherapy. *Journal of Personality Disorders, 15*(2), 110–122.

Okonski, V. O. (2003). Exercise as a counseling intervention. *Journal of Mental Health Counseling, 25*(1), 45–57.

Olson, G. A. (1989). Social construction and composition theory: A conversation with Richard Rorty. *Journal of Advanced Composition, 9,* 1–9.

Osipow, S., & Fitzgerald, L. (1993). Unemployment and mental health: A neglected Relationship. *Applied and Preventative Psychology, 2,* 59–63.

Owen, I. R. (1992). Applying social constructionism to psychotherapy. *Counselling Psychology Quarterly, 5*(4), 385–403.

Owens, G., & Chard, K. (2001). Cognitive distortions among women reporting childhood sexual abuse. *Journal of Interpersonal Violence, 16,* 178–191.

Palma, T. V., & Stanley, J. L. (2002). Effective counseling with lesbian, gay, and bisexual clients. *Journal of College Counseling, 5,* 74–89.

Pantony, K., & Caplan, P. J. (1991). Delusional dominating personality disorder: A modest proposal for identifying some consequences of rigid masculine socialization. *Canadian Psychology, 2,* 120–135.

Paradise, L. V., & Kirby, P. C. (1990). Some perspectives on the legal liability of group counseling in private practice. *Journal for Specialists in Group Work, 15,* 114–118.

Parker, I., Georgaca, E., Harper, D., McLaughlin, T., & Stowell-Smith, M. (1995). *Deconstructing psychopathology.* Thousand Oaks, CA: Sage.

Parkes, C. M., Laungani, P., & Young, B. (1996). *Death and bereavement across cultures.* New York: Routledge.

Parron, D. L. (1982). An overview of minority group mental needs and issues as presented to the President's Commission on Mental Health. In President's Commission on Mental Health (Ed.), *Perspectives in minority group mental health* (pp. 52–67). Washington, DC: University Press of America.

Patrick-Hoffman, P. (1984). Psychological abuse of women by spouses and live-in lovers. *Women and Therapy, 3,* 37–48.

Patterson, J. M. (2002). Integrating family resilience and family stress theory. *Journal of Marriage and Family, 64*(2), 349–361.

Patterson, T. E., & Lusterman, D. D. (1996). The relational reimbursement dilemma. In F. W. Kaslow (Ed.), *Handbook of relational diagnosis and dysfunctional family patterns* (pp. 46–58). Oxford, England: John Wiley & Sons.

Pederson, P. (1987). Ten frequent assumptions: Cultural bias in counseling. *Journal of Multicultural Counseling and Development, 15,* 16–24.

Penfold, S. P., & Walker, G. A. (1983). *Women and the psychiatric paradox*. Montreal: Eden Press.

Penn, D., & Wykes, T. (2003). Stigma, discrimination and mental illness. *Journal of Mental Health, 12*(3), 203–209.

Perkins, R., & Repper, J. (1998). *Dilemmas in community mental health practice*. Abingdon, England: Radcliffe Medical Press.

Perry, W. G. (1970). *Forms of intellectual and ethical development in the college years*. Troy, MO: Holt, Rinehart, & Winston.

Pesut, D. J. (1991). The art, science, and techniques of reframing in psychiatric mental health nursing. *Issues in Mental Health Nursing, 12*(1), 9–18.

Peterson, J. V., & Nisenholz, B. (1999). *Orientation to counseling* (4th ed.). Boston: Allyn & Bacon.

Phemister, A. A. (2001). Revisiting the principles of free will and determinism: Exploring conceptions of disability and counseling theory. *Journal of Rehabilitation, 67*(3), 5–13.

Phipps, P. M. (1982). The merging categories: Appropriate education or administrative convenience? *Journal of Learning Disabilities, 15*(3), 153–154.

Piaget, J. (1963). *The origins of intelligence in children*. New York: W. W. Norton.

Pilgrim, D. (2002). The biopsychosocial model in Anglo-American psychiatry: Past, present and future? *Journal of Mental Health, 11*(6), 585–595.

Pilgrim, D., & Bentall, R. (1999). The medicalisation of misery: A critical realist analysis of the concept of depression. *Journal of Mental Health, 8*(3), 262–276.

Porter, R. (2003). *Madness: A brief history*. New York, Oxford University Press.

Pote, H. L., & Orrell, M. W. (2002). Perceptions of schizophrenia in multi-cultural Britain. *Ethnicity and Health, 7*(1), 7–20.

Powell, R. A., & Boer, D. P. (1995). Did Freud misrepresent memories of sexual abuse as fantasies? *Psychological Reports, 77, 563–570.*

Prieto, L. R., & Scheel, K. R. (2002). Using case documentation to strengthen counselor trainees' case conceptualization skills. *Journal of Counseling and Development, 80,* 11–22.

Proctor, E. K., & Morrow-Howell, N. (1993). Classification and correlates of ethical dilemmas in hospital social work. *Social Work, 38*(2), 166–178.

Raingruber, B. (2003). Nurture: The fundamental significance of relationship as a paradigm for mental health nursing. *Perspectives in Psychiatric Care, 39*(3), 104–117.

Ramchandani, P., & Stein, A. (2003). The impact of parental psychiatric disorder on children. *British Medical Journal, 327*(7409), 242–244.

Raskin, J. D. (2001). On relativism in constructivist psychology. *Journal of Constructivist Psychology, 14*(4), 285–313.

Regier, D. A., First, M., & Marshall, T. (2002). The American Psychiatric Association (APA) Classification of mental disorders: Strengths, limitations and future perspectives. In M. Maj & W. Gaebel (Eds.), *Psychiatric diagnosis and classification* (pp. 47–77). New York: John Wiley & Sons.

Reich, J., Nduaguba, M., & Yates, W. (1988). Age and sex distribution of DSM-III personality cluster traits in a community population. *Comprehensive Psychiatry, 29,* 298–303.

Reich, W. (1999). Psychiatry as en ethical problem. In S. Bloch, P. Chodoff, & S. A. Green (Eds.), *Psychiatric ethics* (3rd Edition) (pp. 193–224). New York: Oxford University Press.

Reid, P. T. (1993). Poor women in psychology research: Shut-up and shut-out. *Psychology of Women Quarterly, 17,* 133–150.

Reiser, D. E., & Levenson, H. (1984). Abuses of the borderline diagnosis: A clinical problem with teaching opportunities. *American Journal of Psychiatry, 141,* 1528–1532.

Rest, J. (1979). *Development in judging moral issues*. Minneapolis: University of Minnesota Press.

Richardson, J. (1999). Response: Finding the disorder in gender identity disorder. *Harvard Review of Psychiatry, 7*, 43–50.

Ridley, C. (1998). Multicultural assessment: Reexamination, reconceptualization, and practical application. *Counselling Psychology Quarterly, 11*(4), 827–903.

Ridley, C. R. (1995). *Overcoming unintentional racism in counseling and therapy: A practitioner's guide to intentional intervention.* Thousand Oaks, CA: Sage.

Riedl, R. (1984). The consequences of causal thinking. In P. Watzlawick (Ed.), *The invented reality: How do we know what we believe we know? Contributions to constructivism* (pp. 69–94). New York: W.W. Norton.

Rieker, P., & Carmen, E. (1986). The victim-to-patient process: The disconfirmation and transformation of abuse. *American Journal of Orthopsychiatry, 56*, 360–370.

Rigazio-DiGilio, S. A. (2000). Relational diagnosis: A constructive-developmental perspective on assessment and treatment. *Journal of Clinical Psychology, 56*(8), 1017–1036.

Rigazio-DiGilio, S. A., Ivey, A. E., Locke, D. C. (1997). Continuing the postmodern dialogue: Enhancing and contextualizing multiple voices. *Journal of Mental Health Counseling, 19*, 233–255.

Ritchie, M. H. (1994). Cultural and gender biases in definitions of mental and emotional health and illness. *Counselor Education and Supervision, 33*, 344–348.

Robertson, J., & Fitzgerald, L. F. (1990). The (mis)treatment of men: Effects of client gender role and life-style on diagnosis and attribution of pathology. *Journal of Counseling Psychology, 37*, 3–9.

Robins, L. N., & Helzer, J. E. (1986). Diagnosis and clinical assessment: The current state of psychiatric diagnosis. *Annual Review of Psychology 1986.* New York: American Psychological Association.

Rodgers, R. F. (1989). Student development. In U. Delworth & G. R. Hanson (Eds.), *Student services: A handbook for the profession* (pp. 117–164). San Francisco: Jossey-Bass.

Rogers, C. R. (1942). *Counseling and psychotherapy.* Boston: Houghton Mifflin.

Rogers, C. R. (1951). *Client-centered therapy: Its current practice, implications, and theory.* Boston: Houghton Mifflin.

Rogers, C. R. (1961). *On becoming a person: A therapist's view of psychotherapy.* Boston: Houghton Mifflin.

Rogers, C. R. (1987). The underlying theory: Drawn from experience with individuals and groups. *Counseling and Values, 32*, 38–46.

Rogers, E. S., MacDonald-Wilson, K. L., Massaro, J. (2003). Identifying relationships between functional limitations, job accommodations, and demographic characteristics of persons with psychiatric disabilities. *Journal of Vocational Rehabilitation, 18*(1), 15–25.

Rogler, L. H. (1996). Hispanic perspectives. In J. E. Mezzich, A. Kleinman, H. Fabrega, & D. L. Parron (Eds.), *Culture and psychiatric diagnosis: A DSM-IV perspective* (pp. 39–41). Washington, DC: American Psychiatric Press.

Root, M. P. P. (1985). Guidelines for facilitating therapy with Asian American clients. *Psychotherapy, 22*, 349–356.

Root, M. P. P. (1989). A model for understanding variations in the experience of traumata and their sequelae. Paper prepared for the Eighth Advanced Feminist Therapy Institute, Banff, Canada.

Root, M. P. P. (1992). Reconstructing the impact of trauma on personality. In L. S. Brown & M. Ballou (Eds.), *Personality and psychopathology: Feminist reappraisals* (pp. 229–265). New York: Guilford Press.

Rorty, R. (1979). *Philosophy and the mirror of nature.* Princeton, NJ: Princeton University Press.

Rosenbaum, J. E., & Miller, S. R. (1996). Gatekeeping in an era of more open gates: High school counselors' views. *American Journal of Education, 104*(4), 257–280.

Rosenberg, C. E. (2002). The tyranny of diagnosis: Specific entities and individual experience. *Milbank Quarterly, 80*(2), 237–261.

Rosenhan, D. L. (1973). On being sane in insane places. *Science, 179,* 250–258.

Rosewater, L. B. (1986, August). Ethical and legal implications of the DSM-III-R for feminist therapists. In R. Garfinkel (Chair), *The politics of diagnosis: Feminist psychology and the DSM-III-R.* Symposium presented at the Convention of the American Psychological Association, Washington DC.

Rosewater, L. B. (1987). A critical analysis of the proposed Self Defeating Personality Disorder. *Journal of Personality Disorders, 1,* 190–195.

Ross, N. M., & Doherty, W. J. (2001). Validity of the global assessment of relational functioning (GARF) when used by community-based therapists. *American Journal of Family Therapy, 29*(3), 239–254.

Rothblum, E. D. (1982). Women's socialization and the prevalence of depression: The feminine mistake. In The New England Association for Women in Psychology (Eds.), *Current feminist issues in psychotherapy* (pp. 5–13). New York: Haworth.

Russell, D. (1986a). *The secret trauma: Incest in the lives of girls and women.* New York: Basic.

Russell, D. (1986b). Psychiatric diagnosis and the oppression of women. *Women and Therapy, 5,* 83–89.

Rutter, M. (2002). The interplay of nature, nurture, and developmental influences: The challenge ahead for mental health. *Archives of General Psychiatry, 59*(11), 996–1000.

Ryan, T., & Bamber, C. (2002). A survey of policy and practice on expenses and other payments to mental health service users and careers participating in service development. *Journal of Mental Health, 11,* 635–645.

Sadler, J. Z. (2002). *Descriptions and prescriptions: Values, mental disorders, and the DSMs.* Baltimore, MD: Johns Hopkins University Press.

Sadler, J. Z., & Hulgus, Y. F. (1994). Enriching the psychosocial context of a multiaxial nosology. In J. Z. Sadler, O. P. Wiggins, & M. A. Schwartz (Eds.), *Philosophical perspectives on psychiatric diagnostic classification* (pp. 261–278). Baltimore, MD: Johns Hopkins University Press.

Sadler, J. Z., Wiggins, O. P., & Schwartz, M. A. (Eds). (1994). *Philosophical perspectives on psychiatric diagnostic classification.* Baltimore, MD: Johns Hopkins University Press.

Saleebey, D. (2001). The diagnostic strengths manual? *Social Work, 46*(2), 183–188.

Sanford, N. (Ed.). (1962). *The American college.* New York: John Wiley & Sons.

Santiago-Rivera, A., Arredondo, P., & Gallardo-Cooper, M. (2002). *Counseling Latinos and la familia: A practitioner's guide.* Thousand Oaks, CA: Sage.

Sarbin, T. R. (1997). On the futility of psychiatric diagnostic manuals (DSMs) and the return of personal agency. *Applied and Preventive Psychology, 6,* 233–243.

Sarbin, T. R., & Mancuso, J. C. (1980). *Schizophrenia: Medical diagnosis or moral verdict.* Elmsford, NY: Pergamon Press.

Saul, C. (2002). Mapping training to support the implementation of the national service framework for mental health. *Journal of Mental Health, 11*(1), 103–117.

Sayed, M. A., & Collins, D. T. (1998). West meets East: Cross-cultural issues in inpatient treatment. *Bulletin of the Menninger Clinic, 62*(4), 439–455.

Scheflin, A. W. (2000). The evolving standard of care in the practice of trauma and dissociative disorder therapy. *Bulletin of the Menninger Clinic, 64*(2), 197–235.

Scheidt, C. E., Seidenglanz, K., Dieterle, W., Hartmann, A., Bowe, N., Hillenbrand, D., et al. (1998). Basic data for quality control of out-patient psychotherapy. Results of a survey of 40 psychotherapeutic practices. Section 1: Therapists, patients, interventions. *Psychotherapeutics, 43*(2), 92–102.

Schmolke, M. (1999). Ethics in psychiatric diagnosis from a psychodynamic perspective. *Psychopathology, 32*(3), 152–158.

Schott, S. A., & Conyers, L. M. (2003). A solution-focused approach to psychiatric rehabilitation. *Psychiatric Rehabilitation Journal, 27*(1), 43–52.

Schwartz, M. A., & Wiggins, O. P. (2002). The hegemony of the DSMs. In J. Sadler (Ed.), *Descriptions and prescriptions: Values, mental disorders, and the DSMs* (pp. 199–209). Baltimore, MD: Johns Hopkins University Press.

Schwartz, S., Weiss, L., & Lennon, M. C. (2000). Labeling effects of a controversial psychiatric diagnosis: A vignette experiment of late luteal phase dysphoric disorder. *Women and Health, 30*(3), 63–75.

Schweder, R. (1985). Menstrual pollution, soul loss, and the comparative study of emotions. In A. Kleinman & B. Good (Eds.), *Culture and depression* (pp. 182–215). Berkeley: University of California Press.

Schweder, R. A. (1991). *Thinking through cultures: Expeditions in cultural psychology.* Cambridge, MA: Harvard University Press.

Scott, R. W. (2000). *Legal aspects of documenting patient care* (2nd ed.). Gaithersburg, MD: Aspen Publishers.

Seem, S. R., & Johnson, E. (1998). Gender bias among counselor trainees: A study of case conceptualization. *Counselor Education and Supervision, 37,* 257–268.

Segal, L. (1986). *The dream of reality: Heinz von Foerster's constructivism.* New York: Norton.

Seligman, L. (1990). *Selecting effective treatments.* San Fransisco: Jossey-Bass.

Seligman, M. (2003). Positive psychology: Fundamental assumptions. *Psychologist, 16*(3), 126–127.

Seligman, M. E. P., Walker, E. F., & Rosenhan, D. L. (2001). *Abnormal psychology.* New York: W. W. Norton.

Serafica, F. C. (1997). Psychopathology and resilience in Asian American children and adolescents. *Applied Developmental Science, 1*(3), 145–155.

Sexton, T. L. (1994). Systemic thinking in a linear world: Issues in the application of interactional counseling. *Journal of Counseling and Development, 72,* 249–259.

Sexton, T. (1997). Constructivist thinking within the history of ideas: The challenge of a new paradigm. In T. L Sexton & B. L. Griffin (Eds.), *Constructivist thinking in counseling practice, research, and training* (pp. 3–18). New York: Teachers College Press.

Shankman, S. A., & Klein, D. N. (2002). Dimensional diagnosis of depression: Adding the dimension of course severity, and comparison to the DSM. *Comprehensive Psychiatry, 43,* 420–426.

Shaywitz, S. E., Shaywitz, B. A., Feltcher, J. M., & Escobar, M. (1990). Prevalence of reading disability in boys and girls: Results of the Connecticut longitudinal study. *Journal of American Medical Association, 264*(8), 998–1002.

Sheehy, G. (1976). *Passages: Predictable crises of adult life.* New York: Dutton.

Sheehy, M., Goldsmith, L., & Charles, E. (1980). A comparative study of borderline patients in a psychiatry outpatient clinic. *American Journal of Psychiatry, 137,* 1374–1379.

Sherer, R. A. (2003). The mental health care parity debate continues. *Psychiatric Times, 20*(5), 1–3.

Shergill, S. S., Barker, D., & Greenberg, M. (1998). Communication of psychiatric diagnosis. *Social Psychiatry and Psychiatric Epidemiology, 33*(1), 32–39.

Sherman, J. A. (1980). Therapist attitudes and sex-role stereotyping. In A. M. Brodsky & R. T. Hare-Mustin (Eds.), *Women and psychotherapy: An assessment of research and practice.* New York: Guilford Press.

Shields, S. A. (1995). Functionalism, Darwinism, and the psychology of women: A study in social myth. In J. S. Bohan (Ed.), *Re-placing women in psychology: Readings toward a more inclusive history* (pp. 49–70). Dubuque, IA: Kendall/Hunt.

Sinacore-Guinn, A. L. (1992, October). *Cultural considerations in diagnosis: A multi-faceted approach.* Paper presented at the conference of the Chicago School of Professional Development on "Cultural Impact: Meeting the Challenge of Growing Up in a Changing America," Chicago, IL.

Sinacore-Guinn, A. L. (1995). The diagnostic window: Culture- and gender-sensitive diagnosis and training. *Counselor Education and Supervision, 35*(1), p. 18.

Sinacore-Guinn, A. L., & Bahr, M. (1993a, April). *Diagnosis and culture: Working toward an integrative assessment model.* Paper presented at the annual meeting of the Great Lakes Regional Conference for Counseling Psychology, Division 17, American Psychological Association, Bloomington, IN.

Sinacore-Guinn, A. L., & Bahr, M. (1993b, August). *Cultural considerations in the assessment of children.* Paper presented at the national convention of the American Psychological Association, Division 16, Toronto, Ontario, Canada.

Sinaikin, P. M. (2003). Categorical diagnosis and a poetics of obligation: An ethical commentary on psychiatric diagnosis and treatment. *Ethical Human Sciences and Services, 5*(2), 141–148.

Skene, A. (2002). Rethinking normativism in psychiatric classification. In J. Z. Sadler (Ed.), *Descriptions and prescriptions: Values, mental disorders, and the DSMs* (pp. 114–127). Baltimore, MD: Johns Hopkins University Press.

Skodol, A. E., & Bender, D. S. (2003). Why are women diagnosed as borderline more than men? *Psychiatric Quarterly, 74,* 349–360.

Slife, B., & Ruberstein, J. (1992). Do diagnostic labels hinder the effective treatment of persons with mental disorders? In *Taking sides: Clashing views on controversial psychological issues* (pp. 77–96). Guildford, CT: Dushkin.

Slimak, R. E., & Berkowitz, S. R. (1983). The university and college counseling center and malpractice suits. *Personnel and Guidance Journal, 61*(5), 291–296.

Smith, D. (1981). Unfinished business with informed consent procedures. *American Psychologist, 36,* 220–226.

Smith, D., & Kraft, W. A. (1983). DSM-III: Do psychologists really want an alternative? *American Psychologist, 38,* 777–785.

Smith, H. B. (1999). Managed care: A survey of counselor educators and counselor practitioners. *Journal of Mental Health Counseling, 21*(3), 270–284.

Smolak, L. (2002). The relationship of gender and voice to depression and eating disorders. *Psychology of Women Quarterly, 26*(3), 234–242.

Snyder, C. R., & Lopez, S. J. (Eds.) (2002). *Handbook of positive psychology.* New York: Oxford University Press.

Snyder, D. (1992). *The misdiagnosis of men in gender nontraditional roles.* Unpublished manuscript.

Spaulding, W., & Strachan, E. (2003). Response to Holloway and Szmukler. *Journal of Mental Health, 12*(5), 449–451.

Spence, J. T. (1985). Achievement American style: The rewards and costs of individualism. *American Psychologist, 40,* 1285–1295.

Sperling, M. B., & Sack, A. (2002). Psychodynamics and managed care: The art of the impossible? *American Journal of Psychotherapy, 56*(3), 362–378.

Sperry, L. (2002a). DSM-IV: Making it more clinician-friendly. *Journal of Individual Psychology, 58*(4), 434–441.

Sperry, L. (2002b). From psychopathology to transformation: Retrieving the developmental focus in psychotherapy. *Journal of Individual Psychology, 58*(4), 398–421.

Spitzer, R. L. (1975). On pseudoscience in science, logic in remission and psychiatric diagnosis: A critique of ""On Being Sane in Insane Places."" *Journal of Abnormal Psychology, 84,* 442–452.

Spitzer, R. L., & Fleiss, J. L. (1974). A re-analysis of the reliability of psychiatric diagnosis. *British Journal of Psychiatry, 125,* 341–347.

Spitzer, R. L., Williams, J. B., Kass, F., & Davies, M. (1989). National field trial of the DSM-III-R diagnostic criteria for self-defeating personality disorder. *American Journal of Psychiatry, 146,* 1561–1567.

Sporakowski, M. J. (1995). Assessment and diagnosis in marriage and family counseling. *Journal of Counseling and Development, 74,* 60–64.

Sprinthall, N. A., & Thies-Sprinthall, L. (1983). The teacher as an adult learner: A cognitive-developmental view. In G. Griffin (Ed.), *Staff development: Eighty-second yearbook of the National Society for the Study of Education* (pp. 13–35). Chicago: University of Chicago Press.

Sprock, J., & Yoder, C. (1997). Women and depression. *Sex Roles, 36,* 269–303.

Spruill, D. A., & Benshoff, J. M. (2000). Helping beginning counselors develop a personal theory of counseling. *Counselor Education and Supervision, 40*(1), 70–81.

Steen, M. (1991). Historical perspectives on women and mental illness and prevention of depression in women, using a feminist framework. *Issues in Mental Health Nursing, 12,* 359–374.

Steinberg, L. (1990). Autonomy, conflict, and harmony in the family relationship. In S. Freedman & G. Elliott (Eds.), *At the threshold: The developing adolescent* (pp. 255–276). Cambridge, MA: Harvard University Press.

Steyn, B. J., Schneider, J., & McArdle, P. (2002). The role of disability living allowance in the management of attention deficit/hyperactivity disorder. *Child: Care, Health, and Development, 28,* 523–528.

Stirman, S. W., DeRubeis, R. J., Crits-Christoph, P., & Brody, P. E. (2003). Are samples in randomized controlled trials of psychotherapy representative of community outpatients? A new methodology and initial findings. *Journal of Consulting and Clinical Psychology, 71*(6), 963–972.

Stratton, P. (2003). Causal attributions during therapy I: Responsibility and blame. *Journal of Family Therapy, 25*(2), 136–161.

Stravynski, A., & O'Connor, K. (1995). Understanding and managing abnormal behavior: The need for a new clinical science. *The Journal of Psychology, 129*(6), 605–620.

Stone, M. H., Unwin, A., Beacham, B., & Swenson, C. (1988). Incest in female borderlines: Its frequency and impact. *International Journal of Family Psychiatry, 9,* 277–293.

Stout, A. L., Steege, J. F., Blazer, D. G., & George, L. K. (1986). Comparison of lifetime psychiatric diagnoses in premenstrual syndrome clinic and community samples. *Journal of Nervous and Mental Disease, 174,* 517–522.

Sturkie, K., & Bergen, L. P. (2001). *Professional regulation in marital and family therapy.* Boston: Allyn & Bacon.

Sue, D. W., Bingham, R. P., Porche-Burke, L., & Vasquez, M. (1999). The diversification of psychology: A multicultural revolution. *American Psychologist, 54,* 1061–1069.

Sue, D. W., Carter, R. T., Casas, J. M., Fouad, N. A., Ivey, A. E., & Jensen, M. (1998). *Multicultural counseling competencies: Individual and organizational development.* Thousand Oaks, CA: Sage.

Sue, D. W., Ivey, A. E., & Pederson, P. B. (Eds.). (1996). *A theory of multicultural counseling and therapy.* Pacific Grove, CA: Brooks/Cole.

Sue, D. W., & Sue, D. (1990). *Counseling the culturally different: Theory and practice* (2nd ed.). New York: John Wiley & Sons.

Sue, D. W., & Sue, D. (1999). *Counseling the culturally different: Theory and practice* (3rd ed.). New York: John Wiley & Sons.

Sue, S., & McKinney, H. (1975). Asian-Americans in the community health care system. *American Journal of Orthopsychiatry, 45,* 111–118.

Summerfield, D. (2001). The invention of post-traumatic stress disorder and the social usefulness of a psychiatric category. *British Medical Journal, 9,* 61–65.

Super, D. E. (1963). A theory of vocational development. *American Psychologist, 8,* 185–190.

Super, D. E. (1990). A life-span, life-space approach to career development. In D. Brown & L. Brooks (Eds.), *Career choice and development: Applying contemporary theories to practice* (pp. 197–261). San Francisco: Jossey-Bass.

Super, D. E., Thompson, A. S., & Lindeman, R. H. (1988). *Adult career concerns inventory.* Palo Alto: CA: Consulting Psychologists Press.

Surrey, J., Swett, C., Michaels, A., & Levin, S. (1990). Reported history of physical and sexual abuse and severity of symptomatology in women psychiatric outpatients. *American Journal of Orthopsychiatry, 60,* 412–417.

Sweeney, T. J. (1998). *Adlerian counseling: A practitioner's approach* (4th ed.). Philadelphia: Accelerated Development

Swenson, L. C. (1997). *Psychology and law for the helping professions.* Cambridge, MA: Thomson.

Szasz, T. S. (1974). *The myth of mental illness.* New York: Harper & Row.

Szasz, T. S. (2002). *Liberation by oppression: A comparative study of slavery and psychiatry.* New Brunswick, NJ: Transaction Publishers.

Talan, J. (2000). Fighting with care. *Psychology Today, 33*(1), 11.

Taylor, J., Gilligan, C., & Sullivan, A. (1995). *Between voice and silence: Women and girls, race and relationship.* Cambridge, MA: Harvard University Press.

Thatcher, W. G., Reininger, B. M., & Drane, J. W. (2002). Using path analysis to examine adolescent suicide attempts, life satisfaction, and health risk behavior. *Journal of School Health, 72*(2), 71–78.

Thomas, A., & Sillen, S. (1972). *Racism and psychiatry.* New York: Brunner/Mazel.

Thompson, J. W. (1996). Native American perspectives. In J. E. Mezzich, A. Kleinman, H. Fabrega, & D. L. Parron (Eds.), *Culture and psychiatric diagnosis: A DSM-IV perspective* (pp. 31–33). Washington, DC: American Psychiatric Press.

Tomm, K. (1989). Externalizing the problem and increasing personal agency. *Journal of Strategic and Systemic Therapies, 8,* 54–59.

Travis, C. B., & Compton, J. D. (2001). Feminism and health in the decade of behavior. *Psychology of Women Quarterly, 25*(4), 312–324.

Triandis, H. (1994). *Individualism and collectivism.* Boulder, CO: Westview.

Tseng, W. S. (2001). *Handbook of cultural psychiatry.* San Diego: Academic Press.

Tseng, W. S., Asai, M. H., Kitanish, K. J., McLaughlin, D., & Kyomen, H. (1992). Diagnostic pattern of social phobia: Comparison in Tokyo and Hawaii. *Journal of Nervous and Mental Disease, 180,* 380–385.

Tseng, W. S., McDermott, J. F., Jr., Ogino, K., & Ebata, K. (1982). Cross-cultural differences in parent-child assessment: U.S.A. and Japan. *International Journal of Social Psychiatry. 145*(12), 1538–1543.

Tsuang, M. T., & Faraone, S. V. (2002). Diagnostic concepts and the prevention of schizophrenia. *Canadian Journal of Psychiatry, 47*(6), 515–518.

Tsuang, M. T., & Stone, W. S. (2000). Toward reformulating the diagnosis of schizophrenia. *American Journal of Psychiatry, 157*(7), 1041–1051.

Tynerm, J., & Houston, D. (2002). Controlling bodies: The punishment of multiracialized sexual relations. *Antipode, 32*(4), 387–410.

Unger, R. K., & Crawford, M. E. (1992). *Women and gender: A feminist psychology.* Philadelphia: Temple University Press.

Usher, C. H. (1989). Recognizing cultural bias in counseling theory and practice: The case of Rogers. *Journal of Multicultural Counseling and Development, 17,* 16–24.

Ussher, J. (2000). Women's madness: A material–discursive–intrapsychic approach. In D. Fee (Ed.), *Pathology and the postmodern: Mental illness as discourse and experience* (pp. 205–230). London: Sage.

Vacc, N. A., & Juhnke, G. A. (1997). The use of structured clinical interviews for assessment in counseling. *Journal of Counseling and Development, 75,* 470–480.

Vaillant, G. E. (1977). *Adaptation to life.* Boston: Little, Brown.

Valasquez, R. J., Johnson, R., & Brown-Cheatham, M. (1993). Teaching counselors to use the DSM-III-R with ethnic minority clients: A paradigm. *Counselor Education and Supervision, 32,* 323–331.

Valenstein, E. S. (1998). *Blaming the brain.* New York: Free Press.

Vance, E. T. (1997). A typology of risks and the disabilities of low status. In G. W. Albee & J. M. Joffee (Eds.), *The primary prevention of psychopathology: The issues.* Hanover, NH: University Press of New England.

van der Kolk, B. A. (1989). The compulsion to repeat the trauma: Re-enactment, revictimization, and masochism. *Psychiatric Clinics of North America, 12,* 389–411.

van der Kolk, B. A. (1996). The body keeps the score: Approaches to the psychobiology of post-traumatic stress disorder. In B. A. van der Kolk, A. C. McFarlane, & L. Weisaeth (Eds.), *Traumatic stress* (pp. 214–241). New York: Guilford Press.

Van Hoose, W. H., & Kottler, J. A. (1985). *Ethical and legal issues in counseling and psychotherapy* (2nd ed.). San Francisco: Jossey-Bass.

Von Glasersfeld, E. (1984). An introduction to radical constructivism. In P. Watzlawick (Ed.) *The invented reality: How do we know what we believe we know? Contributions to constructivism* (pp. 17–40). New York: W.W. Norton.

Vontress, C. E., Johnson, J. A., & Epp, L. R. (1999). *Cross-cultural counseling: A casebook.* Alexandria, VA: American Counseling Association.

Vygotsky, L. (1978). *Mind in society.* Cambridge, MA: Harvard University Press.

Wakefield, J. C. (1992). The concept of mental disorder: On the boundary between biological facts and social values. *American Psychologist, 47,* 373–388.

Waldo, M., Brotherton, W. D., & Horswill, R. (1993). Integrating DSM-III-R training into school, marriage and family, and mental health counselor preparation. *Counselor Education and Supervision, 32,* 332–342.

Wallston, B. S., & Grady, K. E. (1985). Integrating the feminist critique and the crisis in social psychology: Another look at research methods. In V. E. O'Leary, R. K. Unger, & B. S. Wallston (Eds.), *Women, gender, and social psychology* (pp. 7–33). Hillsdale, NJ: Erlbaum.

Walker, L. E. A (1979). *The battered woman.* New York: Harper & Row.

Walker, L. E. A. (1984). *The battered women's syndrome.* New York: Springer.

Walker, L. E. A. (1985). Feminist therapy with victims/survivors of interpersonal violence. In L. B. Rosewater & L. E. A. Walker (Eds.), *Handbook of feminist therapy: Women's issues in psychotherapy* (pp. 210–221). New York: Springer.

Walker, L. E. A. (1986, August). Diagnosis and politics: Abuse disorders. In R. Garfinkel (Chair), *The politics of diagnosis: Feminist psychology and the DSM-III-R.* Symposium presented at the Conference of the American Psychological Association, Washington, DC.

Walsh, F. (2002). A Family resilience framework: Innovative practice applications. *Family Relations, 51*(2), 130–138.

Walsh, F. (2003). Family resilience: A framework for clinical practice. *Family Process, 42*(1), 1–19.

Walters, M., Carter, E., Pap, P., & Silverstein, O. (1988). *The invisible web: Gender patterns in family relationships*. New York: Guilford Press.

Ward, K. M. (2001). Effectiveness of a model for training direct service personnel in rural and remote locations. *Journal of Intellectual and Developmental Disability, 26*(4), 311–324.

Warren, L. W. (1983). Male intolerance of depression: A review with implications for psychotherapy. *Clinical Psychology Review, 3*, 147–156.

Watzlawick, P. (Ed.). (1984). *The invented reality: How do we know what we believe we know? Contributions to constructivism*. New York: W. W. Norton.

Webb, L. (2002). Deliberate self-harm in adolescence: A systematic review of psychological and psychosocial factors. *Journal of Advanced Nursing, 38*(3), 235–245.

Webster's new world dictionary (3rd college ed.). (1988). New York: Simon & Schuster.

Wehowsky, A. (2000). Diagnosis as care—Diagnosis as politics. *International Journal of Psychotherapy, 5*(3), 241–256.

Weissman, M. M., & Klerman, G. L. (1981). Sex differences and the epidemiology of depression. In E. Howell & M. Bayes (Eds.), *Women and mental health* (pp. 160–195). New York: Basic.

Weisz, J. R., McCarty, C. A., Eastman, K. L., Chaiyasit, W., & Suwanlert, S. (1997). Developmental psychopathology and culture: Ten lessons from Thailand. In S. S. Luthar, J. A. Burnack, D. Cicchetti, & J. R. Weisz (Eds.), *Developmental psychopathology: Perspectives on adjustment, risk, and disorder* (pp. 568–592). Cambridge, UK: Cambridge University Press.

Weisz, J. R., & Weiss, B. (1991). Studying the "referability" of child clinical problems. *Journal of Consulting and Clinical Psychology, 59*, 266–273.

Welfel, E. (2002). *Ethics in counseling and psychotherapy: Standards, research, and emerging issues* (2nd ed.). Pacific Grove, CA: Brooks/Cole.

Westen, D., Ludolph, P., Misle, B., Ruffins, S., & Block, J. (1990). Physical and sexual abuse in adolescent girls with borderline personality disorder. *American Journal of Orthopsychiatry, 60*, 55–66.

Wetterling, T. (2000). Patient education regarding the diagnosis: Results of a survey of psychiatric patients. *Psychiatrische Praxis, 27*(1), 6–10.

Wetzel, J. W. (1991). Universal mental health classification systems: Reclaiming women's experience. *Affilia, 6*(3), 8–31.

Wheeler, B. R., & Walton, E. (1987). Personality disturbances of adult incest victims. *Social Casework, 68*, 597–602.

White, M., & Epston, D. (1990). *Narrative means to therapeutic ends*. New York: Norton.

White, V. E. (2001). Renaming and rethinking the "diagnosis and treatment" course. In G. A. McAuliffe & K. Eriksen (Eds.), *Teaching counselors and therapists: Constructivist and developmental course designs* (pp. 203–218). Westport, CT: Bergin & Garvey.

White, V. E. (2002). Developing counseling objectives and empowering clients: A strength-based intervention. *Journal of Mental Health Counseling, 24*, 270–279.

Widiger, T. A. (1993). The DSM-II-R categorical personality disorder diagnoses: A critique and an alternative. *Psychological Inquiry, 4*, 75–90.

Widiger, T. A. (1995). Deletion of self-defeating and sadistic personality disorders. In W. J. Livesley (Ed.), *The DSM-IV personality disorders* (pp. 359–373). New York: Guilford Press.

Widiger, T. A. (1997). Mental disorders as discrete clinical conditions: Dimensional versus categorical classification. In S. M. Turner & M. Hersen (Eds.), *Adult psychopathology and diagnosis* (pp. 3–23). New York: John Wiley & Sons.

Widiger, T. A. (2002). Values, politics, and science in the construction of the DSMs. In J. Z. Sadler (Ed.), *Descriptions and prescriptions: Values, mental disorders, and the DSMs* (pp. 25–41). Baltimore, MD: Johns Hopkins University Press.

Widiger, T. A., Frances, A. J., Pincus, H. A., First, M. B., Ross, R., & Davis, W. (1994). *DSM-IV sourcebook*. Washington, DC: American Psychiatric Press.

Widiger, T. A., & Sankis, L. M. (2000). Adult psychopathology: Issues and controversies. *Annual Review of Psychology, 51,* 377–404.

Wilkinson, H. (1998). Phenomenological causality: And why we avoid examining the nature of causality in psychotherapy: A dialogue. *International Journal of Psychotherapy, 3*(2), 147–164.

Williams, J. B., Gibbon, M., First, M., Spitzer, R., Davies, M., Borus, J., et al. (1992). The structured clinical interview for DSM-III-R (SCID) II: Multi-site test-retest reliability. *Archives of General Psychiatry, 49,* 630–636.

Williams, R. N. (1998). Science of storytelling? Evolutionary explanations of human sexuality. In B. D. Slife (Ed.), *Taking sides: Clashing views on controversial psychological issues* (10th ed., pp. 79–87). Guilford, CT: Dushkin/McGraw-Hill.

Wilson, J. P. (2001). A holistic approach to healing trauma and PTSD. In J. P. Wilson, M. J. Friedman, & J. D. Lindy (Eds.), *Treating psychological trauma & PTSD* (pp. 28–58). New York: Guilford Press.

Wilson, J. P., Friedman, M. J., & Lindy, J. D. (2001). Treatment goals for PTSD. In J. P. Wilson, M. J. Friedman, & J. D. Lindy (Eds.), *Treating psychological trauma & PTSD* (pp. 3–27). New York: Guilford Press.

Wine, J. D., Moses, B., & Smye, M. D. (1980). Female superiority in sex different competence comparisons: A review of the literature. In C. Stark-Adamec (Ed.), *Sex roles: Origins, influences, and implications for women*. Montreal: Eden Press Women's Publishers.

Winkleby, M. (1993). Homelessness. *Psychology Today, 26*(3), 10.

Winston, R. B., Jr., Miller, T. K., & Prince, J. S. (1987). *Student developmental task and lifestyle inventory*. Athens, GA: Student Development Associates.

Wirth-Cauchon, J. (2000). A dangerous symbolic mobility: Narratives of borderline personality disorder. In F. Fee (Ed.), *Pathology and the postmodern* (pp. 141–162). London: Sage.

Wittig, V. R. (2000). Legislative update. *Perspectives in Psychiatric Care, 36*(3), 107–108.

Woody, R. H. (2000). *Child custody: Practice standards, ethical issues, and legal safeguards for mental health professionals*. Sarasota, FL: Professional Resource Press.

Woody, R. H. (2001). *Psychological information: Protecting the right to privacy: A guidebook for mental health practitioners and their clients*. Madison, CT: Psychosocial Press.

Woolfolk, R. L. (2001). "Objectivity" in diagnosis and treatment. In B. D. Slife, R. N. Willimans, & S. H. Barlow (Eds.), *Critical issues in psychotherapy: Translating new ideas into practice* (pp. 2887–2898). London: Sage.

World Health Organization. (1979). *Schizophrenia: An international follow-up study*. Chichester, England: John Wiley & Sons.

Worell, J. (2001). Feminist interventions: Accountability beyond symptom reduction. *Psychology of Women Quarterly, 25*(4), 335–344.

Wurr, C. J., & Partridge, I. M. (1996). The prevalence of a history of childhood sexual abuse in an acute adult inpatient population. *Child Abuse and Neglect, 20,* 867–872.

Wylie, M. S. (1995). The power of the DSM-IV: Diagnosing for dollars. *Family Therapy Networker, 19*(3), 22–32.

Yahav, R., & Sharlin, S. A. (2002). Blame and family conflict: Symptomatic children as scapegoats. *Child and Family Social Work, 7*(2), 91–99.

Yalom, I. D. (2002). *The gift of therapy: An open letter to a new generation of therapists and their patients*. New York: HarperCollins.

Young, M. E., & Long, L. L. (1998). *Counseling and therapy for couples*. Pacific Grove, CA: Brooks/Cole.

Zanarini, M. C., Frankenburg, F. R., Hennan, J., & Silk, K. (2003). The longitudinal course of borderline psychopathology: 6-year prospective follow-up of the phenomenology of borderline personality disorder. *American Journal of Psychiatry, 160,* 274–284.

Zinbarg, R. E., Barlow, D. H., Liebowitz, M., Street, L., Broadhead, E., Katon, W., et al. (1994). The DSM-IV field trial for mixed anxiety and depression. *American Journal of Psychiatry, 151*(8), 1153–1162.

Zittel, K. M., Lawrence, S., & Wodarski, J. S. (2002). Biopsychosocial model of health and healing: Implications for health social work practice. *Journal of Human Behavior in the Social Environment, 5*(1), 19–33.

Index

About the Authors

Karen Eriksen is the Program Chair for Counseling master's and doctoral programs at Argosy University, Orange County. She received her doctorate from George Mason University and her master's degree from California State University, Fullerton. Her doctoral study emphasized family therapy, counselor education, supervision, and counselor advocacy. She practiced most recently in Virginia while licensed as a Professional Counselor and Marriage and Family Counselor. She spent 18 years as a mental health and community agency counselor, gaining specialties in family therapy, addictions, survivors of sexual abuse, and the intersection of spirituality and counseling. She then re-careered and began teaching counseling in 1993, frequently teaching counseling skills and theories, human development, diagnosis and treatment planning, practicum, and internship. Dr. Eriksen is a Nationally Certified Counselor, an American Association for Marriage and Family Therapy (AAMFT) Clinical Member, and an AAMFT Approved Supervisor. She has written the only book on the process of professional advocacy for counselors, *Making an Impact: A Handbook on Counselor Advocacy.* She has also cowritten three books on counselor education: *Preparing Counselors and Therapists: Creating Constructivist and Developmental Programs, Teaching Counselors and Therapists: Constructivist and Developmental Course Design,* and *Teaching Strategies for Constructivist and Developmental Counselor Education.* Her research area is in counselor preparation. Dr. Eriksen has been active in leadership of several state and national professional associations, including the American Counseling Association (ACA), Virginia Association of Marriage and Family Counselors (VAMFC), Virginia Association of Clinical Counselors (VACC), American Mental Health Counselors Association (AMHCA), Virginia Counselors Association (VCA), Northern Virginia Chapter of Clinical Counselors (NVCCC), and International Association of Marriage and Family Counselors (IAMFC). Dr. Eriksen regularly presents workshops on advocacy and counselor preparation at local, state, and national conferences.

Victoria E. Kress is an assistant professor in the department of counseling at Youngstown State University. She is a Licensed Professional Clinical Counselor, and has 15 years of clinical experience working in various settings such as community mental health centers, hospitals, residential treatment facilities, private practice, and college counseling centers. She has numerous refereed publications in the areas of self-injurious behavior, the *Diagnostic and Statistical Manual of Mental Disorders* (DSM), sexual assault and trauma, and strength-based counseling approaches. She is the recipient of three research and writing awards.

About the Contributors

Montserrat Casado is Assistant Professor and Play Certificate Coordinator of Counselor Education at the University of Central Florida, Department of Child, Family and Community Sciences. Montse is a Licensed Marriage and Family Therapist and a Registered Play Therapist. A native of Barcelona, Spain, Montse has worked in a variety of clinical settings, including schools, mental health agencies and hospital pastoral counseling centers. Some of her areas of interest include resilience, family therapy, play therapy, brief therapy, multicultural counseling and supervision.

Wendy K. Enochs earned her Ph.D. from the University of Arkansas. She is currently employed at Emporia State University where she coordinates the student personnel graduate program. Dr. Enochs has worked as a counselor in mental health centers, a day treatment center, and a psychiatric hospital. She has worked with families, groups, and individuals. In addition, she is trained in critical incident stress debriefing and is a Licensed Clinical Professional Counselor (LCPC) in Kansas and a LPC in Texas. She is also a NCC and an active member of the American Counseling Association and Kansas Counseling Association. Dr. Enochs is currently serving on the board as treasurer for the Association for Adult Development and Aging division of American Counseling Association (ACA), and is a member of the ACA Intraprofessional Committee. In addition, she is a Council for the Accreditation of Counseling and Related Educational Programs (CACREP) Team Member. At the state level, Dr. Enochs is treasurer/secretary for the Kansas Association for Counselor Educators and Supervisors and president-elect of the Kansas Career Association. Dr. Enochs' main areas of interest include crisis counseling, best practices in supervision, college student adjustment, and wellness issues. Dr. Enochs has presented at both the state and national levels on numerous topics.

Colleen A. Etzbach has a doctorate in Rehabilitation Counseling from Southern Illinois University. Currently she is a faculty member at Emporia State University and co-coordinates the rehabilitation program. Dr. Etzbach has worked as a family counselor and rehabilitation counselor. She has worked in a wide variety of settings, including mental health centers and rehabilitation facilities. She is a Licensed Clinical Professional Counselor (LCPC) in Illinois and is a Certified Rehabilitation Counselor. In addition, she is an active member in the National Council on Rehabilitation Education, National Rehabilitation Association, Kansas Rehabilitation Association, and American Counseling Association (ACA). Dr. Etzbach has served as president of the Kansas Rehabilitation Association, as a program reviewer for ACA, and a CORE site reviewer.

Her current areas of interest include psychosocial development, best practices in supervision, and students with disabilities. Dr. Etzbach has presented at numerous conferences at the state and national levels on a variety of issues.

William Etzbach has a master's degree in Rehabilitation Counseling from Southern Illinois University. He is currently employed by SRS in the Emporia, Kansas, Area Office as a rehabilitation counselor and equal employment opportunity (EEO) coordinator. His previous work experience includes working as an outpatient therapist in Illinois and Iowa. As a rehabilitation counselor, Mr. Etzbach works with people who are newly blinded, persons with severe and persistent mental illness, students in transition from school to work, and general cases. He also teaches independent living to people newly blind. And as EEO coordinator, he works to make sure relations between employer and employees in the Emporia area are fair and within legal guidelines. Mr. Etzbach's interest in counseling, especially counseling people with severe and persistent mental illness, began in college. While earning an undergraduate degree in psychology he worked a crisis line at the college.

Kathleen (Ky) T. Heinlen is a Licensed Professional Counselor and works full-time in a secured residential treatment center for adolescents. She teaches part-time and is completing her doctorate at Cleveland State University. She has previously published research on online counseling. Her current doctoral research addresses the needs of caregivers for individuals with traumatic brain injury.

Max Hines is the founder and served as Dean of the Washington School of Professional Psychology in Seattle. He currently serves as Associate Vice President of Graduate and Undergraduate Education at Northwestern Health Sciences University,

Bloomington, Minnesota. Dr. Hines is a Licensed Psychologist in practice for more than 20 years, counseling children, adolescents, adults, couples, families and groups. He is especially interested in boundaries in psychotherapy, has taught ethics for mental health counselors and clinical psychologists for about 15 years, and enjoys the richness of ethical decision making in practice.

Garrett McAuliffe is a professor in the counseling program at Old Dominion University. He graduated with an Ed.D. from the University of Massachusetts at Amherst, and a master's degree from the State University of New York at Albany. He invests his research and scholarly pursuits in multicultural counseling, qualitative research, adult cognitive and moral development, postmodern thinking and social constructionism in counseling, feminist theory, school counseling, and socially critical thinking. He has also cowritten three books on counselor education: *Preparing Counselors and Therapists: Creating Constructivist and Developmental Programs, Teaching Counselors and Therapists: Constructivist and Developmental Course Design,* and *Teaching Strategies for Constructivist and Developmental Counselor Education.*

Debra A. Pender is a doctoral candidate and graduate assistant in the Department of Educational Psychology and Special Education at Southern Illinois University at Carbondale. Ms. Pender is a Licensed Clinical Professional Counselor and National Certified Counselor in private practice and serves as the clinical director of the Southern Illinois Critical Incident Stress Management Team. She has worked in the community mental health field for more than 20 years, specializing in prevention, early intervention, and treatment of trauma stress syndromes. Ms. Pender provides training in trauma intervention education and has presented papers focusing on designing counselor education coursework to prepare counselors for trauma work. She is a member of the American Counseling Association (ACA)'s disaster task force and has been recognized as an "emerging leader" by the Association for Specialists in Group Work.

Robyn Trippany is an Assistant Professor in the Department of Counseling at Troy State University at Montgomery. She received her doctorate in Counselor Education from the University of Alabama in 2001, where she also completed her master's degree in community counseling and bachelor's degree in psychology. Dr. Trippany has presented and published professionally on a variety of counseling issues, including sexual trauma counseling, vicarious trauma, and counselor education and supervision issues. She has clinical experience with both adults and children regarding a variety of clinical issues, including sexual trauma counseling, women's issues, and play therapy, in both the public and private sector.